THE POLITICS OF LABOR IN A GLOBAL AGE

The Politics of Labor in a Global Age: Continuity and Change in Late-industrializing and Post-socialist Economies

Edited by
CHRISTOPHER CANDLAND
and
RUDRA SIL

OXFORD
UNIVERSITY PRESS

OXFORD

UNIVERSITY PRESS

Great Clarendon Street, Oxford OX2 6DP

Oxford University Press is a department of the University of Oxford.
It furthers the University's objective of excellence in research, scholarship,
and education by publishing worldwide in

Oxford New York

Athens Auckland Bangkok Bogotá Buenos Aires Cape Town
Chennai Dar es Salaam Delhi Florence Hong Kong Istanbul Karachi
Kolkata Kuala Lumpur Madrid Melbourne Mexico City Mumbai
Nairobi Paris São Paulo Shanghai Singapore Taipei Tokyo Toronto Warsaw

and associated companies in Berlin Ibadan

Oxford is a registered trade mark of Oxford University Press
in the UK and in certain other countries

Published in the United States
by Oxford University Press Inc., New York

British Library Cataloguing in Publication Data

Data available

Library of Congress Cataloging in Publication Data
The politics of labor in a global age: continuity and change in
late-industrializing and post-socialist economies /
Christopher Candland and Rudra Sil [editors].
p. cm.
Includes bibliographical references and index.
1. Comparative industrial relations.
2. Industrial relations—Developing countries—Case studies. 3. Post-communism.
4. Globalization—Economic aspects. 5. Foreign trade and employment.
I. Candland, Christopher. II. Sil, Rudra.
HD6971 .P55 2001 331′09172′4—dc21 2001016399
ISBN 0–19–924081–7
ISBN 0–19–924114–7 (pbk.)

1 3 5 7 9 10 8 6 4 2

Typeset by Hope Services (Abingdon) Ltd.
Printed in Great Britain
on acid-free paper by
T.J. International Ltd
Padstow, Cornwall

CONTENTS

INTRODUCTION

PART I LABOR IN LATE-INDUSTRIALIZING ECONOMIES

PART II LABOR IN POST-SOCIALIST ECONOMIES

CONCLUSION

LIST OF CONTRIBUTORS

CHRISTOPHER CANDLAND is Assistant Professor of Political Science at Wellesley College where he teaches comparative politics, political economy of development, and South Asian politics. He holds a doctoral degree from Columbia University and has previously taught at the University of California at Berkeley. His research interests include the political economy of development, labor politics, and community development, especially in South and Southeast Asia. His recent publications include book chapters and monographs entitled 'Institutional Impediments to Human Development in Pakistan', 'Can Corporate Codes of Conduct Promote Labor Standards?: Evidence from Thai Footwear and Apparel Industries', and 'Faith as Social Capital: State, Religion, and Community Development in South and Southeast Asia'.

EILEEN M. DOHERTY is Assistant Professor of Political Science at Case Western Reserve University, and holds a secondary appointment at the Weatherhead School of Management there. She is presently completing a book on the management of international financial crises. Her publications include 'Evaluating FDI-Led Investment. The Celtic (Paper?) Tiger', Working Paper 98-1 (Christopher H. Browne Center for International Politics, University of Pennsylvania). She is also coeditor of *Beyond Boundaries? Disciplines, Paradigms, and Theoretical Integration in International Studies* (Albany: SUNY Press, 2000), editor of *Japan's Investment in Asia* (Berkeley: Berkeley Roundtable on the International Economy and The Asia Foundation, 1995). Dr Doherty has previously held appointments as Research Fellow at the Berkeley Roundtable on the International Economy (BRIE) and as Government Relations Analyst at the Japan Economic Institute of America.

LISA E. HALE is currently responsible for political analysis and support for non-proliferation programs at the Los Alamos National Laboratories. She holds a Ph.D. (1999) in Political Science from Northwestern University where her studies encompassed comparative international regimes and political economy. Her dissertation is entitled *Poland's Right Turn: Solidarity as Opposition, Government and Union in the Capitalist Transition*. Dr Hale has previously worked at the Los Alamos National Laboratory as a political analyst and advisor on several projects concerning US science policy and US foreign relations in specific countries.

JEFFREY KOPSTEIN is Associate Professor of Political Science at the University of Colorado at Boulder. His research interests include comparative politics, East European politics, and the political economy of post-communist transitions. He is author of *The Politics of Economic Decline in East Germany, 1945–1989* (University of North Carolina Press, 1997), and has published in a variety of journals, including *World Politics.* He is currently working on a book on overcoming Europe's historical and contemporary divisions.

XIAOBO LU is Assistant Professor of Political Science at Barnard College, Columbia University and a member of the East Asian Institute at Columbia. His research interests include the political economy of post-socialist transition, political corruption, and the role of bureaucracy in economic development. He is the author of the book, *Cadres and Corruption* (Stanford University Press, CA, 2000) and a co-editor of *Danwei: Changing Chinese Workplace in Historical and Comparative Perspective* (Armonk: M.E. Sharpe, 1997).

SCOTT B. MARTIN is Assistant Director of the Institute of Latin American and Iberian Studies at Columbia University where is he is currently finishing a doctoral dissertation in Political Science. He is co-editor of, and contributor to, *The New Politics of Inequality in Latin America: Rethinking Participation and Representation* (Oxford University Press, 1997). He has written extensively on labor and industrial relations in Brazil and Mexico. He has also taught at Columbia, New York University, and the Monterrey Technological Institute (Mexico City campus).

M. VICTORIA MURILLO is an Assistant Professor in Political Science at Yale University. She is author of *Partisan Coalitions and Labor Competition in Latin America* (Cambridge University Press, forthcoming). Her work on unions and market reforms in Latin American has been published in English and Spanish, in edited volumes and journals, such as *World Politics, Journal of Inter-American Studies and World Affairs*, and *Desarrollo Económico*. Dr Murillo holds a Ph.D. from Harvard University and she has previously served as post-doctoral fellow at the Harvard Academy for International and Area Studies.

MITCHELL A. ORENSTEIN is Assistant Professor of Political Science at the Maxwell School of Citizenship and Public Affairs, Syracuse University. He is the author of *Out of the Red: Building Capitalism and Democracy in Post-Communist Europe* (University of Michigan Press, forthcoming 2001), a manuscript which previously won the 1997 Gabriel A. Almond Award of the American Political Science Association for the best dissertation in comparative politics. Dr. Orenstein is currently studying international and domestic influences on the development of post-communist welfare states and is the author of a recent World Bank Policy Research Working Paper 2310 on pension reform in Hungary, Poland, and Kazakhstan. Dr. Orenstein has previously served as Lecturer at Yale University and as Post-Doctoral Fellow at the Watson Institute for International Studies at Brown University. (www.maxwell.syr.edu/maxpages/faculty/maorenst)

RUDRA SIL is Janice and Julian Bers Assistant Professor in the Social Sciences and teaches in the Department of Political Science at the University of Pennsylvania. He is author of *Managing 'Modernity': Work, Community, and Authority in Late-Industrializing Japan and Russia* (Ann Arbor: University of Michigan Press, forthcoming), and co-editor of *Beyond Boundaries? Disciplines, Paradigms, and Theoretical Integration in International Studies* (Albany: State University of New York Press, 2000). Dr Sil's previously published work includes articles in *Polity* and *The Journal of Theoretical Politics*. He is presently working on a comparative-historical study of how transnational and local conceptions of collective 'rights' have affected the patterns and effectiveness of labor-incorporation in India, Japan, and Russia.

CHARLES WEATHERS teaches at Osaka City University and was previously Post-Doctoral Research Fellow at the Institute of Economic Research at Hitotsubashi University in Tokyo. He holds a doctoral degree in Political Science from the University of California at Berkeley. His fields of specialization are Japanese industrial relations and comparative political economy. Dr Weathers' recent publications include an article in *Asian Survey* as well as chapters on contemporary shifts in Japanese labor relations. He is currently working on a manuscript on the development of post-war industrial relations in Japan.

LIST OF FIGURES

LIST OF TABLES

LIST OF ABBREVIATIONS

ACTFU	All China Federation of Trade Unions
AITUC	All India Trade Union Congress
AMIA	Mexican Automobile Industry Association
ANECP	National Agreement for the Promotion of Quality and Productivity (*Mexico*)
APSENAC	All Pakistan State Enterprises Workers' Action Committee
AUCCTU	All Union Central Council of Trade Unions
BIR	Bombay Industrial Relations Act (*India*)
BJP	Bharatiya Janata Party (*India*)
BMS	Bharatiya Mazdoor Sangh (*India*)
CDU	Christian Democratic Union (*Germany*)
CFE	Federal Electricity Commission (*Mexico*)
CFLC	Light and Power Company (*Mexico*)
CGT	General Confederation of Labor (Mexico)
CIOSLt	Center-Left International Trade Union Central
CIPA	bilateral health and safety commission (*Brazil*)
CITU	Center for Indian Trade Unions
CIU	Congress of Irish Unions
CLR	Confederation of Labor of Russia
CMKOS	Czech and Moravian Chamber of Trade Unions
CMM	Chhattisgarh Mukti Morcha (Chattisgarh Liberation Front)
CNSM	National Commission for the Minimum Salary
COPARMEX	Employers' Confederation of Mexico
COR	Revolutionary Labor Confederation
CPI	Communist Party of India
CPI–M	Communist Party of India (Marxist)
CROC	Revolutionary Confederation of Workers and Peasants (*Mexico*)
CROM	Mexican Regional Labor Confederation
CRT	Revolutionary Workers' Confederation (*Mexico*)
CSKOS	Czech and Slovak Chamber of Trade Unions
CT	Congress of Labor (*Mexico*)
CTM	Mexican Workers' Confederation
CUT	Unified Workers' Central (*Brazil*)
CWM	Center for Workers' Management (India)
DIEESE	Inter-Union Department of Socio-Economic Studies
DoT	Department of Telecommunications (*India*)
EEOL	Equal Employment Opportunity Law (*Japan*)

EIU	Economist Intelligence Unit
FDI	foreign direct investment
FDP	Free Democratic Party (I)
FESEBeS	Federation of Goods and Services Unions (*Mexico*)
FIDESZ	Alliance of Young Democrats Party (*Hungary*)
FIE	foreign invested enterprises
FIESP	state industrial federation (*Brazil*)
FITUR	Federation of Independent Trade Unions of Russia
FRD	Front for a Democratic Revolution (*Mexico*)
FSTSE	Federation of Public Services Workers' Unions (*Mexico*)
GATT	General Agreement on Tariffs and Trade
GCTU	General Confederation of Trade Unions (*Russia*)
HMS	Hind Mazdoor Sabha (*India*)
IBEC	Irish Business and Employers Confederation
ICTU	Irish Congress of Trade Unions
IDA	The Industrial Disputes Act (1947)
IISCO	Indian Iron and Steel Company
ILO	International Labor Organization
IMF	International Monetary Fund
IMF–JC	International Metalworkers' Federation—Japan Council
IMSS	Mexican Institute of Social Security
INFONAVIT	Institute of the National Housing Fund (*Mexico*)
INOU	Irish National Organization of the Unemployed
INTUC	Indian National Trade Union Congress
IRC	Interest Reconciliation Council (*Hungary*)
IRO	Industrial Relations Ordinance (*Pakistan*)
ISI	import substitution industrialization
ISITO	Institute for Comparative Research into Industrial Relations
ISO	International Standards Organization
ITGWU	Irish Transport and General Workers' Union
ITUC	Irish Trade Union Congress
JFCA	Federal Conciliation and Arbitration Board (*Mexico*)
JLCA	Local Conciliation and Arbitration Board (*Mexico*)
JUSE	Japanese Union of Scientists and Engineers
KPP	Confederation of Polish Employers
KPRF	Communist Party of the Russian Federation
KUK	Confederation of Arts and Culture (*Czech Republic*)
LFT	Federal Labor Law (*Mexico*)
MITI	Ministry of International Trade and Industry (*Japan*)
MNC	multinational corporation (see also TNC)
MSZOSZ	National Confederation of Hungarian Trade Unions
NAFTA	North American Free Trade Agreement
NCL	National Center for Labor (*India*)
NESC	National Economic and Social Council (*Ireland*)

NFITU	National Federation of Indian Trade Unions
NGO	non-governmental organization
NIRC	National Interest Reconciliation Council (*Hungary*)
NLCC	National Labor Coordination Committee (*India*)
NLO	National Labor Organization (*India*)
NMDC	National Mining Development Corporation (*India*)
OEEC	Organization for European Economic Cooperation
OECD	Organization for Economic Cooperation and Development
OMRI	Open Market Research Institute (*Russia*)
OPZZ	All Poland Alliance of Trade Unions
PDS	Party of Democratic Socialism (*Germany*)
PILER	Pakistan Institute of Labor Education and Research
PNR	National Revolutionary Party (*Mexico*)
POE	privately owned enterprise
PRC	People's Republic of China
PRD	Party of the Democratic Revolution (*Mexico*)
PRI	Institutional Revolutionary Party (*Mexico*)
PRM	Party of the Mexican Revolution
PSE	Pact of Economic Solidarity (*Mexico*)
PSL	Polish Peasant Party
PT	Workers' Party (*Brazil*)
PWC	Pakistan Workers' Confederation
RFE/RL	Radio Free Europe/Radio Liberty
RHSD	Council For Economic and Social Agreement
RMMS	Rashtriya Mills Mazdoor Sangh (National Mill Workers' Union) (*India*)
ROH	Revolutionary Trade Union Movement
RSS	Rashtriya Swayamsevak Sangh
RTK	Russian Trilateral Commission
RUIEE	Russian Union of Industrialists and Entrepeneurs
SAIL	Steel Authority of India Ltd
SAR	System of Savings for Retirement (*Mexico*)
SEWA	Self-Employed Women's Association (*India*)
SIPTU	Services, Industrial, Professional and Technical Union (*Ireland*)
SLD	Alliance of the Democratic Left (*Poland*)
SME	Mexican Union of Electricity Workers
SNTE	National Union of Education Workers (*Mexico*)
SOE	state owned enterprise
Sotsprof	Social Trade Unions (*Russia*)
SPD	Sozialdemokratische Partei Deutschlands (Social Democrats)
STK	councils of labor collectives (*Russia/USSR*)
STPS	Secretary of Labor and Social Welfare (*Mexico*)
STRM	Mexican Union of Telephone Workers

SUTERM	United Union of Electricity Workers (I)
SZOT	National Council of Trade Unions (I)
TIE	Transnationals Information Exchange (*The Netherlands*)
TNC	transnational corporation
TRAI	Telecom Regulatory Authority of India
TUC	Trades Union Congress (*Ireland*)
TVE	township and village enterprises (*China*)
UNCTAD	United Nations Conference on Trade and Development
UOI	Independent Worker Unity (*Mexico*)
UTN	National Union of Workers (*Mexico*)
UTUC	United Trade Union Congress (*India*)
UTUC(LS)	United Trade Union Congress (Lenin Sarani) (*India*)
VTsIOM	All Russia Center for Public Opinion Research
WAPDA	Water and Power Generation and Distribution Agency
WTO	World Trade Organization

Introduction

I

The Politics of Labor in Late-industrializing and Post-socialist Economies: New Challenges in a Global Age

Christopher Candland, Wellesley College and
Rudra Sil, University of Pennsylvania

The increasingly rapid transnational movement of capital, commodities, services, information, and technology force labor institutions everywhere to respond to new challenges and pressures. This is evident in the effects of structural adjustment on political unionism in countries such as India and Mexico, in the shifts in employment practices and labor processes accompanying the privatization of state-owned enterprises in post-communist Europe and in China, and even in unanticipated shifts in industrial relations in Japan. Marked changes in patterns of industrial relations are everywhere an important part of the economic transformations unfolding in these diverse settings.

This volume features several original and timely chapters on the shift in patterns of labor relations worldwide, with a focus on 'late-industrializing', largely post-colonial economies coping with structural adjustment and post-socialist economies coping with the creation of new markets and the dismantling of command economies.[1] The authors examine the processes that are transforming labor institutions—whether at the national, local, or workplace levels—under the conditions of economic reform and increased exposure to international economic forces. Rather than treating these processes of change as dictated from above by political elites, the authors consider the interplay of the multiple political, economic, and social factors that shape the renegotiation of existing pacts and relationships between key economic actors such as labor, management, and relevant governmental actors. Each of the studies

---

[1] The term 'developing' or 'late-developing' is avoided because it begs the question of what constitutes 'development', especially in regions where poverty is increasing and the average quality of life is declining despite aggregate economic growth and technological progress. The historically more descriptive term 'post-colonial' disguises important differences between the experiences of colonized societies and excludes other societies that experienced forms of foreign domination short of colonization. Thus, with some reluctance, we use the term 'late industrializing' to refer to capitalist or mixed economies that have belatedly attempted to overcome relative economic 'backwardness' following a period of colonization or domination under one of the earlier industrializers of the West (without trying to ignore or defeat international capitalism as in the case of socialist command economies).

focuses on the influence of existing economic and social institutions on the process of renegotiation and the emergence of distinctive institutional arrangements. While the essays document that economic adjustment and 'globalization' have weakened organized labor, they also show that distinctive national and local institutions persist in the course of economic reform and contribute to significant and meaningful variations in patterns of labor relations.

In this chapter, we set the stage for the volume by discussing the importance of analysing the experience of workers and the transformation of labor institutions in the new global economy in the light of existing studies of the political economy of late-industrializing and post-socialist countries. We begin by considering two general themes running through each of the contributions to this volume. First, while the study of labor relations is important in its own right, the study of recent changes in industrial relations under conditions of economic transformation is also valuable for illuminating the social forces that frequently influence the politics of economic reform as well as for more effectively bridging the fields of comparative industrial relations and political economy. Second, the comparison of the experiences of workers and the transformation of industrial relations in late-industrializing and post-socialist settings can be employed to systematically test the limits of the currently fashionable concept of globalization. While the concept is valuable for capturing the common pressures facing labor institutions, whether global economic forces erode national or regional differences, undermine the influence of distinctive historical experiences, or produce increasingly uniform policies or institutions needs to be investigated empirically. Following the discussion of these two points of concern, we identify the common set of specific empirical questions addressed by the authors as well as the broader, more theoretically oriented, questions that the authors hope to collectively shed light on by juxtaposing their findings. We then provide brief overviews of the nine studies that follow.

The following four chapters constitute Part I of the volume. These chapters examine shifts in national and local labor institutions in several late-industrializing economies coping with economic adjustment (Brazil, India, Ireland, Japan, Mexico, and Pakistan). The next four chapters constitute Part II of the volume. These chapters examine how post-socialist economies (China, Russia, eastern Germany, and the former communist states of East-Central Europe) are affected by, and respond to, market reforms and new international economic forces. The volume concludes with discussion of some of the key insights gained by comparing these nine studies within and across the categories of late-industrializing and post-socialist economies.

The Politics of Economic Reform: Bringing Society—and Labor—Back in

Significant scholarly study of economic liberalization can be traced to a 1984 conference of political scientists and economists at Columbia University's Lehman Institute, which had been organized in the wake of the debt crisis and the subsequent initiation of structural adjustment measures in Latin America.[2] Much of the earlier literature in the political economy of development focused on the effects of regime characteristics on economic policy and performance, frequently pointing to the benefits of 'bureaucratic authoritarianism' or 'soft authoritarianism' in the implementation of development programs.[3] In contrast, the post-debt crisis studies have sought to identify the concrete political factors in particular countries or regions that influence governments' ability to implement economic adjustment. Some concentrated their attention on 'the packaging of programs or the manipulation of opposition groups' required to adopt and implement unpopular economic programs.[4] Others focused on the political coalitions that facilitated the implementation of structural adjustment programs or the creation of market economies in post-socialist regions.[5] Still others went beyond discussions of coalitions and strategies for designing and implementing economic reforms and were more explicitly concerned with the institutional dimensions of liberalization and transition.[6]

These studies of the politics of economic reform led to an impressive series of volumes that define the political economy of reform as a coherent field of

[2] See the special issues of *International Organization* 39: 3 and 4 (1986); and Miles Kahler, (ed.), *The Politics of International Debt* (Ithaca: Cornell University Press, 1986).

[3] This approach to development has its roots in such studies as Alexander Gerschenkron's analysis of economic backwardness and David Apter's study of mobilization regimes and explicitly informed the studies of bureaucratic authoritarianism in Latin America during the 1970s and the East Asian 'capitalist developmental state' in the early 1980s. See Gerschenkron, *Economic Backwardness in Historical Perspective* (Cambridge: Harvard University Press, 1962); Apter, 'System, Process and the Politics of Economic Development,' in B. F. Hoselitz and W. E. Moore, *Industrialization and Society* (The Hague: Mouton, 1963); Guillermo O'Donnell, *Modernization and Bureaucratic-Authoritarianism* (Berkeley: Institute of International Studies, University of California at Berkeley, 1973); and Chalmers Johnson, 'Political Institutions and Economic Performance: The Government-Business Relationship in Japan, South Korea, and Taiwan', in Frederic C. Deyo, *The Political Economy of the New Asian Industrialism* (Ithaca: Cornell University Press, 1987). Early discussions of regimes types focused on economic adjustment include Jeffrey Frieden, *Debt, Development and Democracy* (Princeton: Princeton University Press, 1991); Adam Przeworski, *Democracy and Markets* (New York: Cambridge University Press, 1991); and Karen Remmer, 'Democracy and Economic Crisis: The Latin American Experience', *World Politics*, 42: 3 (1991), 315–35.

[4] Stephan Haggard and Robert Kaufman, 'Introduction: Institutions and Economic Adjustment', in Haggard and Kaufman (eds), *The Politics of Economic Adjustment* (Princeton: Princeton University Press, 1992), 25.

[5] On the role of political coalitions, see Merilee Grindle and John Thomas, *Public Choices and Policy Change* (Baltimore: The Johns Hopkins University Press, 1991).

[6] See Thomas Callaghy, 'Toward State Capacity and Embedded Liberalism in the Third World: Lessons for Adjustment', in Joan Nelson (ed.), *Fragile Coalitions* (New Brunswick: Transaction Books, 1989), 115–38; and Peter Evans, *Embedded Autonomy: States and Industrial Transformation* (Princeton: Princeton University Press, 1995).

study operating at the intersection of two important disciplines.[7] However, the focus has been almost exclusively on discrete, concretely observable, political and economic variables with no more than a peripheral consideration of the role of the social institutions and social structures, networks and norms underlying these institutions.[8] Scholars of classical political economy (e.g., Karl Marx, Herbert Spencer, Max Weber, Karl Polanyi) were not restricted to strictly political and economic factors. They frequently emphasized the importance of social structures and cultural understandings. Yet, in contemporary studies of economic change, political economy and economic sociology have become distinct subfields. The former tends to neglect social structures, identities, and norms; the latter tends to ignore the role of political structures and processes. Much contemporary literature on the political economy of late-industrializing regions is thus characterized by a strong tendency to view economic adjustment as a process which governments effect upon societies, not vice versa, and to treat policy choices as matters of strategy, relatively unencumbered by the independent interests, expectations, or political pressure from social groups.[9] Similarly, the study of post-socialist transition is frequently viewed by students of political economy and policy advocates alike as a matter of whether competent leaders can be found who understand the dynamics of markets and who possess the will and political acumen to engineer radical market reforms while ignoring social costs and downplaying the social roots of opposition to reform.[10] The chapters in this volume adopt a broader understanding of political economy by explicitly considering the

[7] See Nelson (ed.), *Fragile Coalitions;* Nelson, (ed.), *Economic Crisis and Policy Choice* (Princeton: Princeton University Press, 1990); and Haggard and Kaufman (eds), *The Politics of Economic Adjustment.* More recent studies in the field of contemporary political economy in late-industrializing and post-socialist countries include Stephan Haggard and Chung H. Lee, *The Politics of Finance in Developing Countries* (Ithaca: Cornell University Press, 1993); Anne Krueger (ed.), *Political Economy of Policy Reform in Developing Countries* (Cambridge: MIT Press, 1993); Sylvia Maxfield, *Gatekeepers of Growth* (Princeton: Princeton University Press, 1997); Beverly Crawford (ed.) *Markets, States, and Democracy* (Boulder: Westview Press, 1995); and David Bartlett, *The Political Economy of Dual Transformations* (Ann Arbor: University of Michigan Press, 1997).

[8] On contemporary economic sociology, see Mark Granovetter and Richard Swedberg (eds), *The Sociology of Economic Life* (Boulder: Westview Press, 1992); and Neil Smelser and Richard Swedberg (eds), *The Handbook of Economic Sociology* (Princeton: Princeton University Press, 1993).

[9] Haggard acknowledges that social forces influence policy but insists that as these forces are 'always mediated by institutional settings' the focus should be on placing economic change 'within the context of government strategy'. Note that Haggard's understanding of 'institutional settings' is limited to legal arrangements. [See Stephan Haggard, *Pathways from the Periphery* (Ithaca: Cornell University Press, 1990), 3, 251.] The authors in this volume take legal arrangements as but one dimension of institutional influence over economic reform.

[10] See, for example, Anders Aslund, 'The Russian Road to the Market', *Current History* (October 1995), 311–16; Joseph R. Blasi, Maya Kroumova, and Douglas Kruse, *Kremlin Capitalism* (Ithaca: Cornell University Press, 1997); Jeffrey D. Sachs and Andrew M. Warner, 'Achieving Rapid Growth in the Transition Economies of Central Europe', Discussion Paper 544, Harvard Institute for International Development (July 1996); and David Stark and Laszlo Bruszt, *Postsocialist Pathways* (Cambridge: Cambridge University Press, 1998).

relationships and expectations shared by different social groups which bear on both, the 'political' and the 'economic'.

The research presented here seeks to understand economic policies and institutions as the outcomes not only of political maneuvering or regime features but also of social forces and contests that may not always be manifested as discernible political conflicts or policy choices. In fact, the evidence from the contributions assembled here directly challenges one of the core assumptions of the contemporary studies of the political economy of economic reform, that 'political leadership and organization' matter more than 'social structure'.[11] Where political elites of very different stripes, operating within very different political regimes, may end up adopting broadly similar strategies and economic policies, low levels of state capacity and autonomy are in evidence and where social institutions prove to be unexpectedly resilient. On the other hand, political elites who begin with similar objectives and strategies may end up adopting very different economic policies and institutions, as a result of the unanticipated effects of existing social institutions or the structures, networks or norms underlying these institutions. This points to the need for greater attention to the distinctive historical processes that led to the formation of these social institutions and structures. A better understanding of these processes may shed light on the interests, expectations and interactions of economically important actors seeking to establish new pacts and institutional arrangements as they respond to new conditions in the course of economic adjustment or transition.

The social dimensions of economic development and reform are sometimes difficult to quantify or even translate into discrete variables. Even so, the treatment of the political element in political economy must run deeper than it does in most contemporary studies on the political economy of economic reform. A more complete understanding of the politics in the political economy of reform needs to go beyond the analysis of regime characteristics or political coalitions and strategies. It needs to incorporate the effects of existing social structures and institutional arrangements—whether formal or informal—as these are manifested in the processes of renegotiation and contestation among various social groups and economic actors with different resources in the course of economic reform.[12]

In this regard, analysis of the transformation of labor institutions is particularly worthwhile. Certainly, the study of labor is important in its own right as specialists in industrial relations will quickly point out. However, an additional important advantage of focusing on the experiences of workers and the transformation of labor institutions in the course of economic reform is that it permits us to better understand how social structures shape, and are shaped by, political and economic processes. Workers and their formal and

---

[11] Haggard, *Pathways from the Periphery*, 3.

[12] This is one of the great strengths of the understanding of politics in Peter Gourevitch, *Politics in Hard Times* (Ithaca: Cornell University Press, 1986).

informal organizations represent an important collection of actors who are simultaneously political actors, seeking to advance policies that will protect their jobs, wages, and rights in the course of macroeconomic change, and social actors, whose expectations, norms, and social relations are shaped by wider social structures that extend far beyond their unions, firms, and work. In addition, the study of the political economy of economic reform can be greatly enriched by analysing more thoroughly the process through which formal and informal pacts are renegotiated between workers and labor unions, managerial elites, who are also a part of larger networks, social classes and communities, and governmental elites, who for the most part neither constitute a unitary actor nor remain autonomous from social forces.[13] Thus, by shifting the focus from the engineering of reform from above to the transformation of labor institutions, it is possible to better appreciate how the persistence or legacies of existing institutions—whether these are in the form of the specific characteristics of formal systems of industrial relations, or in the form of informal relationships, norms, and expectations shared by particular groups of workers or managers—shape the dynamics and outcomes of political struggles and social contests in the process of economic reform.[14]

The focus on the experiences and responses of labor within the particular context of economic reform has the added benefit of making more explicit the connections between the fields of comparative industrial relations and mainstream political economy. An earlier generation of scholars did not draw clear distinctions between the fields of industrial relations and political economy; instead, their studies of political and economic development, whatever their other shortcomings, treated the emergence of factories, working-class movements, and new patterns of employment and work as important, if not central, aspects of 'modern' industrial society.[15] Some recent studies of development have also taken for granted the importance of studying the role of labor and

[13] On the general social embeddedness of economic action, see Mark Granovetter, 'Economic Action and Social Structure: The Problem of Embeddedness', *American Journal of Sociology*, 91 (1985), 481–510. On the significance of variations in the capacity of states to act as autonomous, unitary actors, see Peter Evans, 'The State as Problem and Solution: Predation, Embedded Autonomy, and Structural Change', in Haggard and Kaufman (eds) *The Politics of Economic Adjustment*.

[14] On the impact of historical legacies on the world-views of workers and the divergent patterns of industrial relations, see Charles Sabel, *Work and Politics* (New York: Cambridge University Press, 1982), esp. 15–25. See also the pathbreaking (though now outdated) comparative study by Reinhard Bendix, *Work and Authority in Industry* (New York: John Wiley, 1956).

[15] This is evident in the work of many theorists of the 1950s and 1960s who viewed the emergence of a working class and the subsequent transformation of work as intrinsic elements of a broader evolutionary process of political, economic, and socio-cultural 'modernization'. See, e.g., Neil Smelser, *Social Change in the Industrial Revolution* (Chicago: University of Chicago Press, 1959); Clark Kerr, J. T. Dunlop, F. H. Garbison, and C. A. Myers, *Industrialism and Industrial Man* (Cambridge: Harvard University Press, 1960); Ferdynand Zweig, *The Worker in an Affluent Society* (London: Heinemann, 1961); and Alex Inkeles and David Smith, *Becoming Modern* (Cambridge: Harvard University Press, 1974). For a different approach that emphasized the persistence of diversity in industrial relations in the course of industrialization, see Bendix, *Work and Authority in Industry*.

the processes of working-class formation and labor incorporation as part of any attempt to understand the historical processes of political and economic change.[16] This is not the case, however, with the contemporary study of the politics of economic adjustment or transition in late-industrializing post-socialist countries as scholars' narrow understanding of politics frequently results in the failure to adequately incorporate into the analysis of the reform process the experiences and responses of workers, the largest social class to be affected by economic reform and by increasing exposure to international economic forces.[17]

Specialists in industrial relations, for their part, although they locate their empirical observations within the context of the particular political regimes or economic systems in the regions they study, have tended to view the comparative study of labor as a subfield of US industrial relations, a subfield that is 'relatively isolated from the empirical contributions and theoretical insights of related fields, such as political sociology and comparative political economy.'[18] Recent attempts to transform the study of industrial relations into a comparative project that is closely related to the study of international political economy are laudable, but these attempts tend to be heavily influenced by the experiences of advanced industrial countries, that is, in the Organization for Economic Cooperation and Development (OECD) countries.[19] The resulting frameworks, however, are generally limited in terms of whether they

[16] Collier and Collier, for example, have noted that the timing and nature of the incorporation of the labor movement proved to be crucial to subsequent patterns of state-society relations in Latin America for much of the twentieth century. See Ruth Berins Collier and David Collier, *Shaping the Political Arena* (Princeton: Princeton University Press, 1991). Similarly, Rakhahari Chatterji's study of labor formation in three Indian states finds that 'the timing of industrialization as well as the type of industrializing elite made for important differences for the nature of the trade union movement'. Rakhahari Chatterji, *Unions, Politics and the State* (New Delhi: South Asian Publishers, 1980), 207. Another excellent contribution along these lines is Dietrich Rueschemeyer, Evelyn Huber Stephens, and John Stephens, *Capitalist Development and Democracy* (Chicago: University of Chicago Press, 1992).

[17] For example, one excellent study, Gerald Helleiner's *The New Global Economy and the Developing Countries* (Brookfield, VT: Edward Elgar, 1990), traces the effects of international economic forces on late-industrializing economies but makes no mention of labor. Similarly, in the case of post-socialist transitions, the lack of attention to labor except as an input is evident in Blasi *et al.*, *Kremlin Capitalism;* and Sachs and Warner, 'Achieving Rapid Growth in the Transition Economies of Central Europe'; on this point, see also Simon Clarke, Peter Fairbrother *et al.*, *What About the Workers? Workers and the Transition to Capitalism in Russia* (London: Verso, 1993). The volumes cited above in notes 5 and 6 also do not consider workers or labor institutions as significant aspects of the economic reform process.

[18] Kirsten Wever and Lowell Turner, Preface to Wever and Turner (eds), *The Comparative Political Economy of Industrial Relations* (Madison: Industrial Relations Research Association, 1995), v.

[19] See, for example, Sanford Jacoby (ed.), *The Workers of Nations* (New York: Oxford University Press, 1995); Richard Locke, Thomas Kochan, and Michael Piore, 'Reconceptualizing Comparative Industrial Relations: Lessons from International Research', *International Labour Review*, 134: 2 (1995); Wever and Turner (eds), *The Comparative Political Economy of Industrial Relations;* Robert Lawrence, *Single World, Divided Nations* (Washington, DC: Brookings Institution Press, 1996); and Geoffrey Garrett, *Partisan Politics in the Global Economy* (New York: Cambridge University Press, 2000).

can effectively capture shifts in industrial relations in non-OECD countries. While trends in the international economy undoubtedly create some common problems for labor worldwide, the kinds of problems faced by workers and labor institutions dealing with economic adjustment or market transition in late-industrializing and post-socialist settings are quite different and potentially more difficult to resolve. Although there have been important contributions from scholars studying industrial relations in late-industrializing and socialist and post-socialist settings,[20] there has been little cross-regional comparative work done of late on the broader theoretical implications of the similarities and differences in the way in which workers and labor institutions in these settings have been experiencing and responding to the effects of economic adjustment and market transition.[21] By examining the responses of workers and the transformations of labor institutions in the context of the wider transformation of late-industrializing and post-socialist economies, the chapters in this volume offer a modest but important contribution to the development of a more broadly comparative approach to industrial relations, especially in relation to late-industrializing and post-socialist settings, that can be better related to issues and problems of interest to students of contemporary political economy.

[20] On late-industrializing regions, see, e.g., Ruth Berins Collier and David Collier, *Shaping the Political Arena; Chatterji, Unions, Politics and the State;* Jean Carriere, Nigel Hawthorn, and Jacqueline Roddick, *The State, Industrial Relations and the Labour Movement in Latin America* (Basingstoke: Macmillan, 1989); Walter Galenson, *Labour and Economic Growth in Five Asian Countries* (New York: Praeger, 1992); Inga Brandell (ed.), *Workers in Third-World Industrialization* (New York: St. Martin's Press, 1991); and Peter Gutkind (ed.), *Third World Workers* (New York: E. J. Brill, 1988). On labor in socialist and post-socialist regions, see Walter D. Connor, *The Accidental Proletariat* (Princeton: Princeton University Press, 1991); Michael Burawoy and Janos Lukacs, *The Radiant Past* (Chicago: University of Chicago Press, 1992); Simon Clarke (ed.), *Management and Industry in Russia* (Brookfield, VT: Edward Elgar, 1995); Stephen Crowley, *Hot Coal, Cold Steel: Russian and Ukrainian Workers from the End of the Soviet Union to the Post-Communist Transformations* (Ann Arbor: University of Michigan Press, 1997); and Xiaobo Lu and Elizabeth Perry (eds), *Danwei: The Changing Chinese Workplace in Historical and Comparative Perspective* (Armonk: M. E. Sharpe, 1997).

[21] Among the exceptions to this observation are the essays in Stephen Frenkel and Jeffrey Harrod (eds), *Industrialization and Labor Relations* (Ithaca: ILR Press, 1995); Frederic C. Deyo (ed.), *Social Reconstructions of the World Automobile Industry* (New York: St. Martin's Press, 1996); and Peter Waterman and Ronaldo Munck (eds), *Labour Worldwide in the Era of Globalisation* (Basingstoke: Macmillan, 1998). Frenkel and Harrod tend to emphasize the relationship between industrialization and economic growth, with little systematic attention to the specific impact of economic adjustment or transition. The essays in the Deyo volume certainly emphasize the effects of newly emergent flexible production processes, but given the focus on the automobile industry, they only incorporate the experiences of non-OECD countries where automobile factories have been established (such as Korea, Thailand, and Mexico). Our point is not that these volumes suffer from shortcomings, but rather that the framework for our volume has a somewhat different focus and incorporates the experiences of post-socialist transition. As such, the contributions assembled here may be viewed as complementing the volumes edited by Deyo, Frenkel, and Harrod, and Waterman and Munck.

Labor in a Global Economy: The Limits of Convergence

A second common thread running through the essays in this volume consists of the authors' considered reaction to a relatively new trend in the study of international political economy: the expectation of convergence across policies and institutions supposedly as a result of 'globalization'. For some, globalization is a synonym for increasing economic interdependence. In this sense, globalization is simply a new way of referring to a theoretical concept that has been popular since the 1970s and an empirical process that has been under way for several decades with steadily increasing levels of international trade, direct investment, technology transfers, and migration.[22] To others, the term has a more specific meaning, suggesting not only increasing economic interdependence but also a qualitative transformation of the global order and its constituent elements, specifically as a result of the unprecedented level of transnational flows in capital, technology, ideas, and people over the last two decades.[23] In either framework, states are thought to be less capable of intervening in international trade and finance as production and technology become increasingly global and undermine conventional understandings of national sovereignty.[24] Economically important institutions and macroeconomic policies become increasingly homogeneous as individuals, firms, and governments come to appreciate the universal benefits of expanded trade and technology while adopting broadly similar policies and imitating 'best practice' despite cultural diversity.[25] Finally, new, uniform global logics are thought to drive the behavior of transnational and subnational actors.[26]

---

[22] Some of the central defining elements of 'globalization' were anticipated two decades ago in the discussion of 'complex interdependence' in Robert Keohane and Joseph Nye's classic work, *Power and Interdependence* (Boston: Little, Brown, 1977).

[23] See, e.g., Martin Albrow, *The Global Age* (Stanford, CA: Stanford University Press, 1996); and Kenichi Ohmae, *The Borderless World* (New York: Harper Perennial, 1993).

[24] Cerny, for example, claims that '[i]n recent decades, . . . an accelerating divergence has taken place between the structure of the state and the structure of industrial and financial markets in the complex, globalizing world of the third industrial revolution. There is a new disjuncture between institutional capacity to provide public goods and the structural characteristics of a much larger-scale, global economy. . . . [T]oday's "residual state" faces crises of both organizational efficiency and institutional legitimacy'. See Philip Cerny, 'Globalization and the Changing Logic of Collective Action', *International Organization*, 49: 4 (Autumn 1995), 595–625, quote from p. 598. On this point, see also Kenichi Ohmae (ed.), *The Evolving Global Economy* (Boston: Harvard Business Review, 1995); and Ralph Bryant, 'Global Change: Increasing Economic Integration and Eroding Political Sovereignty', *Brookings Review*, 12: 4 (Fall 1994), esp. 42–5.

[25] See, e.g., Jeffrey Sachs and Andrew Warner, 'Economic Reform and the Process of Global Integration', Brookings Paper on Economic Activity, 1 (1995); Vincent Cable, 'The New Trade Agenda: Universal Rules Amid Cultural Diversity', *International Affairs*, 72: 2 (April 1996), 227–46; W. Carl Kester, 'American and Japanese Corporate Governance: Convergence to Best Practice?' in Suzanne Berger and Ronald Dore (eds), *National Diversity and Global Capitalism* (Ithaca: Cornell University Press, 1996), 107–37; and Shigeru Otsubo, *Globalization* (Washington, DC: World Bank, 1996).

[26] See Cerny, 'Globalization and the Changing Logic of Collective Action'; and Kenichi Ohmae, 'Putting Global Logic First', in Ohmae (ed.), *The Evolving Global Economy*.

For many students of industrial relations who subscribe to this thesis, integration into the global economy is expected to produce a convergence in patterns of labor relations and work organization as a result of similar pressures on existing social pacts. As economic adjustment leads governments and employers to curtail many of the welfare benefits and employment guarantees previously offered to employees, especially employees in large public sector firms, the expectation is that the old labor institutions and understandings will give way to new universal logics for reorganizing labor relations and production processes. According to one scholar, for example, throughout the world,

corporatist bargaining and employment policies are everywhere under pressure . . . in the face of international pressure for wage restraint and flexible working practices. The provision of education and training increasingly is taking priority over direct labor market intervention, worker protection, and incomes policy.[27]

Others emphasize the significance of similar trends worldwide towards supposedly homogeneous employment practices, forms of employee participation, patterns of work organization, and other labor processes. In this context, the shift to a new age of post-Fordist production is often interpreted as a universal phenomenon as more and more firms are expected to respond to the pressures of an increasingly competitive global economy by imitating each others' best practices and adopting similar flexible labor systems or lean production techniques.[28] Moreover, the employment practices and production techniques of Japanese firms in particular—what some refer to as 'Toyotaism'—have been treated by many as a model for post-Fordist industrial relations in both advanced post-industrial countries and late-industrializing countries.[29] In the light of these shifts in employment patterns, wage bargain-

[27] Cerny, 'Globalization and the Changing Logic of Collective Action', 612. Among the key works that first noted the weakening of corporatism and decline in union membership during the 1980s in Western Europe are Scott Lash, 'The End of Neo-Corporatism? The Breakdown of Centralised Bargaining in Sweden', *British Journal of Industrial Relations*, 23 (1985), 215–39; and Peter Swenson, *Fair Shares: Unions, Pay and Politics in Sweden and Germany* (Ithaca: Cornell University Press, 1989).

[28] The idea of a new age of 'flexibility' in production was first anticipated in Michael Piore and Charles Sabel, *The Second Industrial Divide* (New York: Basic Books, 1984). For other works on the appearance of 'flexible specialization' and 'lean production', see Kester, 'American and Japanese Corporate Governance'; Stephen Wood (ed.), *The Transformation of Work* (London: Unwin & Hyman, 1989); Paul Blyton and J. Morris (eds), *A Flexible Future* (New York: De Gruyter, 1991); Joseph Tidd, *Flexible Manufacturing Technologies and International Competitiveness* (London: Pinter, 1991); Ash Amin (ed.), *Post-Fordism: A Reader* (Oxford: Blackwell, 1994); and John Paul MacDuffie, 'International Trends in Work Organization in the Auto Industry: National-Level vs. Company-Level Perspectives', in Wever and Turner (eds), *The Comparative Political Economy of Industrial Relations*.

[29] One of the first arguments about the possibility of an 'organization-centered' Japanese model of labor relations and work organization was Ronald Dore, *British Factory, Japanese Factory* (Berkeley: University of California Press, 1973). That argument was framed within the context of late-developers engaging in 'catch-up industrialization' as part of the second industrial revolution (i.e., Fordist mass production). More recent arguments focus on Japanese lean production techniques and flexible employment practices in both late-industrializers and advanced

ing, and production systems, even neo-Marxists and labor sympathizers adopt a 'global' perspective, arguing that international standards must be introduced or that workers must adopt international strategies to protect their rights and livelihoods.[30] In all of these arguments, we often find implicit assumptions—and sometimes explicit claims—about an underlying evolutionary dynamic at work whereby national and regional variations are regarded as becoming progressively less significant in economic life compared to the homogenizing effects of increasingly uniform institutions, practices, and policies in a more thoroughly integrated global economy.

Arguments about convergence are certainly not new in the fields of political economy or industrial relations. In earlier theories of modernization and development, for example, national societies were regarded as distinct social systems that were becoming increasingly differentiated as they gradually became modern industrial societies characterized by increasingly homogeneous social structures, economic systems, political systems, and even value-systems.[31] In studies of industrial relations, some scholars explicitly argued that industrialization was producing a convergence across societies through interrelated processes leading to similar class structures, similar labor processes and work experiences, similar distributions of power and wealth, and even similar attitudes and values among factory workers everywhere.[32]

In contrast to these earlier theories, the new arguments about convergence involve a very different logic and a very different theory about the sources of

countries. See, e.g., Nick Oliver and Barry Wilkinson, *The Japanization of British Industry* (Oxford: Blackwell, 1988); Martin Kenney and Richard Florida, *Beyond Mass Production* (New York: Oxford University Press, 1993); Raphael Kaplinsky, 'Technique and System: The Spread of Japanese Management Techniques to Developing Countries', *World Development*, 23: 1 (1995), 57–71; and, for a more critical review of such arguments, Tony Elger and Chris Smith (eds), *Global Japanization?* (London: Routledge, 1994).

[30] See, e.g., Ellen Meiksins Wood, Peter Meiksins, and Michael Yates (eds), *Rising From the Ashes? Labor in the Age of 'Global' Capitalism*, special issue of *Monthly Review*, 49: 3 (July–Aug. 1997); Terry Boswell and Dimitris Stevis, 'Globalization and International Labor Organizing: A World-System Perspective', special issue on 'Labor in the Americas', *Work and Occupations*, 24: 3 (Aug. 1997), 288–307; Terry Collingsworth, J. William Goold, and Pharis J. Harvey, 'Time for a Global New Deal', *Foreign Affairs*, (Jan.–Feb. 1994), 8–13; and Michel Hansenne, 'Promoting Social Justice in the New Global Economy', *Monthly Labor Review*, 117 (Sept. 1994) 3–4.

[31] These arguments were mostly based on the 'structural-functional' framework developed in Talcott Parsons, *The Social System* (New York: Free Press, 1951); and Parsons and Edward Shils, *Toward a General Theory of Action* (New York: Harper & Row, 1951). See also Walt Rostow, *The Stages of Economic Growth* (Cambridge: Cambridge University Press, 1962); Daniel Lerner, *The Passing of Traditional Society* (rev. edn.) (New York: Free Press, 1964); and Marion Levy, *Modernization and the Structure of Societies* (Princeton: Princeton University Press, 1966).

[32] See, e.g., the classic arguments on convergence in John Dunlop, *Industrial Relations Systems* (Carbondale: Southern Illinois University Press, 1958); and Kerr *et al.*, *Industrialism and Industrial Man.* For theories suggesting that workers experienced 'embourgeoisement' as a result of their increasing affluence and their increasing abilities to exercise discretion in the control of machines, see respectively Zweig, *The Worker in an Affluent Society;* and Robert Blauner, *Alienation and Freedom* (Chicago: University of Chicago Press, 1964). The argument on the increasingly similar modern attitudes and values among workers in industrial factories is from Inkeles and Smith, *Becoming Modern.*

change. The impetus for change is to be located at the global level, not at the societal level. The mechanisms for convergence now involve not increasing differentiation of societies or factory systems but the worldwide spread of markets, the transnational flows of capital, technology, ideas and people, and the imitation of best practices in designing institutions and policies.[33] But, as with the earlier theories of convergence, arguments about the harmonizing or homogenizing effects of 'globalization' need to be treated not as axiomatic propositions but as hypotheses to be evaluated in the light of the concrete historical experiences, actual evidence of institutional change, and the specific responses of key actors at national and local levels.[34]

The convergence view of globalization may be least applicable in the context of analysing the experiences of workers and the nature of labor institutions since, as one specialist of industrial relations notes, there exists '. . . a basic tension inherent in the process of economic globalization: capital—that is, money and corporations—is becoming more international, while labor remains rooted in particular places called nations'.[35] Indeed, most workers are concerned with basic issues such as wages, working conditions, and welfare—issues that can only be understood within the framework of particular historical experiences and concrete institutional frameworks at the national or regional level.

Increasing levels of economic interdependence have produced new pressures on existing institutions and policies for dealing with the complex relationships among labor, management and the state. Pressures for wage restraint, the decline in welfare benefits and employment security, the relative decline in the size and power of many trade union federations, the growth of underemployment and the informal sector, and a growing gap in incomes and status within the labor force—confront labor worldwide. In this context, the idea of globalization is meaningful for systematically capturing and comparing the dilemmas facing workers, unions, firms, and managers around the world. What this suggests for the level of homogeneity in the institutions, norms, decision-making processes, and policy outcomes across nations, sectors or regions, however, is very much an open question to be analysed in concrete empirical contexts.

---

[33] Such arguments on the standardizing effects of globalization are seen by critics as indicative of a return to convergence theories and universalism in social science theorizing (at the expense of historical contexts and cross-national variations). See, e.g., Robert Boyer, 'The Convergence Hypothesis Revisited: Globalization But Still the Century of Nations?' in Berger and Dore (eds), *National Diversity and Global Capitalism*, 29–59; and Jeffrey C. Alexander, 'Modern, Anti, Post and Neo', *New Left Review*, 210 (March–April 1995), esp. 86.

[34] Students of international political economy have already found important differences in the national institutions and policies to persist despite increasing economic interdependence. See, e.g., Boyer, 'The Convergence Hypothesis Revisited'; Robert Wade, 'Globalization and its Limits: Reports of the Death of the National Economy are Greatly Exaggerated', in Berger and Dore (eds), *National Diversity and Global Capitalism*, 60–88; Miles Kahler, 'Trade and Domestic Differences', in Berger and Dore (eds), *National Diversity and Global Capitalism;* and Garrett, *Obstinate or Obsolete? The Nation-State in the Global Economy.*

[35] Sanford Jacoby, Preface to Jacoby (ed.), *The Workers of Nations*, ix.

Comparisons of the experiences of advanced industrial countries have already been invoked to demonstrate the limits of the homogenizing effects of globalization and to document the considerable and persistent variations across nations and regions. Some common trends have been noted through-out OECD countries: the overall decline in union membership, pressures for wage restraint in order to enhance the competitiveness of firms, the increasing focus on the enterprise as the main locus for organizing human resources and making key decisions, and the increased emphasis on flexible labor processes and skill development. These trends, however, do not inevitably erode important and consequential national and regional variations in the relevance of political unionism, patterns of job mobility, employment security provisions, and forms of work organization.[36] Nor is there any indication, as several scholars have recently noted, that corporatist institutions and existing collective bargaining practices are collapsing or in decay in Europe.[37] In fact, as Wever and Turner have noted, the US experience itself demonstrates a high degree of diversity in terms of pressures on different industrial and employment relationships, varieties of regional and local influences on the part of management, labor, and other socioeconomic and political actors, and a broad range of very different kinds of outcomes. Everywhere we see similar kinds of economic and technological pressures working themselves out in very different ways.[38]

In addressing the question of whether distinctive institutional features persist in the face of common global pressures, this volume enters the debate on globalization, but shifts the focus to workers and labor institutions in late-industrializing and post-socialist settings where liberalization and privatization of the economy have exposed previously shielded economic actors to global economic forces at a pace far more dizzying than is the case in advanced industrial countries. By drawing on evidence concerning shifts in such areas as the size and nature of the labor force, the strength and behavior of organized labor and its relations with management and the state, production processes in different sectors, the social relations at the workplace, as well as social pacts accompanying wage and employment practices, it is possible to simultaneously recognize the shared concerns and challenges faced by workers and the institutions both formal and informal in which they participate, while demonstrating the persistence of variations in emerging patterns of

<hr />

[36] See, e.g., Geoffrey Garrett and Peter Lange, 'Political Responses to Interdependence: What's "Left" for the Left?' *International Organization*, 45 (Autumn 1991), 539–64; Locke, Kochan, and Piore, 'Reconceptualizing Comparative Industrial Relations'; and Lowell Turner and Peter Auer, 'A Diversity of New Work Organization: Human-centered, Lean and In-between', in Deyo (ed.), *Social Reconstructions of the World Autombile Industry*.

[37] See, e.g., Peter Lange, Michael Wallerstein, and Miriam Golden, 'The End of Corporatism? Wage Setting in Nordic and Germanic Countries', in Jacoby (ed.), *The Workers of Nations*, 76–100.

[38] Kirsten Wever and Lowell Turner, 'A Wide-Angle Lens', in Wever and Turner (eds), *The Comparative Political Economy of Industrial Relations*, 1.

16   *Candland and Sil*

industrial relations as a result of the persistence or legacies of existing institutional arrangements.

Labor in Late-industrializing and Post-socialist Economies

The preceding remarks should make clear that the studies of industrial relations assembled in this volume are not merely a product of the common professional interests or expertise of the contributors. Only a few of the contributors consider themselves to be industrial relations specialists. However, all the contributors do regard the responses of workers and the transformation of labor institutions as intrinsically important for understanding the economic reform process in the countries or regions they study, and each is deeply committed to systematically exploring the effects of international economic forces on shifts under way in industrial relations.

It is also significant that the contributions to this volume emphasize both late-industrializing and post-socialist settings rather than advanced industrial countries.[39] This is in part a response to the relative paucity of data on the basis of which comparative frameworks can be generated for the analysis of industrial relations in late-industrializing and post-socialist regions (in marked contrast to the rich data available for the comparative study of industrial relations in OECD countries). Several of the contributors to this volume are area specialists who have conducted original field research and careful analysis of primary material for the countries or regions they study.[40] Others are more inclined towards comparative-historical analysis and have combined some field research with the reinterpretation of existing materials for the purpose of developing original approaches to the issues raised in this volume.[41]

Regardless of whether the contributors are specialists in aspects of industrial relations or area specialists or both, the authors frame their country or comparative studies in the context of common related questions so as to pave the way for the creation of a broader framework of analysis and enable the systematic, theoretically significant, comparison of shifts in industrial relations within, between, and across late-industrializing and post-socialist contexts. The authors tackle two sets of specific questions in order to arrive at a better understanding of the similar ways in which workers and labor institutions are affected by economic reform and globalization and the different

[39] Chapter 6, by Charles Weathers, does address shifts in industrial relations in Japan, but this chapter is included for the purpose of stimulating further discussion on the question of whether Japanese industrial relations are stable enough to be regarded as a model for labor reorganization in late-industrializing and post-socialist countries.

[40] This applies to Victoria Murillo, Christopher Candland, Scott Martin, Charles Weathers, Xiaobo Lu, and Mitchell Orenstein and Lisa Hale (authors of Chapters 2, 3, 4, 6, 7, and 10 respectively).

[41] This applies to Eileen Doherty, Rudra Sil, and Jeffrey Kopstein (authors of Chapters 5, 8 and 9, respectively).

ways in which existing institutional arrangements, or at least their legacies, shape the renegotiation of social pacts and the new institutions emerging in the process of economic reform.

The first set of questions is specific to particular empirical contexts and focuses on tracing key aspects of the dramatic changes affecting workers and labor institutions in a given country, region, or sector. What are the specific features of 'labor regimes'[42]—whether formal or informal, whether at the national, regional or sectoral levels—presently emerging in a given late-industrializing or post-socialist region? What changes are evident in the relationships between, on the one hand, labor unions and other working-class organizations and movements, and, on the other, employers, managers, parties, and government officials? How have workers and organized labor—as well as business and government elites—responded to such problems as the decline of wages and employment security, changing skill requirements, or unexpected shifts in the structure of the labor force and in the overall political and economic institutional contexts? What changes are evident in the character of the labor force and patterns of labor representation, and in the social ties binding together different groups of workers and their communities? How have employment practices, production processes, and the level and nature of workforce participation changed at the national, sectoral, and firm levels? To what extent have the formal institutional arrangements and informal social relations formed under previous labor regimes survived in the course of economic adjustment or post-socialist transition? Each of the authors addresses several, but not all, of these overlapping questions about labor in a given empirical context depending on his or her particular expertise and his or her preferred unit of analysis and level of generality.

In addition, each of the authors relates the empirical analysis to a broader, theoretically driven set of questions that is of relevance to the comparative study of labor under conditions of economic adjustment and transition in late-industrializing and post-socialist settings. To what extent can recent changes in industrial relations be traced to increased international economic interdependence, and to what extent do the formal and informal accommodations reached by labor, management, and the state reflect distinctive legacies inherited from past institutional arrangements, or from the social structures, networks, and norms underlying these institutions? More concretely, are there similar policies and institutional arrangements in evidence across the different countries or regions studied, or are the commonalities across cases

---

[42] A labor regime may be defined as the pattern of recruitment and the terms and conditions of employment that structure the articulation of workers' concerns and interests to government and to industry, the two owners and managers of productive assets. Labor regimes are overlapping and multifaceted. Labor regimes operate at national, regional, and local levels in all sectors of the economy, formal and informal. They are structured by a variety of laws and social institutions, and the absence of such laws and institutions. The state's license to permit employers, in the private as well as in public sector, to evade labor regulations is also a determining feature of the labor regime.

limited to the challenges and pressures faced by key economic actors in these regimes? How is the response of workers in different sectors of late-industri-alizing countries similar and different from that of workers previously employed by state-owned enterprises in formerly communist countries? Are these differences significant in light of the more context-specific social struc-tures and historical circumstances shaping the transformation of industrial relations in a given context?

Given the focus on particular countries, regions or sectors, none of the essays attempts to provide globally applicable answers to any of these broader questions. However, the independent conclusions reached by all of the authors point to the remarkable resilience of variations in the content of national, local, and workplace-level pacts even if the labor institutions estab-lished under previous labor regimes are facing similar kinds of pressures. Thus, taken together, the contributions to this volume represent a collective effort to test—and in the final analysis, challenge—the hypothesis that eco-nomic adjustment and globalization are progressively producing greater sim-ilarities in key aspects of labor relations across different societies. The essays also pave the way for systematically comparing the general and particular fea-tures of labor and industry within, between, and across late-industrializing and post-socialist contexts. Some of the similarities and differences that emerge from these comparisons, as well as their potential significance, are considered in the concluding chapter. For now, we present brief overviews of the next nine chapters, considering, in turn, the five essays in Part I that address late-industrializing regions, and the four essays in Part II that focus on post-socialist regions.

Labor and Economic Adjustment in Late-industrializing Economies

To the extent that the evolution of industrial relations in advanced industrial countries are homogeneous at all, the assumption that industrial relations else-where will undergo a similar evolution is unwarranted. In late-industrializers, the combination of weak domestic industry and continued dependence on the formerly imperial economies resulted in the state playing a substantially more active role in economic development and the formation of labor regimes. The state apparatus—whether the political regimes were authoritarian, populist or pluralist—directly shaped the character of organized labor and the scope of its participation in national politics, while national and local institutions, such as labor courts, factory inspection systems, contributed to other stan-dard features of labor regimes across sectors. The state was often the largest employer of industrial workers, and public sector enterprises, which also served as models for employment practices in firms in the private sector as well, set the standard for the recruitment and control of the labor force. In addition, the nature of colonial administration, the character of the independ-

New Challenges in a Global Age   19

ence struggle, the economic ideology that informed the new elites' development strategy, the role assigned therein to labor, and the manner in which
post-independence political regimes structured the trade union movement all
contributed to distinctive features that made it virtually impossible for late-
industrializing labor regimes to retrace the evolution of industrial relations in
the West. Moreover, the persistence of a feudal property structure, a high
concentration of capital, a virtually inexhaustible supply of semi-skilled and
unskilled labor, and conditions of mass urban and rural poverty combined to
make labor markets in late-industrializing economies—to the extent that
these were 'markets' at all—very different from labor markets elsewhere.
Under these circumstances, the kinds of challenges confronting the relatively
affluent, urbanized, educated, and skilled labor force in advanced industrial
countries at present do not bear much resemblance to the pressures facing
workers in late-industrializing economies as existing labor institutions cope
with the partial retreat of the state and the effects of structural adjustment
and increased exposure to the competitive global economy. The chapters in
Part I of this volume are designed to illuminate the common and distinctive
features of labor regimes in late-industrializing economies as they encounter
the effects of economic adjustment and globalization.

In the following chapter, Victoria Murillo examines labor responses to
industrial restructuring, by sector, in Mexico under the Salinas administration. After the debt crisis of 1982, the Institutional Revolutionary Party
(Partido Revolucionario Institucional: PRI) implemented policies of stabilization and structural reforms reversing its protectionist and interventionist
post-war policy. These reforms triggered processes of industrial restructuring
in the private and public sector and challenged the very institutions that had
sustained the historic alliance between unions and the ruling PRI since the
1910 Mexican Revolution. Although the majority of Mexican unions are subordinated to the governing party, some unions chose to negotiate or oppose
the reforms. Murillo's chapter poses a series of questions about union behavior to analyse the responses of the Mexican Workers' Confederation (CTM)
and industry-specific unions in the automobile, education, electricity, oil, and
telecommunication sectors and to explain the variation in the responses of
Mexican unions. Her study focuses on the common behavior of union leaders facing similar challenges. She explains union responses by highlighting the
influence of the competition among unions for the representation of workers
and the competition among leaders for the control of the union as well as the
historical legacies of the PRI-CTM relationship.

Christopher Candland's contribution, in Chapter 3, examines the cost of
labor incorporation in South Asia, focusing on the contrast between political
unionism in India and enterprise unionism Pakistan. In India, an impressive
labor movement based on political unionism developed and exercised some
influence over economic policy. In Pakistan, an assertive and often militant
workers' movement emerged, was severely repressed, and exercised little

influence over economic policy. Candland assesses the ability of trade unions in each country to oppose recent economic reforms, specifically the privatization efforts of each government, in the light of the differing structure of labor institutions, specifically trade union relationships with political parties and workers' representation in trade unions. He finds that Indian unions are losing members as they stick to existing agenda and obstruct economic reform without identifying new strategies. In conclusion, Candland's chapter draws from a debate within the Indian trade union movement concerning the limitations of political unionism and the need for new union strategies. He suggest that a new unionism, with wider networks among other social organizations and deeper roots in local communities, must also include a new political dimension.

Scott Martin's analysis, in Chapter 4, shifts the focus from national systems of industrial relations to the level of the firm, and relies on a detailed comparative analysis of two automobile plants in Brazil and Mexico for tracing changes in labor processes under post-Fordist production systems. Martin notes that analysis of flexible labor innovations seem to be polarized between, on the one hand, critics of 'lean and mean' high exploitation and unilateral managerial domination, and, on the other, advocates or defenders of the potential for improved equity and empowerment under post-Fordist production arrangements. Martin suggests that the impact of flexible production is highly contingent upon the concrete social relations in which the transition takes place at work sites and across local and regional agglomerations of firms. An examination of two plants located within the quintessential globalized industry of automobile assembly and manufacture and in two large late-industrializing countries, Mexico and Brazil, yields the conclusion that the highly varying impacts of flexibilization on systems of worker rights and collective representation in the workplace, or labor regimes, stem from the distinct nature of the transition mode to flexibility in different subnational settings. A comparative examination of two older, so-called 'brownfield' assembly plants, one in each country, demonstrates the sharp contrasts between a negotiated mode of transition to a more flexible workplace in the Brazilian factory, and an imposed, or unilateral, mode in the Mexican facility. These transition modes are then traced to different ensuing trajectories of change in the respective factories' labor regimes. The central explanation for the contrasting transition modes toward high labor flexibility across the two plants is that the capacity of firms and worker representatives to transcend zero-sum conflicts over flexibility and forge innovative new practices hinges upon the character of the social network ties in which, together and separately, they are embedded at the time of exogenous pressures for greater flexibility. Such ties condition their styles of communication, behavior, and interaction as well as the informational and other resources available to them.

In Chapter 5, Eileen Doherty examines the renegotiation of the social partnership between labor, business, and government in the course of Ireland's present industrial restructuring. That we include a study of a European country in this volume might be surprising to some. However, it must be remembered that Ireland is indeed a late-industrializing country. It gained its independence long after Mexico or Brazil. As such, the process of industrialization and the evolution of industrial relations in Ireland are very much comparable to those in other late-industrializing economies. At the same time, Ireland's proximity to Britain and Europe, along with Ireland's membership in the European Union, may confer upon the Irish economy and Irish workers certain distinctive advantages (or disadvantages) that are unlikely to be present in India or Brazil.

During the post-war period, Doherty notes, Irish labor unions have been characterized by fragmentation at the local level—with multiple unions competing for members, industrial unrest at the local level, and tensions between unions—and centralization at the national level. Labor unions have clustered into large umbrella organizations. Moreover, the country has a strong history of corporatism in industrial relations matters. The three stages of 'globalization' in Ireland—the decision to embrace an open economic policy in the 1950s; Ireland's 1973 entry into the EEC; and the deepening of European integration in the 1980s and 1990s—have generated continuous pressures on Ireland to embrace new strategies to accommodate the pressures of market forces. Ireland's response to 'globalization' has not involved a disintegration of corporatist bargains, but rather a renewed focus on social partnership and consensus policymaking. The result of this social partnership has been impressive growth rates since 1987, but a lingering problem of structural unemployment. To address this issue, Dublin has committed itself to the continuation and strengthening of corporatist bargaining, but with an increased emphasis on addressing the problem of social exclusion. It remains to be seen whether social partnership mechanisms can effectively address the problems associated with long-term unemployment and social exclusion or whether Ireland is evolving toward a bifurcated economy, characterized by expanding jobs for skilled workers, but declining prospects for less-educated workers.

Chapter 6, by Charles Weathers, provides a fresh appraisal of one of the few alternatives to Western corporatist models: the Japanese system of labor relations. Despite recent economic problems in Japan, the firm-centered model of labor relations continues to attract attention from industrial relations specialists in late-industrializing as well as post-socialist countries.[43]

---

[43] On the continued interest in Japanese industrial relations and flexible production systems as an alternative model for both advanced industrial and post-colonial or post-socialist settings, see J. Womack, D. Jones, and D. Roos, *The Machine That Changed the World* (New York: Rawson/Macmillan, 1990); Kenney and Florida, *Beyond Mass Production*; Elger and Smith (eds), *Global Japanization?*; Kaplinsky, 'Technique and System: The Spread of Japanese Management Techniques to Developing Countries', and John Humphrey, 'Industrial Reorganization in Developing Countries: From Models to Trajectories', *World Development*, 23: 1 (1995), 149–62; Anita Chan, 'Chinese Danwei Reforms: Convergence with the Japanese Model?', in Lu and Perry (eds), *Danwei: The Changing Chinese Workplace in Historical and Comparative Perspective*; and the discussion of labor relations in Tula in post-Soviet Russia in

Weathers carefully examines whether or not it makes sense to speak of a Japanese model of industrial relations for late-industrializing and post-socialist countries in the light of recent changes in Japanese employment practices and labor institutions across various sectors. Weathers begins by noting that contemporary Japanese political economy may be the ultimate product of 'globalization'. Forcibly opened to the world by the Western powers in the 1850s, the country has since focused its energies on achieving the greatest possible level of economic development. As a result, the union movement has been historically divided between a right wing, which advocates cooperation with management, and a left wing, which makes broader social and political demands. While unions on the right have long dominated organized labor's agenda, even these unions had agreed by the 1980s that the labor movement had done too little to improve working conditions and living standards. However, since the early 1990s, the onset of a severe recession and an era of super-competition in the global economy have prompted both businesses and the right-wing unions to seek comprehensive deregulation of employment systems, against the faltering opposition of the left. As Japan shifts from its 'paradigm' of an industrial relations rooted in mass production and lifetime employment to a more flexible, high-technology based economy, unions are emphasizing new strategies for protecting jobs in their own industries, and the labor movement's influence over general working conditions has further eroded. Post-war Japan's second 'paradigm shift' suggests that there are important limits to convergence, as unions spurn the social provisions of the European Community, and cooperate with business to nurture Asia as an allied production base for Japan. Thus, those who regard the Japanese employment system during the 1970s and 1980s as a model for organizing cooperative industrial relations or establishing flexible labor systems in industrializing societies are having to confront the fact that the model itself is now in flux and is producing pressures not unlike those facing labor regimes in late-industrializing and post-socialist regions.

Labor and Transition in Post-socialist Economies

In many respects, industrial relations under socialist or communist regimes shared important similarities to patterns of industrial relations found in late-industrializing societies. In many respects, the process of economic reforms is now posing similar challenges to workers and organized labor in both late-industrializing and post-socialist settings. However, the dynamics of economic transition from command economies to market economies do result in some distinctive challenges for workers in post-socialist settings.[44] While

Carol Clark, 'The Transformation of Labor Relations in Russian Industry: The Influence of Regional Factors in the Iron and Steel Industry', *Post-Soviet Geography and Economics*, 37: 2 (1996), 88–112.

[44] We discuss the similarities and differences within, between, and across the 'late-industrializing' and 'post-socialist' categories in greater detail in the concluding chapter.

large late-industrializing countries, such as Brazil and India, certainly embraced import-substitution policies in conjunction with economic nationalism, they also had a significant private sector and significant experience with markets. Partly as a result of colonialism and its legacy, and partly as a result of economic policy, they also had a greater degree of exposure to global capitalism than did the communist regimes of Russia, China, or eastern Europe. Although the recent intensification of economic globalization in late-industrializing settings involve the reduction of the public sector and of barriers to international trade and capital flows, economic transformation in post-socialist countries is a far more dramatic event. It involves the creation of a new market economy and the dismantling of a command economy and its explicitly anti-market ideological foundation. It involves large-scale efforts to privatize state enterprises, while establishing stock markets and creating a new class of shareholders in a very short period of time. It involves the creation of new laws and institutions to regulate the transnational flow of goods, capital, and multinational firms for the first time in several decades. And, it involves an unprecedented level of exposure to the international capitalist economy for millions of workers and thousands of managers and bureaucrats who—for better or for worse—were previously unaffected by the international economy. Under these conditions, labor relations are in a far greater degree of flux as trade union federations previously controlled by the communist party-state apparatus have given way to new, independent unions or labor movements while firms lay off redundant workers, income differentials increase dramatically, and unemployment becomes a standard social problem for the first time in decades. What all of this suggests for the direction of labor reorganization and future patterns of industrial relations in post-socialist settings, however, remains very much an open question as evident in the different experiences of workers in China, Russia, and eastern Europe.

In Chapter 7, Xiaobo Lu notes that industrial relations in the People's Republic of China (PRC) were previously characterized by the features common to all state socialist systems—an economy dominated by state-owned enterprises, employee dependence on the enterprise, state-controlled union organizations, and relative labor peace. Communist authorities described labor disputes as 'contradictions between different parts of the same organization'. Aside from sporadic protests by workers, there was no organized labor movement for nearly three decades after the formation of the PRC in 1949. With the economic reforms launched in 1979, however, Chinese industrial relations entered a period of change that brought about increasing exposure to market forces and to the international economy. In keeping with the common themes developed in this volume, Lu questions the assumption that economic interdependence must lead to common institutional outcomes, and proceeds from the premise that political choice as well as institutional legacies of the past in state socialist countries, such as China, affect the sequence and methods of transformation of industrial relations. Lu lays out some basic features of industrial relations under state socialist regimes and in transition economies and argues that although the internationalization of the Chinese economy has had a major impact over the past decade, the character and direction of change in Chinese industrial relations is best understood not as a response to market transition but within the context of a transition from state socialism to 'market socialism'. The pace, scope, and sequence of changes in industrial relations under market socialism over the past decade may reflect in part the responses of key actors to some of the standard pressures of the global economy, but they are also shaped significantly by structural constraints, particularly the institutional legacy of the entrenched *danwei* (work unit) system that stood at the core of the pre-reform Chinese industry. This legacy is evident in the continuing dependence of workers on the intervention of higher authorities to address their grievances and in the active role the state continues to play in the mediation of industrial disputes.

Similarly, in Chapter 8, Rudra Sil argues that while the attempt to integrate the Russian economy into the world market has produced several market-oriented economic institutions that formally appear to converge with those in the advanced industrial West, 'globalization' has had far less of an impact on the prevalent norms and attitudes of key economic actors at the local and regional level where many of the most successful enterprises are focusing their energies. Sil begins with the premise that the privatization program and other market-oriented reforms under Yeltsin, while certainly ushering in a new set of institutions in the post-Soviet era, do not represent a steady, unidirectional process of change leading towards the integration of Russia into the international economy. In the context of industrial relations, he notes that the framework of 'globalization' is at best useful in understanding the demise of the old system of trade unions and industrial management, and that the emerging trends in industrial relations do not represent a uniform transformation that will produce labor institutions similar to those in more advanced industrial societies. This is evident in the failed attempt to develop a tripartite corporatist framework—the Russian Trilateral Commission—for bargaining on key issues, and in the increasing evidence of bilateral dealings and alliances between government actors and the pro-reform and anti-reform segments that cut across the business-labor divide. More importantly, Sil contends, while the old system of industrial relations may not be much in evidence today, a substantial number of industrialists and Russian workers appear to be responding to the transformation of the post-Soviet economy by focusing on regionally based, enterprise-level survival strategies bearing little resemblance to global logics. These three observations set the stage for Sil's general argument that the survival strategies of many managers and workers are nested in informal 'moral' understandings that emerged in the context of enterprise paternalism in the Soviet era and that continue to survive within the context of new economic institutions while demonstrating the same kind of detachment and skepticism seen in regard to the formal system of industrial production in the Soviet era. Although any claims regarding post-Soviet industrial relations must necessarily remain tentative given the extremely fluid situation in contemporary Russian society, Sil offers a plausible alternative interpretation that may also serve as a possible 'corrective' to the prevailing assumptions underlying the study of post-Soviet political economy.

In Chapter 9, Jeffrey Kopstein examines one interesting unanticipated effect of globalization on labor in the case of a unified Germany: the rise of a new particularism in the territory of the former German Democratic Republic. A number of scholars speak of the new divide between eastern and western Germany in terms of ethnicity. Seen more accurately, the source of the new cultural divide in Germany is a conflict between two historically shaped moral economies underlying two very different kinds of social pacts. Despite Stalinist maldevelopment, the economy of the communist East, through everyday labor practices, inculcated a set of egalitarian economic values. For political reasons, the unification strategy after 1991 did not challenge these values but accommodated them. Such a strategy thus guaranteed the persistence and even growth of regional identities among workers in post-unification Germany. The new particularism in other locales, therefore, may stem from the clash not only of civilizations, but rather more prosaically, from the conflict between dominant labor and leisure practices, of notions of what is properly commodified and what is best put outside of markets—practices that are being challenged by global markets and the diffusion of tastes, values, and institutions. Thus, although conditions in eastern Germany have begun to change recently, Kopstein's chapter points to the importance of the enduring constellations of attitudes and expectations fostered by an earlier set of labour institutions.

In Chapter 10, Mitchell Orenstein and Lisa Hale discuss the surprising rebirth of corporatist labor institutions in East-Central Europe. In contrast to Russia, where the attempt to create a tripartite bargaining framework did not go very far, Orenstein and Hale argue that corporatism has become a part of the post-communist institutional framework in the Czech Republic, Hungary, and Poland. While global trends have forced labor into retreat in most countries, in East-Central Europe, organized labor played a major role in the dramatic opening to world markets in 1989. This stands in contrast to Russia where the participation of workers in the break-up of the USSR involved striking coal-miners but not organized labor as a whole. Orenstein and Hale argue that whereas trade unions under communism acted as 'transmission belts' to the working class for state policy and ideology, governments in post-communist Europe needed to develop new roles for resurgent trade unions in a democratic society as they are obliged to reconciling democratic consolidation and liberalization. Therefore, while trade unions had to be reconstituted as independent social and political forces supportive of the new regime, they were also expected to moderate their wage demands so as not to fuel inflation. In all three countries, governments looked to corporatist arrangements for an answer to these seemingly incompatible objectives. Orenstein and Hale note that throughout East-Central Europe, the need to institutionalize a role for trade unions in the emerging democratic society led to a genuinely corporatist forum for indicative negotiation over wages, and the development of progressive social policy. Popular disillusion with structural economic reforms led to corporatist 'pacts' negotiated by the political leadership whether that leadership took the form of Solidarity in Poland or the former communists who came to power in 1993. Even more successful was the low-wage, low-unemployment compromise that underpinned the Czech transformation, providing a formula for a new distribution of social forces over the longer term. Based on his comparisons of the Czech, Polish, and Hungarian experiences, Orenstein and Hale conclude that globalization has generally strengthened trade unions and the pressures for including them in new forms of corporatist intermediation in post-communist Europe. While these new institutions suffer many of the same problems evident under advanced industrial capitalism, albeit to varying degrees, corporatism in East-Central Europe appears to be here to stay.

Conclusion

The studies assembled here share a commitment to systematic analysis of changes in contemporary industrial relations as a result of common domestic and international economic forces. As noted above, while the literature on industrial relations in advanced industrial economies has turned the corner on this point, students of particular late-industrializing or post-socialist countries have produced little comparative work so far on the broader theoretical implications of the similarities and differences in the way in which workers and labor institutions in various countries are experiencing and responding to the effects of the international economy.[45] Significant scholarship has been devoted to the analysis of the political and social development of working classes in both late-industrializing countries and socialist countries. Scholars have recognized that changes initiated by political elites in the process of economic reform produce important changes in the labor force and in the manner in which this labor force can effectively gain representation and leverage in bargaining with other economic actors. They also recognize that these changes, in turn, bring new actors into the political arena and complicate the process of economic reform. While individual essays comparing patterns of labor reorganization have produced significant theoretical insights,[46] many

[45] See the discussion at notes 18–20 above.
[46] See, e.g., Tariq Banuri and Edward Amadeo, 'Worlds Within the Third World: Labour Market Institutions in Asia and Latin America', in Banuri (ed.), *Economic Liberalization: No Panacea, The Experiences of Latin America and Asia* (Oxford: Clarendon Press, 1991), 171–220. Banuri and Amadeo present a useful taxonomy of labor institutions that corresponds to world regions. In East and Southeast Asia, a divided labor movement plays little role in national

volumes attempting to chart the common processes leading to the formation and transformation of the working classes have had to confess their theoretical uncertainty. Very few attempts have been made to systematically chart the relationships between political or economic development and labor regimes across regions or regime-types.[47]

This volume does not offer as a unifying paradigm for the comparative study of industrial relations worldwide. It is, however, designed to combat the aforementioned limitations within the field of comparative industrial relations and, in the process, to better relate the field to some of the theoretical and empirical issues raised in the study of comparative political economy. Four specific points are worth noting in regard to the potential contributions of this volume. First, by comparing post-socialist and late-industrializing countries within a framework that combines industrial relations and broader political economic variables, this volume goes beyond the experiences of advanced industrial economies. Second, this volume elaborates the various historical process and social structures that shaped the distinctive formal and informal institutional arrangements designed to manage the complex relationships between labor, management, and the state in very different kinds of economies. Third, in contrast to those comparative studies of industrial relations that ignore external effects, this study explores how transformations in the global economy have affected existing institutions related to labor-management relations while posing certain common challenges and opportunities for key economic actors in each country. Finally, in contrast to those who view 'globalization' as a dominant force leading to the erosion of distinctive national economic institutions, this study focuses on labor institutions in order to detail how historical legacies and external constraints and opportunities are incorporated into distinctive strategies employed by labor and by other economic actors as they negotiate new pacts and reconsider existing institutional arrangements. The concluding chapter reflects on the extent to which the contributions in this volume have helped to pave the way for a broad, comparative framework with which to understand the relationship

politics (decentralized model); in South Asia, labor organizations exercise political power only through their dependent relationship with political parties or ethnic groups (pluralist model); in Latin America and the Philippines, labor is independent enough and organized well enough to impose 'real costs on the economy in defense of its interests' (polarized model); and in some other regions, a social corporatist model enables labor to function like other functional groups that 'wield power and transact affairs in their own right'. Citations are from Banuri and Amadeo, 'Worlds Within the Third World', 176. However, even this taxonomy, despite its attention to diverse historical, cultural, and political factors, results in reproducing stereotyped regional characterizations and overemphasizes the unity of regional cultures at the expense of distinctions across political regimes and their effects on social institutions.

[47] On this point, see Barry Munslow and M. H. J. Finch, 'Introduction,' in Munslow and Finch (eds), *Proletarianisation in the Third World* (London: Croom Helm, 1984), 1. Examples of such volumes include Brandell (ed.), *Workers in Third-World Industrialization;* Gutkind (ed.), *Third World Workers*; and Rosalynd Boyd, Robin Cohen, and Peter Gutkind (eds), *International Labour and the Third World* (Brookfield, VT: Avebury, 1987).

between international economic forces, economic adjustment, and transition and the general and particular features of industrial relations in a global economy across late-industrializing and post-socialist regions.

PART I

Labor in Late-industrializing Economies

2

Partisan Loyalty and Union Competition: Macroeconomic Adjustment and Industrial Restructuring in Mexico

M. Victoria Murillo, Yale University

Mexico shares with other countries studied in this volume a post-colonial heritage, although like the rest of Latin America, early decolonization mitigated the effects of colonization. Like other late industrializers, Mexico pursued state-led development strategies and, like many other followers of state development, it succumbed to globalization under the pressure of fiscal collapses. The trigger was the 1982 debt crisis, which brought President De La Madrid towards fiscal restraint and trade liberalization seeking macroeconomic stability. His successor Carlos Salinas, inaugurated in December 1988, was a more dramatic market reformer. Like De La Madrid, Salinas belonged to the Institutional Revolutionary Party (PRI), which had been in power since the aftermath of the Mexican Revolution. The PRI had a strong labor component and had championed state intervention and protectionism during the post-war period. Salinas continued and accelerated market reforms and committed himself to a process of economic integration with the United States, which resulted in the signing of the North American Free Trade Agreement (NAFTA).

Globalization and fiscal collapse pushed Mexico toward economic integration, trade liberalization, and privatization, and triggered a process of industrial restructuring, which was especially dramatic in the protected tradable sectors and in the public sector where unionization was the highest.[1] The

An earlier version of this chapter was presented at the 1997 Annual Meeting of the American Political Science Association. I thank Ruth Berins Collier and Mark Selden, who were the discussants of the paper at the 1997 American Political Science Association meetings, an anonymous reviewer from Oxford University Press, and Antonieta Mercado for research assistance. I also thank the Mellon Foundation, the Fundación Harvard en México, the Government Department, the Committee for Latin American and Iberian Studies, and the Harvard Academy for International and Area Studies, at Harvard University, the Instituto Tecnológico Autónomo de México, El Colegio de México, Flacso-México, as well as the Department of Political Science at Yale University for their support.

[1] Nationalized companies were generally organized as large state-owned companies that permitted the organization of nationwide industrial unions (e.g. railroad, oil, and telecommunications). Moreover, unionization is higher in the public sector where unions had a privileged relationship with politically appointed managers. This relationship resulted in union management

impact of globalization for workers in these sectors was dramatic and created a tremendous challenge for unions. Moreover, the policy turnaround of PRI challenged the political influence of unions which had traditionally been compensated for their industrial weakness.[2] Therefore, while globalization created an economic challenge for unions, the policy shift reduced their political influence to compensate for it.

Despite the tremendous challenge, Salinas did not confront important organized labor opposition to his reforms, nor to most processes of industrial restructuring. This development is remarkable considering that he was elected in a contested election where Cuahutémoc Cárdenas, an opposition candidate with a more populist and protectionist program, almost beat him.[3] Cárdenas, the son of the most populist president in Mexican history, Lázaro Cárdenas, split from the PRI in opposition with market-oriented reforms. Lázaro Cárdenas had included labor into the party structure, nationalized oil, and implemented a sweeping land reform and many social policies to protect the poor. Although the Mexican Workers' Confederation (CTM) resented the policies implemented by Salinas and even supported another candidate for the PRI nominee in the 1988 elections, it did not actively organize to oppose his reforms. Partisan loyalty is not a sufficient explanation for labor quiescence because in other countries where labor-based parties implemented neoliberal reforms, such as Venezuela, Argentina, and Spain, organized labor was not as compliant despite its alliance with governing parties. Moreover, while a minority of unions associated with opposition parties actively protested the reforms, a minority of PRI-associated unions rejected pro-market policies or only accepted them after obtaining compensation or achieving policy input. For instance, the National Union of Education Workers (SNTE) could make the government include its demands on the design of education decentralization, and the Mexican Union of Electricity Workers (SME) averted the privatization or liquidation of its company and gained participation in the management of it.

prerogatives and special benefits for the workers of these sectors. See Graciela Bensusán, 'Los determinantes institucionales de la flexibilización laboral', *Revista Mexicana de Sociología* 1 (1994), 53. In 1979, the Mexican Workers' Confederation (CTM) recognized its affinity with state intervention and designed an economic proposal that called for the expansion of state and workers and union property at the expense of private property. See Ignacio Marbrán, 'La dificultad del cambio (1968–1990)', in *El Partido en el Poder* (Mexico City: IEPES, 1990); and Alberto Aziz Nassif, *El Estado Mexicano y la CTM* (Mexico City: Ed. La Casa Chata, 1989), 215.

[2] In the past, unions counted on their political influence to obtain favorable arbitration from a highly interventionist state and from state institutions which included union participation like Arbitration and Conciliation Boards that were in charge of approving collective bargaining contracts and resolving industrial disputes.

[3] Cuahutémoc Cárdenas claimed that Salinas rigged the 1988 elections. Although the fraud was never proven, the number of votes obtained by the PRI (50.36%) was historically low. See Jorge I. Domínguez and James A. McCann, 'Whither the PRI? Explaining Voter Defection in the 1988 Mexican Presidential Elections', *Electoral Studies*, 11: 3 (Sept. 1992), 207. In 1989, the front organized to support Cárdenas' candidacy (Front for a Democratic Revolution, or FRD) gave birth to a new party, the Party of the Democratic Revolution, or PRD.

Union responses had important policy implications. The restraint of the main national labor confederation, the CTM, was instrumental in the acceleration of market-oriented reforms under a climate of labor peace. CTM unions, however, obtained few policy concessions and centered their demands on political resources. Political resources had previously served the CTM well by compensating the industrial weakness of its mostly local and small unions. However, CTM preference for political resources tied it up even more to the governing PRI and further alienated it from other political parties which could have become partners at a time when political liberalization was increasing party pluralism in the electoral arena to the point that the PRI lost the presidency in 2000. Instead, the unions of teachers, electricity workers, and telephone workers studied gave priority to industrial over political identities and attempted to develop alternative strategies to face the effects of political liberalization and state withdrawal.

This chapter examines the responses of Mexican labor organization to a common challenge illuminating the different national trends in the convergent path toward a globalized world economy. It shows the influence of institutional legacies on the demands and strategies of Mexican unions regarding policies that accelerated the impact of globalization on their constituencies and organizations. In particular, it focuses on the effect of partisan loyalties, leadership competition, and organizational fragmentation on the articulation of union demands and strategies highlighting the diversity in the response of national labor confederation and industry-specific unions. The case studies include the PRI-affiliated Mexican Workers' Confederation (CTM), as well as individual unions in the automobile, electricity, education, oil, and telecommunication sectors, each of which were sharply affected by trade liberalization and state reform.

The chapter is organized in five sections. The first section describes alternative explanations for the diversity in union responses under the Salinas administration. The second section focuses on the structure of union organization in Mexico. The third analyzes the macroeconomic reforms of the Salinas administration as well as union responses to such reforms. The fourth describes industrial restructuring and union responses in the education, electricity, telecommunication, automobile, and oil sectors. The last section summarizes the consequences of union responses and provides some concluding remarks.

Alternative Explanationsm of Union Reactions to Salinas Reforms

The acquiescence of the CTM did not surprise the many students of Mexican labor who argued that the non-democratic characteristics of the Mexican political regime and the high degree of state control over industrial relations explains the subordination of the CTM.[4] However, the mechanisms of state control had traditionally been compensated with state concessions for workers and unions. According to Zapata,[5] this corporatist exchange had guaranteed labor peace in Mexico during the post-war era. The subordination of CTM unions during the Salinas administration, however, accompanied reforms which eroded the concessions obtained during the post-war era through that corporatist exchange.

Neocorporatist theories hold that labor tends to be restrained when affiliated labor-based parties are in power, especially when the union movement is centralized and can control the kind of free-riding behavior that brings about militancy.[6] In addition, although the PRI controlled most of the Mexican unions, the fragmentation of the Mexican union movement into several PRI-related national union confederations that compete for the affiliation of more than fifteen thousand individual unions should have hindered the conditions for labor restraint.[7]

The problems of regime-defined and neocorporatist theories to explain both the subordination of CTM unions and the variation in union response within the Mexican labor arena highlight the limitations of national level

[4] Among the authors who point out the high degree of state intervention in industrial relations in Mexico are Ilán Bizberg, *Estado y Sindicalismo en México* (Mexico City: El Colegio de México, 1990); Germán Pérez Fernández del Castillo, 'Del corporativismo de estado al corporativismo social', in Carlos Bazdresch, Nisso Bucay, Soledad Loaeza, and Nora Lustig (eds), *México, Auge y Crisis* (Mexico City: Ed. Fondo de Cultura Económica, 1992); Victor Manuel Durand Ponte, 'El papel de los sindicatos en la política mexicana', *Revista Mexicana de Sociología*, 1 (Mexico City, 1994), 29–44; Bensusán (1994); Graciela Bensusán, 'Institucionalización laboral en México. Los años de la definición (1917–1931)', PhD dissertation (Mexico City: UNAM, 1992); Aziz Nassif (1989); Gerardo Zamora, 'La política laboral del estado mexicano, 1982–88', *Revista Mexicana de Sociología*, 3 (1990); Manuel Camacho, *El Futuro Inmediato* (Mexico City: Ed. Siglo XXI, 1980); Kevin Middlebrook, *The Paradox of Revolution* (Baltimore: The Johns Hopkins University Press, 1995); and Francisco Zapata, 'Labor and Politics: The Mexican Paradox', in Edward Epstein (ed.), *Labor Autonomy and the State in Latin America* (Boston: Unwin Hyman, 1989).

[5] Francisco Zapata, *Autonomia y subordinación en el sindicalismo latinoamericano* (Mexico City: Fondo de Cultura Económica, 1993), 41.

[6] See, e.g., Geoffrey Garret and Peter Lange, 'The Politics of Growth: Strategic Interaction and Economic Performance in the Advance Industrial Democracies: 1974–80', *Journal of Politics* 47 (1985); David Cameron, 'Social Democracy, Corporatism, Labor Quiescence, and the Representation of Economic Interest in Advance Capitalist Society', in John Goldthorpe (ed.), *Order and Conflict in Contemporary Capitalism* (New York/Oxford: Oxford University Press, 1984); and Lars Calmfors and John Driffill, 'Centralization and Wage Bargaining', *Economic Policy*, 3, 1 (1988), 13–61.

[7] The Mexican unionization rate was 18.9% of the economically active population or 30.3% of the salary-earning population in 1974. See Felipe Leal, 'Las estructuras sindicales', in Pablo González Casanova (ed.), *Organización y Sindicalismo* (Mexico City: Ed. Siglo XXI, 1986), 19. There was a wide variation in union density across sectors, from almost 100% in the public administration to 2.9% in the primary sector (27). In addition, the union movement was fragmented into more than 15,000 unions with a predominance of firm and craft unions over activity or nationwide industrial unions, which organized mostly state-owned enterprises. See Cesar Zazueta and Ricardo de la Peña, *Estructura Dual y Piramidal del Sindicalismo Mexicano* (Mexico City: Secretaria del Trabajo y Previsión Social, Centro Nacional de Informacion y Estadisticas del Trabajo (1981), 761–75.

theories. They cannot account for subnational variation. Interest-driven theories derive the policy preference of different actors from their economic interests, explaining policies as a result of these demands.[8] Some of them study the effect of globalization and market-oriented reforms on the economic interest of diverse sectors, such as those exposed and protected or public and private.[9] These theories account for the origin of union preferences by focusing on their interests with regard to economic liberalization and other market reforms. Some authors explain this variation by pointing to the different impact of the same policy in diverse sectors. However, the case studies show that political factors can overcome economic conditions, such as when the CTM violently imposed the subordination of Ford Motors' workers at the Cuatitlán plant to the industrial restructuring they had previously resisted.

Unlike the mentioned literature, my hypothesis seeks to explain union behavior both at the level of national confederations and industry-specific unions. Although my theory implies a simplification of the Mexican reality, it provides a guide to understand union dynamics to which the complexities of specific cases can be added. I argue that union leaders, as political entrepreneurs, want to avoid being replaced as head of their unions, either for ideological or material reasons associated with their leadership positions.[10] Thus, they have to consider workers' preferences to avoid their replacement by election, rebellion, or government selection if they prove unable to control their followers. In addition, union leaders also want to prevent the exit of workers to alternative unions, who compete for the membership of the same workers, because it would hurt their bargaining power. The larger their share of the workers in the involved sector, the larger the value of their restraint. Hence, union leaders fear internal replacement (leadership competition) and external rivals (union competition).

[8] See Peter Gourevitch, *Politics in Hard Times* (Ithaca: Cornell University Press, 1986); Ronald Rogowski, *Commerce and Coalitions* (Princeton: Princeton University Press, 1989); and Jeffrey Frieden, *Debt, Democracy, and Development* (Princeton: Princeton University Press, 1991).

[9] For example, Jeffrey Frieden presents a general argument about sector-driven policy preferences and applies it to unions and exchange rate policies in Frieden. See Jeffrey Friedan, *Debt, Democracy, and Development* (Princeton: Princeton University Press, 1991); and Jeffrey Frieden, 'Labor and Politics of Exchange Rates: the Case of the European System', in Sanford Jacoby (ed.), *The Workers of Nations* (New York: Oxford University Press, 1995). Peter Swenson focuses on cross-class coalitions based on sector-level preferences with regard to collective bargaining decentralization and state adjustment. See Peter Swenson, 'Bringing Capital Back In, Or Social Democracy Reconsidered', *World Politics*, 43: 4 (1991), 513–44. The Latin American literature uses a similar logic to explain populist coalitions between urban workers and industrialists producing for the domestic market based on the transfer of resources from exporting to protected sectors for import substitution industrialization. See Fernando Henrique Cardoso and Enzo Faletto, *Dependencia y Desarrollo en América Latina* (Buenos Aires: Siglo XXI, 1969); and Guillermo O'Donnell, *Modernization and Bureaucratic-Authoritarianism* (Berkeley: Institute of International Studies, University of California, 1973).

[10] Union leaders aim at obtaining material incentives, ranging from their salary to pay-offs, or they could be ideologically motivated.

The cost of organizing unions and even competing for leadership, as well as ideological convictions, had driven Latin American labor leaders to associate with political parties. In many countries, party activists organized the first labor unions. In others, such as Mexico, allied parties in government provided political influence to compensate for their weakness in the industrial arena thus creating a dependence on state resources. Politicians and labor leaders have been long-term allies making partisan loyalty an important consideration in the attitudes of labor unions. Partisan loyalty reduces their incentives for militancy and facilitates their cooperation with incumbent political parties. As a result, not only do labor leaders prefer to have their partisan allies in power, but also incumbent politicians favor their labor associates controlling trade unions because they are more likely to cooperate. In contrast, union leaders associated with the opposition are less likely to cooperate.

Assuming that union leaders are affiliated with the governing labor-based party, two types of competition affect the challenge created by internal or external rivals for labor leaders. Leadership competition influences the possibility of their replacement, thus creating incentives for allied labor leaders to became more demanding or militant to avoid being perceived as having 'sold out' and substituted by new leaders. Union fragmentation within the same sector creates union competition that fosters coordination problems. Union competition is likely to provoke free-riding behavior to attract members from competing unions breaking coordination efforts for the whole group and weakening union bargaining power.

The combination of union and partisan competition introduces incentives for militancy for those union leaders associated with opposition parties. These leaders are also more likely to break coordination efforts involving loyal unions. When competing unions are each allied with the incumbent party, government officials can manipulate competition for state resources allowing one of the allied unions to cut a different deal. This undermines coordination efforts and weakens collective bargaining power. Hence, organizational fragmentation weakens union bargaining power combined with either partisan competition or partisan monopoly.

In short, partisan loyalty facilitates labor cooperation with the government and the restraint of militancy. Leadership competition, however, makes allied union leaders more prone to be demanding and even militant to show that they are better agents of workers than their competitors. Union competition, though, affects their bargaining power and capacity to obtain concessions from the government, either if they exercise restrain, due to their shared partisan loyalty, or if they are militant, probably due to their association with opposition parties. In the next section, I show how institutional legacies affect the existence of partisan attachments, leadership competition, and organizational fragmentation in Mexico. In the third section, I describe how these variables influenced union demands and strategies *vis-à-vis* the challenges created by globalization.

Institutional Legacies, Partisan Loyalty, and Union Organization

The Mexican labor relations system was strongly influenced by the political developments that followed the Mexican Revolution (1910–17). After the Revolution, a one-party dominant system emerged in the 1930s.[11] The PRI embodied the leadership that emerged from the Revolution, and it has been in power since its foundation. President Plutarco E. Calles originally founded it in 1929 as the National Revolutionary Party (PNR). In 1938, President Lázaro Cárdenas reorganized it as the Party of the Mexican Revolution (PRM) with a corporatist organization based on four functional sectors—workers, peasants, the middle class, and the military.[12]

In the 1930s, President Cárdenas institutionalized the alliance between the Mexican unions and the revolutionary party. During his administration, the expansion of the public sector enhanced the power of unions because nationalized companies in monopolistic sectors were generally organized as large state-owned companies that permitted the organization of nationwide industrial unions (e.g., railroad, oil, and telecommunications). In addition, he granted the public sector with monopolies of representation and unions in state-owned companies and the public administration had a privileged relationship with politically appointed managers because they served as tools for policy implementation. This relationship resulted in union management prerogatives and special benefits for the workers in these sectors.[13] Moreover, the expansion of the state to provide social services and regulate industrial relations included union representation within tripartite regulatory bodies, such as the Conciliation and Arbitration Boards which regulate collective bargaining, the 1942-founded Social Security Institute (IMSS), and the 1970-founded Institute of the National Housing Fund (INFONAVIT). These institutions strengthened the authority of labor confederations in charge of their administration while politicizing labor relations by expanding the role of the state in the resolution of collective bargaining. In return for these benefits unions controlled labor militancy. In 1948, after abolishing the military sector, the party was finally renamed the Institutional Revolutionary Party (PRI).

This inclusive authoritarianism combined strong presidentialism, mass mobilization, and electoral manipulation. PRI-related organizations canalized the mobilization of workers and others. Executive discretion overrode

---

[11] For example, Juan Molinar describes how, after 1946, electoral registration was used to limit electoral contestation. See Juan Molinar, *El Tiempo de la Legitimidad* (Mexico City: Cal y Arena, 1991), 37.

[12] On the history of the PRI, see Samuel León, 'Del partido de partido al partido de sectores', in *El partido en el Poder* (Mexico City: IEPES, 1990); Rafael Loyola, '1938: El despliegue del corporatismo partidario', in *El partido en el Poder* (Mexico City: IEPES, 1990); Jacqueline Peschard, 'El partido hegemónico: 1946–1972', in *El partido en el Poder* (Mexico City: IEPES, 1990); Arturo Alvarado, 'La fundación del PNR', in *El partido en el Poder* (Mexico City: IEPES, 1991); and Peter H. Smith, *Labyrinths of Power* (Princeton: Princeton University Press, 1979).

[13] See Bensusán, 'Los determinantes institucionales de la flexibilización laboral', 53.

legal boundaries. And a history of fraudulent electoral practices limited party pluralism. In return for political support, workers and unions obtained benefits including a labor legislation that protected workers' acquired rights and a high degree of subsidies for union organization.[14] In addition, unions were included into the corporatist structure of the party. Due to the 'incorporation' of labor by the PRI and the limits to electoral competition, almost all labor unions are affiliated with the party. PRI governments also resorted to repression to meet the challenges to its control of labor, especially in the 1950s. Labor alliance with the PRI provided labor peace and facilitated the development of a strategy of high growth and low inflation labeled as 'stabilizing development' that characterized Mexico during the 1950s and 1960s. 'Stabilizing development' consisted of import substitution industrialization, state intervention, high public investment, and conservative fiscal and monetary policies.[15]

The institutional legacies of the original alliance created an almost partisan monopoly of Mexican unions. There has been little competition from union leaders affiliated with other political parties. Limited leadership competition provided the PRI with a near monopoly over the affiliation of union leaders with the exception of the small movement of 'independent' unions. Only a minority of 'independent' unions that were not controlled by the PRI rejected corporatist participation in state institutions of tripartite representation which they associated with state control over their autonomy. Some of these 'independent' unions supported opposition parties, such as the Party of the Democratic Revolution (PRD), whereas others remained autonomous from political parties.

Despite PRI predominance, the Mexican union movement was very fragmented at the confederal level. There were six labor confederations associated with the PRI, in addition to the Mexican Workers' Confederation (CTM). These were the CROC (Revolutionary Confederation of Workers and Peasants), CROM (Mexican Regional Labor Confederation), CRT (Revolutionary Workers' Confederation), COR (Revolutionary Labor Confederation), CGT (General Confederation of Labor), and the FSTSE (Federation

[14] For example, monopolies of representation within the bargaining unit, the right to strike and to strike in solidarity, the obligation to negotiate with existing unions, the permission for closed-shop arrangements and for automatic check-off at source, and union participation in the several institutions of labor market regulation and social welfare. See *Ley Federal del Trabajo* (Mexico City: Colección Jurídica Esfinge, 1993); Francisco Zapata, *El Conflicto Sindical en América Latina* (Mexico City: El Colegio de México, 1986); Bensusán, 'Los determinantes institucionales de la flexibilización laboral'; and Ruth Berins Collier and David Collier, 'Inducement versus Constraints: Dissaggregating 'Corporatism'", *American Political Science Review*, 73 (1979), 967–86.
[15] See Bizberg, *Estado y Sindicalismo en México*, 60, and Pedro Aspe, *El Camino Mexicano de la Transformación Económica* (Mexico City: Fondo de Cultura Económica, 1993). Between 1956 and 1972, Mexican economic growth averaged an annual rate of 7% economic growth with an annual rate of inflation of only 3%. See Nora Lustig, *Mexico, the Remaking of an Economy* (Washington, DC: Brookings Institution Press, 1998), 18.

of Public Service Workers' Unions). The latter was the only union allowed to organize public administration employees by the Mexican Constitution (art. 123, clause B). According to Middlebrook, with the exception of the FSTSE, the other national labor confederations registered affiliates in a broad range of economic activities, and the largest confederations—CTM, CROC, and CROM—maintained national presence with important numbers of affiliates registered in every major region.[16] Each of these national labor confederations were effectively competing for the same constituencies despite their common party affiliation. Union competition within the monopolistic party introduced the threat of members' exit to other organizations for union leaders without risking the party control of any of these unions. Union competition among PRI-related national confederations challenged the CTM leadership with the possibility of CTM members exiting to other PRI-affiliated national labor confederations. Such movement, though, did not represent a challenge to the incumbent PRI because all confederations were linked to the party. Thus, while partisan loyalty sustained their cooperation, union competition historically weakened national labor confederations. This institutional context framed the union responses to the challenge of globalization triggered in Mexico by the policy reforms subsequent to the debt crisis.

From Populism to Neoliberalism: The 1982 Economic Crisis

The economic crisis of 1982 marked a turning point in the traditional alliance between the PRI and its affiliated unions. With the oil boom in the 1970s, Mexico increased both its oil production and its external borrowing. The capital inflows combined with exchange rate stability produced a real appreciation of the currency that hurt exporters, induced devaluation expectations, and capital flight. A rise in the US interest rate, along with a deterioration of the terms of trade in Mexican products—especially the decline in the price of oil-triggered the crisis. In 1982, the Mexican government could not service the external debt and asked for a three-month moratorium, devalued the peso, suspended convertibility of dollar deposits, imposed exchange rate controls, and nationalized the banking system thereby alienating the business sector.[17]

With this crisis as a background, President Miguel De La Madrid was inaugurated in December 1982. The fiscal deficit, together with the fall in revenues and rising inflation, highlighted the limits of import substitution industrialization and state intervention. From 1982 to 1985, the government tried to recover business confidence and to control macroeconomic variables with an

[16] Kevin Middlebrook, *The Paradox of Revolution* (Baltimore: The Johns Hopkins University Press, 1995), 178–9.

[17] Carlos Tello and Sylvia Maxfield provide an excellent account of the crisis and bank nationalization. See Carlos Tello, *La Nacionalización de la Banca* (Mexico City: Ed. Siglo XXI, 1984); and Sylvia Maxfield, *Governing Capital* (Ithaca: Cornell University Press, 1990).

adjustment program based on fiscal and monetary retrenchment and wage restraint. After 1985, the government also moved toward trade liberalization to control the prices of the tradeable goods and to increase the competitiveness of domestic production.[18] Inbound production (*maquiladora*) expanded enormously during this period while real wages dropped dramatically.[19]

The government also reduced its deficit by starting to sell state-owned enterprises of minor importance.[20] However, the De La Madrid administration compensated organized labor with welfare concessions administered by unions.[21] These concessions not only eased the impact of the crisis on workers, but also endowed the unions with an intermediary role in the distribution of resources that reinforced their authority.[22]

The orthodox adjustment program could not control the crisis and, in 1987, the fall of the stock market crash started a process of capital flight and high inflation. After the peso was devalued on 15 December 1982, the President, together with business, labor, and peasant leaders, signed the Pact of Economic Solidarity (PSE). The pact, whose architect was Social Planning Secretary Carlos Salinas, established an adjustment plan through income policies based on expected rather than past inflation, price agreements on inputs, and a fixed exchange rate. It also committed the state to restrictive monetary policy, fiscal discipline, including a realignment of public sector

[18] Blanca Heredia, 'Making Economic Reform Politically Viable: The Mexican Experience', in William Smith, Carlos Acuña, and Eduardo Gamarra (eds), *Democracy, Markets and Structural Reform in Latin America* (New Brunswick: North-South Center and Transaction Publishers, 1994).

[19] According to Middlebrook (1995), the hike in the minimum salary ceased to be a reference point for collective bargaining wages and instead became a ceiling. Between 1982 and 1988, the real value of minimum wages dropped by 48.3% and that of contractual wages by 47.6% (Aspe, 1993, 26). The decrease of real minimum wages and real manufacturing wages (ibid. graph 1) was accompanied by a drop in the labor share of the GDP from 35.2% in 1982 to 26.8% in 1988. See Mario Zepeda, 'El Pronasol, la política y la pobreza', *Memoria*, 36 (1990), 6–7. Wage restraint was also enforced by exemplary strikes which were lost by the workers, and which in some cases led to the bankruptcy of state-owned companies (Zamora, 'La política laboral del estado mexicano, 1982–88', 24–48).

[20] Eduardo Vega Lopez, 'La política económica de México durante el período 1982–1994', *El Cotidiano*, 67 (Mexico City, March–April, 1995), 31–3.

[21] The PRI introduced a constitutional reform for social housing, controls on the cost of rents, transportation and basic staples, and increased the share profits for workers from 8 to 10%. See Zamora, 'La política laboral del estado mexicano, 1982–88', 133, and Aziz Nassiff, *El Estado Mexicano y la CTM*, 279–81. The CTM also obtained the extension of the 'social sector' (union and worker property) that reached, in 1984, 400 production firms for basic goods that were distributed in 142 CTM-run shops. See Javier Aguilar García and Lorenzo Arrieta, 'En la fase más aguda de la crisis y en el inicio de la reestructuración o modernización', in Javier Aguilar García (ed.), *Historia de la CTM: 1936–1990*, 2 (Mexico City: Instituto de Investigaciones Sociales, UNAM, 1990), 698–9.

[22] Examples of these policies were a program of incentives to production, distribution, and consumption of basic staples in 1982, a more active role to the National Commission of Minimum Salaries where unions were represented (CNSM), a subsidy to the union-controlled Workers' Bank in order to foster union stores as well as an increase in the funding for tripartite institutions like the INFONAVIT and National Fund for Workers' Consumption Goods (FONACOT) in 1985 (Zamora, 'La política laboral del estado mexicano, 1982–88', and Aziz Nassiff, *El Estado Mexicano y la CTM*).

prices, a retrenchment in and privatization of the public sector, and a larger trade opening that would control the price of tradeable goods. Thus, the PSE marked the beginning of a new strategy of macroeconomic stabilization that was accompanied by an acceleration of the process of structural reforms aimed at reshaping the role of the state as well as the competitiveness of the Mexican economy.[23] These reforms, however, not only challenged the institutions and practices that had previously regulated the relationship between the state and the union movement, but also triggered a process of industrial restructuring in both the private and the public sector.

Labor Response to the De La Madrid Administration

In January 1983, President De La Madrid relaxed a price settlement established the previous month despite wage controls. The CTM threatened a general strike demanding wage-indexation and more frequent minimum wage negotiations. Moreover, it accepted, for the first time, that 'independent' unions join the May Day parade of the 'official' union movement.[24] This timid signal of partisan tolerance challenged the incumbent PRI, afraid of the influence of other parties in the union movement. In addition, CTM affiliates showed their discontent by increasing their share of total strikes between 1983 and 1986.[25] In contrast, the share of strikes involving unions affiliated with the CROC and the CROM dropped after 1983 (Secretary of Labor and Social Welfare 1989), accompanying their increasing support for the austerity policies of the De la Madrid administration.[26]

The De La Madrid administration took advantage of the competition between labor confederations associated with the PRI. Secretary of Labor and Social Welfare, Arsenio Farrell, rewarded the supportive national union confederations that boycotted CTM wage demands in the Congress of Labor. Farrell's policies ranged from speeding the registration procedures of unions affiliated with compliant national labor confederations, to publicly acknowledging their support as a sign of modernization.[27] This competition with other PRI-related national union confederations made it costly for the CTM to maintain its disagreement in terms of state resources to the point that in

[23] See Aspe, *El Camino Mexicano de la Transformación Económica*, and Nora Lustig, 'The Mexican Peso Crisis: the Foreseeable and the Surprise', Brookings Discussion Papers in International Economics (Washington, DC, 1995).

[24] Middlebrook, *The Paradox of Revolution*, 260–1.

[25] Secretary of Labor and Social Welfare, Annual Reports (Mexico City, 1997).

[26] For instance, in June 1983, the CROC, CROM, CRT, and FTSTE, formed a pro-government bloc opposing the CTM. This bloc signed a National Solidarity Pact, together with government and business, aimed at moderating wage and price hikes. The CTM did not sign the pact and demanded a 50% hike in the minimum wage (Zamora, 'La política laboral del estado mexicano, 1982–88', 135). See also María Xelhuantzi López, 'Reforma del Estado Mexicano y sindicalismo', MA thesis (Mexico City: UNAM, 1992), 253.

[27] See Irma Campuzano Montoya, 'El impacto de la crisis en la CTM', *Revista Mexicana de Sociología*, 52: 3 (Mexico City, 1990), 161–90; and Middlebrook, *The Paradox of Revolution*,175.

1987 it signed the PSE.[28] Salinas would reinforce this manipulation of union competition to control the CTM and to avert opposition to his sweeping reform program.

The Salinas Administration (1988–94)[29]

President Salinas signed, with business, peasants, and labor representatives, a series of pacts that would seek consensus for his policies during his administration. These pacts continued with price negotiation, income policies, increasing deregulation, and fiscal deficit reduction. He accelerated privatization in path and scope, industrial restructuring, and trade liberalization. He championed and signed the North American Free Trade Agreement (NAFTA), reformed part of the social security system, and partially changed the structure of the party as described below.

Stabilization   The stabilization program defined in the annual corporatist pacts of the Salinas administration attacked the fiscal deficit and inflation. It continued with price negotiation and income policies defining a wage ceiling equal to the approved hikes on the minimum wage while promising a restrictive monetary policy and faster trade liberalization to control prices. The government realigned public sector prices, approved a tax reform, and cut subsidies to reduce the fiscal deficit. Meanwhile, the exchange rate served as an anchor against inflation—fixed in 1988 and with a limited crawling peg since 1989.[30] As a result, the reduction of the fiscal deficit was accompanied by a revaluation of the Mexican peso.[31]

The impact of stabilization on the CTM and its constituencies was mixed. The reduction of inflation benefited wage earners that were more hurt by inflation than asset-holders. However, real minimum wages maintained a declining trend and, although the real trend of manufacturing real earnings (considering wages, salaries, and benefits) turned upward, they never recovered their pre-1982 value. Even in the *maquiladora* firms, salaries dropped

---

[28] See Aziz Nassiff, *El Estado Mexicano y la CTM*; and Middlebrook, *The Paradox of Revolution*.

[29] President Carlos Salinas had a six-year term, from December 1988 to December 1994. As with previous PRI presidential nominees, he was elected among other PRI candidates by the governing PRI president in a ritual called '*destape*' (unveiling). The analysis of Salinas' reforms and union responses to these reforms is based on field research done in Mexico in 1993 and 1995. The interviewees (45) included actors of the period and key informants. The three sets of actors were policymakers, managers, politicians and union leaders, from both the PRI and dissidents within the unions analyzed. Key informants were students of the analyzed sectors. The interviews were supplemented by documents, collective bargaining contracts, a press chronology (elaborated by my research assistant, Antonieta Mercado, based on the archives of *Entorno Laboral*), and secondary sources.

[30] See Aziz Nassiff, *El Estado Mexicano y la CTM*; and Middlebrook, *The Paradox of Revolution*.

[31] Lustig, 'The Mexican Peso Crisis: the Foreseeable and the Surprise'.

between 1989 and 1992.[32] Open unemployment and underemployment remained stable and had their lowest value between 1990 and 1992 (Table 2.1), but economic growth was modest, especially if compared with the almost 2% average annual rate of population growth in Mexico during the Salinas administration. The low rate of economic growth, together with the limited compensations offered to wage earners and the absence of unemployment insurance, affected the CTM and its constituencies despite the recovery of purchasing power granted by the success of macroeconomic stabilization. In addition, wage ceilings limited the capacity of unions' bargaining power.

Table 2.1. Mexico: Selected macroeconomic indicators (1980–94)

Year	Real GDP growth (%)	Open unemployment	Under-employment	Minimum real salary[a]	Inflation (% CPI)[b]	Fiscal balance (% of GDP)	Current account balance (US$m)
1982	−1.9	4.3	n.d.	104.7	58.92	−11.98	−5,889
1983	−4.2	5.3	n.d.	84.8	101.76	−8.15	5,886
1984	3.5	5.7	n.d.	71.8	65.54	−7.25	4,183
1985	2.5	3.7	n.d.	70.9	57.75	−7.59	800
1986	−3.6	4.4	n.d.	63.2	86.23	−13.3	−1,377
1987	1.8	3.9	4.0	60.3	131.83	−14.22	4,247
1988	1.3	3.6	3.9	67.4	114.16	−9.61	−2,374
1989	3.3	3.0	3.8	73.6	20.01	−4.99	−5,825
1990	4.5	2.8	3.3	75.1	26.65	−2.8	−7,451
1991	3.6	2.6	3.5	80.1	22.66	−0.23	−14,888
1992	2.8	2.8	3.7	87.8	15.51	1.54	−24,442
1993	0.7	3.4	4.3	94.6	9.75	0.36	−23,400
1994	3.3	3.6	4.4	98.0	6.97	−0.78	−29,418

[a] Real minimum salary is measured with a base of 100 for 1980 and was taken from the Mexican Indicators of ECLAC for 1995.
[b] CPI,

Sources: Inflation, fiscal balance, and current account balance figures are IMF statistics. See International Monetary Fund, *International Financial Statistics, 1996* (Washington, DC: IMF, 1996). Real GDP growth has been calculated using IMF figures. Open unemployment and underemployment (those who work less than 15 hours per week) are rates of the economically active population and have been taken from Salinas for 1982–7 and from Salinas for 1987–94. See Carlos Salinas de Gortari, *Cuarto Informe de Gobierno, Anexo Estadístico* (Mexico City: Poder Ejecutivo Federal, 1992), 331.

[32] CTM, 'Memorias de la CXV Asamblea Ordinaria de la CTM', Annual report (Mexico City, 1993).

The CTM signed all the corporatist pacts of Salinas' administration, preaching their beneficial impact on real salaries,[33] but rejected wage ceilings and demanded higher hikes for the minimum wage from 1988 to 1992.[34] The CTM even denounced wage ceilings in the courts in 1992.[35] In contrast, the CROM, the CROC, and the FTSTE supported the stabilizing pacts without expressing public wage demands.[36] After 1993, CTM wage demands receded and the number of strikes of its affiliates dropped as a proportion of total strikes of PRI-affiliated labor confederations, but the government granted no concessions.

Privatization of State-owned Enterprises   President Salinas privatized very important economic assets, such as the national telephone company, the formerly nationalized commercial banking system, state-owned airlines, steel mills, copper mines, and part of the petrochemical industry.[37] The privatization of state-owned enterprises, according to former Secretary of the Economy Pedro Aspe,[38] sought to balance the fiscal budget and to reshape the state thereby complementing stabilization efforts. The privatization of state-owned enterprises had a tremendous impact on employment and work conditions. Industrial restructuring and labor flexibility in firms designated to be privatized was drastic.[39] According to a high-ranking policymaker,[40] the administration threatened union leaders with firm bankruptcy and the extinction of collective bargaining clauses to persuade them of the need to introduce labor flexibility and to restructure work conditions in the firms designated for privatization.

The privatization program concentrated its impact on the affected workers hurting especially nationwide industrial unions that organized workers in large state-owned enterprises and whose collective bargaining contracts were

[33] CTM, 'Memorias de la CXVI Asamblea Ordinaria de la CTM', Annual report (Mexico City, 1994).
[34] CTM, 'Memorias de la CXI Asamblea Ordinaria de la CTM', Annual report (Mexico City, 1990, 1991, 1992).
[35] *Uno Más Uno* (Mexico City, 15 December 1992).
[36] Press chronology and interviews with Hector Miranda, secretary of National Relations of the FTSTE (14 February 1995), Cuahutémoc Paleta, secretary general of the CROM (1 March 1995), and Mario Martínez D'ector, leader of the CROC in the state of Mexico (3 March 1995).
[37] President De La Madrid had affected minor privatizations that represented less than 0.20% of the annual GDP and less than 1% of the annual public sector income. President Salinas' privatization program was both rapid and financially important. For instance, in 1991, privatization income was 3.83% of GDP and accounted for 14.4% of public sector income (Aspe, *El Camino Mexicano de la Transformación Económica*, 185).
[38] Aspe (1993, 37).
[39] See Miguel Ramírez, 'The Political Economy of Privatization in Mexico, 1983–92', Occasional Paper 1, Latin American Studies Consortium of New England (1993), 20. For example, the state-owned oil company (Pemex) was decentralized in four units while the collective bargaining contract was drastically changed and personnel cut sharply. Rafael Loyola and Liliana Martínez, 'Petróleos Mexicanos: la búsqueda de un nuevo modelo empresarial', *Estudios Sociológicos*, 12 (1994).
[40] Confidential interview (1995).

generous in fringe benefits and union privileges. Despite the conflict in preferences that this policy could have created among different constituencies, the predominance of a coalition of regional unions within the CTM silenced the demands of unions in the state-owned enterprises and forced them into the political logic of subordination, which governed CTM-government interactions.

Trade Liberalization Trade liberalization reduced tariffs from an average of 34% in 1988 to 4% in 1993.[41] Trade liberalization and Mexican integration into NAFTA were aimed at both controlling the price of tradeable products and making the Mexican economy more competitive and integrated into world markets. In addition, trade liberalization and integration promoted the development of the *maquiladora* where employment rose sharply. The export sector benefited from this reform despite the revaluation of the Mexican peso.[42] Trade liberalization thus affected mainly the protected and domestically oriented sectors while benefiting the competitive and export-oriented sectors, particularly those integrated into the US market, such as the *maquiladora*. However, the CTM—as well as the CROC and the CROM—affiliated unions in most sectors and regions, gathering both the losers and winners of this process since their regional union leaders even competed for the potential new recruitment in *maquiladora*.[43] As with privatization, the predominance of regional federations that organized both the winners and losers of trade liberalization and integration averted conflicts of interests within the CTM submerged its policy response within the general dynamics of CTM-government relations and unified CTM response to trade liberalization and integration. Bensusán and García (1993), stressing the unique case of negotiation between the CTM and the government, argues that the CTM, along with the rest of the PRI-related confederations, actively supported NAFTA in exchange for the maintenance of the Federal Labor Law that regulated labor organization.[44] Moreover, the CTM preference for NAFTA was also based on its expectation for increased employment despite the opposition of its American counterparts.[45]

[41] World Bank, *Reformas Laborales y Económicas en América Latina y el Caribe* (Washington, DC: World Bank, 1995).

[42] Mexican exports (freight on board) grew from US$30,692m in 1988 to US$79,418m in 1994 (IMF, 1996).

[43] On that competition, see Jorge Carrillo, 'La Ford en México: restructuración industrial y cambio en las relaciones sociales', PhD dissertation (Mexico City: El Colegio de México, 1993).

[44] Graciela Bensusán and Carlos García, *Opiniones Sindicales Sobre la Reforma Laboral* (Mexico City: Fundación Ebert, 1993).

[45] See also José Domínguez, advisor to the secretary of education of CTM, interviews by author (Mexico City, 21 and 26 Feb. 1995); Janette Góngora and Horacio Vázquez, 'El sindicalismo mexicano ante el Tratado de Libre Comercio', *Trabajo*, 5–6 (1991), 4–6; Bensusán and García, *Opiniones Sindicales Aobre la Reforma Labora*; and CTM (1990, 1991, 1993, 1994).

The System of Retirement Savings   In 1992, with the aim of increasing domestic savings, Congress approved a bill to reform social security by creating a complementary retirement fund under private administration. The System of Savings for Retirement (SAR) was a privately administered pension system of individual capitalization, based on an employer tax of 2% of salary. The SAR complemented the public pay-as-you-go system that was administered by the tripartite Mexican Institute of Social Security (IMSS). This reform of the state system of social security did not affect the public structure of the IMSS, however. None the less, it created a parallel private system without including union representation in management. It was designed as a transitional stage to a future privatization of the public pension system through retirement funds, which would take place during the following administration.

Although the SAR created a complementary benefit paid with employers' taxes, the CTM opposed the SAR. The CTM considered it a first stage in the privatization of social security and demanded that the Workers Bank administers the funds for productive goals or that an unemployment insurance be created using these individual accounts.[46] To the contrary, other PRI labor allies, such as the CROC, the CROM, and some of the new Federation of Goods and Services (FESEBeS) unions, supported the creation of the SAR. The government did not grant CTM demands and only included the CTM, which participated in the administration of the IMSS, in a symbolic advisory committee.

The Reform of the Institute for Housing Funds (INFONAVIT)   The reform of the Institute for Housing Funds (INFONAVIT) was based on a 5% payroll tax from workers earning less than ten times the minimum salary, although the houses built with these funds were intended for workers earning less than five times the minimum salary, with the highest priority to those earning less than two times the minimum salary.[47] The Institute intervened in financing, planning, contracting, building, and distributing housing, and had a tripartite management although unions increasingly dominated it. Indeed, union competition replaced efficiency and solidarity principles in the distribution of housing, and the INFONAVIT became an important source of union financial resources and patronage.[48]

President Salinas designated the SAR to also administer INFONAVIT funds, thereby excluding unions from the administration of funds, the intermediation for housing construction, and the assignation of housing credits

[46] Julián Bertranú, 'La política de la reforma a la seguridad social en México'. Unpublished MS (Flacso-Sede México, Mexico City, 1994), 20.

[47] Nancy Robinson, 'The Politics of Low Income Housing in Mexico: A Case Study of Infonavit, the Workers' Housing Institute'. Unpublished MA thesis (Stanford, CA: Stanford University, 1980), 57.

[48] Ibid. 157.

that had previously been distributed among PRI-related labor confederations.[49] Therefore, this reform to the corporatist structure of welfare had an impact upon the authority structure of unions and affected their capacity to resort to patronage and to create selective incentives.[50] The CTM rejected the reform and proposed, instead, to increase and oversee employer contributions, and to administer funds better.[51] In contrast to the CTM, the CROC, CROM, COR, and even some FESEBeS unions supported the reform.[52] The government disregarded CTM's demands and implemented the reform giving the CTM only small concessions.[53] The INFONAVIT's administrative council restored the old system of union intermediation in credit assignation as a supplement to the new private system in October 1993.[54]

Labor Flexibility Despite the rigidity of the Mexican Labor Code (the Federal Labor Law or LFT), labor flexibility in collective bargaining advanced under the discretion of the Secretary of Labor and Social Welfare (STPS) and the Conciliation and Arbitration Boards. They approved collective bargaining contracts which, contrary to the spirit of the law, reduced fringe benefits and union prerogatives, and increased the flexibility of work conditions.[55] This *de facto* flexibility reduced union influence and transformed the work conditions of union constituencies across sectors. Moreover, in 1992, Salinas signed with business and labor representatives the National Agreement for the Promotion of Quality and Productivity (ANECP), aimed at increasing Mexican productivity and international competitiveness at the micro level. During his administration, labor productivity grew more rapidly in manufacturing than during the previous administration. Yet, because of the revaluation of the exchange rate, the unitary labor cost sharply increased during this period, although was still lower than the US labor cost.[56]

[49] *El Economista* (10 Feb. 1992).
[50] Bertranú, 'La política de la reforma a la seguridad social en México', 22.
[51] *La Jornada*, 11 and 12 Oct. 1991.
[52] Interviews with Hector Miranda, Secretary of National Relations of the FTSTE (14 February 1995), Cuahutémoc Paleta, Secretary-General of the CROM (1 March 1995), Joel López Mayrén, Secretary-General of the COR (29 March 1995), Francisco Hernandez Juarez, Secretary-General of the FESEBeS (19 April 1995).
[53] Bertranú, 'La política de la reforma a la seguridad social en México', 27.
[54] Katrina Burgess, 'Thresholds of Institutional Change: Economic Reform and Party-Labor Relations in Mexico', paper prepared for the conference 'Economic Reform and Civil Society in Latin America' (David Rockefeller Center for Latin American Studies, Harvard University, 12 April 1996), 27.
[55] See Enrique de la Garza, *Restructuración Productiva y Respuesta Sindical en México* and Middlebrook, *The Paradox of Revolution*. This *de facto* labor flexibility resulted from the governmental attempt to divide the reform of work conditions from the reform of labor organization conditions, both of which were regulated by the Federal Labor Law. It was allowed by the discretionary power of the Mexican Executive, which created juridical insecurity in industrial relations.
[56] Productivity in manufacturing increased 10.6% from 1982 to 1988 and 20.2% in the first half of the Salinas administration (1988–92), according to Salinas, *Sexto Informe de Gobierno, Anexo*

De facto labor flexibility affected CTM unions and constituencies across sectors and regions. Between 1988 and 1993, the CTM complained about *de facto* labor flexibility in collective bargaining and in 1982 threatened solidarity strikes against flexibility in the textile industry. In contrast, the CROC and the new Federation of Goods and Services Unions (FESEBeS) were more favorable to labor flexibility and competitive concerns (although the FESEBeS stressed union participation in these changes).

Labor Organization Regulations   The Employers Confederation of Mexico (COPARMEX) proposed a reform of labor legislation in 1991. The COPARMEX demanded the abolition of closed shops, limits to strike activity, the individualization of wage bargaining, and a reduction of union influence in work organization.[57] Their aim was to obtain juridical security and to curb union power by attacking the subsidies for labor organization, such as monopolies of representation, collective wage negotiation, and closed shops.

In 1966, the national labor confederations associated with the PRI had formed the Congress of Labor (CT), an umbrella organization to coordinate their participation in the corporatist institutions of the state and the party. The CTM affiliated 63.9% of CT union members in 1979.[58] However, the CTM could not impose this majority in the CT due to the requirement of unanimous decision-making. Yet, on the issue of labor law reform, the CTM could obtain the unanimous support of CT members, in contrast to what happened with its other attempts to demand policy changes. The CTM could organize a common front against the COPARMEX initiative because all national confederations and PRI-unions also rejected the proposal as being pro-business.[59] The unification of union opposition resulted in the government dropping the reform.

Reform of the Corporatist Structure of the PRI   President Salinas aggressively pursued political reforms within the party as a response to the dismal 1988 electoral results.[60] The PRI had been based on group membership and divided into three functional sectors. Yet, in 1990, the XIVth Assembly of the PRI introduced individual affiliation and established equal representation for the functional sectors and the new territorial structure. The XVth Assembly of the PRI united the peasant and labor sectors of the party in a Worker-Peasant Pact, and created a Territorial Popular Movement and a National

---

Estadístico, 234. The unitary labor cost increased from US$65.3 in 1985 to US$102.4 in 1993, but in the US it was US$107.5 in 1985 and US$105.9 in 1993 (Salinas, *Sexto Informe de Gobierno, Anexo Estadístico*, 234).

[57] Bensusán, 'Los determinantes institucionales de la flexibilización laboral', 58–9.
[58] Zazueta and de la Peña *Estructura Dual y Piramidal del Sindicalismo Mexicano*, 810.
[59] See Bensusán, 'Los determinantes institucionales de la flexibilización laboral'; and CTM, *La CTM y la Economia de los Trabajadores* (Mexico City, 1993).
[60] León, 'Del partido de partido al partido de sectores'.

Citizens Front.[61] The CTM resented these reforms because they attacked their quota in the structure of functional representation, which had traditionally nourished its influence within the party.[62] As a result of this internal conflict within the PRI, the number of labor candidacies for deputies in the PRI slates dropped from 21.4% in 1988 to 15% in 1991, or from 30% to 20% including civil service unions that also belonged to the Congress of Labor (Table 2.2), although this decline ended in 1994.[63]

Table 2.2. Mexico: Labor candidacies in the Institutional Revolutionary Party (PRI) slates (1979–94)

Year	No. of labor candidacies (% of PRI)	No. of candidacies from popular sector belonging to the CT (% of PRI)	No. of CTM candidacies (% of total labor)
1979	70 (23.3%)	24 (8%)	45 (64%)
1982	74 (24.6%)	23 (7.7%)	50 (67%)
1984	72 (24%)	24 (8%)	51 (71%)
1988	75 (21.4%)	26 (9%)	51 (68%)
1991	57 (15%)	17 (5.1%)[a]	44 (76%)
1994	56 (15%)	19 (5.4%)[a]	45 (76%)

[a] The 1991 and 1994 figures for the popular sector correspond only to the SNTE and FSTSE.

Notes: The figures correspond to the Chamber of Representatives and are derived from an interview with Jesús Reyes del Campillo, an expert on Mexican elections, by the author in Mexico City in 1990 and 1991. Since 1988, the total candidacies increased from 300 to 350.

This decline in the political influence of labor until 1993 deepened the competition among labor confederations for the fewer spaces assigned to it within the party and elective bodies. Since the CTM controlled most of the labor sector of the party, the CROC, CROM, COR, FESEBeS, and the FTSTE tried to take advantage of the reforms to improve their relative position at the expenses of the CTM.[64] Their support thus again weakened CTM demands against the changes in the corporatist structure of the PRI implemented from 1990 to 1992. However, after its effective subordination to Salinas' reforms in

[61] Luis Mendez Berrueta and José Quiroz Trejo, *Modernización Estatal y Respuesta Obrera: Historia de una Derrota* (Mexico City: Universidad Autónoma Metropolitana, 1994).

[62] CTM, *Memorias de la CXII Asamblea*.

[63] However, because of the longer terms, the number of senators and governors from the labor sector did not experience this decline (Zapata, 'Crisis en el sindicalismo en México?'). The CTM still held majorities in the IMSS, the INFONAVIT, the FONACOT, and the CNSM, according to Fidel Velásquez (*La Jornada*, 12 April 1992). See Domínguez (1995) and Francisco Zapata, 'Crisis en el sindicalismo en México?' *Revista Mexicana de Sociología*,1 (1994), 79–88.

[64] See note 52.

1993, the CTM recovered institutional space within the party in an alliance with other groups within the party who also felt challenged by the changes in the party structure. These allies took advantage of the upcoming Presidential elections when the reformers would need their support to obtain a return to the corporatist structure of representation for the National Executive Committee of the party. As a result, the XVIth Assembly of the PRI returned the functional representation structure to the National Executive Committee in 1993.[65]

Labor Responses to Salinas' Policies

Although the CTM had supported Alfredo Del Mazo rather than Salinas for the PRI nomination, it did not organize protests against Salinas' reforms and even campaigned in favor of the NAFTA. Government manipulation of union competition, thanks to the party monopoly over labor loyalties, explains the CTM behavior. The Salinas administration manipulated union competition for resources and members taking advantage of the party monopoly, which guaranteed its control over the majority of member unions even if they moved from one national confederation to another. When the CTM expressed its disagreement with government policies, the government used executive discretion to give more resources to the other PRI labor confederations which accepted these policies to make them more attractive for union members and to punish the CTM. To avoid losing resources and member, the CTM subordinated itself to the government and silenced its demands.

President Salinas not only took advantage of the competition among PRI-related national union confederations to control the behavior of the CTM, but also used repression to maintain the party monopoly in the unions. After the Party of the Democratic Revolution (PRD), which emerged from a splinter of the PRI, almost won the 1988 elections, Salinas punished some PRI union leaders who supported the PRD candidate in the elections.[66] He also retained Arsenio Farrell as his Secretary of Labor. The latter continued to reward compliant national union confederations, like the CROC and the CROM, which confronted CTM demands.[67] Simultaneously, Salinas advocated the emergence of a 'new unionism' concerned with work productivity and based on his personal relations with the union leaders who organized the FESEBeS.[68] The FESEBeS obtained its official registration in 1992 against CTM complaints, thus increasing union competition and the number of seri-

[65] Marbrán, 'La dificultad del cambio (1968–1990)'.

[66] For example, Salinas orchestrated the imprisonment, on murder charges, of the powerful state oil workers' traditional leader, Joaquín Hernández Galicia (*La Quina*), who backed Cárdenas.

[67] Domínguez (personal interviews, 1995).

[68] Ruth Berins Collier and James Samstad, 'Mexican Labor and Structural Reform: New Unionism or Old Stalemate?', in Riordan Roett (ed.), *The Challenge of Institutional Reform in Mexico* (Boulder: Lynne Rienner, 1995).

ous challengers to the CTM. In December 1992, the CROC and FESEBeS launched a common front in the Congress of Labor that appeared to be an alternative to the CTM.[69] In addition, in February 1993, a government agency incorporated them into a program for the modernization of unionism, which had been rejected by the CTM.[70] The CROC and the CROM boycotted CTM wage demands in the Congress of Labor, thus hindering the unanimity necessary to have a common front, like the one that rejected the reform of the labor law. In addition, CTM-affiliated unions exited to other national union confederations, especially to the CROC and, to a lesser degree, to the CROM, because they received better treatment from the government.[71] By contrast, the CROC increased its membership and the FESEBeS obtained its registration (despite the complaints of the CTM) while its affiliated unions received industry-specific concessions.

As shown in Table 2.3, although the CTM accepted most of Salinas' reforms due to government manipulation of union competition, the reform of labor regulation was an exception because the common front of all PRI-affiliated labor confederations reduced union competition. Since the CTM built a common front in the Congress of Labor, it avoided the effects of union competition and strengthened union bargaining power *vis-à-vis* the government. As a result, unions obtained the maintenance of the law in return for their active support in favor of the NAFTA.[72] This exceptional case of union

Table 2.3. The Mexican Workers' Confederation (CTM) responses to market-oriented reforms

Reform	CTM position	Competing	Concessions to the CTM
Stabilization	Rejection of wage caps	Support for austerity	No concessions
Privatization	Rejection	Support	No concessions
Trade liberalization	Support	Support	Exchange for Federal Labor Law
SAR	Rejection	Support	No concessions
INFONAVIT	Rejection	Support	Minor concessions after 1993
Labor flexibility	Rejection	Support	No concessions
Federal Labor Law reform	Rejection	Rejection	Reversal
PRI reform	Rejection	Support	Reversal after 1993

[69] *Uno más Uno* (Mexico City, 16 Dec. 1992).
[70] *El Financiero* (Mexico City, 24 Feb. 1993).
[71] The exit of CTM-affiliated unions was reported by several newspapers and collected in my press chronology.
[72] Bensusán, *Opiniones Sindicales Sobre la Reforma Laboral*.

unity further reinforces my theory, since the absence of union competition strengthened union bargaining power.

The subordination of the CTM combined with its centralized control over affiliate unions facilitated the implementation of Salinas' policies. CTM centralized authority derived from the 1947 CTM constitution—which required CTM affiliates to seek the approval of the National Committee for strike actions—as well as from the informal role played by the CTM in collective bargaining.[73] The CTM participated as an informal intermediary in important negotiations with management and the Secretary of Labor and Social Welfare (STPS), and had a majority of labor representatives in both Local and Federal Conciliation and Arbitration Boards (JLCA and JFCA)—which regulated collective bargaining, union registration, and strike approval—as well as in the National Commission for the Minimum Salary (CNSM), which set minimum wages. Its representation in other state institutions, such as the social security and housing institutes, also provided the CTM with selective incentives and other sources of patronage.[74] Moreover, the CTM could not make a credible threat to exit to another political party due to its long partisan loyalty reinforced by Salinas' exemplary punishments to defectors.[75]

The CTM subordinated itself to Salinas' reforms to preclude the loss of further resources that the administration shifted towards rival confederations as well as the exit of more CTM members towards competing confederations. The CTM reflected the fragmentation of the Mexican union movement. Local unions included in regional federations predominated over nationwide industrial unions.[76] As a result, political rather than industrial preferences prevailed in the organization. Political resources were easier to deliver on regional basis and have historically compensated for the industrial weakness of small local unions.

---

[73]   Burgess, 'Thresholds of Institutional Change', 8.

[74]   On the development of such institutions and the influence of the CTM within them see Middlebrook, *The Paradox of Revolution*, 56–70; and Bensusán, 'Institucionalización laboral en México', ch. 6. On the political resources and the authority of the CTM see, among others, Middlebrook *The Paradox of Revolution*; Bizberg, *Estado y Sindicalismo en México*; and Assiz Nassiff, *El Estado Mexicano y la CTM*.

[75]   Moreover, since the PRI was never in opposition, the CTM never had the opportunity to prove its industrial muscle against a non-affiliated incumbent party like other Latin American union movements did (Zapata, *El Conflicto Sindical en América Latina*).

[76]   On the predominance of regional federations over nationwide industrial unions see Zazueta and de la Peña, *Estructura Dual y Piramidal del Sindicalismo Mexicano*, 811–14; and Aguilar, 'En la fase más aguda de la crisis y en el inicio de la reestructuración o modernización', 134. This predominance prevented the CTM from clustering their local industrial unions into nationwide industrial unions to avert a repetition of the 1940s and 1950s when nationwide industrial unions challenged Fidel Velázquez, the CTM perennial leader who was supported by a coalition of regional federations (Camacho, *El Futuro Inmediato*, 112). In the early post-war period, the combination of Communist influence and increased militancy of the nationwide industrial unions also presented a threat to the CTM leadership that was repressed by the incumbent PRI. See Jorge Basurto, *Del Avilacamachismo al Alemanismo (1940–1952)* (Mexico City: Siglo Veintiuno Editores, 1984), 124–32; and Assiz Nassif, *El Estado Mexicano y la CTM*, 98–104.

In short, the government subordinated the CTM by manipulating union competition, restricted within the boundaries of the PRI, which reduced the bargaining power of the CTM and forced its subordination. Only in the case of the attempted reform of the Federal Labor Law a common front of all PRI-related labor confederations reduced union competition and strengthened labor bargaining power averting the reform proposed by the government.

Sector-specific Reforms and Union Reactions

Trade liberalization and integration into world markets triggered industrial restructuring in the automobile, oil, electricity, and telecommunications. While the first two were tradeable goods, the last two sectors provided key infrastructure service for the production of goods and services. In addition, the oil, electricity, and telecommunications sectors were state-owned monopolies until Salinas privatized telecommunications and opened oil to private investment. State reform also affected education where Salinas started a process of decentralization to improve the efficiency of public education thus seeking to build human capital. The following sections describe both the attempts at reforming these industries and the response of unions.

Decentralization of Education: Union Monopoly in a Reformed Reform

Although the Mexican Constitution put primary education under the jurisdiction of municipalities and secondary education and teacher training under the jurisdiction of the states, the Public Education Secretary has expanded and centralized the education system at every level since 1921.[77] While centralization and politicization were blamed on the inefficiency of the system, at the beginning of the Salinas administration, teachers' demands for higher wages and greater democracy within the unions had already generated large protests from regionally based dissidents who forced a change in the union leadership. In 1992, Salinas proposed a decentralization of education that would transfer all schools to the jurisdiction of states. This reform particularly affected the national leadership of the National Union of Education Workers (SNTE) which would lose power to state leaders. Thus, the national leadership unanimously rejected decentralization, afraid of its impact on the authority structure of the union if it were divided into thirty-two units.[78]

---

[77] In 1928, the SEP only controlled 20% of the students and the federal government paid only for 6.1% of education expenditures. By 1991–2, however, the SEP controlled 65% of students and the federal government paid for 80% of education expenditures. See Carlos Ornelas, *El Sistema Educativo Mexicano* (Mexico City: Fondo de Cultura Económica, 1995).

[78] A former policymaker admitted in a confidential interview that the division of the nationwide union into 32 state unions was one of the unachieved objectives of the reform. This objective was perceived by PRI and non-PRI union leaders as well. See José Antonio Rodríguez,

To obtain the support of the union for the transfer of more than 500,000 teachers and 100,000 employees to state jurisdiction in 1992, and for the subsequent General Education Law of 1993, the government granted important concessions to the union. These concessions included the centralization of evaluation, curriculum, and funding for training by the federal government, salary hikes above national wage ceilings, new pension benefits, and pay incentives.[79] In addition, the education budget of states was to be earmarked by the federal government instead of decentralizing financial decisions on education expenditures. This last concession guaranteed new uniform requirements and promotion conditions covering teachers originally under state and federal jurisdiction. In addition, teachers who were formerly under state and federal jurisdictions were included in the same unified districts increasing the influence of the national leadership over the teachers previously under state jurisdiction. These concessions facilitated the decentralization process although substantially modifying its original design. Why was the teachers' union able to extract these concessions from the government?

Teachers' Union: The Emergence of Leadership Competition in a Monopolistic Union   The National Union of Education Workers (SNTE) was a monopolistic union founded in 1943, under the auspices of the PRI-controlled Secretariat of Public Education with the aim of restraining Communist influence and inter-union conflicts in the education sector (Arnaud 1993). Since then, the PRI controlled the union that served as a political machine and as tool for the expansion and centralization of education. In return, union leaders received candidacies in PRI slates and management positions in the Secretariat of Public Education, while centralization strengthened the national leadership of the union, sustained mainly by members under federal jurisdiction.[80] The resulting politicization of the Secretariat of Public

advisor to former Secretary-General of the SNTE Elba Esther Gordillo, interview by author (Mexico City, 4 April 1995); Jesús Martín Del Campo, PRD official and SNTE leader, interview by author (Mexico City, 12 April 1995).

[79] According to José Antonio Rodríguez (personal interview, 1995), advisor to former Secretary-General of the SNTE, Elba Esther Gordillo, teachers' real incomes (including productivity incentives and benefits) increased 150% during the Salinas administration while PRD union leader Jesús Martín Del Campo (personal interview, 1995) claimed that basic real salaries grew 35% between 1988 and 1994. In any case, they fared better than most sectors of the economy that lost purchasing power, although their low wages at the beginning of the administration explain part of the relative increase. See Alberto Arnaud, 'La federalización de la educación básica y normal (1978–1994)', *Política y Gobierno* (Mexico City, 1994), 1, 2.

[80] The control of the union over management positions in education had several consequences. It elicited the loyalty of administrators to the union rather than to the Secretariat of Public Education (SEP), and allowed union leadership to control its members by providing them with power over the specific work conditions of each teacher. See Susan Street, *Maestros en Movimiento: Transformaciones en la Burocracia Estatal (1978–1982)* (Mexico City: Ediciones de la Casa Chata, 1992), 116; and Maria Lorena Cook, *Organizing Dissent* (University Park, PA: Pennsylvania State University Press, 1996), 79. In addition, centralization was statutory imposed. According to Cook, the SNTE increasing control over supervisory appointments coincided with increased restrictions on the internal life of the union. Delegation-level assemblies

Education made the control of education performance increasingly inefficient because supervisors knew that they owed their position to their union careers.[81]

In the 1980s, tighter budget constraints and inflation eroded teachers' real salaries and induced a shift in the expansion of personnel toward management positions granted to union leaders who controlled teachers' discontent with salary deterioration.[82] This situation fueled a regionally—and politically—based dissident movement that toppled the national leadership of the union in 1989.[83] Cook points out that the new PRI leader, Elba Esther Gordillo, had a weak political base and, thus, was forced to include the internal opposition within the national leadership—through mechanisms of proportional representation—to avoid losing control of the union.[84] Moreover, the automatic affiliation to the PRI was abolished, permitting party competition within the monopolistic union.

As a result, non-PRI union leaders, who were regionally based and whose influence grew as a result of the previous process of regional deconcentration, rejected decentralization after obtaining the opportunity to compete for the control of the union and were included into its national leadership.[85] Simultaneously, internal partisan competition increased the incentives for union militancy and the 'price' that the government was willing to pay to retain the union within the PRI ranks.

Leadership competition combined with political monopoly induced the PRI government to reinforce the position of its affiliated leaders within the union by granting them concessions aimed at averting their replacement by non-PRI-affiliated union leaders. Moreover, the new PRI leadership promoted the development of new union services to legitimize its authority.

needed approval from local executive committees and were rarely convened while the national executive committee controlled local electoral processes and the local distribution of finances, and had powers of intervention at the local and delegation assemblies (Cook, *Organizing Dissent*, 80).

[81] Alberto Arnaud, 'La evolución de los grupos hegemónicos e el SNTE', Working paper 3, *Estudios Políticos* (CIDE, Mexico City, 1992); and Cook, *Organizing Dissent*, 85.

[82] Although in the 1980s teachers salaries fell in real and relative terms, administrative expenditures rose to 16% of education spending by 1984. See Ornelas, *El Sistema Educativo Mexicano*.

[83] See Del Campo (personal interview, 1995). According to Cook, *Organizing Dissent*, 270, 'teachers from throughout the country engaged in work stoppages, marches, hunger strikes, and *plantones* in Mexico City and regional capitals from February to May 1989'. Indeed, the largest demonstration of teachers' dissent in SNTE's history occurred in 1989, with more than 500,000 union members joining the work stoppages scheduled in April, more than half of the country's largest union (p. 269).

[84] The new statutes proclaimed proportional representation (SNTE 1992). Dissident 'members enjoyed full participation in the union's first congress after the 1989 mobilization . . . [many of their positions] . . . were incorporated into the documents and resolution of the 1990 congress. It was also important for Gordillo that the SNTE be able to demonstrate to the Salinas government that it could generate new ideas, 'modernize' itself, and do so while incorporating the strongest elements of the opposition' (Cook, *Organizing Dissent*, 279).

[85] Arnaud, La federalización de la educación básica y normal (1978–94), and Del Campo (personal interview, 1995).

These services included a housing fund, a retailing system for consumer durables, training and research institutes, and a political forum to different parties—part of a new strategy of supporting SNTE candidates in every party to promote sectoral interests.[86] This investment in organizational and industrial resources characterized the 'new unionism' attempt to be prepared for a loss in the efficiency of political resources due to the PRI policy shift and the increasing electoral contestation.[87]

Restructuring of Electricity: Economic vs. Political Efficiency

President Salinas' National Program for the Modernization of Energy Industries attempted to raise productivity and quality, improve the efficiency in the use of energy, diversify energy sources, and increase energy investment. As a result, he raised electricity fees and opened energy investment to foreign capital.[88] This program affected the two state-owned enterprises in the electricity sector: the Light and Power Company (CFLC) and the Federal Electricity Commission (CFE). However, the challenge for the CFLC was greater because it had been in a liquidation status for many years and was deprived of public investment, while it subsidized the CFE by buying over-priced electricity. By 1988, the CLCF produced only 5% of its distributed electricity and had accumulated large debts.[89] Moreover, the inefficiency of the CLCF was coupled with a very generous collective bargaining contract that reduced management discretion with a very detailed specification of industrial relations.

While the private sector demanded the privatization of the CLCF, the government introduced a bill to liquidate the CLCF and replace it with a decentralized entity depending on the CFE. There was no mention of the continuity of the collective bargaining contract, or of the Mexican Union of Electricity Workers (SME) monopoly of representation in the firm.[90] The liquidation and merger put at risk both the stability of workers' jobs and the continuity of the union because the monopoly of representation of the CFE was held by a larger union, the United Union of Electricity Workers (SUTERM), which was affiliated with the CTM and very hostile to the SME.

This grim perspective improved when the government agreed to bail out the debts of the firm and to buy a small portion of shares still in private own-

---

[86] Rodríguez (personal interview, 1995).

[87] Although the SNTE attempted to join the FESEBeS, which organized other expressions of the 'new unionism', it was forbidden by the legal obligation of public administration unions to affiliate with the FTSTE. See María Xelhuantzi López, advisor to the Secretary-General of the STRM, Francisco Hernández Juarez, interview by author (Mexico City, 5 April 1995).

[88] Javier Melgoza, 'Avances e incertidumbres en la modernización del sector eléctrico', *El Cotidiano*, 46 (March–April 1992), 45–7.

[89] See Melgoza, ibid. and Melgoza, 'El SME y la productividad: los saldos de la negociación', *Polis*, 93 (1994), 155–92.

[90] Ibid. 165.

ership in order to create a state-owned company different from the CFE in 1989. The SME was promised the monopoly of representation, the continuity of collective bargaining conditions, job stability for workers, and coordination with management for industrial restructuring. The new collective bargaining contract introduced two management-union commissions in charge of increasing productivity and achieving financial viability. These commissions provided the union with information and management rights. Moreover, workers obtained new fringe benefits, such as early retirement for hazardous jobs, and bonuses to pay for housing, education, and household expenses.[91] What conditions explain the bargaining strength of this union in a bankrupt firm?

Electricity Workers: Union Monopoly, Party Competition, and the Emergence of a Political Ally   Internal leadership competition in the SME promoted contestation among different factions regardless of their party affiliation. SME statutes enhanced such competition by introducing a secret and universal vote and a system of first-past-the-post for each leadership position. Additionally, half of the executive committee was replaced every year, thus increasing the opportunities for leadership competition.[92] This electoral structure increased the opportunities of competition for the replacement of leaders. As a result, the union monopoly provided by the closed-shop arrangement was coupled with leadership competition—although without explicit party banners—extended to the workplace where committees with minority representation controlled the implementation of the collective bargaining contract.[93] This competition faced union leaders with the threat of being replaced by discontented constituencies every two years.

In 1987, a combative leadership organized a strike—the first since 1936—and a massive demonstration against the PRI government. The government repressed the strike and took over the company.[94] The SME secretary-general who had led the strike lost the following elections to a more pragmatic leader, Jorge Sánchez. Sánchez bargained with PRI Presidential nominee, Carlos Salinas who preferred granting concessions to this pragmatic leader rather than having the combative leadership winning elections again. In February 1988, Sánchez obtained the endorsement of the SME for Carlos Salinas—despite SME historic independence from the PRI. In return, Salinas granted him with the survival of the company instead of its liquidation, the maintenance of the union monopoly of representation, and new industrial concessions and

---

[91] See SME, *El Nuevo Organismo, Triunfo y Nuevo Reto del Sindicato* (Mexico City: Mexican Union of Electrical Workers, 1994); Melgoza, 'Avances e incertidumbres en la modernización del sector eléctrico', and Melgoza, 'El SME y la productividad', 165–6; and Jorge Sánchez, former secretary general of the SME, interview by author (Mexico City, 7 April 1995).

[92] SME, 1992, preface, art. 23-I-f; art. 34-II.

[93] Melgoza, 'El SME y la productividad', 159.

[94] Melgoza, 'Avances e incertidumbres en la modernización del sector eléctrico', 175.

benefits for members, which built upon the traditional SME culture of productivity.[95]

The threat of leadership competition, which could turn the union into militancy again and disrupt the electricity service in the capital city, enhanced union bargaining power. President Salinas supported this sympathetic union leader in order to prevent more militant leaders associated with the opposition parties from extending their industrial influence in the SME.[96] Like the teachers, the electricity workers of SME took advantage of leadership competition to obtain concessions that influenced policy design. In addition, the investment in organizational or industrial resources was, in both cases, a strategy to survive a future of dwindling political resources.

Negotiating Privatization and Restructuring in Telecommunications

President Salinas announced the privatization of the state-owned telephone company, Telmex, in September 1989. The announcement followed concessions to the union including respect for their previous collective bargaining rights, job stability, and worker participation in the privatization process.[97] The union had been supportive of privatization as an instrument to attract investment to make the company efficient and it had favored the inclusion of new technologies and labor flexibility.[98] Although in 1989, collective bargaining suspended a commission where the union had supervised technological innovations, the commission was reinstalled with more responsibilities which included the design, implementation, and coordination of new programs of quality and productivity in 1990. In addition, the union obtained the permanent hiring of 4,636 workers previously under fixed-term contracts, as well as 467 new workers, generous funds for union social action, investment in training, a 15% hike in wages and a 16% hike in benefits, and an increase from 3% to 4.4% of capital for worker shares.[99]

[95] The sources for this account are Gabriel Pérez, 'El SME ante el reto de la modernización del sector eléctrico', *El Cotidiano*, 58 (Mexico City, Oct.–Nov. 1993), 4–6; Sanchez (1995); and a confidential interview with a high-ranking government official of the Salinas administration (1995). Regarding the SME culture of participation in the industrial organization of the company since 1966, see Melgoza, 'Avances e incertidumbres en la modernización del sector eléctrico', 80, and Horacio Romo, Secretary of External Relations of the SME, interview by author (Mexico City, 7 April 1995).

[96] In fact, Sánchez lost his position to a more combative union leader who strained SME relations with the government at the end of the Salinas administration.

[97] Mateo Lejarza, advisor to the Secretary-General of STRM, interview by author (Mexico City, 1995) and Javier Elguea, director of Inttelmex, training institute of Telmex, interview by author (Mexico City, 1995).

[98] See STRM, 'Comisión de Modernización. Proyecto', XII National Ordinary Democratic Convention of the Telephone Workers (Mexico City 1988). For example, the union took the strategy of adopting modernization by transforming total quality circles into union cells. See Enrique de la Garza, 'Quién ganó en Telmex?' *El Cotidiano*, 32 (Nov.–Dec. 1989), 33–4.

[99] See Oscar Vázquez Rubio, 'Los telefonistas cruzaron el pantano: concertaron con Telmex', *El Cotidiano*, 21, September–October, 1989; De la Garza, 'Quién ganó en Telmex?'; Francisco Hernández Juarez, Secretary-General of the STRM, interview by author (Mexico City, 19 April 1995); and Aspe, *El Camino Mexicano de la Transformación Económica*, 178.

Moreover, the union organized a trust fund that obtained a soft credit from a public bank to buy the stocks that would be paid with the dividends.[100]

The union also participated in industrial restructuring (e.g., in programs for quality, productivity, and training) in return for generous benefits for its members, such as new programs of social welfare for workers.[101] In addition, taking advantage of workers' stock in Telmex, the union organized, with half of workers' stocks, a savings fund to provide soft credits for housing and consumer durables. Union concessions, therefore, not only protected job stability and increased workers' benefits, but also provided the union with a new role in industrial organization and in provision of services to workers. What conditions explained union cooperation and success in obtaining concessions?

Telephone Workers: Leadership Monopoly and the Incentives for Cooperation
The Mexican Union of Telephone Workers (STRM) emerged in 1956 after the unification of the private telephone companies Ericsson and Mexicana.[102] It was a monopolistic union controlled by a traditional PRI leader until 1976 when a rank-and-file rebellion replaced him with a younger leader, Francisco Hernández Juarez. Despite its affiliation with the PRI, Hernández Juarez reformed the union statutes to increase democratic participation, introducing vote procedures for the approval of collective bargaining contracts and strike actions, and forbidding re-election.[103] However, successive changes of statutes had permitted Hernández Juarez to be re-elected three times while he used closed shops to control opposition in extreme cases and maintained an executive group of '*comisionados*' controlling many of the technical decisions of the union.[104] Although dissidents denounced the centralization of resources and the manipulation of unity lists in assemblies as mechanisms to limit leadership competition, they agreed on the responsiveness of the leadership to rank-and-file demands.[105]

Within this context of leadership and union monopoly, Hernández Juarez developed a personal relationship with President Salinas that promoted his union as an example of 'modern' unionism.[106] Salinas rewarded the support

[100] See Mateo Lejarza, advisor to the Secretary-General of the STRM, interviews by author (Mexico City, 27 Feb. and 28 March 1995).

[101] Lejarza (personal interview, 1995) and Pilar Marmolejo, training manager at Inttelmex/Telmex, interview by author (Mexico City, 1995).

[102] María Xelhuantzi López, *Sindicato de Telefonista de la República Mexicana. 12 años: 1976–1988* (Mexico City: Mexican Union of Telephone Workers, 1989), 11.

[103] Ibid. 33–50.

[104] Lejarza (personal interview, 1995); Xehuantzi López, *Sindicato de Telefonista de la República Mexicana*, 53; and Judith Catherine Clifton, 'The Politics of Privatization in Mexico: Telecommunications and State-Labour Relations (1988–1994)', Papeles de Trabajo de América Latina Contemporánea 0397 (Instituto Universitario Ortega y Gasset, Madrid, 1997), 23.

[105] Rosario Ortíz, dissident union leader in the STRM, interview by author. Mexico City, 18 April 1995.

[106] Hernández Juarez (personal interview, 1995) and Collier and Samstad 'Mexican Labor and Structural Reform: New Unionism or Old Stalemate?'

of the union for privatization and its control of labor unrest with important concessions, including an expensive employee-owned stock program. Hence, the loyalty of the union leader to the President, along with the absence of leadership competition and a monopoly of representation, enhanced the bargaining power of the union and facilitated its restraint and cooperation with the process of privatization and industrial restructuring. These concessions, in turn, provided Hernández Juarez with benefits for its constituencies. In addition, like the SME and the SNTE, this non-CTM union invested the concessions obtained in the political arena in organizational and industrial resources.[107] The following two case studies, however, show a much less successful pattern than the previous three.

Ford Motors: Industrial Restructuring under Economic Liberalization

During the period of import substitution industrialization, the automobile industry had both a 60% quota on domestic manufactures and regulated prices. The Salinas administration suppressed the quota and deregulated prices while providing fiscal incentives and promoting labor flexibility to increase international competitiveness.[108] Mexican integration into North American markets and the labor flexibility of the new export-oriented plants of northern Mexico promoted the growth of exports.[109] Therefore, industrial restructuring centered on the old plants of central Mexico—established during the period of import substitution industrialization—which had more rigid collective bargaining conditions, better wages, and more union prerogatives than those in the north.[110]

Following these trends, Ford Motors closed two of its three domestically oriented plants in central Mexico and opened two export-oriented plants in the north during the 1980s.[111] Collective bargaining in the three plants was decentralized, although in all cases it was negotiated with the national union

---

[107] During the Zedillo administration, Hernández Juarez led the organization of an alternative union group, which included 'independent' unions opposed to the PRI. See Lejarza (personal interview, 1995).

[108] See Arnulfo Arteaga, 'Ford: un largo y sinuoso camino', in Graciela Bensusán and Samuel León (eds), *Negociación Colectiva y Conflicto Laboral en México* (Mexico City: Fundación Ebert and Flacso, 1990), 142; and Marisa Von Bulow, 'Reestructuración productiva y estrategias sindicales. El caso de la Ford en Cuahutitlán 1987–1993'. MA thesis (FLACSO-Mexico, 1994), 23.

[109] Automotive exports grew from 173,147 in 1988 to 383,374 in 1992. See Arnulfo Arteaga, (ed.), *Proceso de Trabajo y Relaciones Laborales en la Industria Automotriz en México* (Mexico City: Fundación Ebert and UAM-Iztapalapa, 1992), 23. In 1993, 85% of automotive exports were directed to North American markets. See von Bulow ('Reestructuración', 1994, 15).

[110] Jorge Carrillo, 'La Ford en México: restructuración industrial y cambio en las relaciones sociales'. Unpublished doctoral dissertation (El Colegio de México, Centro de Estudios Sociológicos, Mexico City, 1993); and Fernando Herrera Lima, 'Reestructuración de la industria automotriz en México y respuesta sindical', *El Cotidiano*, 46 (Mexico City, March–April, 1992), 35–7.

[111] Ibid. 381.

and the CTM.[112] However, the remaining plant in central Mexico—situated in Cuautitlán—had higher labor costs and more rigid work conditions than the new ones.[113] The company wanted to change this disparity which reduced productivity and could promote labor unrest in the northern plants.[114]

In 1987, Ford Motors fired all Cuautitlán workers and rehired them under a more flexible collective bargaining contract. This also increased the authority of the national leadership of the union in collective bargaining at the expenses of the local executive committee in Cuautitlán.[115] The 1989 and 1991 contracts increased labor flexibility. This process of industrial restructuring provoked high labor unrest—including work stoppages and violent incidents—from 1989 to 1992 until the intervention of the CTM imposed the subordination of the local union.[116] What conditions explain this shift in union response?

Ford Motors Workers: Partisan Competition, Militancy, and Imposed Subordination   The transformation of the automobile industry in the 1980s extended the influence of the CTM at the expense of non-PRI unions that had been more influential in the 1970s. The CTM controlled only six of the eleven unionized plants in 1976 and eighteen of the twenty-one unionized plants in 1987, including all the unionized plants of the National Union of Ford Motors Company Workers. In addition, 85.5% of CTM members were in export-oriented plants, like Ford's two northern plants in Hermosillo and Chihuahua.[117]

In 1987, the leveling of Cuautitlán work conditions to equal those of the northern plants created a conflict of interest between the Cuautitlán plant and those in the north, and between the Cuautitlán local executive committee and the national leadership of the union.[118] As a result, in 1988, the discontented Cuautitlán workers elected a new local executive committee associated with left-wing parties and hostile to the national leadership.[119] In 1989 and 1990,

[112] Marisa von Bulow, 'Reestructuración productiva y estrategias sindicales. El caso de la Ford en Cuahutitlán 1987–1994', Paper presented at the Latin American Studies Association XIXth International Congress (Washington, DC, 28–30 Sept. 1995), 11.

[113] In 1987, the average wage in Cuautitlán more than doubled that of the northern plants of Chihuahua and Hermosillo (Carrillo, 'La Ford en México', 371; Arteaga, 1990, 150). Collective bargaining conditions established seniority as the main promotion criteria, limited internal flexibility, and granted the union with important management prerogatives exercised by the elected local union executive committees that had replaced CTM-appointed delegates in 1977 (Carrillo, La "Ford en México", 386–7; Middlebrook, *The Paradox of Revolution*, 273). These rigid conditions would be abolished between 1987 and 1991 through collective bargaining (Carrillo, 'La Ford en México', 391).

[114] Arteaga, 'Ford: un largo y sinuoso camino', 148.

[115] Ibid. 153–5; and von Bulow ('Reestructuración', 1995, 13–14).

[116] Ibid. 30–1. Only 35 work days were lost between 1943 and 1987 (ibid. 13).

[117] Carrillo, 'La Ford en México', 375–6.

[118] Ibid. 383; and von Bulow, 'Reestructuración', 14. Von Bulow (1995) also reports the lack of solidarity of other plants with the Cuatitlán conflict.

[119] Ibid. 30.

following this increase in leadership competition, the Cuautitlán plant militantly opposed the policies of the company as well as the national leadership of the union threatening to leave the CTM.[120]

The demand of the local executive committee to exit the CTM introduced the threat of member withdrawal together with leadership competition for the CTM national leaders. This threat—along with its interest in a transformation of the industry which had extended its industrial influence—prompted the CTM to serve as an intermediary in the exchange between the local workers and the company by displacing Ford Motors' union leaders.[121] CTM's intervention was violently imposed upon the local union shifted the union to the national context of CTM competition with other national union confederations. In order to avert the exit of these members, the CTM forced union subordination to industrial restructuring. In return, the government allowed a public ballot procedure supervised by company personnel to decide union affiliation. Such procedures intimidated workers and resulted in a close victory of the CTM. In addition, the government backed a CTM violent internal intervention in the union to limit leadership competition after another non-PRI local executive committee was elected in 1992.[122]

In short, the coincidence between the workers affected by industrial restructuring and a decision-making unit within the union—the Cuautitlán plant—resulted in the election of a non-PRI local executive committee with the consequent rise in leadership competition and opposition to industrial restructuring. However, the CTM and the Mexican government imposed their power over the Cuautitlán workers and forced them into subordination.

Pemex: Industrial Restructuring in the State-owned Oil Company

The Salinas administration reformed the oil industry which was monopolized by the state-owned oil company Pemex. It opened part of the industry to private investment and replaced political criteria with efficiency criteria for management in order to increase productivity, established public bidding for

[120] See also Von Bulow (1995) and the personal interview with Paul Bernardo Diaz (1995), a former local union leader in the Ford plant at Cuahutitlán, interview by author (Mexico City, 28 Feb. 1995).

[121] Ford Motors preferred to negotiate with the CTM (von Bulow, 'Reestructuración', 1995, 14–15). This support coincides with Middlebrook's (*The Paradox of Revolution*, 281–90) claim that labor flexibility was easier to achieve in CTM-affiliated than in 'independent' unions and explains the increase in CTM influence in the automotive industry signaled by Carrillo, 'La Ford en México'.

[122] Reference to Paul Bernardo Díaz, former union leader in the local executive committee of the Ford Motors Workers Union, interview by author (Mexico City, 1995). A man died and several were hurt as a result of CTM-directed violence. Furthermore, the company contributed to the restriction on leadership competition by dismissing non-PRI union leaders after the 1992 election. Thus, both the PRI government and the company were interested in restricting party competition. Moreover, this case contradicts Golden's assumption that unions start strikes to defend their activists at the plant level. See Miriam Golden, *Heroic Defeats: The Politics of Job Loss* (New York: Cambridge University Press, 1995).

contracts with Pemex, and restructured work organization through collective bargaining in 1989, 1991, and 1993.[123] These collective bargaining contracts introduced internal and external flexibility, reduced fringe benefits, and curtailed union prerogatives over hiring and promotion as well as its representation in management. Meanwhile, management cut employment from 210,000 to 106,939.[124] Moreover, in 1993, the government decentralized Pemex into four divisions: refining, exploration and production, gas and basic petrochemicals, and non-basic petrochemicals. These sections did not coincide with those of the union.[125]

Industrial restructuring deeply affected the union. Lay-offs and the shift of workers to managerial categories, which could not be unionized, reduced union membership. The loss of hiring and managerial prerogatives and of the 2% union fee for social welfare applied to suppliers' contracts reduced union industrial and organizational resources. Finally, labor flexibility and the fall in fringe benefits affected union constituencies.[126] None the less, while in 1984 and 1988 the union had expressed strong demands against government attempts to reform the industry, after 1989 the union subordinated itself to government initiatives.[127] What conditions explain the sudden subordination of the oil workers' union?

The Oil Workers' Union: From Partisan Competition to Subordination   In the 1930s, the Cárdenas administration had promoted the unification of all oil workers' unions into the Mexican Union of Oil Workers (STPRM). He had taken advantage of a conflict between the STPRM and the private companies as a legal pretext to expropriate the industry in 1938.[128] This unification created a monopolistic union in the prosperous oil industry. As a result, closed shops arrangements, both for hiring and exclusion, restricted party or

---

[123] See Fabio Barbosa, 'La reestructuración de Pemex', *El Cotidiano*, 46 (Mexico City, 1992), March–April, 21; Pérez, 'El SME ante el reto de la modernización del sector eléctrico'; and Rafael Loyola and Liliana Martínez, 'Petróleos Mexicanos: la búsqueda de un nuevo modelo empresarial' *Estudios Sociológicos*, XII (Mexico City, 1994), 287.

[124] On personnel reduction, see Fabio Barbosa, 'Los trabajadores petroleros hoy', *Trabajo y democracia hoy*, 23 (Mexico City, 1995), 12–13; on other modifications through collective bargaining see Barbosa, 'La reestructuración de Pemex', 23, and Loyola and Martínez, 'Petróleos Mexicanos: la búsqueda de un nuevo modelo empresarial', 288; on the loss of union prerogatives, see ibid. 299–301.

[125] Ibid. 310.

[126] See Gabriel Pérez Pérez, 'El STPRM, bajo las cadenas de la subordinación y el control estatal'. *El Cotidiano*, 67 (Mexico City, Jan.–Feb. 1995), 12–16; Loyola and Martínez, 'Petróleos Mexicanos: la búsqueda de un nuevo modelo empresarial', 295–7; and Fabio Barbosa, 'La reestructuración de Pemex', *El Cotidiano*, 46, (Mexico City, March–April, 1992), 45–8.

[127] See Victoria Novelo, 'Las fuentes de poder de la dirigencia sindical en Pemex', *El Cotidiano*, 28 (Mexico City, March–April, 1989), 23–5; Miguel Angel Cruz Bencomo, 'El quinismo, una historia del charrismo petrolero', *El Cotidiano*, 28 (Mexico City, March–April, 1989), 19–21; Barbosa, 'La reestructuración de Pemex'; and Victor García Solís, Secretary of Social Communication of the STPRM, interview by author (Mexico City, 1995).

[128] Bizberg, *Estado y Sindicalismo en México*, 39.

leadership competition in a union that become increasingly prosperous.[129]
The original structure of the union was based on the compromise of leadership rotation among the northern, central, and southern regions. However,
Joaquín Hernández Galicia (*La Quina*), from the northern region, eventually
dominated the union.[130] He also consolidated the union's autonomy from the
CTM, based on large financial resources, and subsequent contributions to the
CTM, derived from the union's share of supplier contracts with Pemex, and
the 2% union fee for welfare action over any supplier contract.[131] As a result,
the autonomy from the CTM, together with the absence of union or leadership competition, provided the union with strong bargaining capacity. Why
did the union lose this bargaining power?

During the De La Madrid administration the government introduced a
public bidding system for public sector contracts that explicitly excluded
unions, but the STPRM negotiated an exception with the government due to
its strong bargaining power as a monopolistic union controlled by the PRI in
a strategic sector.[132] However, as union companies were less efficient than
their private counterparts and the union contracts were reduced, Hernández
Galicia demanded a larger investment in the maintenance of Pemex infrastructure to be supplied by the union. In addition, he challenged Salinas by
supporting Cuahutémoc Cárdenas in the 1988 elections.[133] Such partisan
challenge could not be tolerated. After the election, Hernández Galicia
threatened to protest against the opening of the basic petrochemical industry
with a general strike in Pemex. Salinas responded by
putting Hernández Galicia in prison in January 1989 under fabricated murder charges. Furthermore, the secretary of labor refused to recognize the transitory leadership elected by the union to replace him. Instead, the government
imposed a new secretary-general controlled by the CTM, Sebastián Guzmán

[129] Cruz Bencomo, 'El quinismo', and Novelo, 'Las fuentes de poder de la dirigencia sindical en Pemex', 19.
[130] Cruz Bencomo, 'El quinismo', 24–6, and Francisco Aldana, 'La renta petrolera y el ascenso del quinismo', in Javier Aguilar Garcia (ed.), *Cuatro Sindicatos Nationales de Industria* (Sinaloa, Mexico: Universidad Autónoma de Sinaloa, 1988), 182.
[131] See also Miguel Angel Cruz Bencomo, STPRM union leader, interview by author (Mexico City, 1995); and Aldana, 'La renta petrolera y el ascenso del quinismo'. Under the leadership of Hernández Galicia, the union also used those resources in shops, farms, and companies to sup-ply Pemex which used the employment of transitory workers who wanted to obtain a permanent position in Pemex (Novelo, 'Las fuentes de poder de la dirigencia sindical en Pemex', 17).
[132] Ibid. 16.
[133] In 1985, Hernandez Galicia allowed union leaders affiliated with the Socialist Workers Party (PST) to hold leadership positions in certain sections (Cruz Bencomo, 'El quinismo', 27). In 1988, he supported Cuahutémoc Cárdenas against Carlos Salinas for the presidency and in most electoral districts dominated by oil workers. Salinas lost the presidential election while PRI–union candidates for representatives and senators were elected. See Cruz Bencomo, 'El quinismo'; Jesús Reyes del Campillo, 'El movimiento obrero en la Cámara de Diputados (1979–1988)', *Revista Mexicana de Sociología*, LII: 3, (July–Sept. 1990), 139–60; and Hebraicas Vazquez, leader of the dissident faction in the STPRM, interview by author (Mexico City, 1996).

Cabrera, who subordinated the union to the government.[134] In this case, as in the Ford Motors' local union, the PRI and the CTM did not tolerate partisan challenges, showing the limits to the partisan plurality within the CTM in accordance to its historic alliance with a party that had relied on electoral fraud in addition to the inclusion of social demands to stay in power for seventy years.

Union Response and Policy Consequences

The CTM competition with other PRI-related national labor confederations for the representation of workers increased government capacity to control each one. The government responded to CTM demands by manipulating union competition for material and symbolic resources. Fearing the loss of resources and a subsequent drain in membership, the CTM subordinated to the government. The subordination of the CTM contributed to the governability of the Salinas administration and to the implementation of his reforms. The preferences of the CTM and its affiliated unions were shaped by the predominance of a cross-regional coalition of regional federations—with political preferences encompassing all its members—over nationwide industrial unions with industry-specific preferences, like the unions of oil workers and Ford Motors workers.

   The non-CTM unions studied responded to the challenged created by globalization according to their own dynamics. Although these unions were atypical, their responses were important due to their strategic position and to the political example they set for other unions. Leadership competition influenced the teachers' militant opposition while union monopoly strengthened their bargaining power to restrict the policy change attempted by the government. The monopolistic character of the union and the permanent threat of leadership competition among SME electricity workers, resulting in militancy when the leader was not an ally of the governing party, increased the responsiveness of Salinas to their demands. This situation allowed the SME to avoid the liquidation of the Company of Light and Power, which would have threatened union survival. In telecommunications, leadership monopoly and union monopoly favored negotiation of the privatization and restructuring of Telmex between the union and the government and resulted in favorable concessions for the union.

---

[134] See Cruz Bencomo (1995) and Vázquez (1995) on the role of Guzmán Cabrera in the subordination of the union. For example, in a General Assembly of 14 July 1992, the new Secretary General Sebastián Guzmán Cabrera, defended the restructuring plan implemented by Pemex while acknowledging the job losses implied in the plan. Simultaneously, one of his union allies proposed to apply the closed-shop separation clause to 'professional agitators' who opposed restructuring (*La Jornada*, 23 July 1992, 13, quoted in Melgoza, 'Avances e incertidumbres en la modernización del sector eléctrico', 184).

Although the capacity of the government to control the CTM reduced the cost of labor peace in terms of concessions, it was a double-edged sword because it did not induce any modernization in CTM union strategies in order to adapt to the more global environment. Concessions to the three non-CTM individual unions in the study were more costly for the government, but they were invested in industrial and organizational resources as an alternative to the dependence on political resources, which had characterized Mexican organized labor. The STRM, SNTE, and SME reinforced their industrial identities by developing industrial and organizational resources that could compensate for a future of dwindling political resources and increasing political pluralism in the electoral arena. The industry-specific constituencies of these unions facilitated their development of strong industrial identities. In contrast, the CTM, because of its cross-sectoral constituencies and a history of successful use of the political resources derived from its alliance with the PRI, was afraid of investing in alternative resources. This preference for political resources was reinforced by the predominant coalition of cross-sectoral regional federations, formed by local unions, within the CTM. Furthermore, the CTM had no experience of using industrial resources to compensate for political resources because the PRI had always been in power. As a result, the alliance of CTM union leaders with the PRI limited the CTM's capacity to bargain with other political parties or to allow partisan competition within its ranks, leaving the organization in a difficult position to deal with increasing political liberalization.[135]

My institutional hypothesis does not contradict the neocorporatist hypothesis of union quiescence with their affiliated parties. However, it explains the variation in union response despite a common party affiliation, a phenomenon that neocorporatist theories can not account for. It also clarifies the mechanisms that induced union quiescence within a governing labor-based party despite union fragmentation. In addition, my argument does not ignore the authoritarian characteristics of this regime and the high degree of state control existing in Mexico that was pointed out both by students of economic liberalization and by Mexican scholars.[136] In fact, regime characteristics are crucial to understanding the capacity of the executive to manipulate union competition among PRI-related national labor confederations, the CTM preference for political influence, and the reactions of the CTM and the gov-

[135] In personal interviews, both PAN Secretary-General Castillo Peraza (Mexico City, 1995) and PRD Secretary of Social Movements Del Campo (Mexico City, 1995) manifested their distrust of the CTM. Both PAN Secretary-General Felipe Calderón (Mexico City, 1995) and PRD Secretary of Social Movements Jesús Martín Del Campo (Mexico City, 1995) manifested their distrust of the CTM in personal interviews.

[136] On the first group see, for instance, Stephan Haggard and Robert R. Kaufman (eds), *The Politics of Economic Adjustment* (Princeton: Princeton University Press, 1991); Haggard and Kaufman, *The Political Economy of Democratic Transitions* (Princeton: Princeton University Press, 1995); and Robert R. Kaufman and Barbara Stallings, 'Debt and Democracy in the 1980s: The Latin American Experience', in Robert Kaufman and Barbara Stallings (eds), *Debt and Democracy in Latin America* (Boulder: Westview Press, 1989). On the latter, see note 4.

ernment to partisan competition in Pemex and Ford Motors. Although international pressures on competitiveness could explain the initial reaction in protected sectors like automobile and oil, where workers and union leaders resisted industrial restructuring, they do not explain their subsequent subordination, imposed by the CTM and the government. However, my hypothesis also accounts for the variation in union responses across Mexican unions that regime theories are not able to explain, such as the better deals obtained by teachers, electricity workers, and telephone workers.

Concluding Remarks

In sum, this chapter shows how the historical legacies on union structure influenced the diversity in union responses to a common challenge triggered by an international shock and by the process of international economic integration. Union responses were not unified even within the same country. The combination of diverse organizational legacies shaped the responses of Mexican unions to a common challenge, while the predominance of industrial over political identities—related to the sectoral composition of union constituencies—enhanced the adoption of innovative resources related to the implementation of these reforms. Thus, distinct historical legacies and institutional mechanisms are crucial in the articulation of union demands and strategies towards industrial restructuring and market-oriented reforms, which are sweeping the world as a result of economic integration and globalization.

The findings of this chapter reinforce the theme of this book concerning the importance of historical legacies, union organization, and political dynamics in shaping union responses to market-oriented reforms and industrial restructuring. My hypothesis explains why the Mexican CTM responded differently from other national confederations facing the common threat of globalization and the policy shift of allied labor-based parties implementing neoliberal policies. The combination of partisan monopoly and union competition explains the subordination of the CTM to Salinas. This hypothesis is also useful for understanding the variation across Mexican unions in their strategies for confronting this common challenge. Leadership competition was a key variable for understanding the attitudes of unions while organizational fragmentation influenced their bargaining power as shown in the cases of teachers, electricity workers, and telecommunication workers. Although these variables explain the initial reaction of oil and Ford Motors workers, other institutional variables related to the characteristics of the Mexican regime should be added to understand their subsequent subordination.

Among the institutional variables important for study, this chapter highlights the influence of organizational legacies in the opportunity for both leadership competition and organizational fragmentation to emerge.

Historical legacies related to the previous use of political resources are also important for understanding the choices of union leaders. The CTM leaders—with sunk costs in political resources—reinforced their partisan identities following a strategy that had been successful since the origins of the organization. In contrast, non-CTM unions attempted to develop alternative strategies that reinforced their industrial identities based on their sector-specific constituencies and their autonomy from the CTM to bargain with the government. These sector-specific strategies were aimed at compensating for possible losses in political resources after the Salinas administration. Each of these different strategies emerged from a previous history of interaction between the respective union and the governing PRI, as well as from the diverse internal composition of these unions. The consequences were remarkable because the non-CTM unions led a process of union renovation that would take place during the following administration when fourteen unions organized the Union Forum, which later evolved into a new central organization, the National Union of Workers (UTN) that broke with the 'official' labor movement and joined other 'independent' unions.

Finally, the costs of bargaining proved to have positive side effects. Although the exchange was particularly affected by the bargaining capacity of the union, the process of bargaining itself influenced the attitudes of union leaders towards union modernization. The restraint of the CTM was not very costly for the government in terms of concessions because the CTM was forced to close a 'bad deal'. However, it did not provoke innovations within the organization like those experienced by non-CTM unions which were in a stronger bargaining position than the CTM. These developments show the importance of bargaining itself in the process of union reform as a learning process that changes the attitudes of the involved parties. In sum, this chapter highlights not only the importance of incentives on union leaders and the weight of historical legacies in their responses to industrial restructuring and market reforms, but also in the resolution of the tension between industrial and partisan identities and their ability to renovate union strategies in order to adapt to globalization.

3

The Cost of Incorporation: Labor Institutions, Industrial Restructuring, and new Trade Union Strategies in India and Pakistan

Christopher Candland, Wellesley College

Within the last two decades, transnational consumption networks have widened and deepened and labor processes have become increasingly informal. Within recent decades, the very nature of production has changed. The ability of trade unions to organize and represent labor in conventional ways is seriously challenged by a trend toward informal, contractless, independent, freelance, home-based, or otherwise unregulated and unprotected employment, and by political appeals to classless identities. Organized labor finds itself in the midst of an historic economic challenge. Not only do labor organizations suffer the general crisis of legitimacy in the conventional organizations of modern political life. They are also shaken from their foundations in an increasingly informal economy.

This chapter covers wide terrain in order to gain a broad perspective on the institutional landscape in which trade unions in industrializing countries are involved and the organizational, and strategic efforts they have effected in response to industrial restructuring and shifting labor force demands. The chapter first examines trade union development in India and Pakistan, countries with broadly similar economies and large labor forces. Focusing on two variables—trade unions' relationships with political parties and the nature of workers' representation in trade unions—two distinct patterns of development emerge. In India, an impressive labor movement based on political unionism developed and exercised some influence over economic policy. In Pakistan, an assertive and often militant workers' movement emerged, was severely repressed, and exercised little influence over economic policy. The chapter then assesses the ability of each labor movement to oppose recent economic reforms, specifically the privatization efforts of each government.

I thank Karamat Ali, Pranab Bardhan, Arun Daur, John Echeverri-Gent, Prem Shankar Jha, Mark Kesselman, Rakesh Mohan, Philip Oldenburg, Gail Omvedt, and Barnett Rubin for helpful comments on the arguments presented here. Much of this chapter draws from Christopher Candland, 'New Social and New Political Unionism: Labor, Industry, and the State in India and Pakistan', in Peter Waterman and Ronaldo Munck (eds), *Labour Worldwide in the Era of Globalisation* (Basingstoke: Macmillan, 1998), 175–96.

The capacity to oppose industrial restructuring is traced to the differing structure of labor institutions, specifically trade union relationships with political
parties and workers' representation in trade unions. In conclusion, the chapter draws from a debate within the Indian trade union movement concerning
the limitations of political unionism and the need for new union strategies.
I suggest that a new unionism, with wider networks among other social
organizations and deeper roots in local communities, must also include a new
political dimension.

Evolution of Trade Unionism in India and Pakistan

India and Pakistan inherited identical colonial labor legislation at
Independence, but the working classes and their organizations were afforded
markedly different roles. The Indian National Congress, which dominated
the independence movement and parliaments in independent India, maintained a strong concern for labor from 1920, with the founding of the All
India Trade Union Congress (AITUC). The All India Muslim League, the
party that successfully petitioned for the creation of Pakistan, had no such
concern for labor and did not develop relations with organized labor in its
campaign for Pakistan.

India and Pakistan exhibit the stark contrasts in regime type and in development ideology that is rarely seen between neighboring countries, except
those created by partition. Pakistan, claiming to be the national right of
South Asian Muslims gave way to decades of military rule within a decade
after its creation in 1947. India maintained a competitive electoral democracy
which predates Independence. Similarly, India and Pakistan adopted
markedly different development strategies. Indian planners were inspired by
Fabian socialism and Soviet industrial achievements and followed an import
substitution strategy for economic development that was politically buttressed by socialist rhetoric. Pakistani planners, in contrast, had no firm ideological moorings and were persuaded by American advisors in the 1950s to
adopt a more export-oriented development strategy and an economic doctrine of 'functional inequality'.[1] Economic development was to be fueled by
the concentration of private capital.

The impact of their divergent economic ideologies is evident in the field of
state-labor relations. Both countries inherited identical regimes of labor legislation. For twenty years after Independence, colonial legislation—notably
the Trade Union Act, 1926, the Industrial Employment (Standing Orders)
Act, 1946, and the Industrial Disputes Act, 1947—provided the basic framework of the Indian and Pakistani labor regimes. The 1947 Industrial Disputes
Act, for example, established permanent administrative machinery for the

[1] Angus Maddison, *Class Structure and Economic Growth* (New York: W. W. Norton, 1971),
136–63.

settlement of labor disputes, laid down deadlines for specific stages of consultation and arbitration, required employers to recognize and to negotiate with trade unions, prohibited strikes and lock-outs during pending conciliation, and provided that industrial disputes in public services be settled by compulsory arbitration.

In Pakistan, however, in 1969, the military government rewrote the colonial era labor legislation and restructured labor institutions. The government of General Yahya Khan ensured that the trade union movement would be factory-based and marginalized from formal party politics. The state promoted trade union multiplicity and restricted the trade unions' national political participation. None of Pakistan's political parties have evidenced interest in alliances with organized labor. India's elected governments, by contrast, encouraged the development of politically powerful trade unions which could serve as electoral vehicles for the major political parties. The participation of industrial labor in the independence struggle secured an institutional role for organized labor in Indian politics. A brief review of Indian and Pakistani labor history bears this out.

As a response to the creation of the International Labour Organization in 1919, the All India Trade Union Congress (AITUC) was founded the following year. Leaders of the Indian National Congress and other nationalist parties played an important role in the development of AITUC. Jawaharlal Nehru, India's first and longest standing Prime Minister, served as AITUC president, as did nationalist leaders of a variety of political persuasions. The Indian National Congress, which dominated the independence movement, and the Communist Party of India, maintained a strong concern for labor. Mohandas Gandhi's strategy of moral resistance to colonial rule, leading to the formation of the Ahmedabad Textile Labour Association in 1920, gave impetus to a tradition of trade unionism that opposes strikes.

Just prior to Independence in 1947, the Congress created its own party-based trade union organization. After independence other political parties, as they gained national standing, sponsored their own trade union wings. When parties split, as did the Communist Party of India in 1964, new trade union organizations were established, as was the Centre for Indian Trade Unions (CITU) in 1970. One of the newer centers, the Bharatiya Mazdoor Sangh (BMS), tied to the ruling Hindu nationalist Bharatiya Janata Party (BJP) and the Rashtriya Swayamsevak Sangh (RSS), is now the fastest growing trade union center in India.

Each major political party maintains a trade union wing, or in Indian parlance, a 'centre'. Presently, there are ten major trade union centers in India, each affiliated in some manner to a political party (Table 3.1).

Between some trade union centers and political parties—particularly on the left, where the organization of working classes is an integral component of the party's program—there is a regular exchange of officials. Inderjit Gupta, for example, rose from General Secretary of the Communist Party of India's All

Table 3.1. India: The ten largest trade union centers and political party affiliations
(listed by date established) (1920–72)

Trade union centers	Political party affiliation	Date established
All India Trade Union Congress	Communist Party of India	1920
Indian National Trade Union Congress	Indian National Congress	1947
Hind Mazdoor Sabha	Janata Dal	1948
United Trade Union Congress	Communist Party of India (Marxist)	1949
Bharatiya Mazdoor Sangh	Bharatiya Janata Party	1955
United Trade Union Congress (Lenin Sarani)	Communist Party of India (Marxist)	1959
National Federation of Independent Trade Unions	Naren Sen (Former Indian National Congress politician)	1967
National Labor Coordination Committee (West Bengal center formerly affiliated to INTUC)	Indian National Congress	1969
Center for Indian Trade Unions	Communist Party of India (Marxist)	1970
National Labour Organization (Gujarat center formerly affiliated to INTUC)	Textile Labour Association	1972

India Trade Union Congress (AITUC) to become the General Secretary of
the Communist Party of India and then India's Home Minister, responsible
for internal law and order. Even officials of the centrist Indian National Trade
Union Congress (INTUC) occupy seats in parliament and in state legislative
assemblies. All trade unions claim to be autonomous from and no more than
ideologically allied to their party affiliates, but each supports party candidates
and uses trade union channels for electoral advancement. The weekly
newspaper of INTUC, for example, the *Indian Worker,* publishes election
material proclaiming that only the Indian National Congress can protect the
working classes. The trade union centers serve as vehicles for successful
organizers to become political leaders.[2] Fifty-two parliamentary seats, nearly
10% of the Lok Sabha, the lower house of the Indian Parliament, were once
considered to be labor constituencies, where political parties vied for candi-

[2] For a study of political unionism in one Indian state, Orissa, see Prafulla Chandra Das,
Trade Union and Politics in India (New Delhi: Discovery Publishing House, 1990).

dates among trade union leaders.[3] One such trade unionist, V. V. Giri, rose to become Minister of Labour and then President of India.

As labor occupied no significant part of the All India Muslim League's imagined community, Pakistan's post-independence economic development strategy gave virtually no attention to labor, except as a factor of production, an industrial input to be drawn from rural areas at subsistence wages. Labor was to assume the role specified by W. Arthur Lewis in his famous neoclassical model of economic growth.[4] This labor extraction approach to development fostered such labor laws as the Essential Services Maintenance Act, 1952. The law prohibits unions and makes absence from or stoppage of work a penal offense in any industry or service designated by the government as 'essential to the life of the community'.[5] It applies today to employees in the banking and finance, broadcasting, post, and telecommunication services, and in the railways and defense industries. The act is in violation of International Labor Organization (ILO) conventions 89 and 96, which the government of Pakistan has ratified, and has repeatedly been cited as such by the ILO.

Repressed and politically disincorporated, the Pakistani trade union movement has nevertheless been influential as a social movement at key phases in Pakistan's political development. In March 1969, popular unrest, in which students, new professional classes, and factory workers played the dominant role, brought an end to General Ayub Khan's decade of martial rule and brought elections for a new constitutional assembly.[6] In response to the political challenge of organized labor, the interim military government, having entrusted itself with the supervision of elections, quickly devised a labor policy to depoliticize labor before the elections.[7] The policy, promulgated as the Industrial Relations Ordinance of 1969, was designed by Deputy Martial Law Administrator, Noor Khan. The Industrial Relations Ordinance (IRO) gave industrial workers the fundamental rights for which they had agitated: the right to form trade unions, the right to collective bargaining, and the right to strike. At the same time, the Ordinance effectively prohibited industry or

[3] Ajeet Mathur [Indian Institute of Technology industrial relations expert] interview (Calcutta, India, 29 Dec. 1991).

[4] Lewis' model postulates two sectors, a capitalist sector and a subsistence sector. 'The former is the *progressive* sector; the latter is *stagnant*' (italics in the original). Because workers are drawn from the subsistence sector, their optimum wages are subsistence wages, 'equal to the average product per man in the subsistence agriculture, plus a margin' just large enough to draw them away from their villages. W. Arthur Lewis, 'Economic Development with Unlimited Supplies of Labour', *The Manchester School of Economic and Social Studies*, 22: 2 (May 1954), 139–91.

[5] Government of Pakistan, *Pakistan Essential Services (Maintenance) Act, 1952*, Sec. 3, Para. 2 (Karachi: Manager of Publications, 1952).

[6] Muneer Ahmed, 'The November Mass Movement in Pakistan,' *Political Sociology* (Lahore: Punjab Adbi Markaz, 1978/1974), 1–56.

[7] In the light of the scholarship that views institutions as historically rooted and thereby not replicable, or path-dependent, it is worth noting that a single set of deliberations and decisions, based on Noor Khan's tripartite meetings in Karachi in May 1969, shaped Pakistan's labor institutions and influenced the character of industrialization for decades to come.

nationwide unions. The Ordinance required that 75% of the members of any trade union have the same employer. But as large nationwide enterprises, such as the railways and postal services, are deemed by the government as essential industries and services, unions may not form in such enterprises. The IRO thereby effectively instituted enterprise unionism in Pakistan.

Noor Khan's inspiration was his experience in Pakistan International Airlines (PIA), the profitable, military owned and operated national airline.[8] When Khan assumed control of PIA in 1959, standard procedure was to imprison workers who attempted to form unions. Khan decided that PIA would run better if these workers were released from jail, brought back to PIA, and permitted to form a union, provided that that the union could be insulated from lawyers, social activists, politicians, and professional trade unionists, and other so-called 'outsiders'. Workers, with no knowledge of legal procedure, were required to represent themselves. The IRO extended PIA's politically insulated enterprise union model to the entire country through a Collective Bargaining Agent (CBA) system. Federations of unions were permitted, but the selection of trade union leaders and the conduct of collective bargaining was restricted to factory-level workers. The CBA system requires that trade unions win a secret ballot election in order to obtain the exclusive right to negotiate with management and to take industrial action. Federations have no legal standing in collective bargaining negotiations (Table 3.2).[9]

Data on trade union and trade union membership growth in Pakistan suggest that the Industrial Relations Ordinance 1969 had a powerful influence on the structure of trade unionism in Pakistan. As a result of Air Marshal Noor Khan's 1969 labor policy, the number of trade unions almost doubled within a year (Figure 3.1). As trade union membership grew steadily, the rapid multiplication of trade unions led to a rapid decline in membership density. The Industrial Relations Ordinance 1969 (IRO) was amended by Prime Minister Zulfikar Ali Bhutto in 1976 with the intention of stopping further multiplication of trade unions. Like the IRO, the effects of the 1976 amendment is

[8] Noor Khan [Air Marshal (retired) and former Deputy Martial Law Administrator (1968–9)], interview (Karachi, Pakistan, 3 April 1995).

[9] Tariq Banuri and Edward Amadeo's definition of a polarized model of industrial relations well describes the Indian trade union movement. The polarized model involves a '[b]road-based labour movement with a long history of mobilization, organization, conflict, and success, but with internal divisions along regional, craft, skill, or industry lines. Thus, while organized labour is capable of imposing real costs on the economy in the defence of its interests, it is not strong enough to impose a co-operative solution at the national level'. Pakistani industrial relations are best described by Banuri and Amadeo's decentralized model: 'Strongly circumscribed and divided labour movement with diffuse influence in some areas of the country; does not play a major role in national politics, nor is able to confront employers in any significant sense. Wage bargaining is always at the enterprise level. Operation of labour laws and labour rights considerably circumscribed. Right to strike strongly limited in practice even when it exists legally'. See Tariq Banuri and Edward Amadeo, 'Words Within the Third World: Labour Market Institutions in Asia and Latin America', in Tariq Banuri (ed.), *Economic Liberalization* (Oxford: Clarendon Press, 1991), 171–220.

Table 3.2. Pakistan: Leading trade union federations (1990)

Federation	No. of affiliated unions	No. of members
Pakistan Trade Union Confederation, Karachi	172	614,800
All Pakistan Federation of Trade Unions, Lahore	n.a.	520,000
All Pakistan Trade Union Confederation, Karachi	25	300,000
All Pakistan Federation of Labour, Islamabad	216	262,000
National Labour Federation of Pakistan, Karachi	230	240,747
All Pakistan Trade Union Federation, Lahore	185	195,600
Pakistan Banks Employees Federation, Karachi	11	158,000
Pakistan National Federation of Trade Unions, Karachi	215	152,300
Sindh Workers Trade Union Council, Karachi	25	19,060
Pakistan Central Federation of Trade Unions, Karachi	45	10,345
Pakistan Mazdoor Ittehad Federation, Karachi	60	9,478

Source: Government of Pakistan, Ministry of Labour, Manpower and Overseas Pakistanis, *Pakistan Labour Gazette* (January–June, 1990), 35.

reflected in membership statistics. Moreover, statistics on Pakistani industrial disputes corroborate trade unionists' contention that the fragmentation of organized labor effected by the CBA system helped to weaken labor power.

Indian figures are inflated because they are reported by unions themselves and are used to determine the number of representatives that the unions will have in official consultative bodies, such as the Indian Labour Conference. Assuming a relatively constant level of exaggeration, neither the number of unions nor membership density underwent dramatic change in the late 1960s or early 1970s (Figure 3.2). Further, we do not find a dramatic decline in industrial disputes in the early 1970s, although Indian trade unionists report that trade unions began to suffer a sharp decline in their collective bargaining power in the mid 1970s. The number of workdays lost, and the number of workers involved in industrial disputes, rose gradually until the early 1980s. The decline in industrial disputes in the early 1980s reflects the success of new

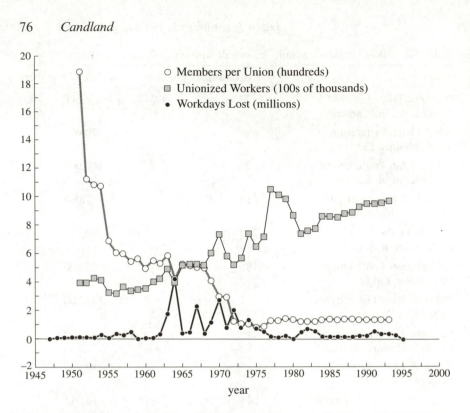

Figure 3.1 Unions, membership, and industrial disputes in Pakistan (1947–97)

Source: compiled from Government of Pakistan, Ministry of Labour, Manpower and Overseas Pakistanis, *Pakistan Labour Gazette* (Islamabad: Printing Corporation of Pakistan Press), various issues.

Note: As East Pakistan became Bangladesh in 1971, data before 1972 are for West Pakistan only. Union density over time cannot be reliably estimated as the definition of employment has changed periodically.

production and employment strategies.[10]

Institutional Impediments and Social Opportunities

The study of economic reform and adjustment to international economic challenges and opportunities suffers from lack of attention to the social institutions that undergird any economy. Often these social institutions must be reformed if economic reform and adjustment is to be effective. Scholarship on the politics of economic reform has typically presumed that adjustment is a process that government effects upon society, focusing on elite political coalitions and on 'the packaging of programs or the manipulation of opposition

[10] Sujata Gothoskar, Priya Halal, Sharad Dudhat, Odile Flavia, and Girish Vaidya, 'Job Losses and Closures: Management Strategies and Union Counter-Strategies', mimeo, 1990.

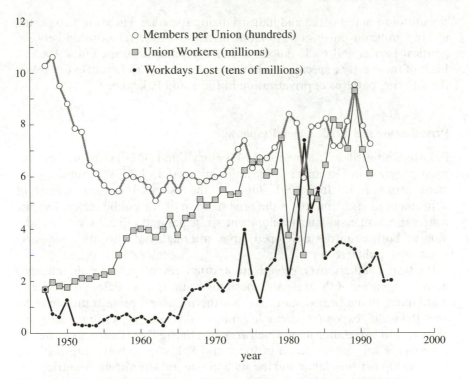

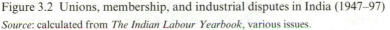

Figure 3.2 Unions, membership, and industrial disputes in India (1947–97)

Source: calculated from *The Indian Labour Yearbook*, various issues.

Note: Union density can not be reliably estimated as the definition of employment has changed periodically.

groups' required to implement unpopular economic programs.[11] The political element in economic reform runs deeper than much of the politics of economic adjustment literature has recognized. The formation, and transformation, of social institutions and their influence over the economic adjustment process demands further study. The comparative historical analysis reported here suggests that social movements and social institutions are central to economic change.

An institution is a custom or practice, established by law or habit. It may be public or private, formal or informal. The social organizations that preserve and enforce these practices are as significant as these customs and practices themselves because, as social organizations change, they help to transform the institutional landscape. Trade unions are a significant social

---

[11] Stepan Haggard and Robert Kaufman, 'Introduction: Institutions and Economic Adjustment', in Haggard and Kaufman (eds), *The Politics of Economic Adjustment* (Princeton: Princeton University Press, 1993), 25.

organisation in industrial and industrializing societies. There are two particularly significant dimensions to labor institutions, the relationship between
political parties and trade unions and the selection of trade union leaders.
Each of these can be specified and measured as variables that help to explain
the differing patterns of privatization in India and Pakistan.

Privatization and Trade Union Response

Pakistan initiated an International Monetary Fund (IMF) structural adjustment program in December 1988; India initiated an IMF structural adjustment program in July 1991. One of the essential conditionalities of
adjustment in each country is the privatization of the public sector. Despite
widely different economic development strategies and official economic ideologies, both countries developed large, although not altogether similarly
structured, public sectors.

Political conflicts over privatization often reveal patterns of influence
between agencies of the state and social institutions. Like Peter Gourevitch's
'hard times' in the United States and Northern Europe, privatization in India
and Pakistan 'expose(s) strengths and weaknesses to scrutiny, allowing
observers to see relationships which are often blurred'.[12] Here we examine the
experiences with privatization in India and Pakistan to better illustrate the
relationship between labor and the state in late-industrializing countries.

The Government of India announced in June 1991 that unprofitable public sector enterprises would, within three years, be cut off from government
subsidies. Unprofitable enterprises were to be privatized. Legal passage for
the privatization of public sector units, long blocked by employment protection legislation, was cleared in December 1991 through an amendment to the
Sick Industries and Companies Act. Despite the policy reforms to facilitate
privatization, privatization is largely absent from India's adjustment program. More than nine years since its implementation, the central government
has not completed the privatization of any of its 248 enterprises. The government has sold shares in public sector units, but most of these shares have gone
to government financial institutions, effectively transferring public debt from
public sector industry to public sector financial institutions. Fewer than three
dozen public sector enterprises have been subject to disinvestment, and these
at an average of less than 10% of equity.

In Pakistan, privatization has been anything but cautious. Rather than
gradually disinvesting shares, the government arranged for the wholesale
liquidation of the public sector. As soon as Nawaz Sharif became Prime
Minister in October 1990, he announced that the public sector would be
privatized and industry deregulated. Sharif declared that Pakistan's
privatization program would be a model for the Muslim world and would

[12] Peter Gourevitch, *Politics in Hard Times* (Ithaca: Cornell University Press, 1986), 9.

rival Margaret Thatcher's achievements.[13] Sharif's Disinvestment and Deregulation Committee, later renamed the Privatisation Commission, recommended that the government 'retire from the production of industrial goods'[14] and approved nearly all central government enterprises for privatization. These included all public sector manufacturing enterprises, all the nationalized banks, and such public sector giants as the Pakistan Telecommunications Corporation. Since the Privatization Commission was established, much of the Pakistani public sector has been sold to domestic and foreign private investors.

Trade unions in both countries have organized national and local strikes, public demonstrations, court challenges, and various local agitations in opposition to privatization. Neither movement has been absent on the streets. But in India, protests have led to reversals of government privatization decisions and to a series of tripartite negotiations to manage industrial restructuring by sector. Tripartite negotiations were begun in December 1991 under the auspices of the prime minister's office.[15] In Pakistan, these protests— sometimes quite militant and prolonged—have led to plant level union-government agreements on industrial restructuring. The Government of Pakistan has privatized dozens of public sector enterprises, from tractor factories to large commercial banks.

Pakistan's enterprise-based trade unions negotiated an agreement with the government that smoothed the way for privatization. Pakistani trade unionists in 115 public sector units scheduled for privatization formed the All Pakistan State Enterprises Workers' Action Committee (APSEWAC) in 1990. APSEWAC was able to negotiate an agreement with the federal government that gives workers of privatizing enterprises the options of retaining their jobs for at least one year after privatization, retiring with a pension amounting to four months' salary for every year worked, or collectively purchasing the enterprise using retirement funds and subsidized bank loans.[16] Workers' representatives formulated business plans for units manufacturing cement, chemicals, and transport equipment.[17] Nine of the sixty-three industrial and financial concerns that were initially privatized are now owned and, in some cases, managed by employee groups.[18] When the privatization

[13] 'Privatization—Need for Checks and Balances', *Economic Review* (Feb. 1992).

[14] World Bank, *Pakistan: Country Economic Memorandum FY93* (Washington, DC: World Bank, 23 March 1993), 49

[15] International Labour Office, 'India: Tripartite Cooperation for Structural Adjustment', *Social and Labour Bulletin* (June 1992), 143–5 and Ajeet Mathur, 'The Experience of Consultation during Structural Adjustment in India (1990–92)', 132: 3, *International Labour Review* (1993), 331–45.

[16] All Pakistan State Enterprises Workers' Action Committee, 'Accord signed with the Govt', mimeograph (1991). The agreement is summarized in Government of Pakistan, *Economic Survey 1991–92* (Islamabad: Government Printing Office, 1992).

[17] Mohammad Yaqoob [Chairman All Pakistan State Employees Workers Action Committee], interview (New Delhi, India, 29 March 1992).

[18] R. Khan [Chief Economist, Pakistan Planning Commission], interview (Islamabad, Pakistan, 29 Nov. 1995).

of Pakistan's entire power sector was threatened by the refusal of 800 workers to allow foreign investors to inspect the Kot Addu power plant, it was the application of the APSEWAC agreement that resolved the seven-month stand-off.[19]

The Government of India, in contrast, has not been able to complete the privatization of a single central public sector unit. The reversal of the government's decision to privatize the giant Indian Iron and Steel Company (IISCO) clearly demonstrates the strength of political unionism labor in India. The government, in a cabinet meeting in November 1993, decided that IISCO should be privatized. The Steel Authority of India Ltd (SAIL), under the financial constraints of a tighter government budget, was unable to finance the necessary modernization. The Communist Party of India–Marxist (CPI–M)-ruled government of West Bengal, where IISCO is located, supported the move. The central government invited bids and accepted that of an Indian industrialist.

The 30,000 workers at the Burnpur-based unit objected to the privatization plan. INTUC, the CPI–M's chief rival in West Bengal, together with other centers, organized a 'lightening strike to oppose the decision'.[20] The unions managed not only to stage a strike throughout the entire public steel sector but also to gain the support of public sector officers' associations. A parliamentary committee, convened to review the privatization decision, recommended that the decision be withdrawn and that SAIL be given the necessary budgetary support to finance IISCO's modernization. The government, despite the Congress Party's majority in the chamber, withdrew from the Lok Sabha, the bill that would have effected the privatization of IISCO. The reversal of the government's decision to privatize the giant public sector enterprise demonstrates the ability of politically affiliated unions, when they are united across party lines and when they form strategic alliances with opposition political parties, to oppose government privatization efforts.

Labor opposition to privatization in India has not been restricted to the traditional mechanisms of strikes and negotiations. Labor agitation has also employed some unusual and ingenious strategies. The Bombay workers of Hindustan Lever, an Indian subsidiary of the giant Anglo-Dutch multinational Unilever, locked out of their factory, produced their own washing detergent powder under the brand name 'Lock-Out'. Selling 110 tons of the powder won the union considerable public attention. Continuing the innovative strategy, the Hindustan Lever Employees' Union runs parallel annual general shareholders' meetings so as to inform investors of various manage-

---

[19] Khurshid Ahmed [General Secretary, Pakistan WAPDA Hydroelectric Central Labour Unions], interview, Lahore, 8 Dec. 1995. It must be admitted that the offer of APSEWAC concessions was not the only motivation to call off the strike. Ahmed reports that the government's threat of army intervention and the possibility that workers would be killed strongly influenced his decision to agree to the privatization plan.

[20] 'Cabinet decides to privatize IISCO', *The Statesman*, (27 Nov. 1993).

ment and financial irregularities.[21] In August 1992, cotton textile mill work-ers from central Bombay marched through the streets in underpants and undershirts denouncing India's commitment to the eradication of poverty as a sham.[22]

The ability of political unionism to resist privatization also may be seen in the trade union opposition to one of the early attempts by a state government to privatize a public sector enterprise. In May 1991, the Janata Dal Chief Minister of Uttar Pradesh, Mulayam Singh Yadav, took out advertisements offering to sell the three cement plants within the Uttar Pradesh (UP) State Cement Corporation. Nine workers' unions joined to win a UP High Court order to stay the sale. Ignoring the stay, the chief minister drew up an agree-ment with the Dalmia industrial group for transferring the plant for a seri-ously undervalued sum. The High Court accordingly began proceedings for a contempt of court case against the chief minister, but the assassination of Rajiv Gandhi, in the middle of India's tenth general election, forced the court to reschedule the case for after July 1991. Before handing over state offices in June, Mulayam Singh Yadav approved the sale of the Dalla plant and began arrangements for handing over the plant to the Dalmia group.

In June 1991, UP government officials and management personnel of the Dalmia group arrived at the factory in Dalla, UP under police escort to trans-fer possession of the premises. Workers feared that they would lose their jobs. They protested at the factory gate, preventing the new management from entering the premises.[23] Police clubbed, tear-gassed, and shot workers, killing twelve and injuring over fifty, six of whom were to die later of their injuries.[24] According to an investigative delegation by members of the Rajya Sabha, police fired without provocation, pursued workers over three days, and assaulted workers and their wives in their homes.[25] Despite the BJP's position in favor of denationalization, sustained popular pressure organized by the workers of the Dalla plant, joined by other state employee unions, forced the BJP government to cancel the sale of the plant.[26]

Efforts to privatize the Bailadila Mines in Raipur, Madhya Pradesh have also encountered significant labor resistance. Mining and quarrying have been the exclusive preserve of central and state governments. The Government of Madhya Pradesh has entertained proposals for opening the mineral rich Chattisgarh area to the private sector. The giant South African diamond mining company De Beers Consolidated Mines Ltd won the con-tract. Nippon Denro is also in negotiation with the government over opening

---

[21] Teesta Setalvad, 'Workers Mean Business', *Business India* (6–19 July 1992), 99–100.

[22] R. Bakshi, 'Bailadila Privatisation', *Trade Union Record* (20 Oct. and 5 Nov. 1995), 35–6.

[23] '9 killed in U.P. Firing on Workers', *Times of India* (4 June 1991).

[24] 'RS Call for Probe into U.P. Firing', *Times of India* (5 June 1991).

[25] N. Siddhanta, 'Brutal Killings at Dalla Cement Factory' (New Delhi: AITUC Publication, Aug. 1991).

[26] Subashini Ali [Communist Party of India Member of Parliament from Kanpur district], interview (Kanpur, India, 22 Dec. 1991).

iron ore mining to the private sector. The Chhattisgarh Mukti Morcha (Chhattisgarh Liberation Front) organized protests against the privatization plan. The Chhattisgarh Mukti Morcha (CMM) is an independent trade union organized by tribal mine workers, formed in reaction to intimidation and periodic killing of laborers and labor leaders by local police and industrialists. Twenty-one workers were killed in 1978 when police fired on non-violent demonstrations against the mechanization of the mines. The leader of the CMM, Shankar Guha Niyogi, was murdered, allegedly by local industrialists in September 1991. Eleven workers were killed and forty injured in 1992 when police fired on a demonstration for a uniform labor law and the prosecution of Niyogi's killers. The CMM Vice-President Sheikh Ansar in March 1996 contemplated contesting a Lok Sabha seat in the April–May 1996 general elections.[27] A mass demonstration was also threatened by the Janata Dal, Communist Party of India, and Communist Party of India–Marxist to prevent Nippon Denro from entering the iron ore mine site at Mine 11B.[28]

The Bharatiya Janata Party (BJP) also opposed the privatization plan, joined by Congress dissidents in the All India Indira Congress (Tiwari) and by Communist Party of India (CPI) activists. They claim that the National Mining Development Corporation (NMDC) has had its proposals for mineral development ignored. The NMDC, with headquarters in Hyderabad, produces 9 million tonnes of iron ore annually in the Bailadilla Sector, one of its major projects, and raises R400 crore (US$123m) in foreign exchange on diamond exports. The NMDC planned to double its iron ore output from the Bailadila mining sector within five years.[29] Internationally, the NMDC has successfully competed with foreign firms in the supply of modernization equipment. At issue in the protests over the privatization proposals are foreign ownership and profit making in an industry where the Indian public sector industry has the capacity to profitably develop the sector. One CMM labor leader complains that 'they [government officials] say De Beers will bring technology. But just ten percent of the royalty from the mine can buy the technology. Why give it to them?'[30]

The conflict over the privatization of Chhattisgarh mining has raised questions about the need for foreign investment and the potential consequence of foreign management in a strategically sensitive sector of the economy. The Bailadilla controversy involves the additional element of a local labor force consisting predominantly of a poor tribal population which has been socially and politically marginalized by local industry, administration, and government. State and higher-caste oppression, now combined with the threat of privatization, forged the local labor force's trade union into a political movement. Labor resistance to the privatization of the Bailadilla Mines is one

[27] Narayanan Madhavan, 'India: Indian Mining Plans Draws Opposition Ire', *Reuters News Service* (31 March 1996).
[28] 'Landmarks', *Business India* (14–27 Aug. 1995), 32.
[29] Bakshi, 'Bailadila Privatisation'.   [30] 'Landmarks'.

instance in a series of opposition efforts by organized labor that dates to the initiation of economic reforms in July 1991.

A stand-off also developed between organized labor and the government over the privatization of the telecommunications industry, formerly in the exclusive purview of the public sector. In January 1994, in the most important component of India's privatization program to date, the central government decided to end the state monopoly in telecommunications. Department of Telecommunications (DoT) unions responded by holding a crippling national strike just before the opening of bids for basic telephone contracts. Labor unions, joined by private firms that were dissatisfied with the tendering procedures, won a Supreme Court ruling in December 1995 requiring the government to address their charges before issuing licenses for telecommunications services to the private sector. The Supreme Court regarded the lack of a regulatory authority to supervise the privatization process as the principal concern.[31] In anticipation of the court's verdict, in January 1996 the central government issued an ordinance establishing a regulatory body, the Telecom Regulatory Authority of India (TRAI), to formulate guidelines for the participation of private companies in the privatization of the central government's telecommunications monopoly. The court's decision constituted a victory for the telecommunications labor unions as it specified that an administered process, subject to the political influence that trade unions could apply, would be established for the privatization of the industry.

Indian trade union centers have also been able to obstruct reform of labor legislation envisioned in the IMF structural adjustment program. One of the most contentious issues in India's labor reform process is the fate of the Industrial Disputes Act, 1947 (IDA). Section 25 of the IDA, originally an ordinance under Indira Gandhi's emergency government in 1976, requires government permission before large-scale lay-offs. International financial institutions and foreign aid agencies have applied intense pressure on the central government for an amendment of the IDA so that employers may terminate employees at their discretion. The adoption of this so-called 'exit policy' has been effectively opposed by the trade union centers.

Although the ability of trade union centers to block a major component of the reform program is an important measure of Indian trade union power, some trade unionists privately admit that opposition to the exit policy may have been self-defeating. Employers have been able to dispense with excess labor through lock-outs, voluntary retirement schemes, subcontracting, and other means.[32] The absence of a legal mechanism for the closure of industry

[31] A scandal broke when Himachal Futuristics Communications, in a consortium with Israel's Bezeq and Thailand's Shinwarta, was awarded licenses for nine of the 21 basic service zones. The Minister of Communications, Sukh Ram, was accused of favoritism in selecting Himachal Futuristics, which is based in the Minister's home state of Himachal Pradesh and successfully bid US$24b for the nine zones, despite having revenues of only US$57m.

[32] Arvind Shrouti, 'New Economic Policy, Changing Management Strategies—Impact on Workers and Trade Unions' (New Delhi: Friedrich Ebert Stiftung, 1994).

has prevented workers from receiving compensation or retraining. Indian trade unions have been able to halt privatization in the public sector and to obstruct labor law reform, but face an altogether different challenge in the increasing informalization of employment and deregulation of the labor market.

Despite the obvious advantages of political unionism in obstructing economic policies, Indian trade unionism is roundly criticized for representing only formal sector workers, being largely concerned merely with wage gains, and seeking to have influence solely through political parties. The contention that political unionism fails to adequately respond to the deep changes that have been occurring in late-industrializing economies, societies, and cultures is now commonplace even among trade unionists.

Brief portraits of industrial relations regimes in three Indian states may help to illustrate the operation of political unionism in India. Karnataka, Maharashtra, and West Bengal have developed markedly different labor institutions. Karnataka and its capital city, Bangalore, is home to a number of large public sector enterprises, particularly in engineering. In the 1950s, the central government opted to locate several strategically significant industries in Bangalore, including Bharat Earth Movers, Bharat Electronics, Hindustan Aeronautics, Hindustan Machine Tools, and Indian Telephone Industries. Karnataka has a reputation for good industrial relations, based on a tradition of stable and strong internal trade union leadership, comparatively low trade union multiplicity, low trade union rivalry, and limited political affiliation.[33] As there are regular trade union elections in Bangalore- and Karnataka-based public sector units, 'it is quite common for workers to refuse to affiliate to a national federation [center] even as they seek outside leadership'.[34] Those trade unions that are affiliated are typically linked either to the Communist Party of India's All India Trade Union Congress (AITUC) or the more militant Communist Party of India–Marxist's (CPI–M) Centre for Indian Trade Unions (CITU). Another significant dimension of Karnataka's industrial relations regime is that successive governments have not typically favored specific labor leaders or specific political parties' labor wings.

West Bengal stands in contrast to Karnataka. CITU grew powerful and militant in West Bengal in the early 1970s. In keeping with Leninist ideology, however, CITU deferred to the Party after the CPI–M's electoral victory in the state in 1977. West Bengal's industrial relations regime is interventionist. 'Almost every industrial dispute in Calcutta goes through the labour department and ends up with the political executive of the state'.[35] At the same time, management has been generally pleased by labor's deference to the stability of West Bengal's government and industry and consequent aversion to

---

[33] A. Ramaswamy, *Worker Consciousness and Trade Union Response* (Delhi: Oxford University Press, 1988), 129–74.
[34] Ibid. 130.
[35] Ibid. 134.

disputes or strikes.[36] The CPI–M's recent overtures to business, and support to privatization and industrial closure plans has provoked criticism from the West Bengal left.[37]

Maharashtra, which is home to one quarter of the country's industry, is characterized by strong independent unions (i.e., unions unaffiliated to a trade union center). One estimate is that 69% of those laborers in the state who are organized are members of independent unions.[38] Maharashtra is also characterized by a corporatist industrial relations regime. The Bombay Industrial Relations Act (BIR) of 1946, which regulates industrial relations throughout the state, requires that a single union in each industry be recognized by government as the sole collective bargaining agent for all workers in that industry. Such recognition is based on unverified membership lists supplied by the unions themselves (the check-off system). This has allowed some affiliated and external unions, such as INTUC's powerful Rashtriya Mills Mazdoor Sangh (RMMS), to dominate industrial relations in their industry, which itself causes considerable industrial unrest.

Ironically, the principal source of the political strength of the Indian trade union movement—its relationship to the major political parties—is also its principal source of shopfloor weakness. The close ties between Indian trade union centers and the major political parties have made the unions dependent upon political party priorities and rivalries. Scholarship on trade unions in India has argued that the Indian unions are politically weaker than their European counterparts because there are too many of them. Lloyd Rudolph and Susanne Hoeber Rudolph refer to this as 'involuted pluralism', adapting Clifford Geertz's concept of 'agricultural involution' to emphasize the effect of excessive multiplicity. Indian trade union multiplicity certainly complicates labor-management negotiations and is often exploited by management'.[39] The weakness of Indian trade unions, however, is a consequence of trade union dependency upon political parties, of which multiplicity is only a symptom. In Pakistan too, more than a dozen unions might be active in a single enterprise. But Pakistan's collective bargaining agent (CBA) system requires management to negotiate with only one, thus regulating shopfloor political rivalry.[40]

While the Indian trade union centers have been powerful in obstructing official national-level privatization, they are socially weak. Privately, trade union officials admit that union membership in trade union centers has

---

[36] Ibid. 175–202.

[37] Nagarik Mancha, *Against the Wall: West Bengal Labour Scenario* (Calcutta: Spokesman, 1991).

[38] Arvind Shrouti [Researcher, Maniben Kara Institute], interview (Bombay, India, 25 June 1996).

[39] Lloyd Rudolph and Suzanne Hoeber Rudolph, *In Pursuit of Lakshmi* (Chicago: University of Chicago Press, 1987), 259–89; Clifford Geertz *Agricultural Involution* (Berkeley: University of California Press, 1963).

[40] In some enterprises, such as Pakistan Steel Mills and Karachi Port Trust, political rivalry between plant unions is high at CBA election time.

dropped. Publicly, social activists and representatives of non-governmental organizations complain that trade union center officials are conservative, uncooperative, and bureaucratic. This is a reflection of the cost of labor's incorporation by political parties.

One of the strongest indications of workers' frustration with political unionism was the Bombay textile strike, the world's largest industrial action, as measured either by the number of workers involved or by the number of workdays lost. One of the chief demands of the striking workers was the de-recognition of the INTUC-affiliated Rashtriya Mill Mazdoor Sangh (National Mill Workers' Union). Under the corporatist Bombay Industrial Relations Act of 1946, a single trade union is recognized for the cotton, woolen, and silk textile industries in the states of Maharashtra and Gujarat. Since 1946, the Congress-affiliated Rashtriya Mill Mazdoor Sangh (RMMS) has been the sole recognized union for sixty mills in Bombay.[41] Textile workers regard the RMMS as an instrument of management not as a union that represents textile workers.[42] Workers were so determined to strike against the RMMS that they enlisted the independent Datta Samant to lead to the strike.[43] Samant, who has since been murdered, was politically independent and militant. The millowners intransigence resulted in the retrenchment of at least 100,000 workers.[44] The strike has yet to be called off. Most of the textile workers moved to poorly paid and unregulated informal work in power-loom sheds. The struggle for independent unionism in the Bombay textile industry suggests that the power of political unionism may be purchased at a rather high price.

Political unionism is increasingly viewed by labor organizers, even within the Indian trade union centers, as a hindrance to their social relevance. In West Bengal, the Communist Party of India–Marxist (CPI–M) government has privatized industry and retrenched labor and the otherwise firebrand Centre for Indian Trade Unions (CITU) has largely conceded.[45] Even trade union officials in the political unions acknowledge that Indian trade unionism is hobbled by a dependent relationship to political parties. One retired INTUC official suggested that the best thing that the Indian trade union centers could do for the Indian labor movement would be to disband.[46]

The costs of incorporation may also be gauged by the importance that Indian trade union centers assign to workers' management schemes as a mechanism for preserving employment in an era of industrial restructuring.

[41] Hariben Naik, [President, Rashtriya Mills Mazdoor Sangh], interview (Bombay, India, 20 April 1992).
[42] Hubert van Wersch, *The Bombay Textile Strike 1982–83* (Bombay: Oxford University Press, 1992).
[43] Datta Samant [President, Kamgar Aghadi (Workers' Party)], interview (Bombay, India, 3 March 1993).
[44] Bakshi, 'Bailadila Privatisation'.   [45] Nagarik Mancha, *Against the Wall*.
[46] Kamal Muzumdar [former INTUC official], interview (New Delhi, India, 28 November 1991).

The official trade unions greet workers' management schemes with no more than rhetorical support, although workers, anxious to retain their jobs, are eager to pursue worker buy-out and worker management schemes. The interest with which Pakistani workers have pursued workers' management stands in stark contrast to the indifference of Indian trade union officialdom. Pakistan trade unionists, who act more often as the leaders of a factory based community than as the officials of a quasi-governmental agency, are often quite aggressive in pursuing workers' shopfloor concerns.[47]

Developing New Trade Union Strategies

Recently, Indian and Pakistani have laid emphasis on advancing trade union independence and internal democracy, organizing informal sector workers, and promoting workers' ownership and management plans and labor education programs. Only the broad contours of these emergent strategies can be suggested here.

At the national level, India's trade union centers have made significant moves in self-transformation. Two of the largest trade union centers, the All Indian Trade Union Congress (AITUC) and the Congress Indian National Trade Union Congress (INTUC), have taken initiatives to 'delink themselves from their parent political organisations'.[48] An even more significant development is the planned merger of the Hind Mazdoor Sabha (HMS) and AITUC. Perhaps the most significant development for trade union independence and democratization as well as for organization of the informal sector is the formation of the National Centre for Labour in May 1995. Made up of nearly two dozen labor unions, it is the only national trade union federation that aims to organize and represent informal sector workers. The National Centre for Labour (NCL) maintains its independence from political parties. The NCL represents nearly 600,000 workers in industries ranging from embroidery, to fishing, forestry, and construction work. Years of careful planning for the organization of the NCL forged a shared perception that 'different sections of the working class[es]' should engage in 'education and information sharing' and joint 'lobbying and interaction [with] . . . government and its regulatory agencies'.[49] The formation of the NCL gives evidence of the resilience and responsiveness of labor to the economic and political challenges facing organized labor.

Indian trade unionists now acknowledge having once ignored the vast informal sector. As AITUC President E. Balanandan put it, the informal sector was viewed as residing 'on the fringes of its parent, the robust organised

---

[47] Zafar Shaheed, 'The Organisation and Leadership of Industrial Labour in Pakistan (Karachi)' Unpublished PhD dissertation (Department of Politics, University of Leeds, 1977).

[48] Mohan Mani, 'New Attempt at Workers' Resistance', *Economic and Political Weekly* (7 October 1995).

[49] Ibid. 2486.

sector'. Balanandan reflects common sentiments among South Asian trade union leaders: the informal sector, based on 'low working capital, cheap labour and scuttling of all labour laws . . . now threaten[s] the very existence . . . of the organized sector'. Trade unions 'must work more systematically to organise the workers in the unorganised sector and bring them into the common struggle, which will give a new turn to the trade union movement in the country'.[50]

The Self-Employed Women's Association (SEWA), one of the members of the National Centre for Labour (NCL), led a successful campaign for the adoption of an International Labour Organization (ILO) Convention on Home-based Workers. The SEWA has a membership of 220,000 women, in block printing, silk screening, garment stitching, and embroidery, 23,000 of whom work at home.[51] Discussions in the ILO raised understanding about the limited protections to this large and growing segment of the informal sector. The implementation of the ILO Home Work Convention will promote the equal treatment and legal protection of home-based informal sector workers.

Another front within Indian trade unionism has pressed for 'the creation of worker cooperatives [as] an alternative form of ownership and control over production'.[52] The movement of plant based trade unionists pursuing workers' management has grown in response to the widespread problem of mismanagement in the private sector. Outstanding credit tied up in sick industries in the private sector was estimated at over US$3bn in 1989 and was expanding at a rate of over 18% per annum.[53] A government commission found that the majority of these industries are unprofitable due to mismanagement.[54]

Kamani Tubes Ltd in Bombay, manufacturer of metal tubes, is the most celebrated workers' management experiment in India. Company performance at privately owned and operated Kamani Tubes began to decline in 1975. 'Internecine feuds and litigation among Kamani family members' and 'imprudent and undesirable management practices' made the enterprise unprofitable.[55] The Industrial Development Bank of India and a national bank devised refinancing and rehabilitation schemes, giving the company fresh capital. Still, Kamani Tubes suffered losses. In 1987, the Kamani

[50] Balanandan, 'Presidential Address to the Working Committee Meeting (annual) of the All India Trade Union Congress', 2 November 1995 (Bhilai), in *The Working Class*, 25: 4 (New Delhi: AITUC, December 1995), 5–6.

[51] Ela Bhatt, 'SEWA is Heading Towards Full Employment at the Household Level', interview with Sindhu Menon, in *Labour File*, 2: 4 (April 1996), 19–22.

[52] Damodar Thankappan [Director, Centre for Workers' Management], letter to P. Chidambaram [Minister of Finance], 15 June 1996.

[53] Omkar Goswami *et al.*, 'Report of the Committee on Industrial Sickness and Corporate Restructuring', submitted to the Union Minister of Finance, Government of India, July 1993, 3.

[54] Tiwari *et al.* (1984).

[55] Government of India, Ministry of Finance, Board for Industrial and Financial Reconstruction, *Industrial Sickness—Case Studies: Metallurgical*, 1: 4, mimeo (July 1991).

Employees Union won a Supreme Court judgment referring the company to the Board for Industrial and Financial Reconstruction. The union devised a plan, approved by the Board, to cut the labor force and finance operations through reductions in salaries and the use of provident funds. The worker-managed company became profitable within two years of operation.[56]

The success of the workers' management experiment at Kamani Tubes led to the formation of the Centre for Workers' Management and to five other successful workers' management operations. Each of these worker-managed manufacturing industries is the result of the workers' struggle to keep a mismanaged private sector enterprise viable. It is curious, given the prevalence of cooperatives in Indian agriculture, that workers' cooperatives in India are rare and given little but rhetorical support by the government and by official trade union centers. The Centre for Workers' Management (CWM) aims to reverse this tendency by giving management education to labor organizers, developing techniques to monitor the financial performance of enterprises, and facilitating the development and adoption of rehabilitation schemes for sick companies.

Advocates for workers' management solutions to sickness in Indian industry continue a long tradition of exposing private and public sector mismanagement. Together with other labor organizers, they argue that as privatization is a method for improving efficiency, not an end in itself, then increased managerial autonomy and new forms of ownership are required. Major business groups are managed privately, without day to day interference by government agencies, despite the fact the government often owns the majority of the assets in their industries. In the public sector, however, the government often fails to appoint directors for long periods and important production and marketing decisions are not made with due consideration to long-term viability. Workers have demonstrated unique perspectives on management and incentives for industrial competitiveness. By force of the new economic policies and accompanying industrial restructuring, Indian trade unions have stepped up their surveillance of company corruption and mismanagement, in both the private and public sector. Trade unions have raised concern in national economic policy debates that the public sector is being treated by some as the private domain of select civil servants, politicians, and businesspeople. The workers' management movement is to a large degree an expression of workers' commitment to responsible industrial development.

The experience of one trade unionist, the president of one of two 'representative' unions at a large Indian public sector unit, suggests the journey that unionists have had to undertake. Bharat Electronics Ltd was disinvested of more than 20% in 1991 in India's first round of public sector

---

[56] The firm is presently in financial difficulty which the workers blame on the non-cooperation of financial institutions, banks, and the state government.

disinvestments and another 5% in 1995. Matthew, the President of AITUC, was elected over the official candidate of the Communist Party of India (CPI), to which AITUC is affiliated. Workers in Karnataka and especially in the Bangalore public sector, where Bharat Electronics is located, have a reputation for preferring the representation of politically unaffiliated leaders over affiliated leaders. Under Matthew's leadership, the union won a Karnataka High Court case against further privatization on the grounds that the management had not formulated a business plan that demonstrated the need for or the advantage of further disinvestment. The Court held that until the central government could show such a plan, it could not initiate further disinvestment.

Employees have also proposed a shareholding plan, under consideration by the High Court. This gives evidence of the commitment of the workers to industrial restructuring and market competitiveness. Matthew argues that the enterprise needs to try 'new forms of ownership and management' and to be 'receptive to collaboration between publics sector units and multinational corporations'.[57] The willingness of the labor leader and of the workers whom he represents to accommodate to the demands of the market reflects the commitment of Indian industrial workers generally to do what is necessary to ensure that their companies and their jobs survive.

One of the challenges these unions face is to demonstrate to government that they have not only the organizational strength and determination to organize strikes and political protests but that they also have the ability to discuss and negotiate credible industrial rehabilitation programs. Indian trade union centers are discussing industrial and labor force restructuring in a series of Special Tripartite industrial rehabilitation commissions. Indian trade union centers are negotiating with government the rehabilitation of the cotton textile, jute, chemical, engineering, electricity generation and distribution, and road transport industries.

Pakistani trade unionists have also been active in developing new union strategies. New varieties of union strategies are emerging in Pakistan, involving inter-federation cooperation, trade union-community alliances, support for workers' ownership and management schemes, and a renewed emphasis on workers' education. At the national level, the most significant recent development in Pakistan trade unionism was the March 1995 formation of the Pakistan Workers' Confederation (PWC). The PWC has coordinated protests across the country against wage compression, rising prices, unemployment, the contract labor system, industrial closures, and underutilization of capacity. The merger is explained by the six participating federations as necessitated by the deep economic, political, and social crisis in which feudalism, corruption, nepotism, and lawlessness have reached

[57] Babu Matthew [President, Bharat Electronics Employees Union], interview (Bangalore, India, 24 June 1996).

historic heights. The PWC represents more than two hundred thousand workers. One of the PWC's objectives is to gain greater influence over economic policy decisions.

The central concern of one of the federations participating in the PWC, the All Pakistan Federation of Trade Unions, is the privatization of the power generation and distribution system (WAPDA). Union leaders claim that the nation will be 'plunged into darkness' if WAPDA is privatized as thousands of villages are not profit-making sites of operation.[58] The Hydro Electric Central Labour Union has met with ministers of the National and Provincial Assemblies to give publicity to the estimate made by a former finance minister that privatization of the power sector would add US$330m to the burden of power consumers annually. The electricity workers union has also fought the privatization of Pakistan's power sector in the courts and protested the privatization plan in the streets.[59]

One of the most significant decisions of the PWC is an agreement not to compete between each other in CBA elections. Pakistani federations calculate that to strengthen themselves they must overcome the divisive logic of factory-level competition. Inter-union solidarity drawn from the plant level promises to have considerable national influence.

New Pakistan trade union strategies have also involved greater emphasis on workers' education. The Pakistan Institute of Labour Education and Research (PILER) has organized workers' education programs since the early 1980s. Trade unionists from all major Pakistani federations participate in the programs, which are 'aimed at enhancing the social and political awareness' of shopfloor-level trade union leaders.[60] Plant-level trade union leaders learn about human rights, labor law, public interest litigation, the environment, economics, and patriarchy.[61]

Another strength of Pakistani unionism, derived in part from its independence from political parties, is cooperation with non-governmental organizations involved in environmental protection. When the private company Dansk Sojakagefabrik (DS) sold an outlawed chlor-alkali plant to the Pakistani company Ravi Alkalis for installation in Karachi, Pakistani non-governmental organizations (NGOs), including the PWC, successfully blocked the deal. Together with Greenpeace International, Pakistani NGOs and trade unions in the Confederation threatened to prevent the unloading at the Karachi port. The plant which uses mercury cell technology, the most

[58] 'Confederation of six workers' groups flay WAPDA privatisation', *Dawn*, Karachi (16 April 1995).

[59] Khurshid Ahmed [General Secretary, Pakistan WAPDA Hydroelectric Central Labour Unions], interview (Lahore, Pakistan, 8 Dec. 1995).

[60] Muttahida Labour Federation, 'An Introduction to the Muttaheeda Labour Federation', pamphlet (May 1992).

[61] Pakistan Institute for Labour Education and Research, 'Trade Union Leadership Development Course'. mimeo (Feb. 1989).

polluting of all chlor-alkali production technologies, had been banned from operating in Denmark on account of workers' health problems.[62]

Conclusion: Trade Union Democracy

The response of trade unionists and labor activists to international economic integration and to more informal labor practices is tempered differently by the political regimes under which labor institutions form. But Indian and Pakistani labor institutions are not replicas of the political regimes that structured them. The Pakistani military imposed regular factory-level, secret-ballot elections upon labor's organizations while Indian democracy promoted top-down, political party control of labor's organizations. It may appear somewhat ironic that an authoritarian regime would institute workplace elections, whereas a democratic regime would promote statism and bureaucracy. The speed of the privatization measures in Pakistan, however, suggests that regular elections are an important mechanism for the depoliticization of the trade union movement. The absence of a system by which workers may select their trade union representatives provides Indian political parties with opportunities to mobilize laborers and politicize industrial restructuring. This is not always in the interest of workers.

Pakistan's industrial restructuring and privatization program has been more extensive yet has involved less labor unrest and better compensation packages. In Pakistan, employers are able to negotiate with legally recognized, workplace-elected trade unions officials in Pakistan. In India, historical disagreements among trade unions, and between them and the government have prevented the adoption of a standard mechanism for trade union recognition. Just as there is no system for the recognition of national trade unions in India, other than through affiliation to a large-enough political party, there is no legal mechanism for trade union recognition at the factory level. As early as 1968, the National Commission of Labour recommended that minimum national membership levels be achieved to acquire consultative status. The recommendation was largely ignored until the early 1980s.[63] Trade union recognition in all but three states is based upon a check-off system. Trade unions claim members and labor officials seldom verify these claims. The absence of elections or other explicit criteria for trade union recognition invites political party manipulation into Indian unionism. A system for the recognition of trade unions by employers was devised by Parliament in 1946. It is widely claimed that this system is not used because it

[62] Beena Sarwar, 'Pakistan: Greens to Blockade Import of Danish Ship', Interpress Services (15 Nov. 1994).

[63] N. Datar, 'Trade Union Recognition' (Bombay: Lala Lajpat Rai College of Commerce and Economics, 1983) 11.1983: 6–7

would expose the unrepresentative character of India's national trade union centers, as when a government verification showed grossly inflated membership claims in 1980[64] and again in 1995. In the 1980 verification, the ten largest trade unions could demonstrate, on average, only 56% of their claimed membership. Recently, the major trade union centers, with the significant exception of INTUC, have expressed support for secret ballot elections, even though such a mechanism for trade union recognition is likely to reduce their membership and their standing in state and central government consultations.

Political unionism has not outlived its usefulness. In South Asia, the social demand for labor to act politically is at a historical high. Trade union response to the limitations of conventional political unionism is not to become apolitical. Given the ability of informal means of production to disorganize workers, the political challenges to organized labor are higher than ever. Methods for effective collective action in India and Pakistan involve more democratic means of decision-making, increased efforts trade union and federation cooperation and mergers, and programs to develop the technical economic and accounting skills with which to better negotiate rehabilitation packages with management, government agencies, and financial institutions. As organized labor in both countries seeks to transform itself, it is developing a new social element to the political work as well as a new political orientation.

The comparative analysis of Indian and Pakistan trade union development and response to new economic realities suggests that the structure of labor institutions in late-industrializing economies is a critical determinant of the pattern of industrial restructuring. A society thick with social institutions is likely to effect economic adjustment only gradually.[65] Some of the new models in economics involve the division of labor, human resource investment, education and training, and learning by doing.[66] Still, much economic theory, notably neoclassical macroeconomic theory, assumes the existence of institution-less labor markets, a condition nowhere in evidence. Late-industrializing economies are at the dawn of a new industrial revolution and a new phase of the commodification of labor. But labor, as Karl Polanyi recognized, will resist complete commodification.[67] How labor resists will differ according to the institutional legacy of past political regimes, but trade unionists in both

---

[64] Ibid. 11.

[65] In the major South Asian economies, the more gradual and the more social contested the process of economic adjustment, the more likely that adjustment will involve increased government expenditure and public commitment to social development.

[66] Robert Boyer, 'Do labour institutions matter for economic development? A "régulation" approach for the OECD and Latin American with an extension to Asia', in Gerry Rodgers (ed.), *Workers, Institutions and Economic Growth in Asia* (Geneva: International Institute for Labour Studies, 1995).

[67] Karl Polanyi, *The Great Transformation* (New York: Farrar & Rinehart, 1944).

India and Pakistan are making efforts toward greater democratization and decentralization as other labor activists are working to achieve greater organizational capacity and more effective political influence.

4

Network Ties and Labor Flexibility in Brazil and Mexico: A Tale of Two Automobile Factories

Scott B. Martin, Columbia University

As economies open, polities decentralize, and economic organization becomes more global and flexible, the fate of workers as economic producers and social citizens in the larger community is increasingly shaped in the workplace and relations with actual or prospective employers. With factories and other places of work increasingly marching to the beats of the 'new economy', the relative homogeneity of conditions of employment and work conditions within countries—at least in their 'advanced' or 'dynamic' sectors—brought by the mass production models, uniform national labor relations regimes, and closed economies of yesteryear has been shattered. To be sure, as many observers note, contemporary trends like decentralized, network-based organization and heightened cross-border integration of investment, trade, manufacturing, and distribution do reshape the workplace in a broadly similar direction, shifting the initiative and rules of the game in a direction favorable to capital. Yet while the fates of the most vulnerable workers do seem 'overdetermined' by structures like export-processing zones in late-industrializing countries and political trends like deregulation, workers in the core or lead firms of sophisticated, high-valued-added activities tend to be in a different position. In a new era of *de facto* self-regulation through socially embedded markets, the relatively autonomy of employment and work practices in these activities—in such key areas as hiring and firing, work hours, and internal job rotation and mobility—naturally grows. The disjuncture with the uniform mass production era norms that still formally anchor most national labor regulatory regimes increases apace, as new 'rules of the game' are written in practice within the firm and inter-firm networks. The authors of these new, decentralized rules are capitalists operating in varying mixtures of unilateralism, conflict, competition, consort, and cooperation with workers and their representatives.

The present study addresses this ongoing, decentralized rewriting of the basic social compacts of global capitalism that is happening in everyday practice, largely in the shadow of formal, national state regulation and of

The author wishes to acknowledge the helpful comments of the editors, the anonymous reviewers, Mark Kesselman, Douglas Chalmers, Eric Hershberg, and Ruth Berins Collier.

encompassing national representatives of state, labor, and capital. It does so through a study of shifting employment and work relations in automobile assembly, a long internationalized and advanced manufacturing sector that has increasingly become globally integrated within cross-border intra- and inter-firm networks and been subject to product and process innovations reshaping work. The focus is on two large late-industrializing countries, Brazil and Mexico, for which autos—as in several other large, late-industrializing and post-socialist economies—has been a critical sector both in their late-industrialization paths of the post-war period and their recent transitions from import-substituting, protected economies toward market-based and more outward-oriented ones. The explanatory puzzle derives from both a pairing of the restructuring experiences of two established, mass production-based, or 'brownfield', manufacturing facilities and from the larger findings of my comparative study of the political economy of work reorganization in this sector in the two countries as a whole as well as the United States (Martin 2000). That is, why, in the face of similar processes of flexible work reorganization, domestic opening, and global firm and industry integration in the first half of the 1990s, do particular factories experience contrasting transitions to greater labor flexibility, with quite different implications for worker participation and equity? In particular, why do some plants, illustrated here by 'M-1' in central Mexico, undergo unilateral, company-controlled processes of restructuring while others, represented here by 'B-1', belonging to a different parent in greater São Paulo, experience bilaterally negotiated restructuring between labor and management? Moreover, in the context of a comparative literature that suggests—in path-dependent fashion—that workers benefiting from 'strong' unions and more inclusionary macro and micro institutions are better positioned to negotiate the terms of productive restructuring than in those with opposite circumstances,[1] how is it that amidst structural workplace change the historically 'weak' (B-1) become stronger while the historically 'strong' (M-1) become weaker?

The explanation that I offer builds on social network analysis, a powerful theoretical current in comparative political economy and economic sociology that is barely tapped in international labor studies. I demonstrate, based on extensive case studies building on fieldwork, interviews, union and management documents, and press accounts, that the capacity of firms and worker representatives to transcend zero-sum conflicts over flexibility and jointly forge innovative new practices hinges upon the character of the social network ties in which they are embedded when pressures for greater flexibility are experienced. These ties are understood not just in dyadic, or bilateral terms, but also in relationship to management and labor representatives' respective links to larger business and labor-popular networks and domains.

---

[1] Lowell Turner, *Democracy at Work* (Ithaca: Cornell University Press, 1991); and Kathleen Thelen, *Union of Parts* (Ithaca: Cornell University Press, 1991).

These structured ties set the constraints and possibilities for work reorganization as they condition the main actors' styles of communication, behavior, and interaction as well as the informational and other organizational resources available to them. Distant ties and sparse network structures reinforced a spiral of conflict and impasse resulting in management's enlisting of coercive state intervention at M-1 in Mexico. At B-1, meanwhile, close ties and dense network structures created a dynamic of conflictual cooperation in which labor and management jointly reshaped a new workplace order through a mixture of negotiation and conflict.

The first section provides necessary background on the auto industry's development in the two countries, establishes the basis for a 'most similar systems' comparison, and develops the concept of labor flexibility. The second introduces the network perspective and elaborates the difference between the two plants in the period leading up to change for each of the three types of ties. In the third section, I explicate how existing structured ties shaped the mid-1992 abrupt imposition of flexible forms at M-1 and the gradual transition to greater flexibility at B-1. After finding wanting alternative explanations based on national labor relations systems and company strategy and culture, I develop broader conclusions. The central point is that for globally, flexibly organized sectors of advanced production, such as autos, the connection to national labor regulatory trends is an increasingly tenuous and mediated one, with much decentralized contingency of outcomes. In such a setting, established practices and norms developed and embedded in subnational, workplace-centered social networks take on central importance in determining the contours of work reorganization.

Historical Background and Key Concepts

The 1980s and first half of the 1990s marked an important if often uneven transition period from import-substituting mass production to flexible, internationalized production for the transnational-dominated auto industries of both Brazil and Mexico.[2] While limited efforts were made to reform work organization and human resource management, major transformations in employment relations occurred only in the 1990s. The auto sector had been key for national development as the respective 'economic miracles' of the previous decades, contributing substantially to industrial GNP—anywhere from 5% to 10%—direct and indirect employment, and economy-wide wage bargaining norms for the private sector. During the two closing decades of the century, shifting parent strategies, liberalizing national policy frameworks, and volatile macroeconomic scenarios combined to create considerable pressures on established, or brownfield, automobile plants to adopt more flexible forms of production and work organization. The respective governments

---

[2] Economist Intelligence Unit, 1995.

moved away from protective import substitution industrialization (ISI) policies and began to embrace liberalization, export orientation, and market
reforms, still authoritarian, one party-dominated Mexico earlier and more
decisively than democratizing Brazil. Auto production formerly destined
exclusively to a protected domestic market, focusing on outdated models and
using antiquated methods and machinery, gave way to a new approach by
auto transnationals (TNCs)—all American- or European-based in both
countries with the exception of one Japanese firm in Mexico—to their
Brazilian and Mexican affiliates. While varying by company and in precise
timing, this approach generally emphasized greater export orientation and
the high-value-added manufacture of newer models; more up-to-date technology and new 'best practice' international methods pioneered internationally
by Japanese firms (such as just-in-time inventory management and statistical
process controls); and pursuit of international quality standards and certifi-
cation (such as the 'ISO' series of the International Standards Organization).
This reorientation of structure and strategy followed a broader trend among
TNCs in some high-end products in the global economy in terms of their relationship with less developed countries, which UNCTAD has labeled 'deep' or
'complex' integration.[3] Both M-1 in Mexico and B-1 in Brazil, plants built in
the prime of ISI in the 1950s, began to take on greater export roles in the
1980s associated with selective modernization of plant and equipment and
limited efforts to restructure workplaces that remained in the mold of vertically integrated mass production.

The parallel restructuring trajectories and ownership and industrial structure profiles of the respective national industries and of the two case-study
factories provide the cornerstone for my use of the 'most similar systems'
research design.[4] The extensive similarities across the two nations and production units are used to isolate the few potentially casually relevant variables
on which they differ. Besides these auto industry characteristics, other broad,
shared features at the national level include: liberalizing ISI-dominated
economies, elite-dominated, transitional political systems, and entrenched,
historic labor relations systems, state corporatist in character. Let me briefly
elaborate on each.

---

[3] United Nations Conference on Trade and Development (UNCTAD), *World Investment Report, 1994* (New York and Geneva, 1994), 163–213. This involves a corporate strategy and organization based on the 'breakdown of discrete functions—e.g., assembly, procurement, finance, research and development—and their location to wherever they can be carried out most effectively in light of the overall needs of the firm as a whole' (p. 139). It is contrasted to both a 'stand-alone' approach in which (as was the case in Brazil and Mexico through the 1970s) over-seas production is intended exclusively or primarily for the recipient country in question, as well as a 'simple integration' form *à la* export processing zones or *maquiladoras* where production of finished goods or inputs is transferred or subcontracted abroad for export to and consumption in the sending country.

[4] Adam Preworski and Henry Teune, *The Logic of Comparative Social Inquiry* (New York: Wiley, 1970).

Auto industry restructuring in both Mexico and Brazil was part of painful, broader processes of growing integration into the global economy and macroeconomic reform and crisis—trade liberalization, privatization, fiscal and state reform, deregulation, anti-inflation packages, and economic integration with their neighbors through trade and investment agreements (the North American Free Trade Agreement and South American Common Market, respectively).[5] To be sure, Mexico moved earlier, more swiftly, and more decisively toward economic liberalization and outward orientation, while Brazil was a relative latecomer within Latin America, moving toward market reforms only in the early 1990s. None the less, the direction of change by the time of the decisive transitions under study was similar. Also common was the fact both M-1 and B-1, like all the surviving brownfields in the two countries, were increasingly diversifying their production mix to include exports (of finished vehicles and motors) while still relying considerably on the substantial internal markets of Latin America's two largest national economies.

In both countries, elite-dominated political systems were undergoing transitions in the 1990s, from protracted, post-revolutionary, single party-dominant authoritarian rule toward greater multiparty competition in Mexico,[6] and from a still fledgling transitional civilian regime emerging out of two decades of military rule toward a more stable if still unconsolidated democracy in Brazil.[7] While Mexico remained a liberalized authoritarian regime or semi-democracy until the victory of opposition presidential candidate Vincente Fox in 2000, Brazil was a formal democracy with serious authoritarian legacies and institutional defects in areas such as rule of law, military prerogatives, and equality of electoral representation among states. The South American country remained, like Mexico, a highly—and increasingly—unequal country in distribution of wealth and income, with 'democratic Brazil' in fact somewhat more unequal than 'authoritarian Brazil' and possessing one of the most polarized income distributions in the world. These substantive characteristics, along with the failure of the inclusionary 'social pacts' or social reforms promised by political elites leading the Brazilian transition of the

---

[5] Haggard and Kaufman, *The Political Economy of Democratic Transitions*, essays in Smith *et al.* (eds), 1994.

[6] Roderic Ai Camp, *Politics in Mexico: The Decline of Authoritarianism* (New York: Oxford University Press, 3rd edn., 1999) and Wayne A. Cornelius, 'Mexican Politics in Transition: The Breakdown of a One-Party-Dominant Regime', Monograph series 41 (San Diego: University of California, San Diego, Center for U.S.-Mexican Studies, 1996).

[7] Scott Mainwaring, 'Brazil: Weak Parties, Feckless Democracy', in Scott Mainwaring and Timothy Scully (eds), *Building Democratic Institutions* (Stanford, CA: Stanford University Press, 1995); Scott Mainwaring, 'Presidentialism in Brazil: The Impact of Strong Constitutional Powers, Weak Partisan Powers, and Robust Federalism', Working papers 225 (Woodrow Wilson International Center for Scholars, Latin American Program, 1997); Guillermo O'Donnell, *Counterpoints* (Notre Dame: University of Notre Dame Press, 1999); and Kurt Gerhard Weyland, *Democracy without Equity* (Pittsburgh: University of Pittsburgh Press, 1996).

[8] Roxborough 'Inflation and Social Pacts in Brazil and Mexico'; and Weyland, *Democracy without Equity*.

1980s,[8] make the formal political system difference between the two countries more one of degree than of kind. None the less, there is a difference in the state's coercive and interventionist power over labor—considerably less in Brazil—that I will consider as an explanatory variable.

Both countries have enduring 'state corporatist' patterns of domination of labor movements and relations dating from the 1930s, which have frequently been compared.[9] Central features are formally tripartite, state-dominated labor court systems; restrictive rules for union recognition and demand-making; and unitary, non-competitive, state-linked union organizations. The historical difference, again, is one of degree rather than kind—union links to a ruling political party with the 'official' labor movement as an important political constituency and hence with some important room for maneuver for labor in political and collective bargaining in Mexico, versus a direct linkage to the state with a heavier dose of bureaucratic control and regulation in Brazil. An important concomitant is historically greater direct presence of unions in the workplace and union weight in shaping practices and relations of work in Mexico as compared to Brazil, particularly in well organized industries like the manufacture of automobiles.[10] Thus, as will be discussed below, the newly militant and democratic unions emerging at plants like M-1 in Mexico during the 1970s achieved extensive influence over work rules;[11] they did so by implicitly mimicking—albeit through collective bargaining with employers rather than political bargaining with the state and party—the gains official unions had made in the post-war decades in many state-dominated sectors under what de la Garza calls the 'contractual pattern of the Mexican Revolution'.[12] Even after a decade and a half of militant, democratic 'new unionism' in the Brazilian auto industry by the early 1990s,[13] in contrast, auto plants such as B-1 did not have contractual protections of a

---

[9] Philippe Schmitter, 'Still the Century of Corporatism?', *Review of Politics*, 36 (1974), 85–131; Ruth Berins Collier, 'Popular Sector Incorporation and Political Supremacy', in Sylvia Ann Hewlett and Richard S. Weinert (eds), *Brazil and Mexico: Patterns in Late Development* (Philadelphia: Institute for the Study of Human Issues, 1982); Ruth Berins Collier and David Collier, *Shaping the Political Arena* (Princeton: Princeton University Press, 1991); and Kenneth Paul Erickson and Kevin J. Middlebrook, '*The State and Organized Labor in Brazil and Mexico*', in Sylvia Ann Hewlett and Richard S. Weinert (eds), *Brazil and Mexico* (Philadelphia: Institute for the Study of Human Issues, 1982).

[10] Ian Roxborough, 'The Urban Working Class and the Labour Movement in Latin America Since 1930', in Leslie Bethell (ed.), *The Cambridge History of Latin America*, v. 4, pt. II (Cambridge: Cambridge University Press, 1997), 307–78.

[11] Ian Roxborough, *Unions and Politics in Mexico* (Cambridge: Cambridge University Press, 1984); Ian Roxborough and Ilán Bizberg, 'Union Locals in Mexico', *Journal of Latin American Studies*, 15: 1 (May 1983); and Kevin J. Middlebrook, *The Paradox of Revolution* (Baltimore: The Johns Hopkins University Press, 1995).

[12] Enrique de la Garza Toledo, *Reestructuración Productiva y Respuesta Sindical en México. México*, DF.: UNAM/UAM-Iztapalapa, 1993).

[13] John Humphrey, *Capitalist Control and Workers' Struggle in the Brazilian Auto Industry* (Princeton: Princeton University Press, 1982); Margaret Keck, 'The New Unionism in the Brazilian Transition', in Alfred Stepan (ed.), *Democratizing Brazil* (New York: Oxford University Press, 1989), 252–98; and Iram Jacomé Rodrigues, *Sindicalismo e Política* (São Paulo: Scritta, 1997).

remotely comparable extent or strength on issues like hiring, firing, promotions, transfers, and disciplinary action. This is the context of the puzzle suggested above regarding historical institutional strengths for unionists in the Mexican plant and weaknesses in the Brazilian plants that belie the trajectories of change toward flexible work organization. Both factories were run by the respective national subsidiaries of two major non-Japanese auto multinationals based in the industrialized world.

Despite the broader national movements from below for change emerging from the 1970s, in which the unions representing B-1 and M-1 workers played key roles, the respective national corporatist systems remained substantially intact in the 1990s. In Mexico, the official, state-linked labor confederations successfully fought off several employer and state efforts (involving proposals for temporary contracts, hourly wages, and greater freedom to fire) to 'flexibilize' the federal labor code.[14] Meanwhile, in Brazil, corporatist pillars such as the Consolidated Labor Laws of the 1930s, state-collected mandatory assessments to fund unions (the 'union tax'), the labor tribunals, and *de facto* and *de jure* restrictions on strikes survived democratization and the 1988 Constitution; nor were most of the meager progressive gains made by labor in the new magna carta translated into implementing legislation.[15] What is more, by mid-decade when negotiated restructuring was still underway at B-1, the terms of the political debate on labor reform in Brazil had shifted radically toward the promotion of 'flexible' reforms and unions had been placed squarely—as in Mexico and many countries around the so-called developing world[16]—on the defensive by government and business legislative initiatives.[17] To be sure, unions were much more mobilized, more politically active on the opposition front, and more autonomous in Brazil; moreover, at least in highly visible, well-organized sectors such as autos, elected authorities (and labor courts) in Brazil were more politically constrained in intervening in heavy-handed fashion on the side of employers (except where wage control, anti-inflation policies were at issue) than were their authoritarian Mexican

[14] Bensusán and García, 'Entre la tradición y el cambio: el corporativismo sindical en México,'; Middlebrook, *The Paradox of Revolution*; and Francisco Zapata, *El Sindicalismo Mexicano Frente a la Restructuración* (México, DF: El Colegio de México, Centro de Estudios Sociológicos/Instituto de Investigaciones de las Naciones Unidas para el Desarrollo Social, 1995).

[15] Armando Boito, 'Reforma e Persistência da Estrutura Sindical Brasileira', in Armando Boito (ed.), *O Sindicalismo Brasileiro nos Anos 80* (Rio de Janeiro: Paz e Terra, 1991); and José Francisco Siquiera Neto, *Contrato Coletivo do Trabalho* (São Paulo: Editora Limitada, 1991). These 'paper' gains included an unrestricted freedom to strike (subsequently curtailed) and shopfloor worker representation in medium and large enterprises (never implemented). Gains that were reflected in practice were extended maternity leave, one-day paternity leave, and a rollback in the state's power to recognize and license unions.

[16] Oscar Ermida Uriarte, 'El futuro del Derecho del Trabajo y las relaciones laborales', in Silvia Portella (ed.), *Sindicalismo Latinoamericao Entre la Renovación y la Resignación* (Caracas: Nueva Sociedad, 1995), 47–56; and Sebastian Edwards and Nora Lustig, *Labor Markets in Latin America* (Washington, DC: Brookings Institution, 1997).

[17] Glauco Arbix, 'Trabalho: Dois Modelos de Flexibilização', *Lua Nova*, 37 (1996*b*), 171–90.

counterparts. This important cross-national difference, within the broader similarity in persistent state corporatist institutional legacies, is a potential explanatory variable for the M-1/B-1 contrast in work reorganization patterns.

Turning now to the crucial concept of labor flexibility, it may be seen as having four basic dimensions: employment, work content, work time, and remuneration. Flexibility in employment refers to a loosening of the conditions under which workers are hired and fired (so-called 'external flexibility') or those under which they are transferred and promoted inside the firm (the workings of 'internal labor markets'). Typical flexibility-enhancing measures include the removal of contractual or other barriers on dismissals, heightened lateral mobility of workers (e.g., across jobs, shifts), greater reliance on performance indicators in determining promotions, and the use of temporary workers. Work content flexibility entails greater breadth and variations in the nature of work. Examples are the broadening or elimination of job hierarchies, so-called 'multitasking' and 'cross-training', and multi-functional work teams.

Flexibility of remuneration can take numerous forms. A classical one now revived in many activities is piecework. More common in capital- and skill-intensive industries like auto assembly is merit- or incentive-based pay. Under so-called 'pay for knowledge systems', a common variant adopted here by M-1, an individual worker's pay level and increment are tied to his or her gradual demonstration of mastery of a designated and graduated series of tasks and professional capacities. Finally, working time flexibility refers to increased variation in the length or period of employees' regularly scheduled working hours.[18] An example relevant to B-1 is fluctuation bands—in this case weekly in nature—whereby employers adjust hours up or down to meet market conditions within established limits and with an overall evening out of hours to a certain baseline number.

Labor flexibility along these various dimensions entails movement away from established mass production or 'Taylorist' patterns of work organization and employment relations. Such patterns were centered on hierarchical command and control, scientific management, elaborate functional division of tasks, and separate of intellectual labor ('conception') from manual labor ('execution').[19] The four dimensions represent a distillation of the key, com-

---

[18] A classic practice is, of course, overtime. However, its effectiveness as the sole form of employment flexibility for employers facing rapidly shifting consumer demand and producing in smaller lots—both attributes of the flexible new economy—is typically limited in high-end activities by legal or contractual norms making it voluntary and/or prohibitively expensive.

[19] It is often forgotten that although such mass production patterns were less universally spread through domestic economies and more weakly tied to 'Fordist' norms and policies of mass production and consumption in late-industrializing countries like Brazil and Mexico, they nonetheless did emerge in high-end activities (and often in the public sector) in these countries during the post-World War II decades. Relatively early industrialization—compared to the other contemporary late-industrializing countries—led by multinational investment was the primary lever for the diffusion of mass production forms.

mon elements of workplace transformation highlighted by the most influential analytical models of contemporary production systems—that is, 'post-Fordism',[20] 'lean production',[21] 'flexible specialization',[22] and 'diversified quality production'.[23] Echoing a theme of many comparative studies of employment relations amidst productive restructuring in advanced industrial contexts,[24] this chapter finds evidence of multiple paths. As in these studies, the metaphor of paths also can be extended backward to encompass different points of departure within the broad commonalities of mass production. In this chapter, however, I depart from most of these institutionalist studies in conceiving such institutional 'legacies' in the form of structured social relations—networks—and as having their primary locus, insofar as productive restructuring is concerned, not at the national level but at the less aggregated level of the firm and place of work and their distinctive and contingent ties with national institutions and actors.[25]

The study identifies two broad, ideal-typical modes of transition to flexible work and human resource arrangements—unilateral restructuring and negotiated restructuring. The first, illustrated by M-1, entails management efforts to force new employment practices on workers without obtaining the prior agreement of their legitimately constituted representatives. Typically, in brownfield settings with established unions, such efforts involve the use or threat of economic coercion through large-scale lay-offs, union-busting, or heightened workplace surveillance and pressure, or the use of state coercion; in many but not all cases, some sort of explicit labor-management confrontation ensues. For its part, negotiated restructuring, represented by B-1, refers to relatively equal exchange situations in which employee spokespersons accept, help implement, and perhaps even champion proposals for changes that alter existing employment practices and standards.

---

[20] Ash Amin (ed.), *Post-Fordism* (Oxford: Blackwell, 1994).

[21] James Womack, Daniel Jones, and Daniel Roos, *The Machine that Changed the World.* (New York: Rawson Associates, 1990); Steve Babson, *Lean Work: Empowerment and Exploitation in the Global Auto Industry* (Detroit: Wayne State University Press, 1995); and Thomas A. Kochan, Russell D. Lansbury, and John Paul Macduffie (eds), *After Lean Production: Evolving Employment Practices in the World Auto Industry* (Ithaca: ILR Press, 1997).

[22] Michael Piore and Charles Sabel, *The Second Industrial Divide* (New York: Basic Books, 1984).

[23] Wolfgang Streeck, 'Lean Production in the German Automobile Industry: A Test Case for Convergence Theory', in Suzanne Berger and Ronald Dore (eds), *National Diversity and Global Capitalism* (Ithaca: Cornell University Press, 1996), 138–70. This chapter adopts an agnostic position on how one should best conceptualize or explain transformations in production systems as a whole, honing in instead on one larger aspect of broader global transformations in production—changes in the organization of work and in associated practices of human resources and industrial relations within firms, and the roles and impacts for workers and unions within these changes.

[24] See, e.g., Lowell, *Democracy at Work*; Thelen, *Union of Parts*; Richard M. Locke, *Remaking the Italian Economy* (Ithaca: Cornell University Press, 1995); and Streeck 1997.

[25] Except Locke. See Richard M. Locke, 'The Demise of the National Union in Italy: Lessons for Comparative Industrial Relations Theory', *Industrial and Labor Relations Review*, 2: 4 (Jan. 1992), 229–49; and Locke, *Remaking the Italian Economy*.

Contrasting Sets of Social Ties

The explanatory framework developed here for understanding dynamics of labor systems transitions toward flexibility at the firm level is derived from the rich tradition of social network analysis, particularly as developed and applied to themes of political economy.[26] Despite ample applications to diverse themes in political economic and economic sociology including the study of labor markets—and despite a clear relevance for understanding contemporary transformation in production and work systems[27]—network analysis has been virtually absent from the study of production politics and employment relations.[28]

Network theory highlights the ways in which social actors interact with each other in a regularized, structured fashion. Actors are constituted, exchange resources, and attach meanings and values to themselves, others, and resources in a socially constructed, iterative process—quite unlike the atomized agent of methodologically individualist conceptions who is assumed to 'pre-form' outside of social relations and autonomous in her preference formation. Network analysts consider that series of encounters between given dyadic pairs and within broader sets of interconnected actors constitute relationships between and among these actors that they term 'social ties' (or 'links' or 'bonds'). They are particularly interested in the character of ties between pairs of actors (dyads)—the frequency of encounters, the extent to which bilateral exchanges (cooperation, transactions) occur, and the affective 'charge' or 'valence' ('intensity') of the relationship, including the degree of trust. To the extent that a particular dyadic link involves frequent encounters and considerable two-way exchange involving at least a modicum of mutual trust, it will be referred to—departing a little from standard net-

---

[26] Works and authors that are particularly influential and/or representative of this rich and diverse tradition are Harrison C. White, *Chains of Opportunity* (Cambridge: Harvard University Press, 1970); Mark Granovetter, *Getting a Job* (Cambridge: Harvard University Press, 1974); Ronald S. Burt, *Toward a Structural Theory of Action* (New York: Academic Press, 1982); and Walter W. Powell and Laurel Smith-Doerr, 'Networks and Economic Life', in Neil Smelser and Richard Swedberg (eds), *The Handbook of Economic Sociology* (Princeton: Princeton University Press/Russell Sage, 1994). An insightful introduction for nonspecialists and especially students of politics is David Knoke, *Political Networks* (Cambridge: Cambridge University Press, 1990). Particularly relevant to political economy issues is his ch. 8 (203–32).

[27] Ibid.

[28] For instance, several recent edited collections of essays on the 'new economic sociology' employing network insights—Neil Smelser and Richard Swedberg (eds), *The Handbook of Economic Sociology.* (Princeton: Princeton University Press/Russell Sage, 1994); Richard Swedberg (ed.), *Explorations in Economic Sociology.* (New York: Russell Sage, 1993); and Mark Granovetter and Richard Swedberg (eds), *The Sociology of Economic Life* (Boulder: Westview Press, 1992)—contain no contributions that examine employment relations. Important exceptions in the use of networks are Locke, *Remaking the Italian Economy*, and Chris Tilly and Charles Tilly, *Work under Capitalism* (Boulder: Westview Press, 1998).

work nomenclature[29]—as a 'close' tie. To the extent that it lacks these attributes, the tie will be characterized as a 'distant' tie.

Dyadic pairs adumbrate into larger network structures linking multiple actors engaged in some common activity (or 'domain'). I will highlight one aspect of these overall configurations, which is their relative density or sparsity of ties. A third network dimension utilized by this study is that of structural position—that is, the extent to which the given network-embedded actor (labor or management in this case) is central or peripheral to the network domain in question.

These three attributes—closeness, density, position—of network ties and structures linking labor and management to each other and to their respective peers are crucial in explanatory terms. Managers' relevant peers are the business colleagues located within the same (transnational or national) organization and the other competing firms that constitute the national (and global) auto industry—social ties in the 'business domain', in short. Social ties in the 'labor-popular milieu' refer to the distinct representatives inside and outside the workplace with a claim to speak for workers in the factories in question, their links to each and to rank and file, and their ties to the larger set of organizations and individuals from labor, popular, and non-governmental spheres with whom they have intense relations.[30] The character and structure of ties shape how the main protagonists actors are constituted (who speaks for workers and management and with what support); their established routines of behavior and interaction ('repertoires'); the resources they bring to bear on their encounters (e.g., information, finances, ideas); and the relevant 'external publics' for their actions in particular firms and places of work (e.g., with whom they compete or seek to influence or lead). In short, I contend, we must understand how labor and management are connected to each other and to their relevant peers in order to explain how and why 'negotiated' versus 'unilateral' scenarios of transition toward flexible work organization occur at the level of factories and firms.

As managers embarked upon efforts to build highly flexible labor systems, they and unionists were embedded in sharply contrasting sets of social ties and relations. Distant bilateral ties prevailed at factory M-1 in Mexico. These distant ties was in turn closely related to the fact that, first, their respective ties to their key social domains were distant—with them often occupying peripheral positions within these structures—and, second, these broader social structures were sparsely structured. In the Brazilian factory of B-1, by

[29] The more conventional dichotomous formulation is 'strong' versus 'weak' ties. However, I avoid this because it so heavily associated with the Granovetter arguments about a particular type of network domain—that of individual job-seekers—in which 'weak' ties are held to be more consequential than 'strong' ties. Below, I elaborate the particular structural configurations of broader networks under which what Granovetter would term 'strong' ties (my 'distant' ties) between a dyad (here, labor and management) are, contra his theoretical argument, in fact conducive to mutually beneficial flows of information and other resources.

[30] Klandermans (1990) terms this an 'alliance system'.

contrast, ties were close between labor and management interlocutors in the period leading up to the transition toward flexibility. In turn, these close plant-level ties ramified outward into densely structured business and labor-popular domains in which they respectively occupied central positions. In the following three sections, divided by network domain, I will describe the nature and formation of ties in the labor-popular milieu, business domain, and bilateral labor-management spheres, respectively. This sets the stage for an elaboration of how these social ties conditioned the factories' distinct transition modes to flexible labor systems.

Social Ties in the Labor-Popular Milieu

The two plants and their respective national industries, as noted above, shared a common historical trajectory of militant unionism with extensive rank-and-file participation growing out of dissident, democratizing movements against corporatist controls in the 1970s (the so-called 'new unionism'). These movements were successful in taking control of undemocratic organizations and making inroads against employers (more so in Mexico) but less so in democratizing larger corporatist systems. However, behind this similarity there lurked significant cross-plant differences in the social ties of newly autonomous labor actors; these differences in turn reflected quite different variations on the theme of union democracy.

In the Mexican case of the M-1 plant, the principal organized voice of workers in establishing the broad parameters of compensation, conditions of employment, and work organization was the leadership of the union, which was an enterprise union.[31] The union negotiated tri-annual collective bargains with management on such issues, as well as annual accords on wage and benefit adjustments. This key actor was distantly tied to a second important set of worker representatives, the directly elected shop stewards who were formally part of the union structure but with an autonomous base of support and selection. Still other distant links tied it to a mistrustful, demanding rank and file itself and to the larger local and national labor-popular milieu.

Distant, or 'arms' length', ties were a persistent feature of relations between rank and file and union leaders that persisted after the union's democratization in 1972, when a dissident movement took the union out of the largest of the 'official' (i.e., ruling party-linked) national labor confederations, the

---

[31] Throughout, the discussion of M-1 draws on not only the authors' fieldwork and interviews but also on studies by several Mexican and foreign scholars. While listed in the Bibliography along with studies of other Mexican plants, they cannot be cited here because their titles would compromise anonimity (except Ludger Pries, with Gabriela García, César Gutiérrez, and Fernando Herrera, 'Relaciones industriales en la industria automotriz', in *Las Relaciones Laborales en el Proceso de Tranformación en América Latina: El Caso de México*. (Bremen: University of Bremen, May 1998); and Yolanda Montiel and Ludger Pries, *Proceso de Trabajo, Acción Sindical y Nuevas Tecnologías en Volkswagen de México* (México, DF: CIESAS/Ediciones de la Casa Chata, 1991)).

CTM (Mexican Workers' Confederation). The dissident movement both gained control of the union and severed its links to the CTM, joining the Independent Worker Unity (UOI), a loose national workers' front primarily centered on the auto industry which grew considerably during this time period. However, the rank-and-file ousted the union's labor lawyer and 'power behind the throne', who headed the UOI, in the early 1980s, establishing a boisterous, rough-and-tumble pattern of internal union politics that would continue. Between 1984 and 1992, two secretaries-general were recalled through general assembly votes; another resigned early in his term; and yet another was roundly defeated when he defied union statutes by standing for re-election. Workers and the militants who competed for their support warred with each other as frequently and as vociferously as they did with management, and intra-union and labor-management conflicts often fed off each other (Montiel and Pries 1992; Pries *et al.* 1998). Tactics of violence and intimidation among activists were a not infrequent part of union life.

Distant worker-leader ties and great dispersion of social ties into shifting, localized, often personality-based leadership cliques of rival stewards and activists characterized the plant. In union elections, held every three years, a 'hyperpluralism' of multiple slates was thus evident, with somewhere between a half dozen and a dozen typically running for the secretary general and other executive committee posts throughout the 1972–92 period. Leadership groups inevitably elected with only a plurality of (first round) votes—having had to gain victory through finalist run-offs—entered office with weak mandates. The weakness of their electoral constituency was compounded by the need for each successive novice, lame duck leadership to 'learn the ropes' and to form alliances with the more stable shop stewards elected by work section (who, by contrast, could stand for re-election) and with union staffers, particularly the powerful chief legal counsel. Complicating the union incumbents' situation considerably were not only the strict non-re-election statutes mentioned above, but also an unusual unwritten labor-management custom whereby, upon completion of their single term, they would receive a generous severance package and leave the company altogether.

This ephemeral nature of incumbents' grip on power undercut their accountability to rank-and-file and generally created strong incentives for opportunistic behavior—such as petty corruption, the cutting of secret 'side deals' with management outside formal bargaining channels, and arbitrary use of their contractual right under the common 'exclusion clauses' of Mexican collective contracts to have workers dismissed from the plant simply by kicking them out of the union. Partly in response to this tendency, three major statutory 'checks and balances' had been incorporated since the 1970s: an elaborate system of sectional and general assemblies with strong powers; a 'contractual review commission' made up of rank-and-file and stewards who accompanied union leaders in all formal negotiating sessions; and a petition procedure allowing for relatively easy holding of recall votes by simple majority-based, general assembly vote. However successful in punishing the actual or perceived leadership abuses at issue, these checks were overly blunt and episodic to serve as continuous channels for accountability. Thus distant, sparse links based on considerable mistrust were manifested in a perpetual cycle that began with institutionally powerful but politically weak leaders who had a strong temptation—bordering on a structural imperative—to utilize their power to commit abuses or cut secret deals with management. Once selective abuses or a particularly outrageous concession crossed a certain intangible threshold of tolerance on the part of mistrustful and vigilant rank-and-file and shop stewards, almost as a matter of course these leaders quickly were ousted and replaced.

A number of features of the plant and the workforce contributed in some measure to the precarious intra-worker and worker-leader ties that characterized M-1. Among rank-and-file, there was a high level of work group identification and cohesion and equally high level of inter-group rivalry. The sprawling division of the plant into nine physically separate (and technologically diverse) workshops, or *naves*; the system of rigid job classifications and well-defined, seniority-based job hierarchy; and the narrow jurisdictions and considerable influence of stewards over workplace issues (scheduling, transfers, promotions, disciplinary proceedings, and the like) all combined to cement the overwhelmingly 'local' loyalties of workers. With their independent power base and greater experience, the numerous stewards were in a position to act as key individual brokers between workers and management and workers and union leaders, and many played this role skillfully. Another source of distant ties within the plant's workforce was the large number of temporary laborers (*eventuales*) employed by the plant, for periods ranging from a few weeks to as long as two years in some cases; the temporaries worked at considerably lower wages and with no guarantee or clear time frame for achieving full-time status. *Eventuales* were viewed as a threat by unionized workers as management sought to reduce staffing levels over the 1980s and into the early 1990s. In the late 1980s, as the share of temporaries in the total work force increased from approximately 20% to a peak of 40%, the union increasingly fought hard to restrict this practice, but with only very limited success.

At the core of the chronic tensions between rank-and-file and union leaders was the fact that formally and procedurally democratic norms and procedures, mixing elements of representative democracy with direct or plebiscitarary democracy, coexisted with near dictatorial *de facto* union powers. Together with the closed shop provision ('exclusivity clause'), the aforementioned exclusion clause effectively enable union leaders to control who entered and exited the factory through control of who was a 'bona fide' union member. While several analysts have understandably hailed the highly pluralistic competition for power at this and other newly democratized autoworkers' unions in Mexico during the 1970s and 1980s as compared to the classic anti-democratic practices of official Mexican unions (Tuman 1998;

Middlebrook 1995), they lose sight of the fact that the democratic reformists did not challenge some of the inherited behavioral and contractual norms of state-dominated unionism. These norms involved practices of clientelism and of elaborate brokering between management and workforce in the setting of work rhythms, selection of new hires, staffing levels, promotions decisions, and other workplace issues,[32] making substantial use of the exclusion clause 'stick' as part of their elaborate 'carrot and stick' arsenal of control. Continued resort to this anti-democratic union governance mechanism against nettlesome rivals, together with occasional petty corruption and malfeasance and secret deal-making outside the normal collective bargaining process, was a key persistent element driving a wedge between rank-and-file and their democratically elected leaders. These vices, persisting within a formally democratic and competitive structure, belied the union's strong rhetorical critiques of state intervention in union and labor affairs and defense of the principle of union democracy. In another bit of irony, statutory elements of direct democracy in union governance, such as prohibitions on re-election and low thresholds for holding and effecting recall votes, had the unintended effect of perpetuating rather than lessening the chronic leader–rank-and-file distance, discouraging effective union leadership, and failing to attack structural obstacles to democracy like the exclusion clause.

Externally, unionists at M-1 had distant links to the rest of the non-official labor movement, even with other independent unions in central Mexico, as manifested in sporadic contacts and sparsely organized activist networks.[33] The union's strong posture and identity as an 'independent union'—present in the unions' very name when reconstituted in 1972 as the '*Sindicato Independiente*' of M-1 Workers and reaffirmed with its departure from the UOI—meant in effect independence from all, including not just political parties and official unions but also opposition-oriented local popular movements and like-minded independent unionists.[34] Finally, on the international front, the M-1 union did have contacts with the national union and locals representing its counterparts in the home country. While they gave solidarity (with protests, brief work stoppages, and other measures) during a long 1987 strike, inter-union exchanges with M-1 were episodic and limited mostly to sharing

[32] Enrique de la Garza Toledo and Alfonso Bouzas, 'La flexibilidad del trabajo en México', Paper presented at the first meeting of the International Working Group on Subnational Economic Governance in Latin America and Southern Europe, Institute of Latin American and Iberian Studies, Columbia University (20–22 Sept. 1997).

[33] The union's engagement in wider labor and political causes was limited to such gestures as rhetorical support for broader inter-union and declarations about the need for a less draconian macroeconomic policy and labor relations reform; participation in the annual anti-government, anti-official labor May Day counter-demonstrations in Mexico City; and a few isolated instances of solidarity received or given to other independent auto unions in Central Mexico amid strikes.

[34] A partial exception took place in the late 1980s, when the union co-founded a 'Coalition of Independent Automobile Unions' (CASIA), a discussion forum intended to facilitate joint strategies *vis-à-vis* company restructuring in the industry that proved stillborn as a genuine inter-union organization.

of information about company performance and strategy.[35] The paucity and distance of outward labor-popular links was both product of and contributor to arm's length social ties within the factory. A fractious organization with high leadership turnover and little institutional continuity was not in a position to form sustained, much less formal, bonds to other organizations and activists. Moreover, the lack of connections to potential external reference points and symbolic and material resources reinforced the salient characteristics of intra-union competition and conflict—fluidity, basis in personality rather than programs, and, most of all, inward orientation.

By contrast, in the period leading up to the transition to greater flexibility at plant B-1 in Brazil, worker representatives were embedded in close, dense labor ties, both locally at the plant and in the municipality as well as at more aggregated levels. Ties were anchored in the São Bernardo union's trajectory as the leading pole of the militant labor resurgence dating back to the 1970s, the aforementioned 'new unionism', and its stature as perhaps the single most influential union within the left-wing Unified Workers' Central (CUT), created in 1983 as Brazil's first contemporary independent labor confederation. In 1976 dissidents had taken over the union from the state-dominated leadership imposed on it, like other unions, following the 1964 military coup. They set out to democratize the union, rebuild ties to workers, and create links with labor activists in other sectors and regions. Under the leadership of President Luis Inácio Lula da Silva, the São Bernardo union led a nationwide wave of strikes between 1978 and 1980 that helped to weaken military rule and attracted widespread opposition support.[36] Lula and other new unionists also joined with activists from the progressive Church, neighborhood associations, and other social movements to found in 1980 the left-wing Workers' Party (PT), which went on to become Brazil's principal opposition party under the new, post-1985 democracy.[37]

Locally, in São Bernardo and the broader ABC region on São Paulo southern flank, labor-popular links were close and enduring on several levels, involving a combination of individual activists who crossed the boundaries of labor and community (and often party, in the form of the PT) politics and of inter-organizational ties among movements. Many of the thirty current and former union leaders, works councilors, and other labor activists whom I interviewed in 1990 and 1992—at B-1, another neighboring auto plant, and at the union itself—had entered activism initially through the Church or neighborhood movements or were still involved in struggles over land use, housing, and other local political issues while also being activists. At the inter-

---

[35] Joint strategic planning, leadership training courses, and thematic seminars—the usual activities of those cross-border ties that are close—were infrequent or totally absent.

[36] Margaret Keck, 'The New Unionism in the Brazilian Transition', in Alfred Stepan (ed.), *Democratizing Brazil* (New York: Oxford University Press, 1989), 252–98; and Maria Helena Moreira Alves, *State and Opposition in Military Brazil* (Austin: University of Texas Press, 1985).

[37] Margaret Keck, *The Workers Party and Democratization in Brazil* (New Haven: Yale University Press, 1992).

organizational level, an enduring relationship of the powerful São Bernardo metalworkers union to popular organizations was born initially of extensive community- and Church-based solidarity for the lengthy mass metalworkers' strike of 1980 against the military dictatorship (Alves 1985). The PT was a key vehicle and reference point for these dense social networks.

Both leader-worker and intra-leadership links at plant B-1 and in the São Bernardo union more generally thus were nested within a dense fabric of party, movement, and non-governmental organization activists in which the union and auto factories such as B-1 were a focal point. Close union-worker ties were manifest in my interviews with a sample of thirteen B-1 workers in mid-1992. First forged in the 1970s under the new unionism, these ties had been deepened and extended to a new generation of workers in part through changes in how the union and worker representation were structured. Under Brazilian corporatism's territorial system of unitary union representation (*sindicato único*), the multicompany, sectoral union formally represented all those working in the broadly defined metalworking industries in several contiguous municipalities, by far the largest of which was São Bernardo. The occupational category of metalworkers included auto assembly, auto parts, machine tools, and metallurgy. Having captured the union in the mid 1970s from the bureaucratic, state-imposed leadership of the harshest period of military role, Lula and the new unionists set out to reverse the tradition of a paternalistic, state-dominated leadership. Elections became open, transparent, competitive affairs, with at least one and often two rival slates (usually linked loosely with rivals from within the CUT's far left wing or from conservative union organizations) opposing the dominant 'Union Articulation' group. Moreover, under an open, slate-based electoral process based on secret ballot and with generally large worker turn-out, this dominant group continued to be returned to office with 90% or more of votes cast throughout the 1980s and 1990s; compared to M-1, opposition currents in union or factor-level works council elections were much fewer in number, cohesive in their identity and make-up over time, but chronically weak given meager worker support.

Despite the Articulation's group's hegemonic status, bureaucratization was avoided. Turnover at the end of electoral mandates was relatively high in union and factory council leadership ranks. There was a continual infusion of 'new blood' from the factory floor through a conscious policy of cultivating new 'organic' leaders from the worker ranks, robust informal norms of cadres rotation and renewal, and formal prohibitions on re-election and informal prohibitions at works councils at factories like B-1. The union had four union presidents from 1976 to the mid 1990s, each bringing fresh faces and ideas to a common, evolving project of activist, participatory unionism as his predecessor moved on to important leadership posts in national party (PT) or labor (CUT) politics. At the same time, the tightly knit but expansive network of activists who led the union and factory councils and norms of democratic participation ensured smooth, open processes of candidate selection, calm transitions, administrative and staff continuity, and considerable institutional capacity for learning and accumulation of institutional memory.

Worker assemblies and successful movements to create factory-level works' councils and to promote unionization were important vehicles for strengthening ties between unionist leaders and rank-and-file. Assemblies were held frequently, voice was given to all viewpoints, and votes contrary to the leadership were scrupulously obeyed—including one witnessed by the author in 1990 in which striking workers at B-1 refused to go back to work despite leaders' recommendations. The chronic structural problem of weak shopfloor presence under Brazilian corporatism began to be addressed in 1981 when B-1 was the first of a number of larger factories in São Bernardo in which union-led workers' movements during that decade successful struggled to achieve company recognition for newly created worker-elected works' councils, or 'factory commissions' (*comissões de fábrica*); they were loosely modeled on a European tradition of plant-level bodies directly elected by all workers. At the level of financing, in the mid 1980s the union refused to continue accepting official 'union tax' revenues assessed by the state on workers, instead adopting a voluntary, dues-based system based in large part on employer check-offs for declared members. This effort went hand in hand with a large-scale membership campaign to convince workers throughout the union's base to join the union and participate actively. Under Brazil's odd corporatist legal norm of 'mandated representation without mandated membership'—contrasting with Mexico's union shop—formal union membership remained a voluntary, individual decision though all workers, unionized or not, were covered by collective bargaining contracts negotiated by unions. By the late 1980s—and in the face of enduring legal incentives for free-riding under national institutions—the union had one of the highest membership rates of any in Brazil, roughly 40%, and at B-1 the figure was 87.3%.[38]

The high degree of identification and interchange between leaders and rank-and-file was closely interrelated with close, solidaristic ties among workers. In interviewing B-1 workers, I found generally approving statements about union and council leaders which went hand in hand with expressions of a strong sense of pride and identity as 'B-1 workers' and 'São Bernardo metalworkers'; both the union and the factory's workforce were considered by most informants to be national leaders (*uma vanguarda*) in the labor movement. In the only groups among whom work group identities were salient— the highly skilled tool and dye workers and equipment maintenance workers—these were not exclusive, but rather translated into a strong, shared self-perception as important leaders in the workplace and in union-led job actions. Solidaristic attitudes toward fellow workers were closely correlated

---

[38] Luiz Paul Bresciani, 'The Challenge to the "ABC" Region: Productive Restructuring and Metal Workers' Strategies in Brazil's Auto Industry Heart', Paper presented at the Fifth Colloquium of GERPISA (Paris, June 1997).

with high levels of involvement in union and factory council activities (e.g., reading of the daily union bulletin, attendance at assemblies, voting in union elections) and consistent union cultivation of an encompassing collective identity. Another factor that most likely contributed to the low incidence of rivalries and competition among workers was the somewhat higher (compared to M-1) levels of mobility across work areas and occupations at this plant.

A key role in the maintenance of close intra-activist and leader-worker ties at the plant and in the union was played by the directly elected works councilors and worker representatives on the bilateral health and safety commission (known by its Portuguese acronym, CIPA), chosen by electoral districts corresponding to work areas. These plant-level activists worked closely with union officials and the single shopfloor union delegate that existed at large plants, such as B-1, in developing negotiation and mobilization strategies; councilors and commissioners worked side by side with union leaders and staffers on a wide variety of technical and strategic issues, sharing an in-factory office-cum-meeting space. While formally autonomous and separate, in practice the boundaries among them were quite porous and practices of consensus formation on strategic issues through democratic internal consensus-building were strongly rooted. It is telling that worker informants often failed to distinguish among the three separate roles of union official, works councilor, and health and safety commissioners as worker representatives, instead referring to incumbents of those roles indiscriminately—and positively—as 'union people' (*pessoal do sindicato*). This close, 'organic' linkage between plant- and union-level representatives—arguably more difficult under conditions of multifirm representation and in the absence of strong formalized institutional linkages—contrasted sharply to the arm's length ties at M-1 under an enterprise union and shop steward structure arguably more conducive in principle to close union-shopfloor leadership ties.

Tight outward links to larger labor-popular milieu, in which São Bernardo unionists were a focal point, both reinforced and reflected close, solidaristic links within the São Bernardo union and at B-1. The union produced both of that independent confederation's first two national presidents and many of its national, sectoral, and state executive office holders. Moreover, São Bernardo metalworker unionists were also prominent leaders of the dominant, center-left political-ideological tendency within the CUT which gave name and orientation to their own ('Union Articulation'). In particular, the union played a leading role in coordinating the activities of CUT metalworkers' unions nationally and in the state of São Paulo, among them CUT-affiliated autoworkers at plants in São Paulo's interior. São Bernardo unionists, both former and present-day, were also prominent within the PT's national leadership and among the party's elected federal, state, and local officials. Despite carefully crafted institutional separations between union and party affairs, strong political affinities clearly remained and the subjective sense of being simultaneously labor (CUT) and party (PT) activists within the broader national context helped cement the tight interpersonal and intergenerational linkages within São Bernardo's activist networks. With popular movement, labor, and party ties mutually reinforcing, the ties were of the deep, multifaceted type that network analysts call 'multiplex'.

At the same time, São Bernardo unionists—again unlike their M-1 counterparts—had close working ties with labor-oriented intellectuals and technical experts from progressive non-governmental organizations at home and abroad. The two prime examples were the local and home office of the Amsterdam-based Transnationals Information Exchange (TIE) and national Inter-Union Department of Socio-Economic Studies (DIEESE), which had a branch office with three full-time staffers at union headquarters. As revealed by my interviews with two union vice-presidents and a union president as well as with a DIEESE economist, these organizations provided invaluable technical assistance and information on technological, economic, and other issues. In fact, these organizations came to be an *ex officio* part of the union's advisory structure, which also included many young non-labor professionals, particularly journalists and labor lawyers, who were recruited into key staff positions.

On the international front, the São Bernardo union had close ties with left-leaning metalworkers' unions in European countries, such as Germany's IG Metall, both directly and mediated through CUT's membership in the international metalworkers' confederation and, starting in 1990, the center-left international trade union central CIOSL. Such links, it is worth noting, were generally opposed by far-left CUT minority currents who rejected organizations that they associated with 'class compromise'. Links with US unions were more distant during most of the period under study, given the traditional anti-communist, 'company unionism' bent of the AFL-CIO until the 1995 change of national leadership.

In sum, the unionists at the B-1 factory and the São Bernardo union were closely tied to each other and to workers, as well to a broad larger national and international labor-popular milieu in which they occupied—by dint of the union's militant tradition and the economic importance of the auto industry—a central position. Their close ties brought them into broader discursive communities and inter-organizational networks that would prove invaluable in rethinking their strategy *vis-à-vis* global industrial restructuring. At the same time, their more distant, 'competitive' ties with far-left CUT rivals who rejected negotiations as a 'sell-out' and with conservative unionists from the CUT's center-right rival confederation, Força Sindical ('Union Force'), provided a mix of incentives and pressures to articulate and obtain tangible results from the stance of 'proactive militancy' (*sindicalismo propositivo*) São Bernardo leaders began espousing publicly in the early 1990s. Workplace restructuring was one of the key arenas where these broader debates and rivalries were played out.

Network Ties in the Business Domain

Let me now consider the character of M-1 and B-1 managers' intra-firm ties and links to competitors and the broader business community. They were generally close in the case of B-1, with dense inter-firm networks in which this company played a central role. At M-1, ties were distant, with sparse inter-firm networks and a peripheral role for this firm.

Turning first to intra-firm ties, it should be noted that in the mass production era there was considerable diversity in transnational corporation (TNC) practices across national and regional subsidiaries and corporate divisions, particularly in the case of late-industrializing countries where penetration of domestic markets was the primary goal—and notably on human resource and industrial relations issues.[39] However, with the adoption of what UNCTAD (1994) calls 'complex integration,' approaches involving tight, intra-firm divisions of labor and the relocation of some strategic, higher-value-added manufacturing and even design processes to late-industrializing countries, TNCs, like the M-1 and B-1 parents, have made efforts at greater internal standardization or, failing that, coordination in areas such as human resource management. However, the pressure toward greater homogenization of human resource practices that complex integration has brought often stands in tension with another evolving feature of TNCs (like other corporations), which is their increasingly network-based internal forms of coordination and decision-making. Particularly with the greater worker performance demands of flexible production, coordination between human resource departments and production staff and supervisors responsible for immediate, day-to-day oversight and direction of workers is of crucial importance for large manufacturing establishments.

Turning first to the M-1 case, human resource and production officials had a distant, often difficult relationship based on a strict functional division of tasks, each enjoying considerable autonomy from the home office.[40] There was little coordination in areas of ostensibly mutual concern such as training programs, screening tests for job applicants, or promotions. Moreover, human resources and industrial relations occupied a marginal place within the multinational affiliate's management hierarchy, manifested in a small, weakly professionalized staff, low budget, and scant prestige. Up until the time of the changes at issue in this chapter, the department's major assignment was the 'negative' one of keeping strikes and other work interruptions to a minimum and bringing them to a swift conclusion when they did occur.

[39] Barbara C. Samuels II, *Managing Risk in Developing Countries* (Princeton: Princeton University Press, 1990).

[40] This section relies on Pries *et al.*, *Las Relaciones Laborales en el Proceso de Tranformación en América Latina*, and the author's interviews in 1996 and 1997 with three high-level managerial informants at the plant.

Besides ties between human resource and production managers and home offices and subsidiaries, another key set of relationships shaping firms' policies towards unions and their workforce involves outward links to other firms operating within the same nation or industry. On this dimension, M-1 managers also had distant ties with their competitors in the Mexican industry as well as with organized business as a whole. This was true both with respect to labor issues and more generally. In the latter connection, studies have shown that auto TNCs producing in Mexico pursued largely individual strategies in seeking to influence and respond to the shifting state's regulatory policies on trade and investment, dating back from the 1960s all the way through the NAFTA negotiations of the early 1990s.[41] In particular, company M-1 frequently had distinct interests and positions from those of its competitors— and closer relations with the Mexican state[42]—due to the more vertically integrated nature of its production processes and its relatively greater emphasis on the local market. Moreover, if the main industry body, the Mexican Automobile Industry Association (AMIA), played a less prominent role on these high-profile regulatory issues than its Brazilian counterpart ANFAVEA/SINFAVEA, it played virtually *no* role whatsoever on coordination or discussion or negotiation of low-profile labor issues.

By contrast, managers at the B-1 plant in Brazil had relatively close internal and outward business links, particularly insofar as labor issues were concerned. Throughout the 1970s and 1980s, informants on both sides told me that relations between the human resource and production divisions were arms' length, with a strict functional separation of tasks similar to that at M-1.[43] However, ties had become markedly closer in the late 1980s in the wake of a 1986 crisis in which the latter—and top officials in the Brazilian subsidiary—had pressured successfully for the disbanding of the works council reluctantly accepted by management under union pressure only five years earlier. Human resource officials worked hard in convincing their production colleagues to accept and cooperate with the re-establishment of the commission, which took place in early 1988. These efforts included industrial relations training courses for line supervisors and production managers. Success in neutralizing 'old guard' resistance from managers steeped in the ways of what one high-level human resources official (a former line worker) called the 'days of the whip' was aided by fortuitous opportunities for personnel changes that arose in the late 1980s and early 1990s due to a cost-driven management downsizing campaign. Also, these changes coincided with the emergence of a new balance in the relationship with the home office on human

[41] Douglas C. Bennett and Kenneth E. Sharpe, *Transnational Corporations Versus the State* (Princeton: Princeton University Press, 1985); Samuels (1990); Laura del Alizal, 'Las reglas de origen en el TLC', in Gustavo Emmerich (ed.), *El Tratado de Libre Comercio: Texto y Contexto* (Mexico, DF: UAM-Iztapalapa), 73–83.

[42] Samuels (1990), ch.7.

[43] Interviews were conducted with twenty human resources, engineering, and production managers at the plant and corporate levels in 1990 and 1992.

Network Ties in Brazil and Mexico

resource mangement, in which the tendencies for considerable centralized control manifest in the early 1980s gave way to improved coordination and more operational autonomy for the branch office by the end of the decade.[44] The upshot of this series of interlocking changes was increased coordination and cooperation in the management of the labor force between human resource and production managers at B-1. This was manifested in a much greater everyday shopfloor presence of human resource officials and their more extensive involvement in trouble-shooting issues that were previously the exclusive or primary domain of foremen and other production managers (transfers, promotions, dismissals, discipline).

Plant B-1 management also had close outward links on labor and other issues, which in large part were the product of automakers' efforts to reform corporatist institutions of business regulation affecting sectoral interests. Brazil's encompassing corporatism includes the compulsory organization of business into its own elaborate series of local *sindicatos*, state industrial federations, and peak industrial confederations paralleling those for workers. In terms of collective bargaining, B-1 and other automakers with plants in São Bernardo would jointly negotiate, through the state industrial federation FIESP, a contract renewal on an annual basis with all firms in the very heterogeneous metalworking branch. In the first half of the 1980s, the São Bernardo union was able to parlay its ties with other CUT-affiliated metalworkers' unions in the state's interior (and employer's ties to each other) into a process of virtually statewide collective bargaining in the metalworking industries. By the second half of the decade, however, there was an increasing tendency for these unions to cut separate, more lucrative deals with auto companies on both wages, working hours, and other issues, sometimes as a group through their own compulsory sectoral organization and sometimes on a firm by firm basis. Not only could automakers afford better terms, but they found it increasingly difficult and cumbersome to work with the other, often smaller firms in the metalworking industries (and vice versa).[45] Moreover, going all the way back to the emergence of the new unionism in the late 1970s, the SINFAVEA's parallel voluntary association (with shared leadership and infrastructure), known as ANFAVEA, had already become an important forum for the inter-firm discussion of industrial relations strategies[46]—a role the AMIA in Mexico had never taken on.

Efforts by automakers such as B-1 to carve out increased autonomy from the FIESP state industrial federation on collective bargaining issues went hand in hand with moves to turn their own two-headed sectoral organization,

---

[44] Samuels (1990).

[45] According to B-1 national human resource managers, the automakers increasingly resented the inordinate voice that the corporatist structures of the FIESP and its metalworking 'Group Five' gave to smaller firms. This, in turn, stemmed from the fact that all employer *sindicatos* are based on the principle of 'one firm, one vote' regardless of size.

[46] Samuels (1990).

ANFAVEA/SINFAVEA, into a more effective organ for the promotion of common interests. This meant supplementing the powerful individual voice and resources wielded by these huge firms (some of the country's largest) with an organization that could provide not only an institutionalized collective automakers' voice, and coordinating forum, on policy issues; it also meant enhancement of service provision on a wide gamut of marketing, information, and regulatory matters. These developments in business representation within the auto industry were part of a more general process of ferment and challenge to existing top-down authority within Brazil's corporatist business structures during this period.[47]

In sum, increasingly close, cooperative ties bound together the most relevant internal bureaucracies for employment relations issues within factory, subsidiary, and home office of B-1, as well as linking them with their counterparts in most other TNCs operating in Brazil and with the sectoral organizations. These contrasted with the distant ties, based on unmediated competition or outright conflict, that prevailed both within the firm and between it and its peers in the M-1 case.

Labor-Management Ties

The third and final contrast in social ties across the two factories during the periods leading up to transitions in their labor systems concerns bilateral labor-management connections—distant at M-1, increasingly close at B-1. Over the course of the 1980s and on into the beginning of the next decade, uneven and incipient efforts at workplace restructuring proceeded in remarkably similar fashion across the two facilities. For a time—up through 1987 or 1988, say—social ties were remarkably similar in their arms' length, adversarial character, but at that juncture a dynamic of formation of closer ties over workplace reorganization emerged at B-1 while the same pattern continued at M-1.

In a model of productive and work organization still characterized by Taylorist mass production, restructuring of work and human resources during this period was 'fine-tuned' at both plants through worker involvement in quality control; limited, selective technological innovations; the initiation of subcontracting of some ancillary services and maintenance work and outsourcing of some parts and components; heavy reliance on overtime work during peak periods and on temporary shutdowns during slack periods (and at M-1 the use of temporary workers as yet another buffer); and somewhat greater emphasis on lateral labor mobility within the plant and on multitasking of workers. The impact on plant performance in terms of cost and quality was relatively limited, however, as the competitive gap separating these

---

[47] Leigh Payne, *Brazilian Industrials and Democratic Change* (Baltimore: The Johns Hopkins University Press, 1994); and Kingstone (1999).

two Latin American facilities from the quickly rising standards in their prime target export markets in late-industrializing countries expanded rather than narrowed. In the case of M-1, the gap between it and the new northern Mexican brownfields set up by its competitors as export platforms for the US market also widened noticeably. Union and worker resistance to these uni-lateral initial reforms, however comparatively tepid, and the deterrent effect this resistance had in discouraging more ambitious proposals, played at least a contributing role in competitive difficulties.

In the late 1980s and beginning of the 1990s, a deep-seated mutual mistrust and adversarial relationship persisted and even deepened at M-1, with ties remaining distant. Meanwhile, at B-1 a new climate of mutual respect and incipient cooperation—which might be called, following Streeck,[48] 'conflict-ual cooperation'—emerged on some important workplace issues. Let me examine M-1 first. At that Mexican factory, disputes over workplace restruc-turing, cost of living raises, and job security were aggravated by the intra-labor conflicts mentioned in the previous section as well as by managers' efforts to both foment and capitalize on these disputes. Both in 1988 and, as will be related below, in 1992 management tried to cut secret deals with union presidents involving labor concessions on highly controversial issues of out-sourcing and teamwork. Executives defended their actions—as the former industrial relations director and current member of the executive council put it to me—that 'with so much turnover and turmoil in the union, we never knew who we were dealing with'.[49]

At B-1, in contrast, representatives from both sides indicated to me in 1990 and 1992 that there was emerging mutual respect and open communication, even amidst conflict. The national human resources manager argued '[t]here is now a very frank dialogue, with mutual respect and understanding.'[50] The plant's human resources director suggested there was 'greater maturity, on both sides, a comprehension on the part of plant management concerning the necessity of movements [strikes]', as well as 'less pressure from pickets and other things [unionists] used to do'.[51] For his part, one of the works coun-cilors at B-1 expressed a widespread view among unionist informants—as well as on the part of rank-and-file—that there was a noticeable shift in the tenor of relations with management. Referring to issues like changes in work layout, scheduling, individual discipline and dismissals, and the like, he indi-cated 'now the company doesn't do anything without consulting us'.[52]

Emerging new ties were particularly evident in labor-management encoun-ters over workplace restructuring. At M-1 there were practically no union-management contacts regarding quality circles (regularized, off-line meetings

[48] Streeck, 'Training and the New Industrial Relations', 225–69, and Wolfgang Streeck, 'Lean Production in the German Automobile Industry: A Test Case for Convergence Theory', in Suzanne Berger and Ronald Dore (eds), *National Diversity and Global Capitalism* (Ithaca: Cornell University Press, 1996), 138–70.
[49] Personal interview, 18 Aug. 1996.   [50] Personal interview, 15 Aug. 1990.
[51] Personal interview, 16 March 1992.   [52] Personal interview, 23 Oct. 1992.

on production improvements, involving managers and workers) and other efforts to encourage worker 'commitment' to improvements in production. At B-1, by contrast, special meetings were called to inform unionists of the purposes behind new 'problem-solving', 'organizational integration', and other participation programs. On an *ad hoc* and irregular basis, unionists began to attend some of the meetings, although they continued to voice their position that these efforts would only work if they linked improvements in quality to improvements in working conditions. By contrast, in the early to mid 1980s quality circles and an employee involvement initiative had been implemented unilaterally and aggressively, with a thinly viewed intention to undercut the base of the newly created works council. Unionists had angrily boycotted and denounced these programs during this period, contributing to their weak results.

The three network domains had interlocking and interactive effects at both factories. Like distant labor ties at M-1, distant business ties also served to reinforce an inward-oriented, ritualized pattern of low-trust, adversarial labor-management relations. In contrast, close business ties together with close labor ties at B-1 fed the formation of closer labor-management bonds, providing important 'external' support, resources, pressures, and information. At the same time, the embedding of close labor-management ties in tight, outwardly ramifying but separate networks served to counteract—particularly for structurally weaker unions in danger of falling into patterns of what Frenkel calls 'cooperative dependence'[53]—the potential that close dyadic ties have for ossification, 'lock-in', and 'in-breeding' in relational and communicative patterns.[54]

Plant M-1: Flexibility through Unilateral Restructuring

The socially embedded networks that underlay labor-management interactions at M-1 perpetuated and exacerbated an arms-length, adversarial relational dynamic as the subsidiary began to respond to competitive and home-office pressures for productive and work reorganization with increasingly serious initiatives, beginning around 1988. The period lasting till mid-1992 was marked by persistent impasse over workplace reform and, from management's relationally colored perspective, a progressive winnowing of options for the improvement of quality and labor productivity and cost containment. In the early months of 1992, a combination of M-1's secret efforts

---

[53] Stephen Frenkel, 'Patterns of Workplace Relations in the Global Corporation: Toward Convergence?', in Jacques Bélanger *et al.* (eds), *Workplace Industrial Relations and the Global Challenge* (Ithaca: ILR Press, 1994), 240–74.

[54] Martin Garguilo and Mario Benassi, 'The Dark Side of Social Capital', memo (1998); Brian Uzzi, 'Social Structure and Competition in Interfirm Networks: The Paradox of Embeddedness', *Administrative Science Quarterly*, 42 (1997), 35–67; and Mark Granovetter, 'The Strength of Weak Ties', *American Journal of Sociology*, 91 (1973), 481–510.

to cut a deal with the union leadership behind its constituents' back and divisive internal union disputes—fueled in large part by such efforts—presented an increasingly aggressive and impatient firm with an opportunity decisively to break the impasse. The firm seized the opportunity, locking out striking workers and seeking and—after some delay—receiving backing from the authoritarian state's federal labor tribunals. This external support enabled the firm to proceed with the technically illegal lock-out; have the collective contract annulled by the labor tribunal; reinstall a union leadership that had just been voted out of office in a recall; reformulate union statutes to weaken worker voice; and—most importantly—implement unilaterally a highly flexible, management-dominated system of work organization and human resources.

Established network structures decisively shaped the complex sequence of events leading to the abrupt imposition of unilateral flexibility in the middle months of 1992. Given unionists' ability to block reform through negotiations and the extensive nature of contractual protections, management sought their formal acquiescence in its reform initiatives in areas such as expanding outsourcing and subcontracting and implementing teamwork. Paradoxically, internal fault lines on the unionist side encouraged managers to seek private deals for concessions with union secretaries-general on several occasions in this period, at the same time that they complicated the ability of these leaders to secure worker acceptance of managerial reforms. Such a backlash occurred in 1988 when the secretary-general was ousted in a recall vote for making secret concessions on subcontracting. After this episode, the new leadership showed a stiffened resolve, fighting hard to win back, in 1989, some of the subcontracting concessions its predecessors had made. For their part, shop stewards and rank-and-file heightened further their usual vigilance toward union leaders and characteristic wariness of company plans. The relational setting was thus marked by continued impasse between 1988 and 1991, both at the level of everyday shopfloor relations and collective bargaining.

As the system of sparse, distant ties in which production politics at plant M-1 was embedded prevented a transition to labor flexibility through conciliation and kept genuine bilateral negotiation outside the actors' repertoire of interaction, bottlenecks in productivity and quality mounted. Meanwhile, the confluence of domestic and international market pressures—and the imminent production launch of a new export model series with greater quality demands—led management to view work reorganization as an urgent priority. In this context, the union election which brought to power new leaders at the beginning of 1992 provided an opportunity for M-1 to retake the initiative. As in 1988, no fewer than seventeen rival slates had competed, but this time none achieved the requisite 30% plurality. In the run-off between the two top vote-getting slates, the winning slate, which had finished second in the first round, triumphed by the narrowest of margins—50.6% versus 49.4%.

This left the new leadership with an even weaker base of support than its predecessors faced upon taking office.

The contract renewal talks a few months hence resulted, after an impasse and a one-day walkout, in no major contractual changes in work rules and a modest pay increase. However, the union's new executive committee negotiated a secret accord (*convênio*) calling for the gradual, experimental implementation of a new labor system based on work teams and performance-based pay and promotions. Reacting to the secret form, sketchy substance, and relational history regarding such secretive deal-making outside established channels, discontented rank-and-file and shop stewards staged a walkout and called a factory-wide general assembly when they learned of the deal. At the assembly, workers voted to oust the secretary-general and name an interim replacement, with about 55% of the unionized workers at the plant signing a petition disavowing the agreement and calling on labor authorities to recognize the new interim leadership until new elections could be held.

Four days into the walkout, the company seized the initiative, petitioning the state-dominated federal labor tribunal to dissolve the union and contract, locking out the workers, and ceasing negotiations. Three weeks later, with the federal government caught in political crossfire but cognizant of the company's open threats to shut down all operations in Mexico and sympathetic to its plan to reorganize the labor system to increase productivity, the tribunal granted the company's petition. With the firm's support, the deposed secretary general was restored to office and achieved official recognition—but only on condition that he ratify a brand new contract and accept new union statutes drafted by the company. Under the new unilaterally dictated rules of the game at M-1, work teams, pay for knowledge, and productivity-based promotions were enshrined, with no union voice in their implementation; the shop steward system was severely weakened (stewards' numbers cut from 200 to 14 and powers narrowly circumscribed and subordinated to the union leadership); and many of the elaborate contractual restrictions on managerial use of the labor force in terms of hiring, firing, transfers, promotions, and so on were eliminated. In addition, the factory's entire labor force having been legally left without work, the company embarked upon a rehiring and retraining process in which some 1,500 older, inefficient, or 'trouble-making' workers were not retained, thus effecting a substantial downsizing. All those rehired did so under the new contract terms. In addition, through statutory reforms, such as consecutive re-election eligibility and a requirement of ten years' plant experience for holding office, the firm sought to strengthen the reliability and malleability of the union executive and to increase its strength while diluting that of rank-and-file and shop stewards.

Elsewhere I discuss these issues in much greater detail.[55] Here, it must suffice to list briefly several of the negative consequences that unilateral flexibility

---

[55] Scott Martin, 'Working in the Global Factory: The Social Embedding of Flexibility', Unpublished PhD dissertation (Department of Political Science, Columbia University, 2000).

brought for workers. On the job autonomy was restricted through a management-controlled variant of teamwork in which team structures were largely management appendages and little discretion was accorded teams over crucial issues like leader selection, job rotation, training, scheduling, and work methods. Accumulated seniority rights were lost by re-hired workers. There was also considerable involuntary workforce reduction, with the already downsized workforce of 12,100 in December 1992 at the restructured, reopened plant cut down to 8,500 by 1996, thanks to a mixture of subcontracting, outsourcing, productivity-induced 'redundancies,' and market volatility. While collective voice was not silenced altogether (as suggested by an August 2000 strike over wages, the plant's first worker stoppage since the late 1980s), the firm cultivated worker commitment and loyalty—keys to labor flexibility in such sophisticated activities as automobile assembly—through primarily individualistic incentives and symbols while unionists were reduced to a subordinate role in the regulation of the employment relationship.[56]

Plant B-1: Flexibility through Negotiated Work Reorganization

Let me turn to how social networks shaped the transition to labor flexibility at B-1 in Brazil. Once management and labor actors felt powerful environmental pressures for improved quality and productivity through greater labor flexibility, the social fabric of increasingly close ties at factory B-1 in São Bernardo pushed them toward a negotiated response. Through a series of company-level agreements reached in 1994 and 1995 they adopted the following major labor systems innovations—a new wage and job classification structure; the joint evaluation and implementation of outsourcing projects; a flexible and reduced work week; and a profit-sharing plan based on productivity, quality, and attendance indicators.[57] There were also other numerous less formal improvements in everyday, informal bilateral cooperation regarding such issues as internal mobility of workers, plant layout and introduction of new technologies, and quality control and improvement. The agreements, while specific to B-1 in terms of actors and substance, resulted from a sort of

[56] Ibid.; and Alejandro Covarrubias, 'Actitudes obreras y compromiso organizacional en la industria automotriz mexicana: Transformaciones bajo sistemas de produccion flexibles', Paper presented at the conference, 'Globalização, Reestruturação Produtiva e Transformação nas Relações Capital–Trabalho no Complexo Automobílistico', Centro Brasileiro de Análise e Planejamento (São Paulo, August 1996), 26–8.

[57] Glauco Arbix, 'Trabalho: Dois Modelos de Flexibilização', *Lua Nova*, 37 (1996*b*), 171–90; Glauco Arbix and Iram Jácome Rodrigues, 'The Transformation of Industrial Relations in the Brazilian Automotive Industry', in John P. Tuman and John T. Morris (eds), *Transforming the Latin American Automobile Industry* (Armonk: M. E. Sharpe, 1998*b*), 77–94; DIESSE (Departamento Intersindical de Estatistica e Estudos Socio-Economicos); 'A Reestruturação Negociada na Industria Automobilística Brasileira', *Boletim DIEESE 168* (March 1995), 18–20; and Márcia de Paula Leite, Roque da Silva, Luis Paulo Bresciani, and Jefferson José da Conceição, 'Reestruturação Produtiva e Relações Industriais: Tendências do Setor Automotivo Brasileiro', *Revista Latinoamericana de Estudios del Trabajo*, 2: 4 (1996), 79–110.

informal, multilevel 'pattern bargaining' in which the four major auto and truck firms having flagship Brazilian factories in São Bernardo—working in tandem and coordinated in part by the ANFAVEA—successively reached broadly similar company- or plant-specific specific agreements on these same four areas between 1994 and 1996. While the direct interlocutors were union officials and the respective factory commissioners, they received substantial technical assistance and support from not only the aforementioned in-house and non-governmental organization (NGO) advisors but also the CUT's National Metalworkers' Confederation and state-level Metalworkers Federation of São Paulo. In the case of working hours there was a framework agreement between the São Bernardo union and automakers' association setting out the principle of linking hours reduction to flexibility without loss in hourly pay, which served as the basis for specific company accords.

These accords, a landmark for the Brazilian context, combined elements of a contingent response to new challenges and opportunities and of the coming to fruition of ongoing learning processes of both an individual and joint nature. These responses and learning processes were embedded in and driven by existing network structures that mediated between changing environmental pressures from domestic liberalization and heightened global integration of Brazil's auto industry, on the one hand, and the strategies and actions of the key actors, on the other. Three particular elements of the relational setting drove the dynamic of conflictual cooperation: internal consensus built around more cooperative approaches to employment relations on both sides; growing but still vigilant and contingent mutual trust;[58] and the network-embedded diffusion from the respective labor and management camps of pressures, concrete proposals, and support for exploration of innovative negotiated solutions to structural problems. Conflict, fed by each side's pursuit of its distinct interests regarding productive restructuring, was still crucial as a motor for negotiation of ever broader and more profound issues. For instance, immediate disputes, including walkouts and protests, about work intensification and excessive overtime—as well as a longer-term debate about work hours flexibility and length of the working week—fed into the working hours agreement of 1995. On the union side, proposals for reducing work hours but allowing for more flexibility were shaped by ties with European unions, especially the German metalworkers who had pursued a similar approach, as well as with staff and ex officio non-governmental advisors familiar with these international experiences, some of whom had taken study trips to Europe. On the other hand, the more arms' length or competitive ties that they had with other actors in the labor realm shaped the pursuit and development of a compelling practical basis in productive restructuring for a type of middle way between counter-productive radical rejectionism and con-

---

[58] This is what Sabel calls 'studied trust'. See Charles F. Sabel, 'Studied Trust: Building New Forms of Cooperation in a Volatile Economy', in Richard Swedberg (ed.), *Explorations in Economic Sociology*. (New York: Russell Sage, 1993*b*), 104–44.

servative conciliation. Moreover, generation of internal consensus necessary
for each side to support and successfully to implement to agreements breaking with historic practices was made possible by close cooperative ties among
unionists, between them and workers, and within B-1.

The labor-management agreements to a large extent reconciled B-1's objectives of creating a more flexible and thus productive and high-quality system
of work organization with worker and union goals of strengthening collective
input into the process, improving working conditions, and improving remuneration and job security. For example, management achieved fewer, broader
job classifications (down from ten to five grades, or steps), consonant with
growing multitasking as well as more merit-based and thus less seniority-
driven promotions; for their part, workers received more opportunities for
upward wage mobility (up from five to eight wage levels per grade) and
greater upward harmonization of occupational wages rates across factories
and firms. Moreover, the employer's long-time demand for 'flextime' in
accordance with variations in production demand was gained but in exchange
for a net reduction in average weekly hours (from 44 to 42), a narrow band of
variation in weekly hours (between 38 and 44), and the suspension of a
planned round of lay-offs now rendered unnecessary. For its part, the outsourcing accord put this contentious issue on a 'technical' plane where the
firm could now present its brief for farming out particular inputs or services
based on cost and productivity considerations; unionists were provided a
hearing on the wisdom of these initiatives and allowed to present possible
alternatives; and displaced workers were guaranteed that—agreement or
not—they would be redeployed and, if necessary, retrained for their new
posts. The profit-sharing accord at B-1, reached under national legislation
legalizing but not mandating such instruments, was among the significant
minority of those reached in Brazilian industry with two features: first, genuine bilateral negotiation and joint implementation and, second, concrete
numerical targets of collective worker performance as the threshold for the
granting of large annual bonuses, that is, truly performance-oriented pay.
Besides these formal agreements, another mutual gain came in the form of a
greater emphasis on training of workers. Involuntary job loss was also limited
in the short to medium term, thanks to the flextime band, occasional generous voluntary buy-out programs, and natural attrition. To be sure, this
certainly was not a panacea of worker empowerment and workplace democracy,[59] and in a technologically dynamic global industry such as autos and
with increasingly fierce competition in a market such as Brazil's liberalizing

---

[59] A more definitive judgment based on the longer term will have to focus on more complex
issues such as the following: how successful labor flexibility is in improving competitive fortunes;
the degree to which worker representatives maintain an independent perspective in shaping
restructuring; the implications of conflictual cooperation in productive restructuring for larger
firm investment strategies affecting the plant; and the impact on automotive workers in supplier
industries of sourcing decisions shaped by unionists.

economy, workers and unions are forced to parry management thrusts in an often defensive fashion. Yet, negotiated reorganization at B-1 during this period left workers better off materially, in working conditions, and in terms of participation than did unilateral restructuring at M-1—and also better than similarly management-dominated (if less coercive) reorganizations which, as I document elsewhere (Martin 2000), occurred at four other Brazilian brownfields and whose existence testifies to the absence of a uniform national auto pattern of plant restructuring.

Assessing Alternative Explanations

Two influential explanatory frameworks—based on national patterns of labor regulation and state-labor relations and on company culture and strategy, respectively—are unpersuasive or incomplete in accounting for the contrasting patterns of transition to labor flexibility across the two plants. Some of the valid causal insights they do generate are best accommodated within a social network perspective.

Let us turn first to the very influential national systems perspective, implicitly or explicitly central to most of the studies in this volume. Turning first to Mexico, however much the superior coercive, but legally sanctioned, resources of the Mexican state help account for the denouement of the crisis, they do not help us understand its outbreak.[60] Nor do they explain why the firm took the unusual and risky measure—in the context of the NAFTA debate and the firm's international stature—of staking its plant's fortunes on an appeal for state intervention. One has to examine the immediate relational setting of labor-management interactions, which was largely inward-oriented and had been consciously insulated by both sides for years from the perceived politicization and clientelism of the larger Mexican corporatist labor order, in order to explain the nature and timing of the crisis. Where the state was not called upon to mediate or resolve bilateral conflicts involving an independent union and work reorganization issues, such as at another central Mexican brownfield owned by another TNC only a few hours away, the record demonstrates that it did not intervene in any heavy-handed fashion during this same period. The authoritarian state in Mexico was able to keep its progressive veneer intact for decades precisely through being extremely selective and judicious in the application of overtly authoritarian means—particularly against high-profile organizations and movements—using them only as a last resort when efforts at containment, conciliation, and mediation failed or overt challenges to the political order were made. Moreover, one must also consider that two important aspects of the relational context—the plant and union's chronic internal divisions and external isolation—both lowered the political

[60] Yolanda Montiel and Ludger Pries, 'Organización del trabajo y relaciones laborales: El reto de la flexibilidad (Avances de investigación)', Working paper (El Colegio de Puebla, Mexico, 1992).

costs of external intervention and help to explain a perplexing puzzle, namely, why, unlike say, coercive military government interventions against a united São Bernardo union in 1980 and 1983 that failed to break it, the Mexican state's heavy hand did not meet with any measurable grassroots resistance from M-1 workers or broader anti-repressive alliance around their dissident leaders.

Turning to a cross-sectoral perspective, de la Garza and Bouzas find that unilateral restructuring was the predominant but not exclusive tendency across established, higher-end firms and industries in Mexico during the first half of the 1990s.[61] In terms of this study, this suggests the considerably less than determinative impact of national labor relations institutions on firm and workplace-level processes of productive restructuring.

Shifting to Brazil, one must temper any tendency to extrapolate workplace outcomes from its comparatively—and only marginally—less confining labor relations environment or the greater strength and independence of its unions. National social pacts had failed roundly on repeated attempts, and tripartite industrial policy pacts at the sectoral level lasted only a few years in the auto-mobile industry (1992–4) and failed to get off the ground in most other sectors.[62] This and economic crisis often left unions, including many CUT-affiliated ones, in an uphill struggle against powerful firms pursuing unilateral restructuring. The state's 1994 withdrawal from tripartism in autos left the actors to their own devices, and in four brownfields where ties, as at M-1 in Mexico, had been and remained weak, similar scenarios of unilateral work reorganization unfolded within the very same national and sectoral regula-tory framework as the negotiated experiments at B-1 and seven other plants.[63] Meanwhile, an inhospitable mixture of enduring corporatist institu-tions combined with neoliberal proposals for labor market flexibility along with macroeconomic and other reforms had emerged by the mid 1990s, and national unionization rates were falling again after the gains of the 1980s. Thus, negotiated restructuring at B-1, as well as at several other auto plants and some firms in other sectors, is best understood as occurring *despite*, not because, of the larger institutions and trends in national labor relations and labor politics.

A second common line of explanation—firm culture, and strategy—also fails to hold up to comparative scrutiny. While firms and subsidiaries may have distinctive approaches to human resource management, they are also known for being pragmatic in adapting to local conditions.[64] I would argue that this adaptiveness is in large measure the result of being embedded, and thus constrained, by local relational settings in both internal and external

---

[61] de la Garza and Bouzas, 'La flexibilidad del trabajo en México'.

[62] Scott B. Martin,'Beyond Corporatism: New Patterns of Representation in the Brazilian Auto Industry', in Douglas C. Chalmers *et al.* (eds), *The New Politics of Inequality in Latin America* (Oxford: Oxford University Press, 1997), 45–71; and Glauco Arbix, *Uma Aposta no Futuro* (São Paulo: Scritta, 1996*a*).

[63] Martin (2000). [64] Samuels (1990).

terms. Management at the Mexican subsidiary of M-1 did not even give serious consideration to doing what its home office had been doing during the 1980s or its Brazilian subsidiary, like B-1, began to do at two plants starting around the same time as B-1—that is, engage workers and their representatives in a serious and wide-ranging dialogue and negotiation over the terms of flexible workplace reform.[65] Meanwhile, negotiated restructuring at B-1 and the firm's other Brazilian assembly plant, as well as in many of its home country factories, coexisted within the same TNC with unilateral restructuring patterns at the firm's central Mexican brownfield and its newer northern Mexican 'greenfield' site. Moreover, yet another TNC in Brazil even had plants that fell on other side of the unilateral/negotiated dichotomy.[66] Therefore, patterns of similarities and differences across and within TNCs and their affiliates in restructuring patterns must be seen in terms of the distinct relational settings in which these corporate actors are situated; these structures mediate shifts or continuities in company strategy, both shaping them in the first place and refracting them in implementation.

Conclusion

Several broader implications emerge from this cross-national, plant-level comparative study of economic transformation deriving from globalization, flexible production, and economic change. The first concerns the broader relevance of the distinction between unilateral and negotiated work reorganization. The finding that restructuring plants may be analytically situated on either side of this dichotomy emerges not just from this and my broader trinational study, but also from comparative cross-national and intra-national plant-level studies of auto industry restructuring in advanced countries by other authors.[67] This leads to a second implication, concerning the need to elevate the importance of the workplace within the analytical instruments and levels of analysis in comparative labor studies. Even outside the leading-edge core economies, new ways of organizing production and work are radically reshaping patterns of work and production throughout the world economy.

---

[65] Turner, *Democracy at Work*; Martin, 'Social Networks and Workplace Citizenship in Brazil's New Democracy'; and Adalberto Moreira Cardoso, 'Globalização e Relações Industriais na Indústria Automobilístico Brasileiro: Um Estudo de Caso', *Avances de Investigacíon. Bremen, Germany and São Paulo: Transformación Económica y Trabajo en América Latina: Proyecto Comparativo Internacional*, 2 (Sept. 1995).

[66] Scott Martin, 'Social Networks and Workplace Citizenship in Brazil's New Democracy'. Unpublished MS (1998).

[67] See, for example, Locke, *Remaking the Italian Economy*; Huberto Juárez Nuñez and Steve Babson (eds), *Enfrentando el Cambio: Obreros del Automóvil y Producción Esbelta en América del Norte* [Confronting Change: Auto Labor and Lean Production in North America] (Puebla, Mexico/Detroit: Universidad Autónoma de Puebla/Wayne State University, Labor Studies Center, 1998), 207–22; Thomas A. Kochan, Russell D. Lansbury, and John Paul Macduffie (eds), *After Lean Production: Evolving Employment Practices in the World Auto Industry* (Ithaca: ILR Press, 1997); and Turner, *Democracy at Work*.

This is particularly true as advanced manufacturing is spread to lower-cost locations in many, particularly larger, late-industrializing and post-socialist economies that offer attractive domestic markets and the combination of low costs with conditions for high-quality, world competitive production. Under certain conditions, I suggest, genuinely democratic, outwardly connected, learning unions are in a position to embrace and shape work reorganization so that it may entail substantial benefits for workers and unions, even as globalization—as it does in the developed world—shifts the general structural economic and political parameters strongly against labor and towards capital. Further, those institutional legacies may have paradoxical consequences in the radically different issue space of flexible production, which privileges network coordination over hierarchy, including among unions; a heavy workplace presence for unions combined with empowering outward links; and a capacity to create new subnational institutions or reinvent and resituate old national institutions and sectoral institutions rooted in national regulation.[68] To the extent that labor scholars are concerned about the fate of workers in such societies, we must follow the comparative literature on the advanced countries of the past decade or so in taking seriously the place of work and employment relations centered on it—at least insofar as we are studying formal-sector workers and higher-end industries, important qualifiers to be sure.

In turn, rediscovering the workplace, or discovering it for the first time, necessarily means posing as a *problématique* the causal relationship in productive restructuring between the workplace, the firm, and local inter-firm networks—subnational categories, in short—and the traditional national-level institutions and actors that have been our privileged site for studying labor politics. Shifting our eyes to the point of production may often reveal a disjuncture between national labor politics and micro and meso developments, and sometimes considerable empirical variation in workplace restructuring trends across firm, sectoral, and regional boundaries *within*, not just across, nation-states—variation that is invisible to the analyst who only focuses on national labor politics.

---

[68] This point builds on the reflections of Sabel (1993*a*, *b*) and Kern and Sabel (1992) while not embracing their unqualified pessimism about the capacity for the reinvention of older, mass production-era institutions. See Charles F. Sabel, 'Can the End of Social Democratic Trade Unions be the Beginning of a New Kind of Social Democratic Politics?', in Stephen R. Sleigh (ed.), *Economic Restructuring and Emerging Patterns of Industrial Relations* (Kalamazoo, MI: Upjohn Institute for Employment Research, 1993*a*), 137–65; Sabel, 'Studied Trust: Building New Forms of Cooperation in a Volatile Economy'; and Horst Kern and Charles Sabel, 'Trade Unions and Decentralized Production: A Sketch of Strategic Problems in the German Labour Movement', in Marino Regini (ed.), *The Future of Labour Movements* (London: Sage, 1992), 217–49. The B-1 case suggests, for instance, that corporatist institutions of business, labor, and labor relations were democratized and reformulated as part of network-like structures that had beneficial consequences for promoting economic, labor-friendly change, at the same time that the absence of a constraining legacy of job control-style Fordist institutions in the workplace also proved helpful.

This observation about levels of analysis leads me to a comment on the 'historical institutionalist' perspective that is of central concern to this volume. Cast in institutional terms, this study argues for a broader, more 'sociological' concept of regularized, persistent patterns of behavior that gives equal attention to formal-legal rules and informal or tacit norms, repertoires, and customs.[69] Social network encounters cross-cut the two types—or better yet, dimensions—of institutionalized behavior, typically exhibiting or embodying elements of both. Labor institutions should also—as Locke argues[70]—be thought of as potentially varying intra-nationally or subnationally. The particular network structures and patterned behaviors of a factory or group of factories or sector clearly instantiate to a greater or less extent elements of the national regulatory framework as it existed at some point of time. Yet those less aggregated, network-based structures and behaviors will tend, as institutions in the broad sense, to persist over time and take on a life of their own, even if the national framework shifts, as was true of M-1 in Mexico—or they may restructure themselves as only a weak, distant, and imperfect echo of those aggregate-level changes, as was true of B-1 in Brazil. In other words, we should bear in mind exactly what it is that is institutionalized in the first place—the actual patterns of interaction and behavior themselves. Then we should inquire as to what institution-creating or institution-disrupting forces—national laws, discretionary government interventions, socio-economic environments, global firm strategies, and immediate network structures, among them—are at work in any given, taking the place of work and firm as our analytical starting point.

As we shift our attention to study how the meta-trends of globalization, democracies, and markets are reshaping workers' lives, we all too readily have continued to ignore the fast-changing world of work and what might be called more broadly 'economic society'. We have treated it as an unimportant or epiphenomenal site not relevant to 'who gets what and how' in the emerging new global order. Old analytical priorities and conceptual habits die hard. Yet we cannot—if we ever really could—understand the unfolding story of worker voice, empowerment, and inclusion or exclusion within a restructuring global capitalism if we do not examine the most direct and immediate ways and arenas in which it affects them. Far from meaning homogenization and convergence as some would have it, globalization and the flexible, decentralizing trends in economic organization that accompany it, are ushering in considerable diversity in on-the-ground practice. Particularly if our goal is to formulate theories that help orient practice, it is thus time that we began expanding our conceptual and analytical toolkit so as to appreciate and explain this diversity. If our goal is to capture and explain these normatively and analytical consequential variations in worker roles in fundamental, perhaps epochal workplace reorganization, a strategy of 'scaling up' from sub-

[69] DiMaggio and Powell (eds), 1991.   [70] Locke (1992, 1995).

national actors and processes to examine their contingent and often very particular forms of articulation with national actors and processes is much more promising than the more conventional one—born of a different world-historical moment—of 'scaling down' from national institutions and processes to 'local outcomes'.

5

Globalization, Social Partnership, and Industrial Relations in Ireland

Eileen M. Doherty, Case Western Reserve University

This chapter examines the evolution of Irish trade unions, as well as the impact of globalization on industrial relations in Ireland. It argues two points. First, Irish trade unions developed in a particular historical context— that of economic and political dependency on Great Britain. Consequently, as Ireland's system of industrial relations evolved, it was both influenced by and continually reacted to the influence of Great Britain. In policy terms, trade unions historically had to balance their wage and other objectives against the broader goal of Irish independence. In organizational terms, Irish trade unions existed (and continue to coexist) side by side with British counterparts. Even after the birth of the Irish Republic in 1921–2, British trade unions continued to organize in Ireland; moreover, unions organized Ireland-wide rather than simply in the twenty-six counties of the Republic. Second, the chapter argues that three stages of globalization—the decision to embrace an open economic policy in the 1950s, Ireland's 1973 entry into the EEC, and the deepening of European integration in the 1980s and 1990s—have generated continuous pressures on Ireland to embrace new strategies to accommodate the pressures of market forces. At the domestic level, this has entailed a commitment to corporatist social partnership bargaining, whereas at the regional level it has entailed a commitment to the deepening of common European social policy.

Irish industrial relations can be characterized as a system of local fragmentation and national centralization. Locally, multiple unions coexist and compete for members, adversarial collective bargaining has been the norm, and industrial unrest has been a persistent element of the economic sphere. Nationally, trade unions have traditionally clustered into large umbrella organizations, with the Irish Congress of Trade Unions (ICTU), the central umbrella organization for labor, embodying the overwhelming majority of Irish unions in the Republic and in Northern Ireland. The counterpart employer's organization is the Irish Business and Employers Confederation (IBEC). Beginning in 1962, and particularly since the 1970s, most pay agreements for the national workforce have been made through centralized tripartite negotiations, or have followed a norm established by such negotiations.

After a hiatus from centralized bargaining from 1982 to 1987, a renewed focus on social partnership and consensus policymaking emerged in Ireland. The national agreements that have been concluded since 1987 are modeled on previous national understandings, but with modifications to reflect and respond to changing competitive challenges. Whereas past agreements focused primarily on traditional issues such as wages, new national agreements have included other 'competitiveness' issues as macroeconomic policy, tax policy, worker training, and small business development. Moreover, while the traditional 'social partners'—government, business and labor—continue to be the primary players in national agreements, more recently the government has experimented with bringing new actors to the bargaining table. Most significant is the inclusion of Irish National Organization of the Unemployed (INOU), a move which explicitly embraces the issues of long-term unemployment and social exclusion as necessary elements of future national agreements.

At the European level, the Irish response to globalization has been to promote the development of a strong common social policy. Unlike Great Britain, who rejected the inclusion of a social chapter to the Maastricht Treaty, Dublin has been at the forefront of the campaign to deepen the European Union's common social policies. In doing so, Ireland has put particular emphasis on the issues of social exclusion and long-term unemployment.

The Theoretical Debate: 'Globalization' and National Market Economies

As the volume of cross-border flows of goods, services, people and capital continues to increase, social science scholars are debating the meaning of the 'globalization' of the world economy. At the heart of this debate lies the question of convergence: to what extent will market forces push differently structured market economies to embrace increasingly similar institutions, practices, and regulations?

At one end of the spectrum is the 'integration' school of thought, which focuses on the transnational forces that are eroding national differences. This is not a new argument. Twenty-five years ago, international relations scholars focused on the effect that multinational corporations (MNCs) and expanding international trade would have on national governance. Vernon argued that MNCs were chipping away at the power of national governments.[1] Keohane and Nye urged us to view the world as linked by a web of transnational interactions, creating a situation of complex interdependence.[2] More recently, Ohmae has offered a variation of the globalization hypothesis, suggesting that

---

[1] Raymond Vernon, *Sovereignty at Bay* (New York: Basic Books, 1971).
[2] Robert O. Keohane and Joseph S. Nye, *Power and Interdependence* (Boston: Little Brown, 1977).

the nation-state, which he calls an 'artifact of the eighteenth and nineteenth centuries' and 'no longer meaningful', is crumbling.[3] For him, the more meaningful unit of analysis is the 'region-state'—a geographical region which may or may not fit within the boundaries of a particular country, but which can on its own participate in the global economy.

Many of the globalization arguments draw heavily on neoclassical economic theories that predict the gradual equalization of the costs of production throughout the world. Fukuyama offers a variation, drawing on the power of ideas (especially Hegelian thought) rather than neoclassical economics, to draw a similar convergence conclusion, but in both the economic and the political realms. He argues that the collapse of the ideological alternatives (fascism and communism) to liberalism means that we have now reached the 'end of history'—a world where democracy and capitalism prevail.[4]

At the other end of the spectrum is the 'national diversity' school of thought. This argument starts with the assumption that there is not—and never has been—one 'capitalism', but rather a wide array of national variations on the broad theme of free exchange. Great Britain and the United States stand as an example of market-oriented capitalism, France and Japan as state-directed capitalism (*étatism*), and Germany as concertational capitalism. From this perspective, it is not at all clear that 'globalization', defined as the political and economic convergence of national systems, is indeed occurring. Rather, it is more appropriate to think of 'globalization' as a synonym for 'liberalization'—a term that can be more precisely defined as the formal withdrawal from government participation in or regulation of markets.[5] According to this view, although economic liberalization pushes countries toward adjustment, there is no reason to expect that particular adjustment strategies will look alike from country to country.[6]

In assessing the impact of globalization on domestic market economies, most studies have tended to focus on one of two aspects. Some focus on the

[3] Kenichi Ohmae, 'Putting Global Logic First', in Ohmae (ed.), *The Evolving Global Economy* (Boston: Harvard Business Review, 1995), 129, 131.

[4] Francis Fukuyama, 'The End of History?', *The National Interest* (Summer 1989), 3–18.

[5] This term may be more precisely defined, but it should be noted that there is little agreement regarding the degree to which national governments are actually withdrawing from markets. Formal liberalization via regional agreements like NAFTA and international trade agreements such as the WTO has been concluded. However, some scholars argue that formal liberalization does not necessarily imply actual liberalization. For a good example of this type of argument, see Steven Vogel's work on financial market liberalization in Japan, which Vogel calls a case of national 're-regulation' rather than deregulation. See Vogel, *Freer Markets, More Rules* (Ithaca: Cornell University Press, 1996).

[6] See, e.g., Robert Wade, 'Globalization and Its Limits: Reports of the Death of the National Economy are Greatly Exaggerated', in Suzanne Berger and Ronald Dore (eds), *National Diversity and Global Capitalism* (Ithaca: Cornell University Press, 1996), 60–88. Sylvia Ostry has discussed the 'systems frictions' that result from the interactions of differently structured national market economies. Ostry, Sylvia, 'New Dimensions of Market Access: Overview from a Trade Policy Perspective', in Eileen M. Doherty (ed.), *Japanese Investment in Asia* (Berkeley: The Berkeley Roundtable on the International Economy and The Asia Foundation, 1995).

effect of globalization on governance structures—institutions, regulations or governmental scope of authority. Others examine the changes in corporate practices and structures. Few studies have focused explicitly on the effect on labor institutions in a globalized economy. To the extent that they have focused on labor, they tend to be grounded in the industrial relations litera- ture, rather than embedded in the debates surrounding the globalization of the world economy. Yet as Jacoby argues, there is an inherent tension between the 'globalization' of capital and the relative immobility of labor.[7] Capital is not nationally bound, while workers generally prefer to live and work in their country of national origin, even when governments liberalize restrictions on the movement of people across nations (as the EU did in 1992). What, then, is the impact of globalization trends on national labor practices and institutions? Are we seeing a convergence? This chapter constitutes a first step in identifying the policy responses of Irish unions and government actors to the pressures of globalization. Clearly, one cannot address the convergence question with a single case study. However, this chapter provides one case which, when compared with other countries examined in this volume, offer insights regarding the trajectories of industrial relations in an era of increas- ing economic interactions.

Industrial Relations in a Colonial Context

Given the historical and colonial ties between Ireland and Great Britain, it is not surprising that Irish trade unions developed in a manner broadly similar to those of Great Britain. The level of unionization in Ireland is high, with roughly half of the national workforce represented by a union. Moreover, the great majority of unions in Ireland are affiliated with the Irish Congress of Trade Unions (ICTU), the central umbrella organization for labor. The sys- tem of industrial relations in Ireland can be characterized as voluntaristic, antagonistic, non-participative, inflexible, institutionalized, and centralized.[8] At a conceptual level, collective bargaining is defined as a *voluntary* process among social partners; indeed a norm against extensive legal regulation of the collective bargaining process emerged over time. Industrial relations also rest on the assumption that the interests of management and labor are inherently *antagonistic*, and therefore must be resolved through collective bargaining. Taken further, this assumption suggests that although collective bargaining may permit the emergence of sustained cooperation, the underlying relation- ship between management and labor remains inherently conflictual. At the level of the workplace, the system is *non-participative* in that both employers

---

[7] See Sanford Jacoby, Preface, in S. Jacoby (ed.), *The Workers of Nations* (New York: Oxford University Press, 1995).
[8] The characterization of Irish industrial relations is taken from Ferdinand von Prondzynski, 'Ireland: Between Centralism and the Market', in Anthony Ferner and Richard Hyman (eds), *Industrial Relations in the New Europe* (Cambridge: Blackwell Business, 1992).

and unions have been suspicious of formal worker participation mechanisms, and consequently, few consultative mechanisms have been created at the level of the workplace. It has also been *inflexible*, in that rigid job descriptions have limited the emergence of flexible work practices.[9] Moving from the workplace to the national level, there is a significant level of *institutionalization* (e.g., the existence of strong encompassing organizations and state-supported dispute resolution agencies) and *centralization* (e.g., the reliance on national agreements and other centralized mechanisms as means of resolving industrial disputes).[10] Taken together, these characteristics suggest a labor relations system that is fragmented at the local level, but well-organized and strong at the national level.

Ireland's experience differs from that of Great Britain in two significant ways. First, in Ireland, British unions competed with Irish unions for membership. Second, in Ireland, the political focus of the left wing was not as sharply on industrial labor as it was in Britain. Labor issues competed with other agricultural issues and nationalist concerns for a place on the activist political agenda. The fact that Ireland was primarily an agricultural economy—combined with the serious agricultural crises that occurred during the mid-nineteenth century—meant that landlord-tenant and land tenure issues were high priorities for activists. Moreover, many of the political organizers who might have focused on union issues were involved in the Republican movement. Consequently, a strong Labour Party did not emerge in Ireland in the way that it did in Great Britain. Rather, the broad-based catch-all party, Fianna Fail, has tended to capture labor votes, despite the existence of an Irish Labour Party which is formally linked to trade unions.[11]

'Combinations' of working men appeared in Ireland in the early eighteenth century, although they had been ruled illegal under both English and Irish law since the sixteenth century.[12] The combinations occurred primarily among journeymen who wanted to protect themselves against unfair masters. The Irish Parliament responded by passing a series of prohibitive laws: in 1729, 1743, 1756, 1757, 1763, 1772, 1780, 1787, and 1792.[13] These laws were largely ineffective, although they did force labor organizations underground.

---

[9] The extent to which this remains true is a matter of debate among industrial relations scholars. As will be discussed below, as employers, and particularly multinational corporations, increase their focus on achieving flexibility to retain competitiveness, job descriptions and terms of employment have changed dramatically in recent years. This, of course, is not always to the advantage of the workers. For the increase in part-time workers and the 'casualization of employment' in Ireland, see Denis O'Hearn, *Inside the Celtic Tiger* (London: Pluto Press, 1998).

[10] Because centralization in Ireland is much stronger than in Great Britain, it is the one characteristic that Prondzynski suggests does not fit the British experience. As will be discussed below, centralization in Ireland has increased over time.

[11] See Kieran Allen, *Fianna Fail and Irish Labour* (Chicago: Pluto Press, 1997).

[12] For a history of Irish labor, see Douglas McLernon, 'Ireland' in Joan Campbell (ed.), *European Labor Unions* (Westport, CT: Greenwood Press, 1992).

[13] Ibid. 239.

Trade unions were not legalized until after the 1800 Act of Union. A number of legislative acts, starting in 1824, repealed the statutes that had outlawed combinations of men. In the latter part of the century, laws were passed to offer some protection to the collective rights of workers. Under the Trade Union Act of 1871, Irish law gave legal status to unions and employers' trade associations. This law provided the framework for the evolution of twentieth-century industrial relations. Trade unions and trade associations could not be held responsible for restraint of trade; issues of intra-union affairs were exempted from normal legal channels; trade unions could participate in a voluntary registration system in order to receive legal benefits and to receive a negotiating license from the Ministry for Industry and Commerce; trade unions also had the same right to buy and sell land for the benefit of their members as corporations enjoyed (under the Companies Act of 1862).[14] Thus, the legal framework for industrial organization was in place by the late nineteenth century, although union activity remained quite limited.

A key feature of Irish trade unions has been the fragmentation of membership. This is partly a function of the competition between Irish-based and British-based unions for membership, thereby leading to a situation in which multiple organizations claim to be the representatives of a given group of workers. In the late nineteenth century, attempts were made to form umbrella organizations that would give some cohesion to the trade union movement. In 1863, the United Dublin Trades Association was established; this organization affiliated itself with the British Trades Union Congress (TUC) in 1868. After a couple of faltered attempts to establish an independent Irish umbrella organization, the Irish Trade Union Congress (ITUC), the predecessor of today's umbrella organization (ICTU), was formed in 1894.

During the latter part of the nineteenth century, there was little cross-fertilization between Irish nationalism and trade unionism. After the failure of the Fenian rebellion in 1867, and the setback it created for the Irish nationalist movement, British trade unions were the most important impetus for worker organization. This led one observer to note that 'during the latter half of the 19th century, the entire movement took on the appearance of a foreign organisation spreading its tentacles over the country. . . .We have not yet escaped from the latent hostility to working-class organisation arising from the suspicion that it is of alien origin'.[15]

Irish trade unions flirted with the idea of radical socialism briefly in the early twentieth century, but this did not last long. Unlike in Great Britain, no deep relationships developed between unions and a Labour Party; nor did union leaders embrace socialism with the same enthusiasm that their British counterparts did. In Ireland, a more pressing political issue became interwoven in labor union policies: the cause of Irish nationalism. The importance of

---

[14] Ibid. 242.
[15] J. M. MacDonnell, *The Story of Irish Labour* (1921; Cork 1974), p. 21 as quoted in Munck, Ronnie, *Ireland: Nation, State, and Class Struggle* (Boulder: Westview Press, 1988), 52.

the nationalism issue meant that any attempt to bring a socialist agenda to Irish unionism would be fused with discussions of Republicanism.[16] Indeed, the Irish Republican and socialist leader James Connolly argued that 'The cause of labour is the cause of Ireland, the cause of Ireland is the cause of labour. They cannot be dissevered'.[17]

In the early years of the twentieth century, the causes of trade union socialism and Irish nationalism were clearly intertwined. For example, in 1909 labor leader Jim Larkin founded the Irish Transport and General Workers' Union (ITGWU), which based the concepts and goals of general unionism on a combination of James Connolly's political ideals and broad support for Irish nationalism.[18] In this sense, the union was to lead the fight of both industrial and political goals. As a first step in that process, Larkin declared the unacceptability of continuing 'the policy of grafting ourselves on the English Trade Union Movement'.[19] After an unsuccessful eight-month strike in Dublin during 1913–14, Larkin left for the United States. Then, in 1916, the failure of the Easter Uprising resulted in the execution of James Connolly. The loss of these two leaders, who had insisted so strongly on the fusion of political and social goals, ended whatever chance there was for socialism to prevail as the predominant ideological force of Irish unionism.

During this period, the goals of nationalism explicitly overshadowed those of labor. During the war for independence that began in 1919, membership in the ITGWU swelled from 5,000 to 100,000 in the three years through 1919.[20] However, Sinn Fein leader de Valera is famed to have insisted that 'Labour must wait', and indeed, Labour Party candidates withdrew from the 1918 general elections in order to allow nationalist Sinn Fein candidates a clearer shot at winning.[21] In short, trade unions deferred to the broader goal of national independence.

By 1921, the year in which the Irish Free State was created by treaty with Great Britain, the radical syndicalist elements within the labor movement had taken a back seat to more mainstream collective bargaining strategies. Yet, the newly independent Ireland did not provide a conducive environment even for unions who were interested in a more moderate collective bargaining approach. First, there was a shortage of industrial jobs in the country. The economy was underdeveloped with over 50% of the 1.3 million workforce employed in the agricultural sector. Lack of jobs in Ireland prompted widespread emigration at an average rate of 33,000 people per year from 1921 to 1931. Second, the government gave priority to the agricultural sector, a policy that Minister for Agriculture Patrick Hogan called 'helping the farmer who helped himself and letting the rest go to the devil'.[22] Industrial policy, to

[16] See Munck, *Ireland*.
[17] James Connolly, *Worker's Republic 1916* quoted in Munck, *Ireland*, 50.
[18] McLernon, 'Ireland', 244.   [19] Quoted in Munck, *Ireland*, 53.
[20] Ibid. 57.   [21] Ibid. 57.
[22] Jonathan Haughton, 'The Historical Background', in J.W. O'Hagan (ed.), *The Economy of Ireland* (New York: St. Martin's Press, 1995), 28.

the extent that it existed, was dominated by an emphasis on free trade, limited government spending and taxation, modest state intervention in productive sectors, and parity.[23] The policy was not simply one of neglect, but rather, was explicitly anti-union. Soon after the creation of the Free State, the government denied its postal employees the right to strike. When the employees went on strike anyway, the government used military force to suppress the action.[24] Third, internal disputes within the union movement further weakened trade unions. The split between Irish and British unions continued to be a problem, more pronounced by the fact that Irish unions as a percentage of overall membership increased steadily after the creation of the Free State. Nor was there unity within Irish unions. Larkin returned to Ireland in 1923, but when a leadership dispute arose in the ITGWU that he had established, he was expelled from the union. He established an alternative organization, the Workers' Union of Ireland. The leadership disputes marred the credibility of the movement, and prompted an overall drop in trade union membership.

With the advent of the Great Depression, government policy shifted away from economic openness. Policies of protectionism and self-sufficiency became the norm in Ireland, as they did in other European countries and in the United States. In the Irish context, however, the emphasis on self-sufficiency was aimed largely at reducing economic dependence on Great Britain, which market accounted for the vast majority of Irish exports. As Ireland turned toward protectionism, tariffs rose to a high of 45%. These were the highest tariff levels in Europe, after Germany and Spain, twice as high as US rates, and 50% higher than British levels.[25] The combination of the Depression, economic protectionism, and the trade war exacerbated the plight of unions. Unemployment nearly quintupled, reaching roughly 14% of the labor force by 1935.[26] Competition between British and Irish unions, the proliferation of small, fragmented unions, and the anti-labor stance of the new Irish government led to disunity within the trade union movement.

The economic hardship of the war years only made things worse. During the war, real gross national product (GNP) fell and unemployment continued to be a major problem. Unemployment rates were more than 15% in 1939 and 1940, partly because emigration to the United States was not an option. However, emigration to Great Britain continued. Unemployment declined

---

[23] Haughton, 'The Historical Background', 28.   [24] McLernon, 'Ireland', 245.

[25] At the same time, an economic war broke out between Ireland and Great Britain. The ruling party, Fianna Fail, refused to pay land annuities to Great Britain, which had been aimed at repaying money lent under a number of pre-Independence land acts. Britain retaliated with targeted sanctions on Irish agricultural exports, and Dublin retaliated with sanctions on British cement and coal. The trade war was resolved with an Anglo-Irish Trade Agreement, which included a £10m payment by Ireland to Britain and the agreement by Britain to cede control of the treaty ports. Haughton, 'The Historical Background', 30–1.

[26] Haughton notes that this was also partly a reflection of the reduced opportunities for emigration to the United States.

after 1940, and stood at just over 10% in 1945.[27] Given the low growth and high unemployment rate, the war years saw a rash of industrial unrest. Indeed, some have argued, despite the fragmentation of unions, labor unrest rather than opposition parties posed the greatest challenge to President de Valera and the ruling Fianna Fail party during that period.[28]

Trade union leaders attempted to mitigate the fractiousness of the labor movement by creating new encompassing institutions. In the 1930s, an Advisory Council of Irish Unions was formed. Yet again, the nationalist issue became a point of contention. In this instance, it was the presence of British-based trade unions in the umbrella organization. Thus, in 1945, the Advisory Council of Irish Unions broke away from the ITUC, and renamed itself the Congress of Irish Unions (CIU). The underlying basis of the dispute the inclusion of British unions in the umbrella organization, with the CIU arguing that 'the opinions and aspirations of Irish Labour cannot be expressed by the Irish Trade Union Conference, which is controlled by British Trade Unions'.[29] Accordingly, the CIU supported the creation of an all-Ireland trade union movement which included Northern Ireland but not British-based unions.[30] The split between the Irish unions launched a decade-long dispute, which was not resolved until 1959 with the establishment of the Irish Congress of Trade Unions (ICTU), an umbrella organization of Irish- and British-based members from both the Republic of Ireland and Northern Ireland.

Globalization, Stage 1: The Post-war Shift toward Open Economic Growth

After World War II, Ireland's strategy of self-sufficiency was reconsidered, and ultimately dismissed as unfeasible. The Irish economy was in a serious crisis. Domestically, the country was suffering industrial stagnation, slow economic growth, and staggering emigration flows. Internationally, rising US imports created a dollar shortage in the country, which was exacerbated by the fact that the overwhelmingly agricultural orientation of the economy allowed Ireland to earn very little foreign exchange through exports. The results were serious balance of payments difficulties by the early 1950s.

Economic crises create windows of opportunity for dramatic policy shifts. In Ireland, the post-war economic downturn constituted just such a crisis. During the early 1950s, the Department of Finance prevailed over the Department of Industry and Commerce in its call for deflation rather than industrial expansion. But four years of deflationary policies during the period 1952–6 resulted in negative growth rates, falling employment, serious discontentment among Irish business and labor, and more than a 2% drop in popu-

---

[27] Haughton, 'The Historical Background', 33.

[28] See, for example, Dermot Keogh, *Twentieth Century Ireland* (New York: St. Martin's Press, 1995).

[29] Quoted in Munck, *Ireland*, 63.   [30] McLernon, 'Ireland', 246.

lation due to emigration.[31] Irish citizens continued 'voting with their feet' in search of job opportunities in Great Britain, the United States and elsewhere, and emigration steadily whittled away at the country's population figures.[32] If Dublin was to restore economic health and stem the tide of emigration, an expansionary policy was necessary.

Internationally, Dublin faced incentives to pursue this expansion through open economic policies. Strong pressure came in the form of the United States European Recovery Program (Marshall Plan), announced in 1948, which was explicitly designed to promote industrial expansion. But there were strings attached to the aid: Marshall Aid assistance was linked to membership in the Organization for European Economic Cooperation (OEEC) as well as the gradual loosening of trade restrictions among member countries. Thus, already by the early 1950s, Ireland was in a position in which it had ready access to aid flows for industrial expansion, but was constrained in the choice of policies by international pressures for liberalization.

Given this context, Irish policymakers had to develop a strategy which would simultaneously be liberal in orientation, export-oriented, and capable of creating domestic jobs. Ideally, said Taoisach John Costello in an October 1956 speech, expansion could be achieved with policies to 'favour home investment rather than foreign investment'.[33] But the prognosis for a domestic investment-led strategy seemed dim. Ireland's Industrial Development Authority (IDA), which had been created in 1949 to encourage industrial development and export expansion in the country, issued a series of pessimistic reports suggesting that domestic capital was inadequate for national development purposes. Given the paucity of domestic capital, alternative agents of modernization had to be found. The obvious candidates were foreign manufacturers. Thus, policymakers began to focus on multinational corporations as the key to job creation, industrial development and export expansion. As one 'early and influential' advocate of investment-led development argued:

By far the most hopeful means of getting good management, technical knowledge, and capital all at once is from subsidiaries of large foreign companies . . . a plant which is paid for by foreign capital is a great deal better than one which has to be paid for from the scanty saving of the Republic.[34]

---

[31] Denis O'Hearn, 'The Road from Import-Substituting to Export-Led Industrialization in Ireland: Who Mixed the Asphalt, Who Drove the Machinery, and Who Kept Making Them Change Directions?' *Politics & Society*, 18: 1 (1990), 26–7.

[32] Ireland's population has fluctuated wildly throughout history, moving from a level of roughly 8 million in the 1840s to a nadir of 2.8 million in 1961, to roughly 4.5 million today.

[33] O'Hearn, 'The Road from Import-Substituting to Export-Led Industrialization in Ireland', 28.

[34] Charles Carter, 'The Irish Economy Viewed from Without,' *Studies*, 46, 137–43, quoted by Denis O'Hearn, 'The Irish Case of Dependency: An Exception to the Exceptions?' *American Sociological Review*, 54 (1989), 581.

Added to this sentiment was the popular conviction that it was better to find ways to attract foreign industry than to let thousands of young people emigrate in pursuit of jobs. The idea was simple: better to bring foreign jobs to the Irish people rather than send Irish people to foreign jobs.

The strategy was coherent, consistent, and efficiently implemented. The IDA quickly gained a reputation as a world-class operation, channeling information and incentives to foreign firms interested in establishing operations in Ireland. After 1956, the country moved quickly to attract foreign investment to the country. Dublin expressed a firm commitment to drawing foreign manufacturing firms, especially US firms, into Ireland, with the hope that those firms would create jobs for Irish workers and export the bulk of their goods, thereby ameliorating the country's balance of payments difficulties. The government structured tax and other incentives to draw foreign multinational corporations into Ireland. The incentives were targeted explicitly at export-oriented industries, especially in sectors that were not already well served by Irish industry. High technology firms were given high priority, while non-manufacturing activities received low priority. Thus, the IDA actively identified, contacted, and lobbied US electronics and other high-tech firms. It did little to encourage foreign real estate investment; moreover, it designed separate and less concessionary investment regimes for extractive industries, such as mining and exploration, or service industries, such as banking. While the latter industries were not actively discouraged, Dublin's incentive structures were aimed clearly at foreign export-oriented manufacturers.

Moreover, Ireland was the first country to establish an export processing zone. The Shannon Free Trade Zone, located at Shannon International Airport, was established in 1947 and was augmented in 1958, when the government passed legislation that empowered the local development authority, the Shannon Free Airport Development Corporation to set up an industrial estate next to Shannon International Airport in the western part of Ireland.[35] Government legislation also provided that the profits from all exports from the industrial estate were tax-free for twenty-five years. Profits on exports from outside the estate were given tax-free status for ten years. The tax exemption was extended twice and lasted until the mid 1980s, when the government decided to replace export profit tax relief with a 10% corporate tax. The free trade zone continues to be attractive to US firms, which use its facilities to import duty-free components and materials; to process, sort, and repackage goods; to store items with low inventory costs; and to re-export goods to other EC countries.

Since the policy shift in 1958, investment incentives in Ireland have remained extremely generous. The IDA provides information, advice, and

[35] Leslie Sklair, *Foreign Investment and Irish Development*. Progress in Planning series 29, 3 (New York: Pergamon, 1988), 153.

financial assistance to MNCs who are interested in establishing operations in Ireland. US investors are the primary focus and US firms are given national treatment, including access to government loans and grant aid. This means that there are no general restrictions on the foreign majority ownership in Irish companies or other properties, nor are there nationality requirements regarding directors and shareholders of Irish firms. Irish law gives duty-free status to raw materials and partially finished items that are processed and re-exported. Moreover, taxation policies are highly favorable to foreign investors. In addition to a 10% corporate income tax for export-oriented manufacturing, foreign nationals enjoy favorable personal income tax regulations.[36] Specific investment incentive packages are negotiated on a case-by-case basis with the IDA, but can include any number of concessionary elements. These include tax-free grants for employee training, accelerated depreciation, low-cost facilities for rent or sale in industrial estates, and export-risk guarantee programs.

But for FDI-led economic development to work, Dublin needed to offer a stable investment environment. This required an industrial relations strategy that allowed the flexibility to rationalize industry in an increasingly competitive market environment, but without creating excessive unrest at the enterprise level. To meet these challenges, the Fianna Fail government embraced a social partnership strategy. Events in the private sector created a conducive environment for this kind of approach. With regard to management, the early 1960s witnessed a strengthening of the employers' umbrella organization, the Federated Union of Employers (now the Federation of Irish Employers). With regard to labor, the resolution of internal leadership disputes had culminated in the creation of ICTU in 1959, as well as a gradual decline in the overall number of unions.[37]

In this context, the Fianna Fail government moved to create a variety of social partnership institutional mechanisms.[38] These institutions were designed to incorporate union leaders more closely into policy discussions, and consequently, to ensure that union leaders would support economically painful policies which were aimed at increasing productivity and enhancing Irish economic competitiveness. Thus emerged the Commission on Industrial Organisation, which sent consultation teams to employers' 'Adaptation Councils' and parallel 'Trade Union Advisory Boards' in order to make

[36] Non-residents are taxed only on the portion of their income earned in Ireland. Moreover, individuals who work for foreign firms without legal resident status are taxed on a remittance basis only. Additional tax incentives for firms include tax programs to encourage business development and job creation; tax breaks for investment in basic R&D; and tax incentives for expenditures that encourage urban renewal and development. See the Irish Trade Web, 'Overview of Taxes', http://www.itw.ie/Itw/taxes.html

[37] It is important to note that this decline in the number of unions did not result in a drop in the overall unionization rate. Rather, it reflected a strengthening rather than weakening in union organization. See Cormac O'Grada, *A Rocky Road: The Irish Economy Since the 1920s* (Manchester: Manchester University Press, 1997), 99–100.

[38] See Allen, *Fianna Fail and Irish Labour*, particularly ch. 5.

recommendations regarding the process of rationalization and restructuring in various industries. The Employer-Labour Conference was also created in November 1961, with the explicit goal of issuing guidelines for pay negotiations, and in so doing, to move the issue of wage bargaining into the realm of national policy. In 1963, the National Industrial and Economic Council was established, which comprised ten employer representatives, ten union leaders and government representatives. The Council issued reports on national economic conditions, which in turn served as the background information for the Employer-Labour Conference's wage recommendations and for national economic planning efforts.

The new social partnership institutions were symbolic in that they represented a conscious turn in Ireland toward cooperative policymaking. In fact, some have argued that the primary contribution of these institutions during the 1960s was rhetorical, that is, they shifted the terms of debate away from class conflict and toward a team vision of industrial policy.[39] One government official went so far as to portray the National Wage Recommendation of 1964–6 as heralding the end of the old idea of class war.[40]

Such optimism was premature. Beneath the rhetoric of cooperation laid significant dissent. The 1964 national agreement provoked suspicion among local labor leaders, who were accustomed to more traditional collective bargaining. During 1964–71, Ireland experienced nearly twice the average number of annual strikes than it had during the previous seven-year period.[41] There was record-level strike activity in such sectors as public transportation, electricity supply, and over such fundamental issues as union recognition (particularly in multinational corporations). These struggles took place in the context of an international trend toward greater civil rights activism, and particularly in the Irish context, the re-emergence of the Troubles in Northern Ireland. This social environment only reinforced the sense of militancy among workers in the Republic. Union leaders were therefore pulled in two directions, with the reality of increasing labor militancy, on the one hand, and the promise of national social partnership, on the other.

The unrest reached a critical point in 1969, with the outbreak of a maintenance workers' strike. Standing out in stark relief during this strike was the rift that had gradually emerged between national union leaders and local workers. This was especially apparent when national union leaders brought a negotiated settlement to the strikes. The strikers rejected the settlement offer, and instead, convened a rank-and-file committee to lead the strike. Official leaders were thenceforth ignored. When the numbers of picketers rose into the tens of thousands, employers backed down and agreed to an enormous 20% pay increase. The success of the strike notwithstanding, ICTU president Jimmy Dunne warned against perpetuating this 'do-it-yourself band of trade unionism which treats with contempt all the institutions, practices and proced-

---

[39] Ibid. 118.   [40] Ibid. 119.   [41] Munck, *Ireland*, 64.

ures that our trade union movement has created in this country over the last sixty years'.[42] For ICTU leaders, the extreme nature of the strike, and particularly the erosion of union discipline, swung the pendulum firmly away from supporting militancy and toward centralized bargaining. In response to the maintenance strike, ICTU supported the Fianna Fail government's decision invigorate the institutions that had been created in the early 1960s. The functions of the Employer-Labour Conference were expanded to include monitoring and enforcing union members' adherence to procedure during labor grievances. Furthermore, legislation, in the form of the Trade Union Bill of 1971, strengthened existing labor unions by making it more difficult to create a legal breakaway union.[43]

In short, the turn toward foreign investment-led growth in 1958 created the necessity of adopting policies that increased productivity in Ireland, partly through the rationalization of industry. New collaborative institutions were created in the early 1960s, but were almost immediately threatened by heightened labor militancy. With the specter of rank-and-file unrest hovering in the background, there was the real possibility that industrial instability might spill over into other social and political arenas. In such an event, the foundation of Ireland's economic development strategy would entirely collapse. It was in large part for this reason that the social partners refocused attention on social partnership by strengthening the existing social partnership mechanisms.

Globalization, Stage 2: Entering the EEC

In 1973, Ireland joined the European Economic Community. This gave the country a stronger relationship with Europe as a whole rather than simply with the United Kingdom. The economic strategy was also an extension of the FDI-led development embraced after 1958. While joining the EEC would put more competitive pressure on Irish indigenous industries, it would also encourage non-EEC countries to establish manufacturing facilities in Ireland for the purpose of exporting to the rest of the Community. Most attractive was the possibility of increased investment by US firms, who viewed Ireland as an attractive environment because the country's political stability, well-educated labor force, and English-speaking environment.

The IDA predicted that joining the EEC would allow Ireland to generate 10,000 new manufacturing jobs a year.[44] Government policies optimistically forecast new surges of FDI into the country, and in anticipation of these investments, poured money into establishing engineering and other technical

---

[42] Quoted in Allen, *Fianna Fail and Irish Labour*, 144.
[43] Allen, *Fianna Fail and Irish Labour*, 144–6.
[44] Kieran A. Kennedy, 'Ireland: The Revolution Unfinished', in Kieran A. Kennedy (ed.), *Ireland in Transition* (Cork: Published in collaboration with Radio Telefis Eireann by the Mercier Press, 1986), 43.

institutes throughout the country. But accession to the EEC coincided with the 1973 oil shock. When the first oil shock hit after 1973, the chinks in the development strategy started to show. A slowdown of manufacturing production coincided with a leveling off of new investment activity. Downsizing became a priority for firms which were struggling to survive in the recessionary environment, and job shedding occurred to a greater extent among foreign owned firms than indigenous firms. Jobs lost in foreign-owned firms during the 1973–80 period constituted 29% of 1973 total foreign sector jobs. Among indigenous firms, the percentage of jobs lost in the same period was only 16%.[45]

Unemployment, declining union membership, industrial unrest, and broad dissatisfaction with centralized bargaining plagued the labor movement. The economic crisis pushed unions toward a strategy that they had been discussing, but had not been able to achieve: amalgamation. Simply in order to survive, some smaller unions began to merge. Even so, the most significant of these mergers did not occur until 1990, when the two largest general unions, the ITGWU, and the Federated Workers' Union of Ireland, both of which were members of the ICTU, merged to form the Services, Industrial, Professional and Technical Union (SIPTU).[46]

At the level of national bargaining, the social partners continued to rely on National Understanding throughout the 1970s. The aim of these agreements was mainly to sustain more harmonious industrial relations, rather than to promote an economic objective like full employment or low inflation.[47] Initially, the National Understandings focused on the traditional issue of wages, setting a national norm for pay increases, but also explicitly allowing for local-level bargaining to achieve further increases.[48] The reaction, not surprisingly in a recessionary environment, was the continuation of local level activism and renewed militancy, even as union leaders relied on national-level bargaining to improve industrial relations.

The social partnership agenda expanded under the National Understanding of 1979, which also incorporated government commitments regarding income tax concessions and social welfare policy in exchange for traditional wage restraint. Again, however, the policy coincided with an international crisis. The second oil crisis hit Ireland even harder than the first. Moreover, the subsequent rise in global interest rates pushed the debt-laden government,

---

[45] Telesis report, 294, 362, 415–16 as cited in Sklair, 192.

[46] The creation of SIPTU in 1990 brought more than 70% of general workers and more than 50% of trade union members in the Republic of Ireland into the same union. McLernon, 247.

[47] O'Grada, *A Rocky Road*, 101.

[48] While general pay increases are negotiated centrally, 'special' increases—that is, increases that are not related to inflation but are rather in response to such things as productivity increases or changes in working practices—are negotiated at the level of the firm. Matters of local procedure and other conditions of employment are similarly also dealt with locally. It should also be noted that industry-wide bargaining, which is common in some other countries, is not an important part of the Irish industrial relations system. Prondzynski, 'Ireland: Between Centralism and the Market', 76.

which has relied heavily on deficit spending during the 1970s, into fiscal crisis. By 1980, public debates raged over the appropriate path to decreasing national debt and implementing fiscal adjustment measures.

Double-digit unemployment also plagued the economy. Traditionally, an outlet for economic hardship in Ireland has been emigration. Yet in times of global recession, as in the Great Depression, World War II, and the recession of the early 1980s, emigration has tended to decline. In the 1980s this was not so much because the United States and Great Britain blocked immigration, as they had in earlier times, but rather because economic opportunities in those countries did not seem significantly brighter than they did in Ireland. Against this backdrop of unemployment (which soared from 7.8% in 1979 to 18.2% in 1985), deepening recession, and fiscal crisis, the National Understanding broke down in 1982. The next five years, 1982–7, saw no centralized bargaining.

Globalization, Stage 3: Renewing Social Partnership and Deepening the EU Commitment to Domestic Partnership

The period since 1987 has been one of a twofold focus in Ireland: a renewed commitment to economic adjustment through social partnership; and a renewed commitment to European integration. In 1987, the Irish government, business and labor leaders made an explicit commitment to centralized bargaining as the way to deal with the economic decline, alarmingly high emigration figures, inflation, steep unemployment, and rising interest rates.[49] The result has been a new generation of national agreements. The broad approach is consistent with Ireland's foreign investment-led development strategy, and consequently, an overall theme in negotiating national agreements has been to devise ways to make Ireland an attractive partner in the international economy. The new generation of national agreements have retained their traditional focus on wage restraint, price stability, taxation policy, and job creation. However, since 1987, centralized discussions have also included a range of other social and economic issues, most significantly the broader issues surrounding unemployment and anti-poverty programs. The new generation of national agreements are the Programme for National Recovery, 1988–90; the Programme for Economic and Social Progress, 1991–93; the Programme for Competitiveness and Work, 1994–96; and Partnership 2000, 1997–1999.

The result of the 1987 turnaround was the stabilization of the economy and several years of economic growth. Unemployment fell, but continued to hover in double digits. By mid-1996, unemployment stood at 12.4%, down from over 15% in 1994 and approaching the average for the European Union,

---

[49] Ireland Department of Finance press release, 'Opening of Discussions on a New National Programme', 23 Oct. 1996.

but still considered a major policy problem in Ireland.[50] Moreover, union leaders argued that tax reductions should be implemented to soften the impact of wage restraint. Moreover, long-term unemployment meant that some groups were left out of the economic boom.

Consequently, when Dublin opened discussions on a new national program in 1996, which would continue the emphasis on economic stability, low inflation, and wage restraint, the government also voiced a commitment to prioritizing social inclusion. Moreover, the Irish National Organization of the Unemployed (INOU) was included for the first time in national level negotiations.[51] Finance Minister Ruairi Quinn, at the opening of the discussions on a new national program, stressed the need to

not only continue the partnership approach to the management of the economy, but . . . [also the need to] develop and widen the process of social partnership to achieve social inclusion and fairness and to reinforce the conditions we have created for securing economic growth.[52]

Partnership 2000, a national agreement on pay, working conditions, and social policy, was approved in 1997. Like other national agreements, the primary aim behind Partnership 2000 was to ensure future economic growth. The agreement includes pay increases, tax reduction, and the expansion of jobs programs. On pay issues, ICTU negotiated annual pay increases, along with a local bargaining clause that allows for further increases. Tax reduction measures were estimated to add an average 14% to the take-home pay of most workers. On jobs creation, the agreement provided for the expansion of an existing pilot program to provide jobs for the long-term unemployed, from its initial 1,000 jobs target to 10,000 jobs. For business leaders, the agreements provides the benefit of continued industrial peace, pay increases that keep Irish wages competitive with other EU nations, and beneficial changes in tax policy.

More importantly, however, Partnership 2000 is aimed at extending social partnership more deeply into local-level industrial relations. This was a pri-

---

[50] According to Central Statistics Office figures for May 1997, unemployment dipped below 250,000 for the first time in six years. The reduction of unemployment continues to be an important priority, however, especially long-term unemployment. Government officials recognize that most of the people who move off the Live Register and back to work are those who have been unemployed for less than a year. Department of Social Welfare press release, 'De Rossa Welcomes Live Register Drop of 7,000' (6 June 1997).

[51] The extension of the centralized approach to industrial policy and labor relations is also reflected in the establishment in 1993 of the National Economic and Social Forum. The Forum consists of three strands: first, legislators from all political parties; second, the 'traditional social partners' of employers, unions and farmers; and third, a representative group of citizens outside of or under-represented in the paid labor force—including the unemployed, people with disabilities, young people, the elderly, disadvantaged communities, environmental advocates, and women.

[52] Ireland Department of Finance press release, 'Opening of Discussions on a New National Programme: Concluding Remarks of Mr Ruairi Quinn T.D., Minister for Finance at the opening of Discussions on a New National Programme', 23 Oct. 1996.

ority for ICTU, a strategy to ensure that the labor movement does not become marginalized locally, despite national-level cooperative mechanisms. Consequently, the national agreement provides that, during local-level pay negotiations, trade union leaders will be able to put forth broader issues such as work organization, company policies, and the structure of the bargaining process. The agreement also provides for the establishment of a National Centre for Partnership and Change, with membership including IBEC, ICTU, the Labour Relations Commission, and other government agencies, to provide joint training for trade union officials and human resource managers.[53]

The agreement was by no means embraced wholeheartedly, however. Labor leaders cautioned that the three national agreements negotiated since 1987 had involved sacrifices by the trade union movement.[54] According to ICTU general secretary Peter Cassells,

the last three agreements have served the country well and brought some benefits to working people and their families. But at this stage of the process it is clear that the process of social partnership either develops or it dies. It can be developed by deepening the democratic content through real partnership at company level and by widening the scope through the inclusion of more flexible systems of rewards, like profit sharing.[55]

Irish Business and Employers Confederation leaders disputed the claim that national agreements involved labor sacrifice, arguing that the economic crisis of the early 1980s should not be viewed as the era of hardship for labor.[56] The controversy went deeper than the traditional business/labor cleavage, however. Negotiations on Partnership 2000 sparked some cynicism in among the Irish public; newspaper articles began to discuss the way that the public viewed 'social partnership' as a venue for narrowly focused unions to pursue their independent deals with the government as a precondition for accepting the national agreement.[57]

The grievances of labor leaders regarding partnership lie mainly at the local levels. During the Partnership 2000 negotiations, ICTU leaders argued that although IBEC is committed to social partnership, that commitment does not

[53] 'New Pact Aims at a Wider Social Contract', *The Irish Times on the Web* (19 Dec. 1996).

[54] The initiative was approved by ICTU by a vote of 217 against 134—a margin that has a high 'No' component. ICTU General Secretary Peter Cassells argued that the 'No' votes reflected union dissatisfaction at the local-level implementation of previous national agreement, especially in power-sharing issues. 'Cassells Defines ICTU Priorities', *The Irish Times on the Web* (31 January 1987).

[55] ICTU General Secretary Peter Cassells, remarks at the special delegate conference of the ICTU, 26 Sept. 1996, as quoted in the *Irish Times on the Web*, 27 Sept. 1996.

[56] 'ICTU and Employers at Odds on Effect of Pay Deals', *The Irish Times on the Web*, 1 Nov. 1996.

[57] See, e.g., 'Social Partnership Disillusions Workers', *The Irish Times on the Web*, 29 Jan. 1997. The criticisms were sparked by the fact that the Government agreed to create 3,000 new jobs for primary teachers in exchange for the teachers' union's seventeen votes in ICTU's vote on national agreement.

extend to all of IBEC members—and does not translate into union recognition by IBEC's constituent corporations. IBEC leaders countered that parallel problems exist at the local level for management. That is, although ICTU has embraced social partnership, its member unions do not always seem to share that attitude.[58] Another local issue priority is the issue of union recognition. The refusal by some MNCs to recognize trade unions has increased fears within ICTU that the labor movement may become increasingly marginalized. Partnership 2000 established a study group, comprised of the ICTU, IBEC, IDA, Forbairt, Department of the Taoiseach, and the Department of Enterprise and Employment, to consider possible solutions to the problem.[59]

Deepening Integration of the EU

At the same time that Ireland renewed its commitment to social partnership mechanisms at the domestic level, it has also reaffirmed its support for European-wide partnership on social issues. Most relevant for industrial relations, the Social Chapter of the Maastricht Treaty, which was adopted by eleven EU member states in 1989, aimed at deepening European cooperation by accepting qualified majority voting in such areas as labor market conditions, wages, working conditions, collective bargaining, equal opportunity issues, freedom of movement, health and safety issues, and job retraining. When Great Britain opted out of the social chapter, the other eleven moved to attach the social chapter as a protocol to the Maastricht Treaty and continue working toward harmonization of social issues.

Since that time, Ireland has been in the forefront in pressing for European cooperation on social issues. Dublin has advocated the EU go even further than adopting the social chapter. During the Maastricht negotiations, Dublin proposed the idea of an employment chapter in the Treaty in order to coordinate member country efforts to create sustainable employment in the EU. When this initiative failed, Ireland attempted during its Presidency of the EU to launch a new EU Poverty Programme. However, the initiative was blocked because there were questions regarding the legal basis in the Maastricht Treaty for programs to combat poverty and social exclusion. Dublin has also argued that social considerations must be formally integrated into the economic programs mandated by the EMU process.[60] As Social Welfare Minister De Rossa argued:

It is essential that we effectively challenge, both at national and EU level, the common perception that social protection is only a burden on the economy. It is this percep-

[58] 'Fear of Failure to Aid Case for New PCW', *The Irish Times on the Web*, 26 Sept. 1996.
[59] 'New Pact Aims at a Wider Social Contract', *The Irish Times on the Web*, 19 Dec. 1996.
[60] Department of Social Welfare press release, 'Ireland Puts Social Exclusion on the IGC Agenda—De Rossa', 25 April 1997. See also 'EU Treaty needs Jobs Chapter, says Fitzgerald', *The Irish Times on the Web*, 27 May 1997.

tion, often too readily accepted by commentators, that helps to fuel the often strident demands for unacceptable cutbacks in social welfare, health and other social services. In fact, appropriate levels and new forms of social protection, including non-cash supports as well as traditional financial provisions are an essential backdrop to the modern, dynamic and flexible labour markets of social Europe.[61]

Despite the limited progress that the EU has made in developing social and employment policies, European-wide initiatives have already translated into significant domestic change in Ireland. The most significant example occurred in 1997, when Ireland took legislative action to implement the European Working Time Directive. The result was the most comprehensive employment legislation in Ireland since the 1930s. The European initiative directed countries to adopt regulations that limit the working week to an average of 48 hours, outlaw zero-hour contracts, provide for premiums for Sunday working, and extend holiday entitlements. One of the most controversial aspects of the labor law in Ireland was the 48-hour working week provision. Employers objected that the provision excessively restricted the flexibility required to meet changing competitive conditions or seasonal demand changes. The government argued that the legislation was sufficiently flexible since it did not place a 48-hour limit on any given week, but rather allowed the 48-hour limit to be averaged over four-, six- or twelve-month increments, according to the particular needs of any given business. Opponents of the legislation emerged from both sides of the social spectrum. Employers argued that the bill threatened to impede Irish competitiveness, while low-paid workers feared that the legislation would prevent them from earning much-needed overtime income. Other critics of the legislation included the Building Materials Federation, the Irish Concrete Federation, the Irish Farmers' Association (which argued that applying a 48-hour working week would be unworkable in the agricultural sector), as well as many MNCs.[62] Despite critics of the legislation, Dublin obtained a consensus among the umbrella organization social partners, IBEC and ICTU, to support the measure. Implementing legislation was drafted with extensive input with industry (including MNCs) and labor leaders. A monitoring group comprised of both industry and labor groups was also established to oversee the implementation of the bill.

In an ironic twist that was not lost on Irish nationalists, Irish leaders suggested that Dublin's implementing legislation, the Working Time Bill, might profitably be used as a model for Britain. Prior to the Labour Party victory, Great Britain had refused to adopt the Working Time Directive, on the

[61] Department of Social Welfare press release, 'De Rossa Calls for Release of EU Funding for Poverty Programme and Welcomes Major EU Debate on Modernising and Improving Social Protection Systems', 17 April 1997.

[62] Hewlett Packard, for example, issued a statement that although the company was delighted with its operations in Ireland, and planned to continue investing in the country, it was 'gravely concerned' about the impact of the Working Time Bill. 'Government Rules Out Changes to Work Bill', *The Irish Times on the Web*, 25 Feb. 1997.

grounds that it had opted out of the Social Chapter, and therefore was not bound by the EU directive. This changed for two reasons. First, the European Court of Justice ruled that because the length of the working week is a health and safety issue, as well as a social matter, opting out of the Social Chapter was not sufficient reason to ignore the Working Time Directive. Second, the change in British government from the Conservative Party to the Labour Party created a more sympathetic environment for working time legislation. Equally significantly, some Irish commentators began to cite Ireland's social partnership approach as a model for other European countries. Even Irish Labour Affairs Minister Fitzgerald noted publicly that the Blair government had expressed interest in the partnership approach, an important change from the fragmentation that occurred as a consequence of the Thatcher reforms.[63]

Conclusion: Successes and Lingering Issues

In broad economic terms, it is hard to deny that the reaffirmation of social partnership in 1987 has been a phenomenal success.[64] In the seven years to 1995, economic growth averaged over 5% annually. According to Irish government officials, this is the most successful rate among EU member countries.[65] Inflation has remained between 2% and 2.5%, and total employment increased by 1.75% annually (again a high rate compared to other EU countries). The government budget deficit has remained around 2–2.5% of GDP. The reasons for these successes have been attributed to appropriate economic policies (by different governments), as well as strategic use of EU structural funds. The succession of national agreements reflected and reinforced the importance of social partnership in gaining a policy consensus on national economic goals, wage restraint, and a commitment to economic growth and job creation.[66]

Another criterion of success for Ireland has been the extent to which the country has decreased dependence on Great Britain. On this score, too, the figures appear encouraging. Ireland is the location for nearly 25% of all available US manufacturing investment in Europe, though the country accounts for only 1% of Europe's population.[67] There has also been some success in

---

[63] Department of Enterprise, Trade and Employment Press Release, 'Labour Affairs Minster Welcomes British Commitment to Working Time Directive', 8 May 1997.

[64] For a skeptical view, see O'Hearn, *Inside the Celtic Tiger*.

[65] Growth figures have been even more impressive recently. According to official statistics, during the period from 1994 to 1997 Ireland's real GDP growth rate has averaged 8.4%, compared to an EU average of 2.3%.

[66] Department of Finance press release, 'Speech by Minister to the European Parliament (regional affairs committee)', 5 July 1996.

[67] Department of Finance press release, 'Address by Mr Ruairi Quinn, Minister for Finance, to the IBEC Annual Business Conference on Thursday 29th May 1997, Dublin Castle, "Celtic Tiger in a Global Jungle"', 29 May 1997.

export diversification. The UK continues to be the most important export destination, accounting for 25% of Ireland's exports, but this is a significant drop from the 37% share that the UK accounted for in the early 1980s. Exports to other EU countries increased from 32% in 1983 to nearly 47% in 1995. Ireland has also looked beyond Europe; trade with Singapore increased by 93% in 1995, and by 75% with Malaysia during that same year.[68]

Looking underneath the macroeconomic figures to more specific numbers highlights some lingering problems in Ireland, however. A major problem facing Ireland is long-term unemployment (defined as unemployment lasting longer than three years), particularly among workers without a university education. Youth unemployment is almost twice the rate of adult unemployment. A major fear is that unemployed youths will drift into the category of long-term unemployed. The government has recognized that economic growth will not in itself allow long-term unemployed workers to find jobs. As Minister Fitzgerald said:

Creating new jobs through economic growth is clearly important. But it is not enough in itself to tackle the problem of long-term unemployment. The rising tide does not lift all boats. Indeed, the experience of European recession and recovery has been that long term unemployment continues to rise during the recovery period.[69]

The government's strategy for dealing with this problem has been to broaden the social partnership to include representatives of the unemployed. It remains to be seen, however, whether social partnership mechanisms effectively address the problems associated with long-term unemployment and social exclusion, or whether is Ireland evolving toward a bifurcated economy, characterized by expanding jobs for skilled workers, but declining prospects for those less-educated.

Another problem is the lingering dissatisfaction among workers at the local level. As noted above, there has long been at least a partial disconnection between the policies of the umbrella organizations and local unions, a characteristic that poses a continuing threat to the cohesion of the labor movement. The generation of national agreements since 1987 has relied heavily on labor wage restraint (usually in return for tax concessions), in combination with government economic restraint programs designed to keep inflation low and to preserve the economic viability of Ireland as a host for multinational investment activities. After a decade of national economic prosperity, there are increasingly vocal demands that workers share a greater portion in the benefits of economic growth. It remains to be seen whether the economic gains associated with social partnership will abate local tensions over time, or

[68] These high percentage increases are partly attributable to the low base figures, of course. Department of Finance press release, 'Address by Mr Ruairi Quinn, Minister for Finance, to the IBEC Annual Business Conference on Thursday 29th May 1997, Dublin Castle, "Celtic Tiger in a Global Jungle" ', 29 May 1997.

[69] Department of Enterprise, Trade and Employment Press Release, 'Address by Minister Fitzgerald at INOU Conference', 1997.

will create new divisions between national and local union leaders. It is also possible that dissatisfaction at the local level may put pressure on national leaders to take a more confrontational position in future bargaining.

Nor are there many cooperative local mechanisms to resolve tensions. Rather, social partnership has been almost entirely a centralized process, involving the creation and strengthening of national-level institutions to facilitate the emergence of corporatist agreements regarding a range of economic and social issues. Grassroots labor critics argue that the national-level partnership has entailed disproportionate labor concessions, which have not only posed an economic burden on workers, but which have also weakened the ability of unions to organize and establish social partnership mechanisms at level of the shop floor. While Partnership 2000 took first steps toward facilitating the emergence of enterprise level partnerships, little progress has thus far been achieved in doing so. Although the National Economic and Social Council (NESC) and ICTU have both endorsed the idea of building stronger enterprise-level industrial relations partnerships, little has been done to date. Part of the problem is the long-standing tradition of pluralist collective bargaining at the local level, combined with a strong historical distrust among union members and employers for collaborative mechanisms. Another part is a lack of vision as to how such collaborative mechanisms might work. According to the NESC, enterprise-level partnerships must be created 'not by imposing a single structure or model, but in ways that recognise the need to tailor the partnership approach to fit different employment settings and take account of existing arrangements'.[70] Such a broad approach may well be appropriate, but the quotation also reflects the current paucity of positive suggestions for industrial social partnership schemes. Thus, a lingering question is the degree to which social partnership at the national level will be sustained in local-level bargaining and institutions.[71]

A third question concerns the impact of multinational corporations on the evolution of industrial relations. While space considerations preclude a detailed discussion of the role of foreign direct investment in Irish economic development, it is hard to overstate their importance in Ireland today. Many of these firms accepted 'sweetheart deals' before investing, in which no-strike agreements were exchanged for union recognition. Others have refused to allow unionization at all, and given the national development strategy of creating an attractive climate for foreign investment, Dublin never insisted on unionization as a condition for investing in the country. Moreover, for these firms, 'flexibility' is becoming a catchword for competitiveness. The emphasis on flexibility has resulted in a trend toward part-time or temporary work. Some have created a two-layer employee system, with one group of perman-

---

[70] Quoted in Patrick Gunnigle, 'More Rhetoric than Reality: Enterprise Level Industrial Relations in Ireland', *The Economic and Social Review*, 28: 4 (1997), 183.

[71] For a good discussion, see Gunnigle, 'More Rhetoric than Reality'.

ent workers and a 'buffer' of part-time or temporary workers.[72] These factors have led to a decline in overall unionization rates. Whether this trend will continue, or will be significant, remains to be seen. Given Ireland's historically high unionization rates, it is a matter of concern for labor leaders.

The continued problems of social exclusion, the national/local disconnection within the labor movement, and the impact of MNCs on unionization levels are all putting pressure on Ireland's social partnership model. One cannot help but wonder what would happen to social cohesion in the event of a strong economic downturn. So far, however, the strategy remains firmly in place. Industrial relations in Ireland are predicated on the continuation and strengthening of corporatist bargaining on such issues as wages, working conditions, social policy, tax policy, job creation, and other national economic policies. Globalization, as reflected in Ireland's reliance on foreign investment to spur trade and economic growth, as well as in the of deepening European integration, has prompted the reaffirmation of corporatist bargaining arrangements.[73] In this sense, Ireland stands in stark contrast to Great Britain, where the Winter of Discontent (marked by a rash of strikes during the winter of 1978–9) led to the election of Margaret Thatcher, the resultant splintering of unions, and the demise of negotiations regarding such issues as incomes policies. In Ireland, the national agreements themselves have evolved and adapted to changing competitive conditions, but the commitment to corporatism has not wavered. Both Irish government and EU analyses of Ireland's economic performance during the past ten years have laid heavy emphasis on social partnership as the key to sustaining economic growth. For example, the official government website for Ireland credits 'the Irish Model . . . of social partnership' with resulting in 'industrial peace, high economic growth, moderate wage increase, progressive tax reductions, and job increases'.[74] Similarly, the 1996 European Commission Report on Ireland noted that 'the basis for the Irish success lies in a comprehensive macroeconomic strategy involving the social partners. The strategy is strongly stability oriented and is complemented by a successful policy of industrial development'.[75] In Ireland, globalization has gone hand in hand with increased social partnership.

[72] O'Hearn argues that the unions themselves bear some responsibility for these changes. The current generation of national agreements has allowed for local bargaining in order to secure pay increases over and above the rate set at the national level. Often, the local pay agreements incorporated trade-offs for higher pay, in the form of more subcontracting and more part time, temporary, and fixed-contract work. O'Hearn, 'The Road from Import-Substituting to Export-Led Industrialization in Ireland', 1998.

[73] The alternative, free collective bargaining, has been repeatedly dismissed by political leaders as creating social and economic instability. Taoiseach Bruton has labeled free collective bargaining a process of 'leapfrogging claims' as different groups of workers vie with each other in their demands on employers or the government. 'Renewing the Partnership', *The Irish Times on the Web*, 30 Jan. 1997.

[74] Website address: http://www.irlgov.ie

[75] 'Ireland in the Transition to EMU', European Commission Report on Ireland, 1996, as cited in Ireland Department of Finance press release, 'Minister for Finance Welcomes European Commission Report on Ireland in the Transition to EMU', 4 June 1996.

6

Globalization and the Paradigm Shift in Japanese Industrial Relations

Charles Weathers, Osaka City University

Japan's political economic institutions manifest the opportunities and the pressures of decades of globalization. Forcibly pressed into the world economy in the early 1850s, the country acted quickly to adapt organizations, institutions, and technologies from economically advanced Western economies in an effort to protect its independence and bolster its prestige. Following World War II, catch-up efforts steadily evolved into efforts to overtake, as new means of organizing production increased manufacturing efficiency, so that Japan now ranks with the United States as one of the world's two economic superpowers. Today, Japan is not only an exemplary case of adaptation to globalization, but is also itself a major force driving globalization through its advanced production and personnel management techniques, and its competitive pressure. None the less, the nation's economic decision makers often prefer to emphasize Japan's vulnerability in order to stimulate and mobilize the nation's economic energies.

The mainstream, or non-radical, unions of organized labor have historically supported national economic strategies by promoting cooperative labor-management relations and, during the post-World War II era, by helping to raise productivity. The ideal of lifetime employment has served for nearly four decades as the dominant paradigm for expressing close labor-management cooperation based on a common commitment to the enterprise. In recent years, however, the economic conditions that lent some substance to the ideal have been breaking down, prompting employers to introduce a new paradigm, inspired in large part by the United States, emphasizing flexibility, labor mobility, and individualistic competition. At the core of a deepening dilemma for Japan's major unions is that they remain committed to cooperation with employers even though employers are attempting to reduce their commitment to workers. Further, while the emerging paradigm should favor many skilled employees, it is also likely to create pressures to reduce the pay and benefits for the mass of less-skilled or unskilled workers.

Although the nation's employment paradigm is changing, its basic economic strategies remain constant. From the beginning of economic modernization in the 1870s, national leaders have emphasized the development of high-value-added manufacturing industries in order to achieve maximum economic independence from the West. They have also tended to insist that the demands of economic development leave little leeway for improving working conditions. The invocation of the threat of foreign economic domination has continued despite rapid post-war growth, rising affluence, and even the attainment of massive trade surpluses in the mid 1980s—in the 1960s, the threat was economic liberalization; in the 1970s, the oil price hikes; in the mid 1980s, the rapid appreciation of the yen; and, in the 1990s, globalization, or what the Japanese more often term internationalization (*kokusaikai*) or the era of super-competition (*dai-kyoso jidai*). Each economic threat or disruption is portrayed as a threat to jobs and livelihoods justifying further rationalization in order to protect enterprises and maintain industry's ability to export. The prolonged economic recession of the 1990s has once again triggered the crisis consciousness of managers, prompting a management campaign aimed at cutting labor costs and rationalizing employment practices in order to bolster international competitiveness. Yet there are numerous signs that it is Japan's aggressive export-oriented practices that are creating or contributing to many of the country's present economic ills; if so, the rationalization campaign will simply repress wages and working conditions for marginal workers instead of generating growth.

This chapter examines the strategies debated and implemented by the Japanese union movement in the 1990s, along with the historical and institutional foundations of those strategies. Most importantly, it highlights the divisions among the unions. The so-called right-wing unions based primarily in manufacturing industries have committed themselves to close cooperation with managers in promoting productivity and economic competitiveness; left-wing unions in sectors less exposed to international competition have preferred to place greater emphasis on raising wages or improving the quality of life.[1] Right-wing, or cooperative, unions, being located in the strategic sectors of the economy, have exercised the strongest influence in determining the priorities for the union movement as a whole, or have at least made it difficult for labor to resist concerted pressures by employers and by conservative-dominated governments. The commitment of cooperative unions to help managers improve productivity has helped to generate rapid economic growth and prosperity, but it has also helped to relegate organized labor to a subordinate position and contributed to steady organizational decline. As the first non-Western country to achieve economic modernity, Japan presents the troubling dilemma that labor organizations that commit themselves to promoting national economic development may fail to promote social development as well.

---

[1] The terms 'right wing' and 'left wing' are used here as convenient descriptive, not pejorative, terms, as is often done in historical accounts of Japanese labor.

The Institutional Foundations of Enterprise-based Labor Relations

Japan's process of economic modernization made it difficult to organize the working class. The government steadily repressed leftist or labor activists, its fear of all dissent typically leading it to target moderates as well as radicals. But if national leaders were wary of democratic institutions, they were eager to embrace capitalism. They noted that capitalism had driven the development of the powerful states of the West, and accordingly encouraged the rapid development of the modern business corporation.[2] The Japanese pattern of development accordingly conferred high status on the company. As Thomas Rohlen notes, the company steadily supplanted the village as the nation's social as well as economic organization during the twentieth century.[3] Companies gained a privileged status as the leading agents of national modernization, and large companies, along with the government bureaucracy, provided the major source of secure, well-paid jobs and upward social mobility. Before 1945, however, the benefits were limited primarily to white-collar workers.

One result of the importance accorded to firms was that, much as in the United States, large enterprises developed relatively quickly, and were well established before workers began to attempt to organize. Moreover, employers consistently opposed the efforts of reformist national bureaucrats to enact factory laws, arguing that their fledgling enterprises could not incur the expenses and still survive foreign pressure.[4] They also opposed governmental efforts to encourage cooperative labor organizations. Instead, employers sought to nurture close labor-management ties through such means as stronger job security or management-led employee associations. Such efforts had little success with regard to production workers, partly because companies lacked the resources necessary to follow through on their pledges during economic downturns,[5] but they provided a preview of the highly successful strategies of the post-war era.

After the war, American occupation authorities conferred strong powers on unions, which in turn momentarily created the tantalizing possibility of spearheading a major revolution in the social and economic order through such innovations as the establishment of a 'livelihood wage' based on worker need. But US priorities in the occupation soon changed, partly because of the unexpected radicalism of labor, but also because the United States decided to rebuild Japan's economy and reintegrate the country into the international economic system. Occupation officials began to urge government and busi-

---

[2] Rodney Clark, *The Japanese Company* (New Haven: Yale University Press, 1979), ch. 2.

[3] Thomas P. Rohlen, *For Harmony and Strength: Japanese White-Collar Organization in Anthropological Perspective* (Berkeley: University of California Press, 1974), 13.

[4] Sheldon Garon, *The State and Labor in Modern Japan* (Berkeley: University of California Press, 1987).

[5] Andrew Gordon, *The Evolution of Labor Relations in Japan: Heavy Industry, 1853–1955* (Cambridge: Council on East Asian Studies, Harvard University, 1985), chs 2–6.

ness leaders to take stronger stances against unions. From 1948, the government revised the labor laws and purged radical labor leaders, while managers launched an offensive to restore managerial prerogatives in workplaces. The United States supported the offensive with a draconian anti-inflation policy that badly depressed the economy, further sapping union strength and making it easier for managers to justify dismissals. By the mid 1950s, many of the country's original enterprise unions had been replaced by cooperative new unions (or second unions) following disputes with managers. Once a firm's militants were ousted and the workforce suitably downsized, management invariably pledged to protect the jobs of the remaining workers in return for their cooperation. By the mid 1950s, the contemporary Japanese Employment System was basically established, with its components of strong job security, seniority-based pay and promotions—a remnant of the livelihood wage system won by unions just after the war—and cooperative enterprise unionism. The ideal of mutual commitment between employee and employer became tied to the tradition of the company as a leading social and economic institution.[6]

During the 1950s and 1960s, the major manufacturing firms developed new labor management practices aimed at nurturing a commitment to improving productivity among production employees. One was egalitarian promotion systems that motivated workers to strive for promotions and weakened their ties to unions. Many new labor management practices were first developed in the steel industry, which then enjoyed a status as the country's leading industry, and commanded considerable resources to implement its strategies. The Japan Productivity Center, whose establishment was encouraged and partly financed by the United States, played an important symbolic role in promoting productivity-raising consciousness among workers as well as managers. Soon after its founding in 1955, the Center signed agreements with right-wing unions pledging that increases in productivity would be used to raise living standards, and would not eliminate workers' jobs.[7]

Quality control (QC) circles became one of the innovations that helped to define Japanese labor management practices. The primary developer of QC circles, the Japanese Union of Scientists and Engineers (JUSE), heightened the effectiveness of their creation by turning it into a nationwide movement. JUSE organizers also emphasized the importance of quality control in enabling companies to survive (and to continue exporting) by cutting costs and raising quality. The movement also proved effective at instilling feelings of social solidarity among participating workers and encouraging them to feel that they were engaged in broad social movements that transcended their

---

[6] Ibid. ch. 10.

[7] On the promotion of productivity consciousness, see Andrew Gordon, 'Contests for the Workplace', in A. Gordon (ed.), *Postwar Japan as History* (Berkeley: University of California Press, 1993).

firms and contributed to the advancement of society.[8] Similarly, individual companies have often meshed themes of self-protection and contribution to the community through responsibility to one's employer. One prominent example is Matsushita Electric, which often emphasizes how its high-quality low-cost products have improved the quality of life.

The course of the union movement has strongly reflected the success of managers and their associations in nurturing the productivity consciousness. Further, just as the steel industry played a leading role in developing labor management innovations that helped to raise productivity, it was the steelworkers' unions that became the leading advocates of supporting managers. By 1960, the Federation of Steel Workers' Unions was under the control of the right-wing activist Miyata Yoshiji. Miyata expounded a doctrine that extolled cooperation with management. His labor unionism called on workers to help increase output, or 'expand the pie', in order to raise living standards for themselves and society at large. Unions would exercise a checking (*chekkingu*) function to ensure that the fruits of growth would be fairly distributed. Japan's mainstream labor leaders had historically advocated cooperation, but what distinguished Miyata's approach was the emphasis on enterprise-based cooperation. While Miyata rejected the left-wing assumption of class struggle he also ignored the labor movement's historical dream of creating strong industrial and national level labor federations.[9]

From his base in the nation's leading industry, steel, Miyata became the leading figure in the establishment of the International Metalworkers' Federation–Japan Council (IMF–JC) in 1964. The IMF–JC and its major industrial unions—primarily the Federation of Steel Workers' Unions, the Federation of Shipbuilding and Engineering Workers' Unions, the Confederation of Automobile Workers' Unions, and the Electrical Electronics and Information Workers' Unions—served as pillars of the vision of enterprise-based cooperative unionism aimed at protecting jobs by increasing productivity. The industrial unions are dominated by their strongest enterprise union affiliates. Toyota Motor Union, for example, controls the top executive positions in the Confederation of Automobile Workers' Unions. Although the IMF–JC has no authority, it strengthened the influence of cooperative doctrines in the union movement, and has served as an important forum for coordinating wage and economic policymaking.[10]

[8] See Robert E. Cole, *Strategies for Learning: Small-group Activities in American, Japanese, and Swedish Industry* (Berkeley: University of California Press, 1989), esp. 280–92.

[9] Miyata Yoshiji, *Kumiai Zakkubaran* [Speaking Frankly about Unions] (Tokyo: Toyo Keizai Shimposha, 1982); and Takagi Ikuro, 'Nihon rodo kumiai undo ni okeru "uha" no keifu: Sodomei to JC-gata no doshitsusei to ishitsusei'. [The genealogy of the 'right-wing' of the Japanese labor movement: Sodomei and JC-type homogeneity and heterogeneity], in Shimizu Shinzo (ed.), *Sengo Rodo Kumiai Undo shi Ron* [Debates on the Post-war History of Labor Unions] (Tokyo: Nihon Hyoronsha, 1982). However, probably Japan's most influential post-war labor leader, Miyata maintained a low profile.

[10] Sources on the IMF-JC include Yoshimura Yosuke, *Daikigyo Roshi no Kenka Matsuri* [Ritualistic Quarrels Between Labor and Management at Large Companies] (Tokyo: Japan

The evolution of the IMF–JC is indicative of the unexpected ways that foreign influences have often influenced the formation of Japanese institutions without altering the basic strategies of the actors. The American and European unions belonging to the International Metalworkers' Federation (IMF) spent years urging Japanese metalworking unions to organize an IMF affiliate. The European members probably hoped that international support would strengthen Japanese unions and help them to win higher wages, thereby diminishing Japan's low wage-driven export pressure. While the rank-and-file were wary, Japanese metalworking union leaders were eager to join, but partly in the hope that stronger international contacts would themselves help to alleviate trade friction. Business leaders appear to have looked favorably upon the IMF–JC's formation for essentially the same reason. They were certainly heartened by the emergence of such a business-oriented organization just as Japan was being forced to liberalize its market to conform to the General Agreement on Tariffs and Trade (GATT) and Organization for Economic Cooperation and Development (OECD) rules (though economic liberalization turned out to be mostly cosmetic).

In principle, the IMF–JC was created to serve as a forum for international exchange among unions, but some union leaders, especially in the Steel Workers' Federation, also had a domestic agenda in mind. They wanted the IMF–JC to serve as a 'third force' in the union movement, or an alternative to the two main national federations, especially the Marxist-oriented Sohyo. Using their bases in the nation's strategic industries, the IMF–JC unions encouraged cooperative practices through their strong influence over its wage and economic strategies. Today's major labor federation, Rengo, is arguably in large part an outcome of their strategies and activities.[11] Despite their professed dislike for ideology, Robert Cole notes that cooperative labor leaders buttressed their position with 'a subtle mixture of nationalism and corporate firm loyalties.'[12] He notes elsewhere that 'union strength tends to be compromised because it becomes a victim of its call for mutual cooperation. The ultimate weapon, the strike is inconsistent with the avowed policy of mutual understanding'.[13] However, thanks to the high growth and strong labor demand (and to the latent threat of revived militant unionism), cooperative unions hardly needed to do more than conduct symbolic strikes to win large raises during the 1960s and early 1970s.

Institute of Labor, 1982), 29–56; and Murakami Kanji, 'IMF-JC no taito' (The Rise of the IMF-JC), *Asahi Jaanaru* (25 June 1967), 94–100. The development of the IMF-JC is believed to have encouraged a shift toward the right in the Electrical Union and in shipbuilders' unions in the mid 1960s.

[11] Onomichi Hiroshi, *Kore ga Rengo da!* [This is Rengo!] (Tokyo: Takeuchi Shoten, 1987).

[12] Robert E. Cole, 'Japanese Workers, Unions and the Marxist Appeal', *The Japan Interpreter*, 6: 2 (Summer 1970), 131.

[13] Robert E. Cole, *Japanese Blue Collar: The Changing Tradition* (Berkeley: University of California Press, 1971), 261.

The IMF–JC unions played leading roles in shaping labor's response to the difficult recession that followed the 1973 Middle East oil embargo, or oil shock. Cooperative unions accepted wage restraint in order to protect national economic competitiveness and protect jobs. Many jobs were in fact lost, but primarily by women and non-regular workers, very few of whom were union members. The cooperative unions thereby helped Japan to maintain a high proportion of manufacturing jobs, while the number of such jobs fell sharply in most Western countries. Determined wage restraint and industrial rationalization helped Japan to generate the most impressive economic revival and growth among industrial economies since the late 1970s.

By the mid 1980s, Japan faced a new kind of economic pressure. Its trade surpluses had reached such proportions that the government reluctantly accepted the need to drastically revalue the yen. That brought on a brief recession, with a greater loss of regular jobs than after the oil shock. What was new was not trade friction, or even revaluation of the yen, but the realization that there might be limits to export-led growth. There was a real fear that Japan might not be able to increase exports, and the concern prompted calls for a shift in economic strategy toward stimulating domestic demand to generate internally led growth. In hindsight, such a course might have brought significant reductions in capital investment and would probably spared Japan much of the economic pain of the 1990s. Instead, the combination of continued wage restraint in manufacturing and financial policies that made cheap capital available to industry led to massive overinvestment by manufacturing firms. At present, the financial system is still in shambles and industry is pleading for the taxpayers and employees to help shoulder the burdens of its excess capacity and debt.

The State of the Unions

The mainstream unions called for a change of economic course in the 1980s, but they lacked the organizational strength or spirit to put pressure on either the government or employers. Their policy of close cooperation with management may have helped protect manufacturing jobs, but it did not prevent one of the worst union organizational declines among industrialized nations. After hovering around 35% for years, the organization rate began to fall slowly but steadily every year from 1975 (when wage restraint was implemented) to the present, reaching an estimated 22.6% in 1997. Government statistics report that the manufacturing workforce peaked at 15.7 million in 1992, which is one reason for the decline, but the organization rate has also fallen in a number of sectors that are not being restructured.

The organizational decline results largely from the dependent status of enterprise unions. They cannot recruit outside of their firms, and they have little incentive to appeal to their own members since most of them are virtually required to join the union, under union shop arrangements, as conditions of employment when they join their firms. As a result, a more serious concern to union leaders than even the steadily falling organization rate is *kumiai-banare* [union leaving], or the extreme lack of interest of members in union activities.[14] Employees have little motivation to join unions on their own as they usually believe that unions have little effect on wages or working conditions. The perception is likely accurate, since researchers consistently fail to find any union effect on wages (though there may be an effect on bonuses).[15] Although there is little if any union effect on pay, union dues are quite high, a disincentive to low-income workers to organize.[16]

The mainstream unions attempted to revitalize their movement in the late 1980s with the establishment of a new national federation, Rengo. The industrial unions of the IMF–JC are concurrently Rengo affiliates. Rengo was initially founded in 1987 by private sector unions. The public sector unions of the left-wing federation Sohyo joined in 1989 following some tense negotiations with the private sector unions. Rengo, which includes just over 60% of organized workers, more or less realized the historical dream of a unified labor movement, though it failed to bridge the gap between the left and right wings. The expansion of Rengo was made possible largely by the increasing moderation of the Sohyo unions, which eliminated most of the ideological distance between them and the cooperative private sector unions. The public sector Sohyo unions were also anxious to gain broader support from other unions to protect themselves from the rationalizing 'administrative reform' policies of Japan's conservative-dominated governments, and accordingly consented to enter the new federation on somewhat subordinate terms. A more positive motivation for Rengo's expansion was the desire of unions to strengthen their proactive policymaking capabilities.[17]

The conditions for a Rengo-boosted revitalization of the union movement appeared in many respects propitious at the end of the 1980s, when Japan's economic prosperity and international prestige reached their peaks. Once again, as had occurred at the end of the high growth era in the late 1960s and early 1970s, there was serious dissatisfaction with the fact that the quality of

[14] Unions launched the so-called Union Identity movement to stimulate interest, but many of the activities, such as redesigning union flags and newspapers, proved ineffective to say the least.

[15] On employee attitudes toward unions, see Tsuyoshi Tsuru and James B. Rebitzer, 'The Limits of Enterprise Unionism: Prospects for Continuing Union Decline in Japan', *British Journal of Industrial Relations*, 33: 3 (Sept. 1995). For an overview of research on the union influence on wages, see Hori Haruhiro, 'Rodo kumiai no keizaiteki kino' [The economic function of unions], *JIL Risaachi*, 29 (Spring 1997).

[16] *Shukan Rodo Nyusu*, (31 May 1993), 3. Dues are high partly because most unions continue to levy archaic strike fund fees, amounting to ¥1,070, even though they virtually never strike. Since Japanese unions almost never strike, the survey calculated that the average union affiliate had accumulated a ¥844,770,000 strike fund.

[17] On the formation of Rengo and its historical background, see Hosei Daigaku Ohara Shakai Mondai Kenkyujo (ed.), *'Rengo Jidai' no Rodo Undo: Saihen no Michinori to Shintenkai* [The Labor Movement of the 'Rengo Era': The Journey Toward Restructuring and New Developments] (Tokyo: Sogo Rodo Kenkyujo, 1992).

life had not kept pace with the country's economic achievements. It became the common wisdom that unions had not done enough to improve working conditions and general living standards,[18] and there was some injured pride in acknowledging that the country's social infrastructure lagged well behind those of Western countries. Union leaders celebrated Rengo's birth with announcements of ambitious programs to organize new workers, obtain higher wage raises, reduce the large differentials in wages and working conditions between larger and smaller firms, and raise living standards in general. However, the establishment of a new national federation was hardly sufficient to overcome union weaknesses.

Like the IMF–JC, Rengo is composed of industrial unions over which it has no authority, and it internalizes the divisions among unions. While the basic ideological differences between the left and right wings have mostly dissipated, important differences of material interest remain. Simply stated, major unions in the manufacturing sector support policies that enhance economic competitiveness, while left-wing unions and those representing service sector and smaller firms prefer policies aimed at increasing purchasing power and improving the quality of life.

Rengo's basic mandated function is to better formulate and head up policy-making initiatives, not to conduct major independent activities, though it is accorded some leeway in the case of social policymaking. Since there are many moderate left-wing officials—some of them formerly with Sohyo—at Rengo headquarters, the federation often disagrees with the IMF–JC on wage setting and economic policy. This does not mean that the federation conducts vigorous policymaking, however. Since its base is divided and its members rarely strike or otherwise exert significant economic pressure, the policy positions that Rengo actually pushes tend to be either useful but limited in scope, such as modest new child care provisions, or overly broad. Critics have likened the policy agenda to 'an array of policy slogans' with 'something to please everyone'.[19] The same sort of contradictions and ambivalence mark the unions' electoral political activities. Both wings of the labor movement have historically been active in electoral politics, notwithstanding the IMF–JC's official opposition to political unionism, and both formally espouse the establishment of a democratic socialist-type party that would challenge the long-dominant conservatives. In practice, one would be hard-pressed to differentiate the agenda of the IMF–JC from that of the government, as discussed below. The left- and right-wing unions have recently

---

[18] One signal of a change in opinion was a 1992 article by a well-known proponent of cooperative industrial relations practices, Haruo Shimada, who mildly criticized the emphasis on competitiveness. See Haruo Shimada, 'Japan's industrial culture and labor-management relations', in Shumpei Kumon and Henry Rosovsky (eds), *The Political Economy of Japan*: Vol. 3: *Cultural and Social Dynamics* (Stanford, CA: Stanford University Press, 1992).

[19] Igarashi Jin, 'Rengo no seisaku seido sanka' [Rengo's policy and institutional participation], *Kikan Rodo Ho* (Autumn 1994), 10.

come together to back the Democratic Party, but its policy agenda is not clear and some of its politicians are hostile to unions.

The divisions between the unions are particularly important in the areas of wage setting and general economic policymaking. Wage setting represents the central dilemma—and illustrates the central contradiction—of the IMF–JC strategy. Metalworking industries set the crucial benchmark for nationwide wage settlements through their own wage agreements in the annual *shunto* (spring offensive) wage setting rounds, giving the major IMF–JC unions a virtual veto power over any ambitious efforts to conduct more assertive wage offensives. The major IMF–JC unions, such as Toyota Union, Nissan Union, Matsushita Union, and Hitachi Union, have tacitly supported strong wage restraint since 1975, and the efforts of unions in private railways and other pivotal service sector industries to gain more influence in wage setting during the 1980s made no headway. One way in which metalworking unions have cooperated with employers to maintain nationwide wage restraint while limiting the cost to their own members has been to disguise portions of real wage increases by providing them through such means as allowances tied to promotions or qualifications.[20]

Wage restraint has effectively supported the economic strategy of maintaining large trade surpluses in high-value-added products by lowering wage costs. However, many observers also believe that it has held down domestic demand to the point that Japan has become incapable of generating internally led economic growth. The unions certainly espouse this view. Even the IMF–JC unions constantly argue that Japanese firms must grant larger real wage increases in order to escape overdependence on exports, stimulate economic growth, and put an end to the long economic slump of the 1990s. It is clear that Japan's aggressive export-oriented strategy tends to become self-defeating because large trade surpluses simply push up the value of the yen, creating pressure for a new round of wage restraint.[21] During wage negotiations, however, the unions either cannot or will not put significant pressures on their firms for significant raises. Unhappy with the IMF–JC's failure to push harder for either substantial wage increases or greater wage equality, Rengo has exceeded its mandate by organizing campaigns to improve wages and working conditions for small-firm employees. Unfortunately, the campaigns have had little impact, and deepening recession in the late 1990s has led to a widening of the manufacturer size-based pay differentials.

While Rengo would like to promote broader social policymaking, manufacturing sector unions are more concerned with economic policies intended

---

[20] The major practitioner of so-called hidden basic wage raises (*kakushi beea*) was the steel industry. The Steel Workers' Federation used to deny that the practice existed, but the IMF–JC now openly supports it, as one of its official recently affirmed in an interview (June 1999).

[21] See the analysis of Japan's national wage strategy and wage growth in Clair Brown, Yoshifumi Nakata, Michael Reich, and Lloyd Ulman, *Work and Pay in the United States and Japan* (New York: Oxford University Press, 1997), ch. 6.

to promote national competitiveness by reducing spending or resolving particular problems that affect their industries. One important way has been to support government policies aimed at economic rationalization. Manufacturing sector unions have not sought substantial wage raises since 1975. Relatively strong restraint was observed even during the boom years of the late 1980s. Instead they have tried to win policy concessions, such as tax cuts, to help maintain employee purchasing power. Thus they have naturally endorsed policies such as administrative reform that are supposed to reduce government spending. It also suits the manufacturing sector unions that such policies tend to weaken certain public and service sector unions, or at least diminish their influence. The IMF–JC tacitly backed the 1980s program of administrative reform, which virtually destroyed Japan's last major militant union in the process of restructuring and nominally privatizing the National Railways.

Industrial unions in manufacturing also lobby for industrial policies that they believe will support companies and thus protect jobs. The Federation of Steel Workers' Unions, for example, has recently requested tax breaks for anti-pollution equipment mandated by new regulations. It argues, plausibly enough, that the burden should be shared because the investment will provide a public good, clean air, and because sharing the cost will avoid jeopardizing jobs in the steel industry. Industrial policy essentially forms the core of the Electronic Union's employment protection policy. To assist the many small and mid-size enterprises in the industry, for example, the union has requested government assistance in relocating production overseas. The Electronic Union is also lobbying for infrastructure investment, including improvements in commuter train networks to relieve passenger congestion, especially in the Tokyo area. The union, as well as managers, fears that many highly skilled workers are growing reluctant to live in crowded cities or endure difficult commutes.

Work hour reduction has been a major policy issue for nearly two decades, and indicates again how international pressures often help to shape domestic debates without exerting much influence on the perceived interests. Long working hours in Japanese factories first provoked anger from trade partners early in the twentieth century, and they once again became a lightning rod for criticism when the trade surplus grew in the early 1980s. The government subsequently decided to try to reduce working hours, but pride and economic concerns were more important than international pressure *per se*. Business wanted to find ways to boost domestic demand because it feared that angry trading partners might impose limits on Japanese exports, and there was also 'the deep-rooted desire to overtake the West—the *oitsuke oikose* [catch up and then exceed] spirit, now transformed from the purely business realm to the field of working conditions'.[22] The interests of workers, or at least the

---

[22] Daniel H. Foote, 'Law as an Agent of Change? Governmental Efforts to Reduce Working Hours in Japan,' in Harald Baum (ed.), *Japan: Economic Success and Legal System* (Berlin: Walter de Gruyter, 1997), 210.

majority, were never the primary concern, and unions were slow to demand work time reductions. In fact, unions generally approved the corporate policies of reducing workforces and lengthening work hours during the 1970s because the remaining workers became nearly indispensable, hence all the more secure. In contrast, American unions want to reduce working hours partly so that firms will hire more workers, hopefully leading to an increase in union membership. Since the Japanese unions were ambivalent, the Ministry of Labor ended up leading efforts to reduce working hours, though with little success. Eventually, it was economic factors that brought significant reductions. First, large firms had to improve conditions, including reducing hours, during the Bubble Economy, the speculative boom of the late 1980s, in order to hire young people. Then working hours fell again when the Bubble Economy collapsed and demand fell off sharply. Consequently, working hours of production workers during the 1990s have primarily been a problem in small firms, where conditions have always been difficult, and where very few workers are organized. The government belatedly established a 40-hour week for smaller firms in 1997 but even then the Ministry of Labor announced that it would not enforce the new regulations, angering the unions that represent small firm employees.[23]

In Japan's world-leading auto sector, unions have been concerned with working conditions mainly in their effect on productivity. Car makers have long had difficulty recruiting workers because of the demanding working conditions, and many observers have attacked such alleged practices as ignoring ergonomics in the design of production processes and putting intense pressure on workers to ignore minor injuries in order to keep production moving with minimum staffing.[24] In 1992, the Confederation of Auto Workers' Unions issued a well-publicized report that indicated a high level of discontent among the industry's employees. However, the report reflected the mood of the Bubble Economy, and it was quickly shelved as the early 1990s recession hit home. Apart from the 1992 report, however, the auto industry unions have usually been passive about working conditions, including the stressful lean production methods pioneered by Toyota. Surprisingly, the notably right-wing Nissan Union was once an exception. It was, in fact, probably the only significant manufacturing sector union in Japan that limited the pace of work or otherwise regulated working conditions during the 1970s. However, the company steadily lost ground to Toyota in terms of production efficiency and market share, and at the beginning of the 1980s management stripped the

---

[23] See Foote, 'Law', on policymaking on working hours. Different, considerably more lenient, regulations have often been applied to smaller firms. On the controversy over the establishment of the 40-hour week in smaller establishments, see *Asahi Shimbun*, (26 February 1997), 4 and 24 March 1997, 34; *Nikkei Weekly* (20 Jan. 1997), 2; *Shukan Rodo Nyusu* (3 March 1997), 3; and *Nihon Keizai Shimbun* (28 March 1997), 2.

[24] Christian Berggren, *Alternatives to Lean Production* (Ithaca: ILR Press, 1992); and Laurie Graham, 'How Does the Japanese Model Transfer to the United States? A View from the Line', in Tony Elger and Chris Smith (eds), *Global Japanization?* (London: Routledge, 1994).

union of most of its powers in order to have a free hand in rationalizing work practices.[25] Coincidentally, the Toyota Union began to call for improvements in working conditions in 1982, but it was concerned that labor shortages would hurt competitiveness. It was only around 1989, at a time when workforce morale was falling and recruiting problems were becoming acute, that Toyota's campaign began to focus more on the well-being of the workers.[26]

Toyota took the lead in redesigning work and production methods in the auto industry, but its objectives shifted as domestic demand plunged in the early 1990s. It became apparent that manufacturing companies had overinvested on a near-disastrous scale in anticipation of continuously rising demand, so Toyota emphasized cost-cutting along with improving working conditions.[27] Instead of automating undesirable jobs, engineers redesigned production using new layouts and low-cost equipment, with added ergonomic features, in order to ease monotony and reduce physical strains. One goal was to employ more women and older workers to make up for labor shortages. Quit rates fell substantially, indicating the considerable effectiveness of the new personnel strategies and plant designs. However, the union does not appear to have played a significant role throughout the industry.[28]

Unions in the electronics sector have played a more important role in improving working conditions. Representing many of the country's most skilled and technically qualified workers, they probably have more leverage than unions in other sectors. Some 60% of the electronics industry's regular employees were university graduates as of 1996, and the ratio is rising. The Japanese Electrical Electronic and Information Union (hereafter, the Electronic Union) is also better funded than other Japanese industrial unions, and it is able to maintain its own modest think tank to study employment problems and directly assist white-collar union members. The Electronic Union is attempting to secure management agreement in restricting out-

[25] Tabata Hirokuni, 'Changes in Plant-Level Trade Union Organizations: A Case Study of the Automobile Industry', University of Tokyo Institute of Social Science Occasional Papers in Labor Problem and Social Policy (1989).

[26] See Takahiro Fujimoto 'An Evolutionary Process of Toyota's Final Assembly Operations—The Role of Ex-post Dynamic Capabilities'. Discussion Paper F-Series, Research Institute for the Japanese Economy, Faculty of Economics, The University of Tokyo (Jan. 1996), 24–5, 29–30, 37; and Jos Benders, 'Leaving Lean? Recent Changes in the Production Organization of Some Japanese Car Plants', *Economic and Industrial Democracy*, 17 (1996), 17. A major problem at Toyota was not so much total turnover, but very high turnover—around 10% annually—of its first-year workers.

[27] Technological change, particularly computerization, had less impact on employment relations during the 1990s than first anticipated. One reason is that the 1991–4 Heisei recession tempered ambitions for investing to upgrade production, and encouraged firms to rely more heavily on outsourcing to cut costs. See Economic Research Institute, Japan Society for the Promotion of Machine Industry, *Engineering Industries of Japan*, 30 (May 1996). On the other hand, outsourcing has emerged as a point of contention between unions and managers in the electronics industry.

[28] On Toyota, see Takahiro Fujimoto, 'An Evolutionary Process', on the technical side, and Asahi Shimbun's 'Yureru Seisan Gemba, Part II', which appeared in October 1994 (especially 14 Oct., p. 13 and 15 Oct., p. 12). See Benders, 'Leaving Lean?' for an overview of the industry.

sourcing, and it hopes to organize non-regular workers, who constitute over half the industry's work force.[29] However, it is unlikely that managers will consent to the organization of non-regular workers.

The enterprise unions in the electronics industry take care not to risk jeopardizing productivity or competitiveness. The policies of Matsushita Electric Union provide an important example. The union takes pride in an agreement it concluded with management to observe strict limits on overtime hours at the firm's VCR factory. The newly instituted system required more automation, tighter scheduling, and closer coordination among the union branches and within management. As a union official acknowledged in an interview, investment in automation is often the main means of resolving problems such as excessive overtime. When seeking to improve conditions, the union emphasizes to management that new equipment necessary to eliminate or ease a stressful job generally pays for itself in around two years by reducing wage costs. In short, reducing overtime at Matsushita, like improving working conditions at Toyota, has relied on new technical inputs to ensure that productivity will be maintained.[30] Personnel changes and innovations at Matsushita, which are generally implemented by management rather than the union, have often served as new standards for the rest of the industry or the country, but successes of the type achieved by Matsushita Union are so firm- or even plant-specific, and so reliant on sophisticated technical inputs, that it appears doubtful that they can serve as useful pattern setters for other companies or industries.

In the case of very depressed industries, unions have sometimes shifted toward helping redundant workers find new jobs. The Nippon Steel Union found that the rapid restructuring of the steel industry that followed the appreciation of the yen in 1985 undermined its standard job protection policies. By 1987, it was obvious that the usual practices of negotiating with management and lobbying national ministries would do little to save jobs. The union therefore began working with regional organizations to help strengthen local economies and create new job opportunities in the hard-hit Tohoku and Hokkaido regions.[31] While innovative in their own ways, however, such policies accept the essentially passive role of unions as protectors of jobs rather than signify a fundamentally new approach.

The Age of Super-competition

The economy fell into a long recession (the Heisei recession) between 1991 and 1994, recovered slightly for two years, and then collapsed into an even worse

[29] Interview, Electronic Union officials, July 1997, Tokyo.

[30] Sources on Matsushita Electrical Union and its policies include Keisuke Nakamura, Helmut Demes, and Hitoshi Nagano, 'Work Organization in Japan and Germany: A Research on VCR Production (1)' (Tokyo: Deutsches Institut für Japan-studien, 1994), and an interview at Matsushita Electrical Union headquarters (Dec. 1997).

[31] Totsuka Hideo and Hyodo Tsutomu (eds), *Chiiki Shakai to Rodo Kumiai* [Regional Society and Labor Unions] (Tokyo: Nihon Keizai Hyoronsha, 1995).

recession in early 1997. Notwithstanding the weak mid-decade recovery, Japan has essentially experienced an eight-year long economic slump. The persistence of the slump despite massive trade surpluses suggests that Japan's outwardly oriented economic strategy needs serious readjustment, but the unions remain ambivalent at best. The union movement as a whole has continued to demand a shift to internal demand-led economic policies while the IMF–JC unions in practice have supported the export-oriented economic strategies. Further, the IMF–JC basically support a business movement underway since around 1995 aimed at cutting business costs and deregulating employment practices. In short, far from seeking to stimulate the domestic economy, manufacturing sector unions are joining business and conservative government leaders in support of policies that appear likely to emphasize austerity, with the attendant risk of further dampening consumption and demand.

The rhetoric of internationalization and super-competition that arose in the mid 1990s implicitly emphasized Japan's supposedly increasing vulnerability and supported calls for economic rationalization, even as the massive trade surpluses provided one of the most obvious signs that Japan might still be a net beneficiary of globalization.[32] To a considerable extent, the pressures that have afflicted Japan have arguably been caused by its own economic practices rather more than foreign pressures. Competition intensified in some sectors, such as steel and autos, partly because foreign competitors had rationalized production systems in response to Japanese competition. The press has alluded somewhat half-heartedly to pressure from American financial institutions or institutional investors that are eroding Japanese job security practices, but it is clear that Japanese firms still rely heavily on the US market to maintain current levels of production. Moreover, apart from the likelihood that depressed demand is hurting the economy, a major cause of the 1990s slump is the near-meltdown of the financial system that resulted from the strains and distortions of funneling cheap investment capital to business.[33]

In many important respects, Japan appears to suffer fewer adverse effects from globalization than other industrialized states. Many observers believe, for example, that the globalization of financial flows has diminished national autonomy over fiscal policy, eroding the ability of national governments to conduct Keynesian policymaking, and similarly of unions to use centralized collective bargaining or other means to influence macroeconomies.[34] In con-

---

[32] The trade surplus has averaged a little under US$100b a year from 1992, though exchange rate shifts can create large swings in the figures. By early 1999, the rhetorical focus had shifted away from super-competition to the so-called 3 Ks, or *kajo* (excess), which mean excess capacity, excess employees, and excess debt. It is an ironic reference to the 3 Ks during the year of prosperity and labor shortages in the late 1980s, when employers worried that manufacturing jobs were too dirty (*kitanai*), difficult (*kitsui*), and dangerous (*kiken*) to attract young workers.

[33] R. Taggart Murphy, *The Weight of the Yen* (New York: W. W. Norton, 1997).

[34] For an overview of the impact of globalization on industrial relations in industrialized countries, see Sanford Jacoby, 'Social Dimensions of Global Economic Integration', in Jacoby (ed.), *The Workers of Nations* (New York: Oxford University Press, 1995).

trast, Japan has been able to spend tax dollars prodigiously to stimulate the economy during the 1990s, but has poured the money primarily into public works, as well as farm communities and the small business sector, all of which happen to be closely tied to conservative politicians. Conversely, the unions have not, as discussed here, made a concerted effort to use wage raises to reflate the economy. An increase in immigration is cited as a manifestation of globalization that brings difficult social strains and raises welfare costs in many countries, but Japan still puts tight official restrictions on foreign workers while tacitly allowing small firms to employ them illegally. Foreign workers, who can almost never blend into the general population, accordingly receive low pay and few benefits, and rarely remain long in Japan or bring their families. Finally, outward foreign direct investment has certainly contributed to job losses, but the proportion of FDI by Japanese manufacturing industry is, despite its high profile, far less than those of major competitors such as the United States or Germany. Further, Japanese firms are believed to keep sophisticated manufacturing processes at home when possible. This is becoming more difficult in the electronics industry, as discussed below, but officials of America's Union of Automobile Workers claim that Japanese investment in the United States creates only one-third as many jobs as comparable investment by American firms since many high-value-added parts are still made in Japan.[35]

Much of the present strain in the employment system results largely from changes in the industrial structure, which largely reflect technological advances, rather than from globalization. Japan experienced high growth and institutionalized its basic employment practices when steel and shipbuilding were the country's leading industries, then managed to maintain relatively high growth and employment levels into the 1980s, thanks to rising demand for autos and electronic products. The lifetime employment paradigm functioned partly because it was so flexible. Companies were legally required to protect employment, but had great leeway in using transfers and adjusting pay to do so.[36] The paradigm also functioned in large part because the government's industrial policies were effective in promoting the development of the nation's industrial base, notably the metalworking industries. The exemplary case was the steel industry, Japan's most prestigious sector for most of the twentieth century. Major steelmaking firms, enjoying the backing of the Ministry of International Trade and Industry (MITI), routinely colluded to minimize competition so that they could collectively maintain high levels of investment—as Japanese observers put it, the industry was not really competitive. By 1980,

---

[35] Interview, Sept. 1998.

[36] See the study of so-called employment adjustment in several major industries during the recessions of the mid 1970s, mid 1980s, and early 1990s in Hiroyuki Chuma *Kensho—Nihon-gata 'Koyo Chosei'* [Investigation: Japanese-style 'Employment Adjustment'] (Tokyo: Shueisha, 1994). Using comparative analysis, Chuma also posits that Japanese job security is no stronger than in most Western European countries.

however, the auto and electronics sectors were eclipsing steel in terms of importance and prestige, thanks to their greater potential for new product development and technological innovation. The appreciation of the yen in the mid 1980s accelerated industrial change by forcing some industries to locate significant portions of production offshore for the first time.

The emerging industrial structure is less stable than before, and the divergence from reality of the lifetime employment paradigm, which emphasizes the protection of jobs in particular companies, has grown steadily. The dynamism of autos and electronics largely reflects the fact that they are more changeable and adaptable than steel. Coordination was once relatively easy to achieve in steel because there is little product differentiation, enabling producers to agree fairly readily to limits on production and investment when demand fell. But production development and differentiation are more critical in other technologically advanced manufacturing industries. The auto and electronics industries, with their numerous major firms and myriad supplier networks, also have structures far more complex than that of the steel industry with its compact core of five major firms. Subcontractors play a much less important role in steel than in autos and electronics, meaning that steel firms draw much less benefit from the low-wage, low-cost subcontracting firms. Toyota has also recently stepped up the hiring of contract (short-term) employees in order to hold down long-term wage costs. Finally, offshore investment enables the auto and electronics industries to adjust flexibly to currency swings and trade friction, and to gain direct access to foreign markets, while the massive fixed costs of steel production limit the usefulness of overseas investment.

The electronics firms have been forced to steadily abandon the principle that Japan must maintain maximum economic independence and keep core manufacturing processes at home. Computer makers until recently kept production in Japan in order to maintain quality, but fierce price competition forced them to start procuring parts from offshore suppliers in the mid 1990s. Toshiba even found that it could engage in joint ventures with foreign partners to enhance technical capabilities without sacrificing quality.[37] As a result of such trends, Electrical Union officials expect virtually all good manufacturing jobs in their sector to move offshore in several years.[38] Facing this discouraging prospect, the union has energetically backed measures to help companies cut labor and other costs.

In the mid 1990s, the media began to echo the views of employers that Japan is confronting an era of super-competition. A basic scenario holds that the primary manifestation is a great widening of performance differentials among economic sectors and firms.[39] The greatest disparity, according to the

[37] Economic Research Institute, *Engineering Industries*, ch. 3.
[38] Interview, Electrical Union officials, June 1997.
[39] The scenario is succinctly laid out by Nakatani Iwao, the most prominent individual proponent of economic rationalization and reform, in a newspaper editorial, 'Nikyokubun ga susumu Nihon keizai' [The progressive bipolarization of Japan's economy], *Asahi Shimbun* (20 March 1997), 4.

scenario, is between competitive, internationally oriented industries such as autos and electronics, and domestic-oriented sectors such as finance, real estate, and construction. Long protected by government regulators, the latter sectors are experiencing great difficulty in coming to grips with the pressures of the market. The second dimension of disparity is within industries. Even in the dynamic auto industry, firms such as Toyota and Honda have affirmed their positions as elite global manufacturers, while Nissan and Mazda have faded. A third dimension of differentials is between large firms and small and mid-sized firms. Smaller firms have been hit especially hard by the slump, partly because larger firms have stepped up the use of non-Japanese suppliers and opted for more in-house production.[40]

The scenario has some glaring problems—such as ignoring the fact that the government protects the strong (autos) as well as the weak (finance)—but it illustrates the type of logic often marshaled by economic opinion leaders calling for reform in the 1990s. The desire for reform was stimulated in large part by a series of scandals that undermined confidence in the government, reinforcing the widespread perception that 'reform' was necessary to reduce tax burdens, restore job security, and improve the quality of life. In reality there has been relatively little economic reform despite the hue and cry, largely because business leaders routinely demand reform but use their ties to the government to forestall it in their own sectors. Similarly, manufacturing sector unions oppose reform of their own sectors.[41]

While business leaders have largely fended off reform of their own sectors, they have made steady progress in fostering a steady restructuring of employment practices and regulations. The leading proponent of deregulating employment practices has been the hardline employers association, Nikkeiren. Like Rengo and the IMF–JC, Nikkeiren has no authority and perhaps little influence but serves as a useful indicator of its affiliates' opinions. In 1995, Nikkeiren began to issue well-publicized reports, such as *New Age Japanese-style Management*, which urged employers to implement more flexible employment practices and cut labor costs through such measures as making greater use of specialists, contract workers, temporaries, and part-timers. The thrust of Nikkeiren's arguments was that employment could be stabilized and living standards improved only if wage and employment systems were made more flexible and the nation's high-cost structure broken down. Employers seeking to revise the wage system have been seeking to eliminate the practice of linking wages in *shunto* (spring wage offensive) and to eliminate or reduce the importance of seniority pay. Almost all employers would also like to make greater use of merit pay, although most firms have been

---

[40] According to the Small and Medium Enterprise Agency, the production indicator of SMEs for April–June 1997 stood at 95.5 (1990 equals 100) while that of large firms was 105.8. *Asahi Shimbun* (7 Aug. 1997), 8.

[41] Steven K. Vogel, 'Can Japan Disengage? Winners and Losers in Japan's Political Economy, and the Ties that Bind Them', BRIE Working Paper 111 (Dec. 1997).

cautious about moving too fast because comprehensive merit pay systems remain untested. Other parts of the emerging paradigm are vague, but some managers have stated that they will exercise their social responsibility to protect jobs in the future by improving training to enable individual workers to find new jobs throughout their careers on their own. It is also often assumed that the government will improve its retraining and other capacities for facilitating a mobile workforce.[42]

Employers have spent decades modifying the basic wage setting structure. Two main objects are seniority-based wages, the importance of which has decreased steadily over the years, and the linking of wage settlements within and across industries. Employers often argue that the practice of linking wage settlements, which lies at the heart of the annual *shunto* national wage setting system, threatens jobs by raising costs for weaker firms. By linking wage settlements, *shunto* has helped to minimize wage differentials and to raise low-end wages. *Shunto* operates through a process of pattern setting in which the wage settlements of major firms, especially in metalworking industries, have served as benchmarks for other firms and industries. The *shunto* framework has given unions an opportunity to help raise wages of millions of non-union workers, but it has weakened rapidly in the 1990s because of economic changes and the determination of employers to cut costs. A breakdown of *shunto*, which now appears likely,[43] would deprive organized labor of one of the few remaining mechanisms that enables it to either put pressure on managers or to use positive appeals to capture the public's attention. None the less, the IMF–JC unions have been ambivalent about raising wages, and they have supported policies that have indirectly weakened *shunto*. One example is deregulation, which has forced cost-cutting rationalization on sectors such as telecommunications, electric power, and private railways. These sectors, being subject to little if any foreign competition, until recently awarded wage raises higher than the official raises in the metalworking sector. The private railway unions were militant, by Japanese standards, about wages because their members regarded themselves as underpaid. However, the recent increase in cost pressures has led service sector firms not only to hold down wage increases, but to dismantle or reduce the importance of industry-level wage setting, weakening the wage setting influence of the individual enterprise unions. The unions directly affected are unhappy since performance of the firm tends to reflect demand factors more than worker effort or efficiency. However, the outcome suits the IMF–JC, which believes that service sector firms and unions have not tried hard enough to raise productivity, but have

---

[42] For samples of management opinions, see Nikkeiren's monthly organ, *Keieisha*, which is a principal forum for discussing new pay and personnel policies. See also Committee for the Study of Labor Issues, Japan Federation of Employers' Associations (Nikkeiren), 'Structural Reform—The Search for a Third Option. Employment Stability and Improved National Quality of Life', Nikkeiren Position Paper for 1997.

[43] The current state of *shunto* is examined in detail in Charles Weathers, 'The 1999 Shunto and the Restructuring of Wage Setting in Japan', *Asian Survey* (Nov./Dec. 1997).

instead passed higher wage costs on to customers. This practice, it feels, not only raises the cost of living but also damages competitiveness. Other unions have retorted that IMF–JC unions do not bargain hard enough, and that the high productivity gains made possible in manufacturing through automation cannot be achieved in service sector industries.

IMF–JC unions have also generally supported the use of merit pay and other means of linking wages more closely to individual or firm performance.[44] The Electronic Union has been a strong advocate of pay systems intended to increase productivity despite dissent from a few of its affiliates. Japanese firms have used merit pay since the 1950s, but have increased its weight only slowly over the years while reducing that of seniority-based pay.[45] The use of merit pay has increased more quickly in the 1990s because of the growing importance of white-collar and highly skilled occupations. Until recently, manufacturing was so important to the national economy that employers cared relatively little about the notoriously low productivity of Japanese white-collar employees. That is changing now, especially in electronics, which has evolved from a primarily blue-collar sector into a largely white- or gray-collar sector. However, the shift in pay systems appears likely to reduce union influence over pay further as it is difficult for unions to exercise a voice in individualized pay systems.

In addition to revising pay systems, businesses and some government agencies have been revising regulations governing working conditions to further increase flexibility and cut costs. The Ministry of Labor has greatly expanded the number of job categories to which discretionary pay can be applied, an important change given the growing importance of white-collar sectors. In discretionary pay systems, employees are paid only for contracted hours and do not earn overtime. While the system facilitates flexible deployment of white-collar workers, and will let some workers set their own hours, it can also mean more unpaid overtime. In addition, companies such as Toyota are making increasing use of contract workers (generally on three- to five-year contracts) in order avoid taking long-term responsibility for employees.

Working conditions for women are another issue where divisions among unions leave employers and the government relatively free to shape new policies. Social and economic changes have improved the job prospects for women over the past two decades, as more firms have given women opportunities to pursue professional careers, but deregulation and cost-cutting strategies have recently relegated many others to poorly paid and insecure positions.[46] Japan passed the Equal Employment Opportunity Law (EEOL)

[44] Ishida Mitsuo, 'Jinji shogu no kobetsuka to rodo kumiai kino' [The individualization of personnel treatment and labor union functions], *Nihon Rodo Kyokai Zasshi*, 460 (Oct. 1998), 40–8.

[45] Okunishi Yoshio, 'Kigyo-nai chingin kakusa no genjo to sono yoin' [Intra-firm wage differentials and their causes], *Nihon Rodo Kenkyu Zasshi*, 460 (Oct. 1998).

[46] See Makoto Kumazawa, *Portraits of the Japanese Workplace*, Andrew Gordon (ed.); Gordon and Mikiso Hane (trans.) (Boulder: Westview Press, 1996), ch. 7, on female workers in

in 1986 in order to demonstrate compliance with international norms on female equality but the law was limited to encouraging employers to make efforts to put an end to gender-based workplace discrimination. At the same time that the EEOL was being passed, the legislation on dispatch (temporary worker) agencies was revised, and a number of banks promptly dismissed some of their female employees and 'rehired' them through dispatch agencies that were wholly owned subsidiaries of the banks.[47] Further deregulation of dispatch agencies in the 1990s has enabled more companies to replace regular employees with dispatch workers, 80% of whom are women. The liberal newspaper *Asahi Shimbun* has reported that companies frequently commit violations such as assigning work not specified in contracts and dismissing dispatch workers before contracts run out as rules are not enforced.[48]

The government liberalized the archaic laws limiting working hours for women in April 1999. The auto companies were the leading advocates of liberalization because they want to employ more women in factories;[49] they were supported by the Confederation of Auto Workers' Unions and other manufacturing sector unions. Unions, such as Zensen Domei, which represents large numbers of women in the textile and service sectors, were concerned that liberalizing laws governing women without improving general standards risked worsening working conditions for all employees, but failed to exercise much influence on the debate.[50]

Conclusion

Viewed in the context of globalization, a dilemma for Japanese labor is that foreign capital is creating little of the direct pressure at present on wages, working conditions, and job security, because the present recession is largely a result of the collapse of domestic demand. None the less, employers are attempting to restructure employment and wage practices to further develop national competitiveness, and many unions are strongly supporting these efforts, despite the likelihood of increasing differentials. Compared to late-industrializing or post-communist nations, of course, the basic welfare of workers in Japan is well protected, but many union leaders have shown surprisingly little concern for quality of life issues, much less the tougher issues of differences in wages and working hours. Despite nearly fifteen years of debate about whether the appropriateness of the nation's economic course, and eight years of economic stagnation, many leading unions remain com-

post-war Japan, and the business weekly *Nikkei Bijiness*, (27 Jan. 1997), 22–35, on the deregulation of women's jobs. Women account for around 27% of Rengo members, but only 2.4–5.8% of the members of its three major committees. *Shukan Rodo Nyusu* (14 April 1997), 4.

[47] Kumazawa, *Portraits*, 181.   [48] *Asahi Shimbun* (16 May 1999), 3.
[49] Interview, Association of Automobile Manufacturers Associations officials, June 1999.
[50] *Asahi Shimbun* (17 July 1997), 3.

mitted to supporting the goals of raising productivity and strengthening the competitiveness of individual firms and entire industries.

The post-war employment system proved effective in contributing to rapid development by promoting cooperative workplace relations, making it possible for firms to conduct long-term training and deploy workers flexibly. Lifetime employment was a misleading term in many respects, but it proved an effective symbol for the exchange of security in return for loyalty and commitment to enterprises. Even with the fading of the lifetime employment paradigm and the shift in preference toward flexible employment practices, many major unions have not yet altered their basic strategy of closely supporting individual enterprises in order to protect jobs. The position of other unions has become more contradictory. Rengo unions have supported the view that Japan should put greater emphasis on domestic growth and reduce its export orientation, but many of its unions have also supported employer initiatives for cost-cutting and rationalization, policies that are intended in part to hold down domestic consumption in order to support an export-oriented strategy. Advocates of rationalization argue that Japanese employment practices are too rigid and labor costs too high to allow Japanese firms to remain competitive, and that firms must utilize flexible, individualistic, and competition-oriented practices to survive and to generate jobs and growth. Yet the 1990s have shown that Japan can run a massive trade surplus, hold down wages, and still fall into severe recession, bringing the argument into question.

Japan has established a model for countries wishing to modernize and avoid dependence on foreign capital, even if its particular developmental approach cannot be duplicated. Its model of labor-management relations is more ambivalent, especially for workers. Studies of manufacturing in late-industrializing countries sometimes note that higher skilled workers benefit most from inward foreign direct investment and more technologically advanced production systems; lesser skilled workers receive little if any benefit.[51] In many respects, this pattern has been evident in Japan as well in the large differentials in wages and working conditions that exist according to firm size, educational background, and gender. The ongoing campaign to cut labor costs may well exacerbate those trends and further marginalize the influence of organized labor. Japan's unions have helped to achieve impressive economic gains for their country, but their failure to sustain a meaningful social agenda may prevent the majority of wage earners from sampling the full benefits of economic success.

---

[51] Ishac Diwan and Michael Walton, 'How International Exchange, Technology, and Institutions Affect Workers: An Introduction', *The World Bank Review*, 11: 1 (1997).

Part II

Labor in Post-socialist Economies

7

Transition, Globalization, and Changing Industrial Relations in China

Xiaobo Lu, Barnard College

As a country undergoing rapid political, social, and economic changes, China faces a two-pronged challenge—the economic regime transition from the state socialism characterized by state ownership and central planning to a capitalist economy based on private ownership and the market, and an economic growth increasingly defined by export and international markets. These two parallel processes—transition and globalization—are taking place while the political regime remains authoritarian. The records are impressive; the economic reforms launched since 1978 have transformed China's economy. Chinese economic growth since then has exceeded all expectations, with real gross national product (GNP) growing almost 9% annually during the period between 1982 and 1996. In less than twenty years, China jumped from below the top twenty-five trading economies rank to the eleventh largest trading economy in the world in 1998.

As becomes increasingly clear, globalization affects the economic transformation that China, and indeed all former state socialist economies, is engaged in. The experiences of the transforming regimes, such as China's, have raised some important questions, which bear broad theoretical and policy significance. What impact has globalization had on the transition from state socialist economies? What are the dynamics between these two processes? What makes the experience of former state socialist countries unique among countries that are under the similar impact of globalization? Among the many aspects of globalization's impact that one may analyze, the issue of how labor institutions respond to the pressure of globalization offers a significant case through which these questions may be addressed.

By examining some basic features of Chinese industrial relations under state socialism and the emerging labor institutions, this chapter intends to take a close look at how the two parallel and sometimes intertwined processes of economic transition and globalization have had affected the relations among the state, enterprises, and workers. It argues that as both are important factors in

An earlier, substantially different version of this chapter was published in Francis Adams, Satya Gupta, and Kidane Mengisteab (eds), *Globalization and the Dilemmas of the State in the South* (Basingstoke: Macmillan, 1999).

recasting industrial relations in China, the broad economic transition from state socialism has been a defining element while the internationalization of the Chinese economy has had some impact. Neither the changing international political economy nor the transition has diminished the role the state has played, and will continue to play, a significant role in redefining and managing industrial relations. The pace, scope, and sequence of change in industrial relations are determined not only by leadership choice, but also by historical and structural constraints derived mainly from the pre-reform past, key among which are the entrenched *danwei* (work unit) system, weak trade unions, and abundant labor supply.

Chinese Industrial Relations under State Socialism

For nearly three decades, industrial relations in the People's Republic of China (PRC) were characterized by what was common in state socialist systems—an economy dominated by state-owned enterprises, employee dependence on the enterprise, state-controlled union organizations, and relative labor peace. Despite sporadic working- class protests in PRC history since 1949, there were no organized labor movements.[1] Labor disputes were usually described as 'contradictions between different parts of the same organization' by the communist authorities. As a visiting delegation of American labor arbitrators discovered more than a decade ago, when contradictions did occur they could be solved by education, the existing system of regulation, demotion, or reduction in wages.[2]

Under state socialism, the state was the dominant part of the state-enterprise–worker relationship. David Stark, in an analysis of the nature of state socialism, puts such relationship in a broad context:

With nationalization of banking and industry and the near elimination of small private proprietors in agriculture and services, the modern redistributive economy represents an unprecedented concentration of ownership of productive assets. But there is one asset, vital to our understanding of the dynamics of state socialism, that has not been nationalized . . . Labor remains de facto and de jure the property of individuals and households.[3]

---

[1] Some scholars identify several major conflicts between workers and the government that occurred during the past four decades (see, e.g., Anita Chan, 'Revolution or Corporatism? Workers and Trade Unions in Post-Mao China', *The Australian Journal of Chinese Affairs*, 29 (1993), 31–61; and Elizabeth Perry, 'Labor's Battle for Political Space: the Role of Worker Associations in Contemporary China', in Deborah Davis, Richard Kraus, Barry Naughton, and Elizabeth Perry (eds), *Urban Spaces in Contemporary China* (Washington, DC: Woodrow Wilson Center Press, 1995). Yet these were exceptions rather than defining events that have changed history. More importantly, each of these conflicts ended with further tightening of state control over the trade unions.

[2] I.B. Helburn and John Scharer, 'Human Resources and Industrial Relations in China', *Industrial and Labor Relations Review*, 38 (1984), 3–15.

[3] David Stark, 'Bending the Bars of the Iron Cage: Bureaucratization and Informalization in Capitalism and Socialism', *Sociological Forum*, 4 (1989), 637–64.

Both trade unions and enterprise management played an auxiliary role, as part of the state-sponsored production process. Under state socialism, the labor process was combined with a specific political economy in which the party/state apparatus appropriates and distributes resources through centralized planning and command. It produced a distinctive labor process characterized by the dual control system of managers and party mobilized to meet production targets through a variety of mechanisms.[4] The state-controlled employment and work compensation. Enterprises had limited autonomy to hire and fire, while workers had little freedom in choosing their jobs.

Profitability was not the only, nor even the most important, goal for firms in state socialist systems generally. They sought, rather, full employment and job security. Most urban workers had lifetime employment. Enterprise paternalism—firms provides social services and welfare including housing, vacation facilities, food subsidies—can be found in many transition economies, ranging from the well-developed Russian industrial system to less industrialized economies such as Vietnam (Lu 1997). In the former Soviet Union, enterprises provided their employees and families with many services and subsidies—what Russian scholars called the 'social sphere'—that are either the government's responsibility or are delivered by private businesses in capitalist countries.[5] Enterprise paternalism has contributed to labor peace and dependent relations of employees on their factories, posing barriers to collective action by labor.[6]

State socialist industrial relations were also defined by the absence of a labor market. Labor was not regarded as a commodity whose value could be dictated by supply and demand. Relationships between workers and their employers were often purported to be those between individuals and organizations or citizens and the state, not employee and employer or labor and management. More emphasis was given to employee participation in industrial affairs than to confrontation between labor and management. Given the existence of a bargaining relationship between enterprises and the state, the incentive was strong for 'triple alliance between managers, unions, and party within the enterprise' to promote the interests of the enterprise before the central planners.[7] As a result, the direct producers—the purported 'masters of the nation' and 'masters of the enterprise'—were deprived of any institutionalized way of defending their interests against managerial despotism.[8] If and

[4] Chris Smith and Paul Thompson (eds), *Labor in Transition: The Labor Process in Eastern Europe and China* (London: Routledge, 1992).

[5] Richard Bird, Robert Ebel, and Christine Wallich (eds), *Decentralization of the Socialist State: Intergovernmental Finance in Transition Economies*. (Washington, DC: The World Bank, 1995).

[6] Stephen Crowley, 'Barrier to Collective Action: Steel Workers and Mutual Dependence in the Former Soviet Union', *World Politics*, 46 (July 1994), 589–615.

[7] Michael Burawoy, 'View From Production: The Hungarian Transition from Socialism to Capitalism', in Chris Smith and Paul Thompson (eds), *Labour in Transition: The Labour Process in Eastern Europe and China* (London: Routledge, 1992).

[8] Ibid.

when labor disputes did occur, they were presented and handled as any other disputes in an administrative organization—that is, by individual petitions to higher levels of organizational leadership.

Trade unions served a political role, functioning as a 'transmission belt' between the state and workers.[9] Unions were nonetheless reduced to a minimal welfare organization with limited roles in industrial relations. Occasionally, trade unions would become more participatory at the enterprise level and adversarial at the national level. The many 'trade union reforms' in these socialist countries never went beyond the model of 'dualistic functions'—that is, as 'transmission belt' of the state and advocates of workers interests.[10] Only near the end of communist rule in many former socialist states did the official unions—for example, the Polish OPZZ and Soviet AUCCTU—begin to shed their 'transmission belt' function and become genuinely adversarial.

The nature of the relationship between the state and trade unions in particular and communist politics in general has been analyzed in the light of 'state corporatism'.[11] It was argued that communist states adopted corporatist rule by creating vertical functional institutions and placed them under central control, with the express purpose of pre-empting the horizontal coalescing of class interests. This argument overlooks, at least in the Chinese case, the fact that the cellular structure of work units—mostly in China but also in other former state socialist systems—have exerted a more defining impact on state-union-worker relations. Workers' interests were more fragmented between or within different enterprises[12] rather than 'organized into a limited number of singular, compulsory, non-competitive, hierarchically ordered categories'.[13] The communist state relied on neither corporatism nor pluralism.[14] Instead, it relied heavily on the *danwei* system, which generated cellular social and political dynamics. When they did occur, labor protests as well as protests by other social groups, often took place with workers from

[9] Malcolm Warner, *The Management of Human Resources in Chinese Industry* (New York: St. Martin's Press, 1995); Anil Verma, T. Kochan, and R. Lansbury, *Employment Relations in the Growing Asian Economies* (New York: Routledge, 1995).

[10] Chan, 'Revolution or Corporatism?'

[11] Daniel Chirot, 'The Corporatist Model and Socialism', *Theory and Society*, 9 (1980), 363–81; Valerie Bunce and John Echols, 'Soviet Politics in the Brezhnev Era: "Pluralism" or "Corporatism"', in Donald Kelly (ed.), *Soviet Politics in the Brezhnev Era* (New York: Praeger, 1980); Alex Pravda and Blair Ruble, *Trade Unions in Communist States* (Boston: Allen & Unwin, 1986); Chan, 'Revolution or Corporatism?'

[12] See, for example, Perry's finding that during two of the four major labor unrest periods (i.e., 1956–7, 1966–9) a main cause of grievance was differential treatment of temporary, contracted workers and permanent workers in the same enterprises (Perry, 'Labor's Battle for Political Space').

[13] Philppe Schimitter, cited in Chan, 'Revolution or Corporatism?', 35.

[14] Though sharing some common denominators, there are some generic differences between pluralist and cellular politics. They both have a multiplicity and competition of social interests. Yet, in pluralist society, competition is open and encouraged. Public policy is a result, not an arbitrator, of competition among different interests. In a cellular polity, competition is not open and encouraged. Order and maintenance of boundaries of each cell are emphasized.

one enterprise during the Maoist period.[15] Rarely were they organized by unions or joined by workers from other enterprises.

While China shared many features of labor relations in a typical state socialist system, it also had some unique characters of its own. Perhaps the most significant of all is the *danwei* system, which made both entrance and exit extremely difficult for urban employees, leading to a situation approximating what Starks called the nationalization of labor. It also helped to create divisions within the working class—between newer and older workers, between locals and outsiders, and between permanent and temporary and contract laborers. Except for a short period during the rapid industrialization in the late 1950s and early 1960s, Chinese enterprises maintained a system of enclosed welfare communities, which prohibited people from freely coming in.[16]

As *danwei*, the Chinese enterprise had multifunctions beyond a simple production-centered, profit-generating entity. This system, which some scholars call a 'total institution',[17] once had three major roles: full employment and job security, welfare and social service deliverance, and political control.

State enterprises provided the largest share of urban employment opportunities nationwide. In the 1970s, enterprises were even allowed to hire children of employees who had graduated from high school in order to reduce urban unemployment. One consequence of such policies was the creation of excess labor in almost all state-owned enterprises (SOEs). Unless a worker committed serious criminal acts, he or she could not be discharged. The *danwei* was a 'cradle to grave' institution where workers were permanently attached to the work unit. Under central planning, China's urban working population had to be absorbed by *danwei* of all kinds including industrial units. Except for a small group, most people of working age in the cities were permanent employees. Contract-based employment was rare before the reforms.

Chinese enterprises took on responsibilities to provide social services and welfare, which would otherwise be provided by the private sector or the government. Some enterprises still spend as much as 40% of their profits on social services. By the mid 1980s, over 70% of SOEs ran schools of some kind while roughly 40% of all hospital beds were in the state-owned industrial system.[18]

---

[15] Xiaobo Lu and Elizabeth Perry (eds), *Danwei: The Changing Chinese Workplace in Comparative and Historical Perspective* (Armonk: M. E. Sharpe, 1997).

[16] According to internal official documents, there were incidents where large numbers of workers left their state-owned factories to join better-paid collective enterprises in 1960. In some cases, over one hundred workers quit their jobs *en masse* in one factory. Some state-owned enterprises also tried to hire workers from other factories without official approval. This prompted the government to issue an order to regain tight control of labor mobility and remuneration. See Zhonghua Quanguo Zonggonghui [All China Federation of Trade Unions], *Jianguo Yilai Zhonggong Zhongyang Guanyu Gongren Yundong Wenjian Xuanbian* [Selected CCP Central Committee Documents on Workers' Movements] (Beijing: Gongren chubanshe, 1989), 860–70.

[17] Warner (1995).

[18] Naughton (1997). One large state enterprise in Shanghai owns more than 20 buses for the sole purpose of transporting its workforce to and from their factory jobs, being used only twice

In some cases, large enterprises spend as much as 20% of annual profits on social services. In these firms, shopfloor workers, technical assistants, and administrative and social service staff each account for one-third of total employees.[19]

Pensions and employee health costs are covered by enterprises. Currently some 30 million public sector retirees are paid this way nationwide. For enterprises, retiree pensions are actually a part of their payroll (albeit at retiree scales), creating heavy financial burdens. It is common among SOEs for retirees to account for as much as one third of employee payrolls. In some enterprises, the ratio of workers and retirees can even be 1 : 1, and the pensions are larger than the total amount paid to working employees. These entitlements squeeze enterprises for more resources, which are already in dire need of capital reinvestment to upgrade outdated production equipment. According to official figures, the total payroll spending on excess labor and pensioners by SOEs nationwide was yuan 160bn (US$19bn) in 1995, while SOE profits totaled only yuan 110bn (US$13.2bn) in the same year.[20] In addition, SOE spending on employee health care reached unmanageable heights by the early 1990s. In 1994, the total of health care spending by the state sector amounted to yuan 55.8bn (US$6.7bn).[21]

The *danwei* system also afforded an effective mechanism with which the state was able to monitor the political loyalty of its citizens, particularly party members. The enterprise was laced with political organizations that served to prevent organized opposition and to recruit and co-opt members of the workforce.[22] If a worker engaged in independent political activities, he or she would be unable to transfer and find work elsewhere. Each unit was responsible for its members; the activities its members engaged in outside of their units were also reported back to the unit. In this way, the regime was able to inhibit, albeit not entirely prevent, large-scale organized opposition. Such political dependence of workers on management was what distinguished it from such capitalist systems as Japan's where large firms also created social dependence by employees by offering welfare benefits and services. The combination of both political and social dependence created by the Chinese *danwei* system posed barriers to collective action, in contrast to the former Soviet Union where enterprise paternalism was largely attributed to labor shortages, and disincentives for participating in collective action was mainly economic in nature.[23]

a day for less than two hours in total while public buses are extremely crowded. See Lu and Dittmer (1996).

[19] Weizhong Fang (ed.), *Guanyu Gaohao Guoyou Qiye de Diaocha* [Investigations on How to Improve SOEs] (Beijing: Zhongguo wenshi chubanshe, 1995).

[20] *Jingji Ribao* [Economic Daily], 22 Aug. 1996.

[21] *Renmin Ribao (RMRB)* [People's Daily], Beijing, 6 April 1996.

[22] Andrew Walder, *Communist Neo-Traditionalism: Work and Authority in Chinese Industry* (Berkeley: University of California Press, 1986).

[23] Xiaobo Lu, 'Enterprise Paternalism and Transition to Market Socialism: the Political Economy of State Sector Reform In State Socialist Systems', *Mondes en Développement*, 25 (1997), 41–56.

Although state socialist countries varied in the degree of worker depend-ence on the enterprise, Chinese workers experienced extreme political and social dependence on the enterprise.[24] Compared to Russian enterprises which have long faced labor shortages, Chinese enterprises were more exclu-sive and their employees more permanent. Chinese workers were more tied to the enterprise than their counterparts in other state socialist countries. The dynamics of power relations within enterprises were different in China and the Soviet Union. While Chinese workers were very much at the mercy of managers, Soviet workers had more control of the labor process. Herein lies one of the key differences between industrial relations in China and other state socialist countries—the labor supply. Due to labor shortages, Soviet enterprise managers competed constantly with incentives of welfare provi-sions to attract employees, especially skilled ones.[25] Persistent labor short-ages, not legal guarantees, made it very difficult to dismiss a worker. In this sense, though Russian and Chinese enterprises were quite similar in their wel-fare functions, they existed for opposite reasons. Labor shortages during the early years of rapid industrialization prompted Soviet enterprises to become 'Bolshevik fortresses'[26] in order to keep skilled workers from leaving, whereas the Chinese brick-walled 'small societies' or 'mini welfare states' were designed to keep unwanted rural labor from entering. It has been argued that because of the need to woo workers in Russia, such welfare provisions became necessary and managers worked hard to take care of the interests of their employees to such an extent that there was a certain degree of depend-ence on employees. Dependence was found to be more mutual between man-agement and workers in Soviet enterprises.[27]

Another possible difference between the Chinese and other socialist states is the relative high degree of egalitarianism among urban workers and man-agers in China. Often described as 'eating from the same big pot', this remu-nerative structure also reinforced the enclosed character of the *danwei*—only those who were in the 'big pot' could have a share. Those who were outside the *danwei*, mostly peasants without city residency, were shut out.

Compared to other former state socialist countries, China also had more controlled and less functional workers' councils and trade union systems dur-ing the Maoist period. Even though workers' councils—which was suppos-edly a 'basic form of democratic management and an authoritative body for workers to participate in decision-making and to monitor managers'—were revived after the reforms began in the late 1970s and had been established in almost all SOEs by 1986, they have largely met for the sake of formality and

[24] Walder, *Communist Neo-Traditionalism*, 16–18.
[25] Flitzer, 'Economic Reform and Production Relations in Soviet Industry'.
[26] Kenneth Straus, 'The Soviet Factory as Community Organizer', in Lu and Perry (eds), 1997.
[27] Stephen Crowley, 'Barrier to Collective Action'; and Flitzer, 'Economic Reform and Production Relations in Soviet Industry'.

are basically being used as rubber-stamp bodies. More recently, a survey found that with the SOE reforms many newly transformed 'modern corporations' (65% of those surveyed) have reduced the authority of workers' councils.[28] In many instances, they only deal with social and welfare issues such as employee housing allocation. They are rarely taken seriously by either workers or managers as having any major influence. At best, they were, and still are, 'consultative forums that impose limited obligations on top management'.[29] If the experience of other transition economies can offer any perspective for Chinese enterprises after privatization, *de facto* or *de jure*, it is the diminishing role of the workers' councils.[30]

The stature of trade unions in China was even more precarious throughout PRC history than their counterparts in other former state socialist countries. Though there were times, as in the early 1950s, when the leadership of the All China Federation of Trade Unions (ACFTU) leaned toward being more of a 'workers' interest representative and protector', trade unions were often subject to political wrangling, their orientation dictated by the political needs of the day. From time to time, unions were accused of being 'economistic'—that is, in putting the short-term interests of workers before the long-term interests of the nation. They ceased to exert their 'representative functions' after the radicalization of the Chinese political leadership in 1958. A typical statement of the function of labor unions would read,

the most fundamental and important mission of trade unions is to organize and educate workers in order to improve productivity and guarantee fulfillment of the state production plan. On the basis of improving production, unions shall pay attention to the mundane interests of workers and serve their needs. Unions shall lead workers to fight for the future of socialism.[31]

In a 1958 speech to purge former leaders of the ACFTU, the new chairman stated,

labor unions must summit themselves *unconditionally* to the Party leadership. Union work is part of the Party's mass work. Unions at all levels (from the ACFTU on down) should be *in essence the union affairs department of the Party committee*. All must work under the unified leadership of the party, serving the needs of the core tasks and political mission of the Party [emphasis added].[32]

The desired relationship between the communist party, management, trade unions, and ordinary workers was made clear in another speech by an official in 1957. 'The director makes the report, the party committee gives instructions, the trade union issues the call, the masses give the pledge'.[33] Indeed,

[28] Liu Jiang *et al.*, *1996–97 Zhongguo Shehui Xingshi Fenxi yu Yuce* [Analysis and Predictions of China's Social Situation in 1996–97] (Beijing: Zhongguo shehui kexue chubanshe, 1997).
[29] Smith and Thompson, *Labor in Transition*, 237.
[30] Florek (1992), 112.
[31] Zhonghua, Selected CCP central committee documents on workers' movements, 662.
[32] Zhonghua, Selected CCP central committee documents on workers' movements, 669.
[33] Li Xue-feng, as quoted in Smith and Thompson, *Labor in Transition*, 235.

trade unions became instrumental in Maoist attempts to radically transform Chinese urban society. In one of the most telling instances, unions played a significant role in carrying out a massive downsizing of the urban workforce in 1959 without instigating social unrest. In this what communist leaders themselves later marveled at as an 'incredible achievement', the government was able to lay off nearly 10 million workers, many of whom had to relocate to the countryside. Unions helped to arrange the lay-offs.[34]

Trade unions' political role of serving the needs of the regime was often overshadowed by its welfare caretaker role at the enterprise level. Working closely with management, they were an important part of 'enterprise paternalism' that the *danwei* system was known for. Some summarized this role figuratively as 'issuing film tickets, managing meal coupons, and collecting bathing tickets'.[35] But again, even in such capacity, unions' role was mainly redistributive rather than representative.

Economic Transition and Emerging Labor Relations

The reforms of the last two decades have drastically changed China's industrial relations. There is today a relatively open labor market in which employers can hire freely without being dictated to by the state. The Chinese state still plays a significant role in managing labor relations, as do states in large industrializing countries. A recent national survey of business managers found that over half of them regard government labor agencies as 'intervening too much'.[36] However, state concerns and priorities have changed. With a gradualist approach and a 'growing out of plan' strategy, the Chinese government has been pushing a comprehensive reform of the state sector since 1992. No longer are the full employment and job security policies endorsed. At the firm level, Tayloristic management practices are adopted. Unlike other industrializing countries such as Thailand and Malaysia,[37] however, its concerns have been less about cost containment than trying to attract more foreign investment. The most challenging task for the Chinese state has been redefining industrial relations under an emerging market economy. In the face of the twin challenges, the state realized that industrial relations 'have become more diverse and complicated', and that they are no longer a simple state-worker relationship. The rise of the non-state sector, particularly foreign invested enterprises, has made the management an independent actor

---

[34] Zhonghua, Selected CCP central committee documents on workers movements, 718.

[35] Warner (1995), 36.

[36] According to this survey, tax agencies as a whole had the highest number of complaints of 'government over-intervention' (60%), while labor agencies had the second highest (55%) among all such functional departments. See *Zhongguo Jingji Nianjian* [Economic Statistic Yearbook of China] (Beijing: Zhongguo tongji chubanshe, 1996).

[37] Stephen Frenkel and Jeffrey Harrod, *Industrialization and Labor Relations: Contemporary Research in Seven Countries* (Ithaca: ILR Press, 1995).

whose interests and positions must be reckoned with. Furthermore, as the state sector reforms widens, unemployment puts additional pressure on the government to steer clear of an increasingly treacherous course. The basic thrust of the efforts by the government has been to construct a legal framework aimed at effectively regulating increasingly divergent interests among the state, corporations, and workers.

A series of new labor legislation, including the Labor Law—which, after fifteen years, thirty drafts, and a few political near-deaths, took effect on 1 January 1995—began to lay a basic framework of regulating emerging labor relations in a market economy. It is no coincidence that only after the adoption of the objective of a 'socialist market economy' at the 14th Party Congress in 1992 that the Labor Law received the final push in the National People's Congress, the legislature. In the next few years, the government plans to set up a comprehensive structure of labor regulations that will suit the needs of a market economy.

A major change from the pre-transition period is the 'contractualization' of labor. Beginning in 1983, new employees were required to be hired on a contract basis while employees who had been hired previously remained permanent. This created a dual-track system of 'tenured employees' (*guding zhigong*) and 'contracted employees' (*hetong zhigong*). Instead of state guarantee and assignment of employment, now all industrial workers are to be hired on a contract basis.[38] For the first time in PRC history, employers can legally discharge someone for economic reasons, while employees have the right to resign. Neither were legitimate nor practical under the old labor regime, for employers could exact a heavy cost on individuals who wanted to transfer out of the enterprise with such tactics as holding on to employees' personnel records or taking back housing. Gradually, the tenured workers are also being transformed into contracted workers. By end of 1998, 98% of urban industrial workers have become contractual employees, while half of the entire workforce is now contract-based (Table 7.1).[39]

With the new Labor Law being enacted, a whole array of institutions began to emerge including minimum wage regulations, social security funds, labor mediation and arbitration bodies, and a labor law enforcement monitoring system, called the 'labor supervision agency'. Both Enterprise Labor Mediation Committees and Labor Arbitration Commissions were re-established in 1987 after a thirty-two year absence. Currently there are 270,000 Labor Mediation Committees and 3,159 Labor Arbitration Commissions nationwide.[40] The

[38] The evolution of contractualization is indicative of the gradualist approach to reforms by the Chinese leadership. Beginning in the mid 1980s, *new* employees of SOEs and some foreign firms were to have contracts with their employers. Employees previously hired were not included. With the promulgation of the new labor law in 1995, all employees are now required to enter into contracts with their employers.

[39] See *Renmin Ribao (RMRB)* [People's Daily], Beijing, 7 July 1997 and 22 June 1999.

[40] *Renmin Ribao (RMRB)* [People's Daily], Beijing, 25 July 1997.

Table 7.1. China: Employees on labor contracts (percent of total employees)

Year	All sectors	SEUs[a]	CEUs[b]	Other
1983	0.6	0.6	0.3	n.a.
1984	1.8	2.0	1.0	8.4
1985	3.3	3.7	2.2	11.4
1986	4.9	5.6	2.7	14.5
1987	6.6	7.6	3.6	18.1
1988	9.1	10.1	5.8	20.7
1989	10.7	11.8	7.0	25.1
1990	12.1	13.3	8.1	26.3
1991	13.6	14.9	8.9	28.0
1992	17.2	18.9	11.0	29.8
1993	21.0	21.9	15.5	37.4
1994	25.9	26.2	20.1	45.6
1995	40.9	40.1	37.4	62.8

[a] SEUs = state economic units. This category includes both enterprises (*qiye*) and non-production (*shiye*) units.
[b] CEUs = collective economic units.

Source: *Zhongguo Tongjin Nianjian* (1996); *Zhongguo Laodong Nianjian* (1995–6); *Zhongguo Gonghui Nianjian* (1994).

most significant change, however, is the introduction and gradual phase-in of collective bargaining and contracts.

With these institutions functioning, cases of labor dispute and violation of labor law rose dramatically in the last few years. Between 1987 and 1993, there were over one million labor dispute cases.[41] According to the latest official statistics, 1998 saw a 31% increase from 1997 in labor dispute cases, involving 359,000 employees—an increase of 62%.[42] In 1996, 196,700 cases of labor law violation were brought up and handled by labor supervision agencies. This represents a 264% increase from 1995. Among these cases, 117,800 were assessed administrative penalties including, 83,000 fined, 1,729 closed for rehabilitation, and 412 had their licenses revoked.[43] In addition to those investigated by labor supervisory agencies, labor-related litigation also increased. Before the Labor Law went into effect in 1995, some 10,000 labor litigation cases were brought to court annually. Since 1995, however, courts have handled three times as many labor-related litigation cases each year.[44] In 1998, 58,205 cases of labor litigation were brought to the courts (Table 7.2).[45]

[41] Jiaxin Wang (ed.), *Zhongguo Laodong Nianjian 1992–1994* [Chinese Labor Yearbook]. (Beijing: Zhongguo laodong chubanshe, 1996).
[42] *Renmin Ribao (RMRB)* [People's Daily], Beijing, 22 June 1999.
[43] *Renmin Ribao (RMRB)* [People's Daily], Beijing, 9 July 1997.
[44] *Renmin Ribao (RMRB)* [People's Daily], Beijing, 15 Aug. 1996.
[45] *Renmin Ribao (RMRB)* [People's Daily], Beijing, 21 March 1999.

Table 7.2. China: Labor dispute cases brought to labor
arbitration commissions (1992–8)

Year	No. of cases	Collective disputes (% of all cases)
1992	8,150	548 (6.7%)
1993	12,358	684 (5.5%)
1994	19,096	1,482 (7.7%)
1995	33,033	2,588 (7.8%)
1996	n.a.	n.a.
1997	67,625	4,108 (6.1%)
1998	94,000	6,762 (7.2%)

Source: *Zhongguo Laodong Nianjian* (1992–4), (1995–6); *Renmin Ribao (RMRB)* [People's Daily], 25 July 1997; *RMRB*, 22 June 1999.

State Sector Reform

China has adopted a gradualist strategy in reforming its inefficient state sector, which offers both opportunities and predicaments. The government has been able to maintain relative labor peace during the reforms due in part to its refusal to push for wholesale privatization of the state sector and its active role in building up a social safety net. Deliberate avoidance of potential labor unrest has also meant the delay or slow-down of the state sector reforms in the past decade, further worsening the entrenched problems of the state-owned enterprises (SOEs). Facing competition from newer, more efficient domestic firms in the private sector, especially foreign invested firms, as well as international competition, those SOEs that are old and cumbersome, burdened by non-production responsibilities can no longer contribute to the economy. The number of loss-making industrial enterprises has risen steadily since the early 1990s. On the other hand, with the intensified SOE reform efforts after 1995 and despite the efforts by the state to control the pace and scope of these reforms, relatively peaceful labor relations appear to have become increasingly confrontational. It is workers in the state sector, not conservative leaders, who are now the most vocal opponents of the rapid transformation of SOEs. Recent reports indicate that because strong resistance from workers, state authorities in some areas could not move forward with privatization plans as endorsed by the 15th Party Congress in September 1997.[46]

Although the state sector as a whole still is able to maintain labor peace, it is no longer immune from worker protests and strikes. Labor unrest has thus become a serious potential threat to the regime. A deputy minister of labor

[46] *Shijie Ribao (SJRB)* [The World Journal], New York, 24 Oct. 1997.

admitted that in recent years, labor collective actions, including strikes, protests, and collective petitions, have been rising. Mostly caused by unsolved labor disputes, these actions 'bear not only economic but also political implications'.[47] Most labor collective actions were in the form of petitions and sit-ins at government offices, and street protests. In 1996, there were 3,000 street demonstrations by workers, among which some three hundred were large-scale, involving more than a thousand people. Some of these labor protests involved workers from several factories, a unprecedented occurrence in the PRC where most labor collective actions, with the exception of the Cultural Revolution, were enterprise-based 'cellular protests'. In Xi'an, hundreds of textile workers from different mills have staged collective petitions almost weekly since 1996.[48] In the first six months of 1997, there were already 1,400 such marches, among which two hundred were large scale. The most recent one was a massive street demonstration in July 1997 by several thousand workers out of jobs due to the closure of a few state-owned textile mills.[49]

Globalization and Chinese Labor Relations

The Internationalization of national economies has affected industrial relations in many countries. But the reasons why the consequences of such impact differ lie in, among other things, how the state in these countries has responded to both internal and external pressures. Since the early 1980s, there has been a steady inflow of foreign direct investment (FDI) into China. By the end of June, 1997, foreign invested enterprises (FIEs), which include equity and contractual joint ventures, and wholly foreign owned firms, have amounted to 293,556, with half of them already in operation, and utilized foreign investment totaling US$197.9bn. Today, foreign owned assets account for 13% of total social assets in China and FIEs account for as much as 47% of China's total imports and exports.[50]

Another dimension of China's economic internationalization is the growth of export-oriented manufacturing. Today, five major manufacturing sectors in China—garments, office equipment, leather products, electronics, and textiles—export over 30% of their products overseas (Table 7.3).[51]

Compared to state-owned enterprises, FIEs enjoy considerable autonomy in the management of their labor forces.[52] While most domestic companies were still under strict state plans in the late 1970s, foreign companies were the

---

[47] Wang, *Zhongguo laodong nianjian 1992–1994* [Chinese Labor Yearbook].
[48] Jiang *et al.*, *1996–97 Zhongguo Shehui Xingshi Fenxi yu Yuce* [Analysis and Predictions of China's Social Situation in 1996–97].
[49] *Shijie Ribao* (*SJRB*) [The World Journal], New York, 22 July 1997.
[50] *Renmin Ribao* (*RMRB*) [People's Daily], Beijing, 31 July 1997.
[51] *Renmin Ribao* (*RMRB*) [People's Daily], Beijing, 28 July 1997.
[52] Jude Howell, 'The Myth of Autonomy: the Foreign Enterprise in China', in Smith and Thompson (eds), 1992.

194   *Lu*

Table 7.3. China: The structure of foreign investment in China (1995)

Sector	Number[a]	Total investment (%)
All sectors	233,564	100
Manufacturing	166,786	71.4
Services	16,802	19.3
retail and restaurants	(13,280)	(5.6)
real estate	(15,131)	(6.4)
social services	(14,769)	(6.3)
health and welfare	(509)	–
education and entertainment	(1,524)	–
finance	(85)	–
Agriculture and fishing	5,661	2.4

[a] This category indicates officially approved foreign investment enterprises (FIEs) including both those in operation and those in the process of becoming operational.

Source: *Zhongguo Jingji Nianjian* (1996).

first—according to the 1979 Joint Venture Law—to have the power to 'hire and fire' and to determine wages and bonuses as the market dictated. The impact of FIEs on Chinese industrial relations was particularly salient in the early years of the reforms when industrial relations in the state sector remained virtually unchanged. Despite the absence of a labor market, FIEs were permitted to freely hire people and set higher wages. Because many workers hired by FIEs had come from the state sector, FIEs, within certain limits, began chipping away at the enclosing walls of the *danwei*. They contributed to increasing labor mobility, a precursor to a fully-fledged labor market a decade later.

The presence of foreign companies also created new industrial relations distinct from those in the SOEs. The clashes between two kinds of management highlighted the early period. Since most of the early FIEs were in the form of joint ventures,[53] Chinese managers and workers alike in these companies often found that the new practices in labor management by their foreign partners 'ignored human feelings' and were at odds with what they had been used to. It was within the early joint ventures where conflicts between the new practices based on emerging labor relations and the old institutions of state socialism first unfolded. Many of these joint ventures were formed in existing state-owned enterprises. As often was the case, one shop or division would be converted into a joint venture, with the rest of the larger enterprise remaining

[53] In China, there are three types of foreign investment companies: *equity joint ventures*, where the Chinese and foreign partners jointly invest in and operate the corporation sharing profits, losses and risks; *contractual joint ventures*, where Chinese and foreign partners cooperate in joint projects, sharing output, earnings or profits according to contracts; and *wholly owned foreign enterprises*.

state-owned. This in effect created the coexistence of two kinds of labor relations in what previously had been one company, causing tension between workers of two different types of enterprises over different remuneration and management techniques. The situation began to change with more wholly foreign owned firms in operation as a result of government determination to bring in more foreign investment. One of the direct factors was the decentralization of the foreign investment approval process and the opening up of more sectors to overseas investors. Competition to attract foreign investment among local governments led to more accommodating and less restrictive postures toward foreign investors. In the early 1990s, some large joint ventures sent managers to the United States, Singapore, Thailand, and the Philippines to learn about labor relations management in multinational corporations.

Today, among the estimated 100 million employed laborers who work for private companies, 5.6 million are in FIEs.[54] The novel concept of differentiation and conflict of interests between capital and labor derived from privately owned domestic or foreign companies prompted the government to re-evaluate existing industrial relation regulations. Since the early 1980s, FIEs have provided a testing ground for many new labor regulations. From the very beginning, the Chinese government has attempted to regulate labor relations in FIEs as a part of its efforts to direct and regulate foreign investment. It adopted a dual-track policy—that is, the sequence and process of implementing labor regulations is different when applied to the state and non-state sector, especially FIEs. In addition to the labor regulations that are applied to all types of companies, there are special regulations on FIE labor relations. They are primarily concentrated around occupational safety,[55] remuneration,[56] and enforcement of written contracts.

In fact, the rules for collective bargaining and contracts, and the decision to begin pilot projects for setting up collective bargaining mechanisms were both aimed at the foreign-owned companies. Beginning in 1994, collective bargaining first began to be implemented on a limited scale in FIEs. So far, the state sector has not yet started such a process.

Foreign invested companies in China are characterized by a large number of small-sized firms in Hong Kong, Taiwan, South Korea, and even Thailand.

---

[54] Jiang *et al.*, *1996–97 Zhongguo Shehui Xingshi Fenxi yu Yuce* [Analysis and Predictions of China's Social Situation in 1996–97].

[55] With the inflow of foreign capital to China and increasing numbers of FIEs, there were increasing cases of physical abuse, longer working hours, delayed payment or impoundment of workers' salaries, and poor work conditions before 1994. The Ministry of Labor issued a 'Regulation on Labor Management in FIEs' in 1994 to address this and other related issues.

[56] In 1991, the Ministry of Labor issued a ruling putting a salary ceiling on workers in FIEs in order to avoid too large a gap between employees in the SOEs and FIEs. A year later, a vice-premier revised it by saying that the salary ceiling is only applicable to the FIEs not operating efficiently. For profitable FIEs, such a salary cap 'can be broken': Wang, *Zhongguo Laodong Nianjian 1992–1994* [Chinese Labor Yearbook], 205. This indicates that the government has been struggling to come to terms with the socioeconomic effects of the new market economy.

Large multinational corporations (MNCs) only entered China later, in the 1990s. Compared to small-sized family-owned businesses by Taiwanese, Hong Kong, and Koreans, larger foreign companies invested in by MNCs generally have better working conditions and labor practices. Labor disputes have taken place mostly in the small Korean, Japanese, and Taiwanese firms. Before 1993, foreign investment predominantly concentrated in labor-intensive manufacturing such as garments, footwear, and toys. Although in recent years with government policy to attract more technology—and capital-intensive investment—more and more foreign investment goes into infrastructure, services, and energy sectors (see Table 7.3). Labor-intensive manufacturing still remains the dominant sector where most FIEs are located. Factories in these industries tend to hire non-skilled labor from the countryside. One study estimates that about 80% of workers in FIEs are from rural areas, while 15% are laid-off workers from SOEs.[57] This has created a situation where workers face low wages, unpaid overtime work, poor working conditions and welfare provisions, and even physical abuse that mirrors Dickensonian factories in early capitalist development. At the same time, there is a shortage of local managers who are well trained and experienced.[58]

Despite the fact that in some provinces, as many as 96% of foreign invested companies have organized unions,[59] most FIEs still have a low rate of unionized labor. As Table 7.4 indicates, only 1% of existing unions in China in 1993 were in FIEs. Out of 170,000 FIEs, employing over 10 million workers, labor unions barely covered 12% of the labor force.[60] Among the cases of violation of the labor laws, 52% were by non-state companies.[61]

The Impact of the State Socialist Legacy

As other new institutions emerging as a result of gradual reform of the old system, the implementation of labor laws has faced resistance and distortion. One of the major targets of these new regulations is malpractice in the non-state sector including foreign invested enterprises (FIEs) and domestic private firms, the sources from which the new labor relations themselves are perceived to have originated. Unions, though numerous, still have limited functions in representing workers' interests *vis-à-vis* those of the state and management. Trade unions, especially those in the state sector, are not armed with their most powerful weapon, collective bargaining. Most labor protests and strikes, increasing rapidly in recent years, are spontaneous and not organized by unions.

[57] Lianjie Ma and Haning Chen, 'Lun waishang touzi qiye de laozi guanxi' [Labor relations in foreign invested enterprises], *Jingji Wenti* [Economic Problems], 4 (1996), 31–8.
[58] *Economist*, 23 June 1997.
[59] See *Renmin Ribao (RMRB)* [People's Daily], Beijing, 9 June 1997.
[60] *Beijing Review*, 11 July 1994.
[61] *Renmin Ribao (RMRB)* [People's Daily], Beijing, 8 April 1997.

Table 7.4. China: Unions at the firm level (1993 and 1998)

Year	1993	1998
State-owned enterprises	478,753	n.a.
Collectively-owned enterprises	116,591	n.a.
Township and village enterprises	19,566	76,000
Shareholding firms	3,272	n.a.
Privately owned enterprises	224	29,132
Foreign invested enterprises	8,260	53,634
Total	626,666	586,000[a]

[a] The decrease in the total number of unions between 1993 and 1998 may be due to the fact that the number of SOEs decreased. According to one report, 24,000 SOEs were eliminated in 1998. See *RMRB*, Beijing, 7 August 1999.

Source: *Zhongguo Gonghui Tongjinianjian* (1994); *Renmin Ribao (RMRB)* [People's Daily], Beijing, 15 October 1998.

Many state-owned firms have been slow in implementing contracts because of the large number of workers who are reluctant to give up lifetime employment. The long-standing reliance on the enterprise has put workers, especially non-skilled ones, in a weak bargaining position. On the other hand, the power of managers has been greatly enhanced. In many firms, what Andrew Walder called 'social and political dependence on the enterprise'[62] which characterized pre-reform industrial relations has actually been intensified.[63] Given the abundant labor supply, some employers, mostly non-state sector firms, require workers to pay a 'job security deposit' (*fengxian diyajin*) as part of their job commitment to the firm. According to an official report, the government discovered yuan 230m worth of such funds nationwide and ordered employers who collected job security deposits to return the monies to employees.[64] Cases of 'internal takeover' by factory managers—*de facto* privatization and its labor relations consequences—have been reported.[65] After 1996, when labor contracts expired in some SOEs, many managers tried to avoid renewing contracts and to lay off older employees by replacing them with cheaper temporary workers from the countryside.[66]

Chinese industrial relations are as much political as economic. After the collapse of the former communist regimes in Eastern Europe and the 1989 mass demonstrations in China, the Chinese communist leadership became highly vigilant against further possible social unrest. Putting laid-off workers

---

[62] Walder, *Communist Neo-Traditionalism*.

[63] Bojun Wang, 'Shichanghua dachao zhongde zhigong quanyi baozhang' [Worker rights protection in the market reform], *Taosuo yu Zhengming* [Inquiries and Debates], 4 (1995), 23–7.

[64] *Renmin Ribao (RMRB)* [People's Daily], Beijing, 8 April 1997.

[65] Liu Jiang *et al.*, *1996–97 Zhongguo Shehui Xingshi Fenxi yu Yuce* [Analysis and Predictions of China's Social Situation in 1996–97].

[66] Ibid.

'on the street' would present a serious risk to the stability of the communist regime itself. In this regard, enterprise reform advocates face opposition from both conservatives and SOE workers who, being used to guaranteed employment and social welfare, are making every effort to hold on to such benefits. Indeed, much of the resistance to SOE reform comes from the workers of these enterprises whose lives are dependent on their units. Leaving the factory would mean, in many cases, losing health care, housing, and other benefits.

The state remains highly suspicious of any attempt to organize labor groups without official sanction. The feared scenario is one of independent labor unions challenging the legitimacy of official unions and the authority of the regime as in the case of Solidarity in Poland. In this sense, the role of the unions has changed the least. Trade unions remain mainly welfare caretaker and a political 'transmission belt' of the state. Although labor unions in non-state sectors were once fewer in number, in recent years there has been a steady increase reflecting both the rapid growth of the sector and the extra attention given by the government to the new labor relations in capitalist firms (see Table 7.4). In 1992, a labor union law was promulgated, replacing the previous law of 1950. The new law ostensibly stipulates some roles that are comparable to any free union movement.[67] Yet few resources are guaranteed with which such active roles can be made effective.[68] The fact that recent years have seen a dramatic increase both in labor disputes brought to labor arbitration bodies and labor law violations handled by courts, as well as in collective actions, indicates that the internal problem-solving mechanism between management and employees remains ineffective with a weak union role in representing the interests of workers.

The most indicative of the role of the union is the institutions of collective bargaining and contracts. Although collective bargaining and contracts are not entirely novel to state socialist systems including China,[69] during the Maoist period the interests of state, enterprise, and the workers were sup-

[67] *Renmin Ribao (RMRB)* [People's Daily], Beijing, 9 April 1997.

[68] Perry, 'Labor's Battle for Political Space'.

[69] Collective contracts did once exist in the 1950s in some SOEs before China's economic system was completely transformed to that of state socialism. In 1953, there were 103,000 firms in 33 cities—all private businesses—that had signed collective contracts: *Zhongguo Laodong Tongjin Nianjian* [Labor Statistic Yearbook of China] (Beijing: Zhongguo laodong chubanshe, 1996). The main purpose of the collective contracts, however, was not regulating labor relations. As the Ministry of the Textile Industry stated in a proposal to the CCP Central Committee to implement a pilot project of collective contracts, 'primarily, such contracts should put in writing the specific targets under production planning as the goals of joint efforts by workers, staff, and technicians. Secondly, they should stipulate the kinds of measures to solve specific potential problems that may occur in pursuing production goals . . . Fourthly, they should specify measures to enforce labor discipline . . .': Zhonghua Quanguo Zonggonghui [All China Federation of Trade Unions], *Jianguo Yilai Zhonggong Zhongyang Guanyu Gongren Yundong Wenjian Xuanbian* [Selected CCP Central Committee Documents on Workers' Movements], 193–4). In this document, labor protection and welfare issues are listed as the sixth or later in the order. It is apparent that the collective contracts then—which in later years were not implemented—were not intended to be labor-oriented.

posed to have merged. Comprehensive installation of these institutions remains a politically delicate matter. At a labor bureau chiefs' meeting in 1994, the minister of labor revealed that whether and how to implement collective bargaining was highly controversial during the drafting of the Labor Law. Opponents of a rapid implementation of collective bargaining argue that many SOEs have very murky property rights which may lead to positioning the government, rather than management, at the opposite end of the bargaining table.[70] The government, it is argued, may risk being made a political adversary of the workers. The government eventually decided not to push too hard in the first few years after the Labor Law took effect while allowing a few experiments.[71] Only after 1994 did the government allow a gradual implementation of these institutions.

Even though collective bargaining is being established and collective contracts are being actively promoted in firms of all types including SOEs, the government tries to avoid a direct reference by using the term 'equal *consultation*' instead. To the government, contract *negotiation* is not to be regarded as a bargaining process, which implies a confrontational stance among parties. Progress has been made in establishing bargaining and collective contracts. The ACFTU organized workshops to train union negotiators. By the end of 1995, only 350 firms had experimented with collective bargaining and contracts, most of them in the non-state sector.[72] By the end of 1997, 236,068 firms had established collective bargaining and contract mechanisms, covering 60.72 million employees.[73] Currently, 70% of the industrial workers in the state and collective sectors are on collective contracts.[74] Still, labor disputes continue to be individual-based and unions' roles are limited. As Table 7.2 shows, while the number of labor dispute cases involving collective disputes have been on the rise, they remain constant in proportion to individual disputes.

Ideological constraints still exert influence on the future direction of the current transition, especially the nature of 'market socialism', a frequently used yet contentious concept. Some leaders insist on the bottom line that to maintain the 'socialist nature' of the Chinese economy (i.e., market socialism), public ownership must be the main form of property rights.[75]

---

[70] *Zhongguo Laodong Tongjin Nianjian* [Labor Statistic Yearbook of China] (Beijing: Zhongguo laodong chubanshe, 1996).

[71] See Wang, *Zhongguo Laodong Nianjian 1992–1994* [Chinese Labor Yearbook]. One incident illustrates the wariness of the state about unsanctioned calls for collective bargaining. In March 1994, a 39-year-old street vendor was detained for interrogation because he printed T-shirts with the slogan 'collective bargaining is a worker's right'. (Website: http://www.clean-clothes.org/1/s-asia)

[72] *Zhongguo Laodong Tongjin Nianjian* [Labor Statistic Yearbook of China] (Beijing: Zhongguo laodong chubanshe, 1996).

[73] *Renmin Ribao (RMRB)* [People's Daily], Beijing, 26 Sept. 1998.

[74] *Workers' Daily* (29 March 1999).

[75] In China, the 'public sector' or 'public ownership' refers to both state-owned and collective enterprises. The latter is a somewhat ambiguous category.

Privatization is seen only as a secondary means. Most SOEs, large or small, are not to be privatized.[76] Despite the continuing growth of the private sector in China's economy, the public sector, especially SOEs, remains dominant. Not only does it employ 90% of the urban working population among which 67% are employed by SOEs, but the public sector remains the single largest contributor to the national economy. SOEs still contribute 60% of annual national revenue.[77] For many urban workers, the lack of guaranteed jobs still violates the social contract of the People's Republic.[78] Not very long ago, guaranteed employment was the main indicator of workers' 'masters of the nation' status and a cornerstone of state socialism.

Structural constraints also hamper the recasting of industrial relations in an emerging market economy. China faces immense employment problems because of continuous and severe labor market supply pressures, large-scale rural development, rising urban unemployment, and labor redundancy, as well as growing income and social inequalities between different segments of the population. Surplus labor from both the countryside and the industrial sector will generate tremendous pressure on the government, which intends to keep the targeted unemployment rate under 5% before 2001. In 1995, there was already an excess labor force of 175 million people—almost half the agricultural labor force—in the rural areas. Real unemployment rate in the agricultural sector is about 34.8%.[79] Hundreds of millions of farmers will have to leave agriculture by the year 2000, for better or worse. It is estimated that in order to revitalize the inefficient state sector, 20–25% of the urban state sector labor force—some 15–30 million employees—must be laid off.[80] In the first nine months of 1997, more than 8 million state sector workers were either unemployed or semi-unemployed.[81] China must also find ways to accommodate millions of mobile workers from rural areas who are outside the *danwei* social benefits system.

[76] There is a significant difference in the use of the concept 'privatization' between the Chinese and the Russians. Russians use it to mean any form of 'destatization' including shareholding, collective enterprises, and even changes in SOE management styles. Chinese, however, apply the concept only to refer to transfers of state assets to private citizens through transactions. For ideological and practical reasons, the Chinese leadership regards it as highly significant that a distinction be drawn between 'privatization' (or the more recently invented term 'socialize') and the 'private economy' (i.e., capitalism). The latter is regarded as an ultimate deviation from the goals of socialist revolution.

[77] *Renmin Ribao (RMRB)* [People's Daily], Beijing, 20 May 1996 and 3 July 1996.

[78] Douglas Guthrie also found that at the firm level such a sense of social contract, remains strong among both managers and workers. See Guthrie 'Organizational Uncertainty and Labor Contracts in China's Economic Transition', *Sociological Forum*, 13 (1998), 457–94.

[79] *Qiaobao* [Overseas Chinese Daily], New York, 4 Nov. 1997.

[80] *Qiaobao* [Overseas Chinese Daily], New York, 4 November 1997; *Liaowang* [Outlook New Weekly], Beijing, no. 25, 1996; and Fang, Weizhong, *Guanyu Gaohao Guoyou Qiye de Diaocha* [Investigations on How to Improve SOEs], (Beijing: Zhongguo Wenshi Chubanshe, 1995).

[81] *Ming Pao*, 4 Oct. 1997.

Conclusion: Labor Relations with Chinese Characteristics?

Despite some major changes, contemporary Chinese labor relations, under the impact of transition and globalization, are still evolving. On the one hand, the pressure of economic globalization has rendered many of China's existing industrial enterprises inefficient and has forced the reform leadership to step up its efforts to transform the state sector, risking social unrest and deterioration of the state-worker relations. There are, as a result of the reforms and integration of Chinese economy with the world economy, more and more new labor institutions have emerged. On the other hand, globalization has not been the sole source of change for its scope, pace, and sequence. Existing political, ideological, and structural factors remain significant in the reformulation of labor relations in China. This challenges the conviction that increasing globalization and transition to a market economy would inevitably produce greater convergence in labor institutions and processes. The case of changing Chinese industrial relations shows that there is no reason to believe that any degree of globalization will soon fundamentally transform China's labor relations. For a long time to come, the transformation of Chinese labor relations will likely maintain four important characteristics that have already emerged in the past decade.

First, the state occupies the center stage in reformulating industrial relations and reconstructing labor institutions. As a large industrializing country, China's labor process and industrial relations are defined by the economic and political transitions. This makes China, along with some other former state socialist countries, distinct from both industrialized capitalist societies and newly industrializing countries. Industrialized countries have experienced a relatively reactive state during early industrialization when pre-industrial employment relationships based on personal status were replaced by contractual arrangements. Reacting to the relegation of labor to treatment as a commodity, the state first acted to countermand the harshness of certain of these contractual arrangements—mostly what it deemed 'abuses' of the market system—including restrictions on child and female labor, working hour limits, and occupational safety.[82] In the late stages of industrialization, however, the state became more active. It expanded the scope of its intervention to take on issues such as unemployment compensation, job training, and workplace discrimination. This process—what some scholars call the 'juridification of labor relations'[83]—took more than a century to evolve.

For newly industrializing countries, such sequencing does not always apply. Patterns of late industrialization in so-called developing countries have resulted in many cases in labor repression by the state. External competition

---

[82] John Niland, Russell Lansbury, and Chrissie Verevis (eds), *The Future of Industrial Relations.* (Thousand Oaks: Sage, 1994).

[83] S. Simits, 'The Juridification of Labor Relations', *Comparative Labor Journal*, 7 (1986), 93–142.

and cost-cutting measures affected labor relations in these countries.[84] For China, the 'juridification of labor relations' process has been more intense—the state has taken on virtually simultaneously all the formidable tasks which its Western counterparts did incrementally and sequentially. Unlike in many industrializing countries, however, globalization and external competition and cost-cutting were not the determinant factors for the state's role in labor relations in China. The active role of the state in a transition economy is rather dictated by the needs of both dismantling the old labor regime dominated by the state itself and reconstructing a new one that still requires some intervention from the government.

Second, China's gradualist strategy of transition has meant careful avoidance of large-scale social unrest. Such a strategy is under increasingly salient effects from globalization. Many existing socialist enterprises must be transformed into 'modern corporations' in order to compete in an increasingly competitive international economic environment. Yet at the same time, a transition of such scale may also cause dislocations for millions of workers who are used to lifetime employment and welfare benefits provided by their enterprises. In the near future, such deterioration of conditions for the working class will continue, given the needed structural reforms and China's ample labor supply. To delay the industrial reforms any further, as Chinese leaders well understand, could mean an incomplete transition to 'market socialism' and loss of competitiveness in face of the prospect of further globalization of the international economy of which China seems to have become an inseparable part. The looming World Trade Organization (WTO) accession and financial crisis in Asia add urgency to reformers' determination to accomplish state-sector reform. At the 15th Party Congress in September 1997, it was decided that a final push for the state-sector reform with more radical measures such as closure, merger, and selling-off should be accomplished by the year 2000. However, as a sign of how deeply Chinese economy has integrated into the world market, the recent economic crisis in Asia with the prospect of more competitive exports and the threat of an economic slow-down may adversely affect China's ambitious plan.

Third, as in other transitional economies, changes in China's labor relations are very much affected by its state socialist past. Although China has been relatively successful in constructing a comprehensive institutional framework to manage industrial relations in a market economy, new institutions none the less have emerged with the influence of existing labor institutions, among which the most defining one is the cellular system of the *danwei*. Some paternalistic features of firms are likely to remain, albeit to a lesser

---

[84] Frederick Deyo, *Beneath the Miracle: Labor Subordination in the New Asian Industrialism.* (Berkeley: University of California Press, 1989); Frenkel and Harrod, *Industrialization and Labor Relations: Contemporary Research in Seven Countries*; Juliet Schor and Jong-Il You (eds), *Capital, the State and Labour: A Global Perspective* (Brookfield, VT: Edward Elgar, 1995).

degree. Expectations of firms in delivering certain welfare and social services remain strong among urban employees.

Under state socialism, workers' interests were purported to be indistinguishable and inseparable from those of the state. Even though unions and workers councils nominally existed, they rarely engaged in real negotiations or dispute mediation with management. Such a lack of experience and procedures in internal negotiations and mediation has shown its effect in the increasing amount of external arbitration and court cases as well as 'petitions to higher authorities' (*shangfang*), a common mode of expressing grievances since pre-revolutionary times and other forms of demonstration. This has two consequences: first, the state has to be more active than it intends to be in resolving labor disputes; and second, labor peace becomes more difficult to maintain in the absence of an effective internal mediation mechanism.

The role of labor unions will likely remain weak as they are only slowly gaining some say in representing workers' interests. State management of industrial relations that are emerging as a result of transition and globalization appears to be active but indirect—that is, actively legislating and enforcing labor laws while leaving actual negotiations and mediation to employers and employees. As its efforts in the past few years indicate, the Chinese state is trying to set up a tripartite framework of labor relation maintenance. Undoubtedly, the government is granting, albeit ever so cautiously, some new powers to officially sanctioned labor unions. It will allow a more active role for trade unions in representing and protecting workers interests *vis-à-vis* capital and management. The key, however, is the autonomy of trade unions which traditionally were ineffective and at the mercy of the government. The 'depoliticization' of trade unions is underway. It is unlikely, however, that unions will gain full autonomy from the state in the near future. They will not be allowed to organize collective actions such as large-scale strikes.

Finally, Chinese industrial relations have always been, and will continue to be affected by the abundance of labor supply. For many years, low labor costs have fueled the rapid growth of export-oriented industrialization. The main concerns of the governments in regulating emerging labor relations have had less to do with pressures to suppress labor costs in order to attract more investment, as in many other newly industrializing countries. The vast labor pool China possesses simply makes such concerns irrelevant. For the Chinese state the primary concern has been, and will continue to be, how to protect the working class which is in a perennially disadvantageous position. Moreover, as the structural reforms deepen, unemployment pressure will remain present for a long time to come.

Economic globalization and liberalization have transformed China's labor relations. Such a process has rendered itself gradual, at times treacherous, and constrained. It is by no means finished business. Labor relations in China still continue to evolve as the state sector reform unfolds and the Chinese economy becomes even more intimately linked to the world economy.

Despite the seeming convergence to the capitalist economic system, it is too early to foresee if Chinese labor institutions and processes will eventually become a mere copy of those in the industrialized countries. Perhaps the more likely outcome will be a set of labor institutions and processes that grow out of the historical, ideological, and structural conditions akin to the so-called 'market socialism with Chinese characteristics'.

8

Privatization, Labor Politics, and the Firm in Post-Soviet Russia: Non-market Norms, Market Institutions, and the Soviet Legacy

Rudra Sil, University of Pennsylvania

'Globalization', if it is regarded in the broad sense as a long-term process of increasing international interaction and interdependence, can actually be said to have begun in Russia well before the Soviet Union collapsed. One can make the case that the emphasis on common 'global challenges' in Gorbachev's new thinking, Brezhnev's quest for *detente* with the United States and greater involvement in the Third World, and Khrushchev's recognition of 'many roads to socialism'—or, even the communist internationalism of the early twentieth century and the Russian Empire's quest for modernization since the time of Peter and Catherine—all served at different times to increase Russia's political, social, and economic contact with the outside world. As a result of this steady exposure to global forces, it might be argued that the Soviet leaders, not unlike their Tsarist predecessors, found themselves unable to control the flow of ideas, goods, and people that would lead to sweeping political and socioeconomic transformations.

Thinking about 'globalization' in such broad terms does provide food for thought at a certain level of abstraction. It is not terribly helpful, however, if we are to attempt to understand the dramatic changes that have taken place in Russia over the past decade and to characterize the direction of this change. However important the incremental changes over the past decades or centuries may have been in paving the way for recent events and trends, the problem has to be understood from the point of view of the actors involved and their experiences within particular institutional contexts. And if the concept of 'globalization' is to carry any meaning for these actors, then it must be cast at a more concrete level, in terms of the discernible impact of the flow of goods, services, technologies, and, especially, institutional models across the

This chapter has its origins in a talk given at the University of California at Berkeley on 14 May 1997 entitled 'Post-Soviet Labor and the (Im)Moral Economy of Soviet Industry'. I am grateful to the Center for Slavic and East European Studies at Berkeley and the Berkeley Program in Soviet and Post-Soviet Studies for sponsoring the talk. The chapter also benefited from helpful comments from Tadashi Anno, Hilary Appel, George Breslauer, Stephen Crowley, Stephen Hanson, Barbara Lehmbruch, Sven Steinmo, Carrie Timko, Edward Walker, and this volume's reviewers.

borders of the new Russia. Thus, it is the economic reforms and socioeconomic conditions of the past decade, together with the social cleavages and coalitions formed in response by key political and economic actors in concrete institutional arenas, that provide the basis for assessing the extent and impact of 'globalization' in post-Soviet Russia in this chapter.

What follows is an attempt to make sense of some of the unexpected patterns and trends in post-Soviet industrial relations against the backdrop of the privatization program, the success of which would be a necessary foundation for Russia's integration into the global economy. The chapter is divided into four sections that address four related points cast at different levels of generality; these points collectively demonstrate that economic institutions in post-Soviet Russia, far from converging with institutions in advanced industrial economies, reflect the influence of distinctive institutional legacies. First, in terms of the national economy, the privatization program and other market-oriented reforms under Yeltsin—while increasing the exposure of most Russians to foreign actors, goods, and ideas—did not lead to market capitalism, economic growth, or integration into the global economy. Second, in terms of industrial relations, there was little evidence of movement towards Western-European corporatist models as Russian reformers had hoped; instead, the main division was between pro-reform and anti-reform elements of both labor and business, with trilateral collective bargaining giving way to *ad hoc* bilateral contacts between the state and leaders of the trade union federation derived from the Soviet-era unions. Third, in any case, it is now evident that large-scale trade unionism has become progressively ineffectual and irrelevant as workers have increasingly turned to spontaneous or locally organized activities to air their grievances. Fourth, while the Soviet command economy has been formally dismantled, many workers and managers appear to be behaving according to non-market norms and social relations at local and enterprise levels. I conclude with the argument that these norms and relations may well reflect the enduring legacy of the informal understandings and collusive practices that workers and managers relied on to get by under the uncertain conditions created by the formal Soviet system of production.

The Broader Context: The Failed Promise of Privatization

Small steps towards market-oriented reform were actually in evidence five years before the Soviet Union collapsed. As early as November 1986, Mikhail Gorbachev had authorized the Law on Individual Labor Activity, defining a minimal realm for private transactions among individuals and legalizing a significant portion of what had been a quasi-legal shadow economy under Leonid Brezhnev. In 1987, Gorbachev's Law on Enterprises reduced the level of state controls over enterprise activity, enabling direct links between customers and suppliers. By May 1988, the Soviet Law on Cooperatives had legalized the formation of cooperative shops—jointly owned by the state and private individuals—in limited sectors of the economy, primarily dealing with food services and small-scale consumer goods. In 1990, however, Gorbachev rejected the 500-day plan for a rapid transition to the market (crafted by Stanislav Shatalin and his team of economists), opting instead for a more gradual package of reforms and convincing more radical reformers that neither Gorbachev nor the USSR Supreme Soviet were prepared to dismantle the command economy entirely.

Within the Russian Federation, however, 1990 marked the stirrings of a bolder vision of market-oriented reform that would theoretically pave the way for capitalism and new economic relations with the outside world. The Russian Federation parliament, chaired at the time by Boris Yeltsin, who had already resigned from the USSR politburo, approved the Shatalin Plan. The Russian Federation subsequently passed new laws in 1990 and 1991 legalizing previously prohibited forms of private ownership, including limited liability companies and limited partnership enterprises as well as joint ventures with increased foreign ownership. Yeltsin brought into his government such pro-market reformers as Anatoly Chubais, Chair of the Committee on Privatization of State Enterprises from November 1992 to November 1994, and Boris Fedorov, the Finance Minister through January 1994. Despite the concerted effort of a new generation of economists and politicians, however, Yeltsin and the Russian parliament could do little more than pass laws and decrees as long as the Soviet Union and its centrally planned economy remained in existence.

New economic institutions emerged only after the failure of the coup attempt against Gorbachev in August 1991 and the subsequent declaration of independence by most of the former Soviet republics. In October 1991, Yeltsin announced Russia's commitment to radical economic reform, centered on the two cornerstones of shock therapy as it was unfolding in Poland: price liberalization and mass privatization. By the end of the year, Gorbachev had resigned as President of the USSR, and the Russian flag flew over the Kremlin for the first time in over seventy years. Yeltsin and his Prime Minister, Yegor Gaidar, wasted no time in enacting radical market reforms. Price liberalization was introduced for most goods on 2 January 1992, and extended to foodstuffs in March. In April 1992, even as the Russian parliament was beginning to raise concerns about skyrocketing prices, Yeltsin announced a program for mass privatization that was seen as the centerpiece of radical reform and rapid marketization in Russia. The process was to take place through the distribution of vouchers to Russian citizens who could use these vouchers to buy shares in former state enterprises. Chubais was appointed to head the committee in charge of privatizing state and municipal property, and within a year, the process was in full swing.

The process did not unfold without several bumps along the way. Buoyed by public frustration with rising prices, parliamentary leaders began to challenge Yeltsin's decrees and call for measures to slow down reform. In the fall of 1993, Yeltsin responded by dissolving the Russian parliament, proceeding to literally blast recalcitrant parliamentarians out of the Russian 'White House' with the aide of the army. This move might well be characterized as a presidential coup against an elected body that was once regarded as the main force for reform, but, among Yeltsin's advisors and Western analysts, it also increased the long-range optimism that the main obstacles to market reforms—the 'old hardliners'—were now being removed, paving the way for the completion of privatization and acceleration of marketization.[1]

Despite the strong showing by nationalist forces, especially by the party of ultra-nationalist Vladimir Zhirinovsky, in new parliamentary elections held in December 1993, the Yeltsin government stayed the course and carried voucher-based privatization through until the end and initiated a program for selling all remaining state and municipal property for cash. The number of private enterprises grew rapidly, and unsold shares went on sale for cash in April 1994. Later that year, Yeltsin sacked Viktor Garashchenko, the head of the Central Bank of Russia who had encouraged printing more rubles to deal with the cash shortage of crisis proportions. In April 1995, the former head of the state's privatization program, Chubais, became Russia's representative to the World Bank and IMF, and the IMF and Russia signed a new agreement for loans totaling US$6.8bn, quadrupling the previous loan amounts involved in previous years. In the course of the following year, the restructured Communist Party of the Russian Federation (KPRF) under Gennadi Zyuganov won a plurality of seats in the December 1995 elections and Zyuganov went on to give Yeltsin a run for his money in the presidential elections of June 1996. Nevertheless, Yeltsin's reaction to these challenges was limited to reshuffling his cabinet, and market reforms continued to move forward throughout 1996. Yeltsin decreed the establishment of mutual funds, the Russian Duma permitted the leasing of state-owned agricultural lands, and the Commission on Securities and Capital Markets was turned into a cabinet ministry. In March 1996, the IMF and Russia signed the largest loan agreement yet, for over US$10bn.

Western advisors initially portrayed the Russian privatization program as the largest and most successful in history. Indeed, between 1991 and the end of 1995, more than 12 million apartments had been turned over to private hands, a total of nearly 800,000 new small businesses were created, and nearly 18,000 mid- and large-sized companies and more than 100,000 smaller shops were privatized through the voucher auctions and subsequent cash privatiza-

---

[1] This parliament was the same body that wanted to go beyond Gorbachev's reforms in 1990 and approved the Shatalin Plan for Russia. However, with many of Yeltsin's former allies and friends objecting to radical reforms, particularly the rapid increase in prices following price liberalization, this same parliament came to be portrayed—both by Yeltsin and the Western media—as a conservative body led by 'old hardliners'.

tion.[2] Although cash privatization moved much more slowly than planned, the Russian government was able to claim that in 1995, the largest state enterprises in the most prized heavy industry sectors were already corporatized and in private hands, and that the non-state sector was responsible for 70% of gross domestic product (GDP). In addition, a third of these firms were now under new directors, while two-thirds of these firms proceeded to introduce marketing departments and change their mix of products.[3]

Through price liberalization, privatization, and growth of foreign investment, the exposure of key economic actors in Russia to international economic forces certainly reached a different order of magnitude compared to any other period in the country's history. Already by the end of 1995, both exports and imports had reached an all-time high, with the trade surplus reaching US$18.3bn. Foreign direct investment had risen from US$1.55bn in 1992 to nearly US$4bn in 1995. Despite the fears spurred by the 1998 Russian financial crisis, these are figures that were inconceivable ten years ago even to the most committed reformers in Gorbachev's administration, and they concretely reflect a qualitative transformation of the Russian economy. There were even some signs that market reforms, together with foreign loans and investment, might pay dividends for Russia's new market economy. Tight monetary policies orchestrated as part of the agreement with the IMF succeeded in bringing down monthly consumer price inflation to 3% by December 1995. Governmental subsidies to enterprises also stood at just 5% at the end of 1994. The budget deficit as a percentage of the GDP was brought down from 30% in 1991 to under 5% in 1995.[4]

It is now clear, however, that the privatization process neither unfolded as planned, nor produced the expected results. While the command economy was broken up, with property rights ill-defined, many of the former *nomenklatura* elites were in a position to convert their social networks and access to information into control of their firms. The formal transfer of ownership did not lead to widespread individual shareholding or to dramatic changes in the internal operations and management structures at the enterprise level; instead, 'insider privatization' allowed networks of former enterprise directors, *nomenklatura* elites, and local bureaucrats to take control of the newly privatized firms.[5] One-third of these firms may have gained new directors, but

[2] See Joseph Blasi, Maya Kroumova, and Douglas Kruse, *Kremlin Capitalism* (Ithaca: Cornell University Press, 1997), xiii–xix, 189.

[3] Blasi *et al.*, *Kremlin Capitalism*, 203–7.

[4] 'Russia: Facts and Figures', *Radio Free Europe/Radio Liberty (RFE/RL) 1996 Country Report* (www.rferl.org).

[5] The process was actually quite simple. Typically, groups of former directors, economic bureaucrats, and political elites, with access to surplus funds and information, were able to acquire the vouchers necessary to control privatized firms through networks of middlemen who had purchased the vouchers from common citizens who were neither well-informed nor sure about what their vouchers or shares in a firm might be worth, at least compared to the hard cash being offered in exchange. For a more detailed look at 'insider privatization', see Pekka Sutela, 'Insider Privatisation in Russia: Speculations on Systemic Change', *Europe-Asia Studies*, 47: 3

fewer than 7% ended up with new directors brought in from outside the original enterprise administration, and just 35% of the firms embarked upon any major changes in technology or the production process.[6] As late as 1996, foreign individuals, firms and banks owned just 1.6% of the shares in the privatized enterprises, and at best a third of the ownership of private enterprises was represented by 'outsiders', namely, Russian citizens, unrelated suppliers, holding companies, banks, mutual funds, pension funds, and foreign individuals, firms, or banks. Nearly 60% of the ownership remained in the hands of 'insiders', that is, among the employees and managers of the former state enterprises, with top-level managers and directors controlling 10% of the total shares. Not surprisingly, the insiders ended up with majority ownership in 65% of the privatized firms while outsiders' managed to gain a controlling interest in only 20%.[7]

Certainly, external relations among firms had to be restructured, but the patterns of exchange appear to have been heavily concentrated among firms carved out of former state enterprises. Far from leading Russia's integration into the global economy, private firms, particularly outside Moscow and St. Petersburg, tended to pursue 'inward'-looking strategies for survival and profiteering, funneling resources from production to exchange and frequently engaging in transactions resembling bartering under 'merchant capitalism' rather than market exchange under industrial capitalism.[8] The Russian Government Committee on Statistics estimates that almost 70% of deliveries were exchanged on barter terms in Russian industry in 1996, with total arrears among companies, excluding arrears to banks, accounting for 23% of the GDP over the twelve-month period.[9] Recent studies further indicate that external relations among firms have been driven primarily by regional factors and regionalized networks,[10] and that regional leaders have contributed to the process of turning Russia into a collection of closed regional markets by adopting a variety of taxes and quality requirements designed to keep products in

(1994), 417–35; A. Schleifer and D. Vasiliev, 'Management Ownership and Russian Privatization', in R. Frydman, C. W. Gray, and A. Rapaczynski (eds), *Corporate Governance in Central Europe and Russia* (Budapest: Central European University Press, 1996); and Bernard Black, Reinier Kraakman, and Anna Trassova, 'Russian Privatization and Corporate Governance: What Went Wrong?' John M. Olin Program in Law and Economics, Working paper 178 (Stanford Law School, Sept. 1999).

   [6] Joseph Blasi *et al.*, *Kremlin Capitalism*, 203–7.
   [7] *Russian National Survey, 1995–96*, cited in Blasi *et al.*, *Kremlin Capitalism*, 193.
   [8] Michael Burawoy, 'The State and Economic Involution: Russia Through a China Lens', *World Development*, 24 (June 1996), 1105–17. The argument that these trends represent a transition to 'merchant capitalism' is from Michael Burawoy and Pavel Krotov, 'The Soviet Transition From Socialism to Capitalism: Worker Control and Economic Bargaining in the Wood Industry', *American Sociological Review*, 57 (Feb. 1992), 16–38.
   [9] See Tony Weselowsky, 'Russia: The Roots of Labor Malaise', *Radio Free Europe/Radio Liberty (RFE/RL) Report* (11 Feb. 1998).
   [10] See Carol Clark, 'The Transformation of Labor Relations in Russian Industry: The Influence of Regional Factors in the Iron and Steel Industry', *Post-Soviet Geography and Economics*, 37: 2 (1996), 88–112.

other regions out, sometimes in defiance of Russian law, which gives federal bodies the authority to determine product standards.[11]

From the point of view of the people caught in this confusing transformation, the more important facts have to do with the ability of the average Russian to live a decent life. In these regards, too, the promise of privatization has been far from fulfilled. As a whole, the GDP growth rate declined dramatically between 1991 and 1998, with agricultural output and industrial output both dropping steadily, sometimes precipitously.[12] The first half of 1999 showed a modest gain of 1.5%, with industrial output and the trade balance both posting significant gains, but this has come at the expense of a mounting foreign debt and the ruble's value, which had declined nearly 75% since August 1998. More importantly for the average Russian, the lag between the rises in wage levels and consumer prices translated into a dramatic drop in real wages, with the real value of average wages and pensions plummeting by 78% and 67%, respectively, between 1991 and 1997, while wage arrears mounted from 2 trillion rubles (US$350m) in 1992 to more than 50 trillion rubles (US$9bn) in February 1997.[13] Following the 1998 financial crisis, real incomes fell a further 35.9% by September 1999, with the unemployment rate climbing to over 12% in a country accustomed to full employment in the late Soviet era.[14] And with the social security system in Russia still underdeveloped and underfunded those without employer-provided benefits, the unemployed and early retirees particularly, found themselves with little or no assistance from either national or local governments.[15]

The effects of the growing unemployment level, the decline in wages, and the problem of arrears are evident in the plummeting standard of living. As of July 1999, official statistics found 52 million people, nearly 35% of the population, receiving incomes below the subsistence minimum of 872 (redenominated) rubles per month (about US$36).[16] This poverty has disproportionately affected both skilled and non-skilled workers who together account

[11] Robert Orttung, 'Russia Becoming a Series of Closed Markets', *Open Market Research Institute (OMRI) Russian Regional Report* (26 March 1997).
[12] In 1997, there was a brief turnaround with the economy posting gains of anywhere from 0.4% to 0.8%, but these gains were wiped out by the financial crisis and a 4.6% decline in the Gross Domestic Product (GDP) in 1998.
[13] See Blasi *et al.*, *Kremlin Capitalism*, 190; and 'Wage Arrears Mount', *Open Market Research Institute (OMRI) Daily Digest* (16 Dec. 1996).
[14] These figures were reported in 'Russians' Real Incomes Down 14.8% Over Year—Government', *Interfax* (17 Sept. 1999). This unemployment rate is based on methods used by the International Labor Organization which show 9.1 million able-bodied individuals unemployed. The Russian Ministry of Labor and Social Development uses significantly lower numbers by excluding individuals considered to be on unpaid leave.
[15] See Doug Lippoldt, 'Social Benefits in Transition: An Introduction', in Organization for European Cooperation and Development (OECD), *The Changing Social Benefits in Russian Enterprises* (OECD, Aug. 1996; www.oecd.org/sge/ccet/cpru2309/present.htm); and Vladimir Mikhalev, 'Social Security in Russia Under Economic Transformation', *Europe-Asia Studies*, 48: 1 (1996), 5–25.
[16] Nick Wadhams, 'Study: One-Third of Russians in Poverty', *Associated Press* (20 July 1999).

for more than two-thirds of the poorest 25% households.[17] Not surprisingly, the rising poverty has been accompanied by a sharp rise in the death rate, marked by increases in chronic malnutrition, consumption of homemade (often poisonous) alcohol, the number of infectious diseases, particularly tuberculosis, and the number of youth suicides.[18] As a result of such trends, it is hardly surprising that life-expectancy has declined, particularly among males whose life-expectancy has fallen below 60, making debates over reforming the pension system particularly tense as the pensionable age presently stands at 60.[19]

The process of 'insider privatization', the regionally focused barter-based external relations among many firms, and the dramatic decline in production and living standards—all mark the failure of mass privatization to establish a productive, prosperous capitalist economy that can be integrated into the global economy. But, whether socioeconomic trends improve or decline further, there is still the question of whether the collapse of Soviet-era political and economic institutions will pave the way for the emergence of social pacts and economic institutions similar to those found in advanced industrial societies. Certainly, previously shielded economic actors and social groups now face new challenges and constraints similar to those faced by their counterparts in other transition economies. But, to gauge the significance of these challenges and constraints for arguments about convergence, it is necessary to study the behaviors of, and relationships among, key economic actors within concrete contexts. For this purpose, the next two sections focus on post-Soviet labor relations, noting continuities and changes in the institutions that mediate the formal and informal relationships among labor organizations, 'new' business elites, and the state.

---

[17] Skilled workers represent about 43% of the working population but 52% of the poorest 25% households, while unskilled workers represent 10% of the working population but 15% of the poorest 25% households: see Mikhalev, 'Social Security in Russia', 15.

[18] The Russian Health Minister, Vladimir Tarodubov, reports that Russians were 50–100% more likely to die prematurely than inhabitants in Western countries, partly as a result of the collapse of the health care system and the declining access to medicines. See 'Russian Death Rate Almost Twice As High as in West', *Agence France Presse* (13 Nov. 1998); and Anna Blundy, 'Youth Suicides Plague Russia', *The Times* (UK) (3 Nov. 1998).

[19] Between 1990 and 1996, the average life-expectancy at birth for males dropped precipitously from nearly 64 to under 57, rebounding a little over the next two years, while life-expectancy for women dropped less sharply, still standing at over 72; see 'Russia: Facts and Figures'. The life-expectancy for males has serious implications for discussions in government circles about whether to raise the pensionable age, currently 60, to rescue Russia's bankrupt Pension Fund. Government officials have denied that they have such plans, but they have admitted to considering proposals for cutting pensions to working pensioners. There is no retirement requirement for pension eligibility once the pensionable age is reached; cutting pensions of working pensioners would sharply increase the economic hardship for older workers who have already seen real incomes drop precipitously in the past decade. On pension reform, see Mikhalev, 'Social Security in Russia', 22, and 'Pension Reform Debated', *Open Market Research Institute (OMRI) Daily Digest* (5 Feb. 1997).

The Birth of Independent Unionism and the Failure of Tripartism

Despite the talk of 'workers' control' immediately following the 1917 Bolshevik Revolution, by the time Josef Stalin rose to power the USSR (1928–53), trade unions had been turned into 'transmission belts' of the government and the communist party, leading campaigns for 'socialist competition' to stimulate production and productivity, cooperating with enterprise administration to ensure factory discipline, and attempting to socialize a newly recruited workforce.[20] From the point of view of the workers, the most important function that the trade unions served was to manage the social insurance fund for each enterprise, collecting dues and managing the distribution of pensions, disability benefits, as well as a network of health care, educational, and recreational facilities. The official USSR-wide trade union federation, the All-Union Central Council of Trade Unions (AUCCTU), consisted of numerous sectoral federations, each corresponding to branches of the economic ministries. For each branch, the trade union organization at the all-union (Soviet) level was further broken down into regional- and factory-level trade union committees whose leaders frequently cooperated with local communist party officials and the factory administration to maintain order in the workplace.

This top-down system of industrial relations came under pressure in the late 1980s when Gorbachev attempted to boost the performance of Soviet industry by promoting new forms of labor participation. The 1987 Law on Labor Collectives formed new councils of labor collectives (STKs) that would hold elections at the workplace for managerial personnel and take over the function of distributing welfare benefits from party-controlled trade unions. The impact of the law proved to be minimal in the long run, as workers remained skeptical of top-down efforts at stimulating worker participation, and resistance from managers led to the overturning of workplace elections in 1990.[21] Nevertheless, Gorbachev's reforms did put pressure on the tight-knit collaborative relationships among the factory trade union committees, local party representatives, and factory administration. Moreover, Gorbachev's encouragement of 'informal' organizations led to the emergence of several new workers' associations, including the spontaneously organized strike committees that coordinated the miners' strikes of 1989. Threatened by competition from the informal workers' associations and the STKs, the official trade

---

[20] Insightful discussions of how trade unions became 'transmission belts' may be found in Jeremy Azrael, *Managerial Power and Soviet Politics* (Cambridge: Harvard University Press, 1966); Frederick Kaplan, *Bolshevik Ideology and the Ethics of Soviet Labor, 1917–1920* (New York: Philosophical Library, 1968); Margaret Dewar, *Labour Policy in the USSR, 1917–1928* (London: Royal Institute of International Affairs and Oxford University Press, 1956); and Hiroaki Kuromiya, *Stalin's Industrial Revolution: Politics and Workers, 1928–1932* (Cambridge: Cambridge University Press, 1988).

[21] On the difficulties faced by Gorbachev in his efforts to promote greater worker participation and workplace democratization through the 1987 Law on Labor Collectives, see Darrell Slider, 'Gorbachev's First Reform Failure: Work-Place Democratization', *Journal of Communist Studies*, 9: 2 (June 1993), 62–85.

union federation, the AUCCTU, declared itself independent of the communist party and reconstituted itself as the General Confederation of Trade Unions of the USSR (GCTU).

Efforts to devise a new system of industrial relations got under way within the Russian Federation in 1991. In July 1991, Yeltsin, now President of the Russian Federation, issued a decree ending communist party organization at the enterprise level to promote greater enterprise and union autonomy. Following the August coup that would hasten the break-up of the USSR, another decree was issued in November 1991 to establish a 'social partnership' among workers, employers, and the state. Inspired in part by corporatist labor relations in Western Europe, the Russian Trilateral Commission on the Regulation of Social and Labor Relations (RTK) was to be the main institutional manifestation of this new partnership, bringing together representatives of government, the managerial elite, and newly independent trade union federations in order to set the parameters for national, regional, and sectoral agreements that would subsequently guide firm-specific agreements between employers and workers.

First, however, came the question of who would actually represent 'labor'. The Federation of Independent Trade Unions of Russia (FITUR) had been a major component of the official union-wide trade union organization of the Soviet era and, following the collapse of the USSR, inherited the latter's material assets and the right to collect dues at most enterprises. As a result, FITUR ended up with the largest membership of any of the new trade union federations, maintaining its right to manage the dues and the property held by the official Soviet-era unions. But, although FITUR is sometimes seen as a 'remnant' of the old system of industrial relations—indeed, many of the top leaders, such as Igor Klochkov, FITUR's head until 1993, were drawn from the Soviet-era—FITUR's role in post-Soviet industrial relations was not merely an extension of trade union behavior from the Soviet period. For one, even if FITUR's leadership emerged from the Soviet trade union system, it was no longer officially an arm of the state; it was no longer as centralized as the old official unions; and it no longer participated in ensuring orderly production on the shopfloor. Moreover, despite the fact that the FITUR leadership had an interest in protecting its inherited material and organizational resources, the basic issues it advanced in its new role as a representative of workers' interests were essentially the same issues that workers everywhere have been anxious about: timely payment of wages, increased real incomes, social protection, and improved working conditions. Finally, FITUR now had to compete for membership, and this affected the size and nature of its organization and its political posturing as it sought to maintain its membership and resources.[22]

---

[22] Greg J. Bamber and Valentin Peschanski, 'Transforming Industrial Relations in Russia: A Case of Convergence With Industrialized Market Economies?' *Industrial Relations Journal*, 27: 1 (1996), 78.

Meanwhile, a host of new trade union organizations proliferated rapidly in the post-Soviet era, many of them ostensibly supporting Yeltsin's reforms. Such organizations as Sotsprof (Social Trade Unions) and the Independent Miners' Union had their roots in protests against the old system during the period of perestroika, and their commitments became translated into a pro-Yeltsin posture in the post-Soviet era, particularly as these unions had to find ways to gain more prominence *vis-à-vis* FITUR.[23] Other branch-level affiliates of FITUR either defected, as in the case of the Union of Mining and Metallurgy Workers, or acted with increasing independence in organizing strikes and demanding better wages and rights, as in the case of the air traffic controllers who would be crushed by the government. Many of the newer, pro-reform unions joined together in Spring 1995 to form the Confederation of Labour of Russia (CLR), but the combined membership in these unions represented only a tiny fraction of total union membership in post-Soviet Russia. In any case, the CLR proved to be influential only in a few select sectors such as coal mining and transportation, and by the end of 1995, the tensions within the CLR resulted in its fracturing into two separate entities.[24]

These new trade union bodies did reduce the huge membership base inherited by FITUR. The membership was nearly cut in half to 50 million by 1995. But FITUR remained by far the largest and most politically significant component of organized labor.[25] Moreover, despite the decline in centralization, FITUR officials were initially able to communicate their political position into local bread-and-butter issues and orchestrate large-scale rallies and strikes to protest delayed wage payments and declining working and living conditions.[26] It is perhaps for this reason that the Yeltsin administration,

[23] Sotsprof's (Social Trade Unions) support for Yeltsin and its opposition to FITUR's agenda is noteworthy as an instance of white-collar and professional workers seeking to reclaim their rightful place in the workforce. In the Soviet era, the glorification of physical labor over mental labor and the official denial of differences among categories of workers meant that professional or white-collar employees were especially frustrated; in the post-Soviet era, Sotsprof enabled these employees to define and pursue a separate agenda that would lead to greater rewards for their skills. On this point, see J. E. M. Thirkell, K. Petkov, and S. A. Vickerstaff, *The Transformation of Labour Relations: Restructuring and Privatization in Eastern Europe and Russia* (New York: Oxford University Press, 1998), 77–8.

[24] Sotsprof had not formally joined the CLR, but had signed a pact of cooperation with the Independent Miners' Union which was an original CLR member. By the end of 1995, Sotsprof and the Independent Miners' Union, as well as some of their allies, broke away to form a separate confederation. See Bamber and Peschanski, 'Transforming Industrial Relations in Russia', 79–80.

[25] FITUR's claim that it represented 80–90% of all workers was overstated, but in a 1994 survey conducted by the Ministry of Labour and the All-Russian Center for Public Opinion Research (VTsIOM), 50% of the respondents did consider themselves to be FITUR members while only 7.5% considered themselves to be members of new unions; cited in Bamber and Peschanski, 'Transforming Industrial Relations in Russia', 80.

[26] FITUR's continued ability to mobilize substantial segments of the workforce was more recently evident in the 'days of action' it has called every year. In March 1997, FITUR Chairman Mikhail Shmakov claimed that 21 million people had participated of whom 5.1 million had stopped working at least temporarily. The government's Interior Ministry claimed that the number of participants was closer to 2 million. Whatever the correct figures, the numbers cited in both

even if it viewed FITUR's opposition to swift market reforms as motivated by old-fashioned ideological commitments and organizational interests, began to rely increasingly on bilateral dealings with FITUR, marginalizing newer, more reform-minded trade union organizations such as Sotsprof, and weakening the prospects for corporatism under the rubric of the RTK.[27] The story of the failure of the trilateral commission is very much related to the kinds of cleavages and coalitions formed across labor and business organizations, and thus deserves a closer look in the context of particular issues and conflicts.[28]

The RTK consisted of representatives of government, business and labor. The government representatives were primarily drawn from the ministries, with the Labor Ministry particularly well-represented. On the labor side, FITUR ended up receiving nine of the fourteen seats allocated to labor, with the newer unions having to share the remaining seats despite the fierce loyalty some of them demonstrated towards Yeltsin. On the business side, the majority of representatives were linked, either officially or unofficially, to the Russian Union of Industrialists and Entrepreneurs (RUIE) which served as an umbrella organization of associations formed by some of the most powerful directors of the largest state and non-state enterprises; it pointedly did not include many pro-reform employers' associations formed by owners of newer or smaller businesses.[29]

The 2 January 1992 liberalization of prices and its effects on real wages provided the first major issue over which battle lines would be drawn in the RTK. What is noteworthy is that the main conflict was not between labor and business; the dominant cleavages were formed around the question of the pace of market-oriented reforms. Both FITUR and RUIE adopted a critical stance against the government's continuing support for swift market reforms, while the smaller labor organizations, most notably, Sotsprof, and a few of the newer business associations tended to support Yeltsin. It was this cleavage that would continue throughout the time during which the RTK continued to be active, making it virtually impossible for either 'labor' and 'business' to

FITUR and government estimates were larger than the turn-outs estimated at a similar day of protest in November 1996. See Penny Morvant, 'Workers Stage Protests', *Open Market Research Institute (OMRI) Daily Digest*, 28 March 1997.

[27] On the government's assessment that FITUR was the most viable organization representing labor in the management of industrial relations, see Linda Cook, 'Russia's Labor Relations: Consolidation or Disintegration?', in Douglas W. Blum (ed.), *Russia's Future: Consolidation or Disintegration?* (Boulder: Westview Press, 1994), esp. 80.

[28] Much of the discussion in the remainder of this section is informed by the more detailed comprehensive analysis of labor relations in the period between 1992 and 1995 in Walter Connor, *Tattered Banners: Labor, Conflict, and Corporatism in Postcommunist Russia* (Boulder: Westview Press, 1996).

[29] Led by Arkadii Volsky, a former plant director and advisor to Andropov and Gorbachev, the RUIE, like FITUR, cut across both state and private sectors, claiming nearly 3,000 members affiliated with nearly 2,000 of the largest enterprises in Russia. For a lucid discussion of RUIE and other employers' associations, see Paul Kubicek, 'Variations on a Corporatist Theme: Interest Associations in Post-Soviet Ukraine and Russia', *Europe-Asia Studies*, 48: 1 (1996), 39.

behave as unitary actors. By July 1992, FITUR and RUIE had united to form the 'Russian Assembly for Social Partnership', ostensibly to find an alternative route to managing 'class struggle', but, in reality, to block certain components of the government's reform program in order to preserve existing understandings and routines at larger enterprises. The reformist elements among labor and business, similarly, acted in concert in support of Yeltsin, in part because they needed the support of the government in order to demonstrate their relevance and expand their clout *vis-à-vis* the 'Russian Assembly for Social Partnership'. The Independent Miners Union, for example, won substantial wage concessions from Yeltsin in the process of trying to expand its membership *vis-à-vis* FITUR-affiliated unions.

This pro-reform/anti-reform cleavage became even more clearly evident in 1993 when some of the non-FITUR unions attempted to push the government to take over control over FITUR's social insurance fund. Had it been successful, such a move may have transformed the character of organized labor in post-Soviet Russia, reducing FITUR's special position and potentially leading to new peak associations bringing together the various labor organizations. However, this effort was overtaken by the events of Fall 1993 as Yeltsin dissolved parliament and eventually called in the army to forcibly evict recalcitrant parliaments and their paramilitary supporters. During the stand-off, the FITUR leadership and RUIE both objected to Yeltsin's actions, although it is not clear how energetically they were prepared to defend the old Russian parliament. Following the dissolution of the old Russian parliament, there was an opportunity for Yeltsin to go on the offensive against FITUR if he chose to do so, but again, events conspired to preserve FITUR's position.

Late 1993 witnessed a change in leadership in FITUR as the old head, Igor Klochkov, was forced to resign following comments citing the need to defend the Russian parliament. Mikhail Shmakov, former head of the Moscow regional branch of FITUR, eventually took over the leadership and adopted a more conciliatory posture. At the same time, in the December 1993 elections, although the FITUR-RUIE coalition fared poorly—partly as a result of their ties to former Vice-President Aleksandr Rutskoi who had led the defense of the parliament—anti-reform elements did significantly better than pro-reform parties, including those backed by Yeltsin. This setback prompted Yeltsin to respond to FITUR's overtures by allowing FITUR to maintain its property and dues-collecting rights, while establishing a new Service for the Settlement of Collective Labour Conflicts under the Ministry of Labor—although this body would prove to be ineffectual, constrained by the lack of resources. Then, throughout 1994 and 1995, the Yeltsin government moved progressively in the direction of making deals with FITUR, bypassing other trade union organizations and even reducing the number of seats allocated to the latter. The only exception here was the Independent Union of Miners which continued to be an effective independent organization, although it did so by partly cooperating with regional FITUR affiliates over increasingly dismal economic conditions and wage arrears.[30]

At the time of the 1995 elections, FITUR and RUIE joined with a new political party to once again form a large, united bloc. The bloc fared poorly in the parliamentary elections, but it should be noted that much of its expected support went to the newly legalized Communist Party of the Russian Federation (KPRF) under Zyuganov whose agenda shared many of the points on FITUR/RUIE platform. KPRF had explicitly urged FITUR/RUIE not to form a separate party in order to consolidate support, and the FITUR/RUIE-led bloc had responded by noting that it would remain in the elections though it would work closely with the KPRF-led bloc in parliament. But, in the end, it was the latter that actually managed to sustain a well-organized electoral campaign while the former failed to meet the 5% threshold for proportional representation in the Duma.

While their ability to generate electoral support remained weak, FITUR continued to be active and vocal in dealing with specific issues, economic conditions, and the government's policies. The total membership of all of the other non-FITUR trade union federations continued to be significantly smaller when compared to the official membership of 50 million workers claimed by FITUR.[31] FITUR remained the only trade union body able to organize large-scale rallies and strikes, and, as the problem with wage arrears mounted during the mid 1990s, FITUR's affiliates remained the most relevant labor actors in most regions. With FITUR's clout still significant and most workers increasingly frustrated by the rapid decline in their standard of living, Yeltsin's initial quest for corporatism gradually gave way to increasingly high-level contacts between FITUR and the government. As a result, even the most reform-minded trade union groups such as Sotsprof became marginalized, losing some of their seats on the RTK to FITUR. Through 1994–5, *ad hoc* political bargains remained the norm for national-level discussions on labor questions, and the RTK had for all practical purposes become reduced to little more than a 'decorative' body.[32]

One might argue that these trends between 1992 and 1995 represented only temporary phenomena that would give way to more common forms of tripartite collective bargaining as new economic institutions took hold and as busi-

---

[30] For a more detailed analysis of the decline of corporatism in this period, see Connor, *Tattered Banners*, ch. 5.

[31] FITUR's dominance among trade union federations, however, does not extend to its overall clout among the workforce as a whole since an increasing number of workers are either not unionized or belong to small-scale local or branch unions which prefer to act independently rather than as components of federations.

[32] Connor, *Tattered Banners*, 187. The leader quoted is Boris Misnik, head of the Union of Mining and Metallurgy Workers which was originally a part of FITUR but defected in late 1992 to become an independent trade union organization with a more supportive posture towards Yeltsin. Misnik was one of the original signatories to the agreement that established the RTK.

ness and labor came to recognize their respective interests.[33] This is evident, however, only to the extent some of newer unions became increasingly disillusioned and began to throw in their lot with FITUR affiliates, enabling unions to cooperate more at the *regional* level as economic conditions worsened. For the most part, the late 1990s saw little evidence of anything resembling corporatism emerging in post-Soviet industrial relations. The state remained the pivotal actor, and labor relations remained heavily politicized, shaped primarily by support for, or opposition to, the government's economic and social policies. In fact, after 1996, the government, far from retreating from the economy and adopting a neutral role in industrial relations as some expected,[34] sought to rein in organized labor. This was evident in 1997 when the government reportedly pressured the Russian Constitutional Court to repeal a new parliamentary law that required enterprises to pay wages first and taxes afterwards.[35] Then, in 1998, in the aftermath of the financial crisis and the miners' blockade of the Trans-Siberian Railroad, the government initiated deliberations on how to more clearly distinguish trade unions from political parties in order to strictly limit the scope of the former's political activities to labor-related issues.[36] And more recently, the government of President Vladimir Putin has introduced new labor codes that would permit more dismissals and reduce the power of unions to resist them. Employers, for their part, were not able to form anything resembling the apex business organizations found in advanced industrial countries; rather, competing business associations exhibited sharp differences in interests and agendas depending on the extent to which they were part of the business networks that benefited from 'insider privatization'.

Under these conditions, the significance of collective bargaining remains unclear. National-level agreements have consisted of vague promises from the government on the issue of wage payments; the few sectoral or regional agreements concluded among employers and labor organizations have been limited to provisions for minimum wages and measures to ease the impact of mass layoffs. And, in any case, formal agreements have been ignored for the most part, as vividly illustrated by the growing problem of wage arrears.[37] In the early stages of transition, perhaps it was not unreasonable to expect that privatization would lead to a retreat of the state from the economy, greater exposure to global market pressures, the depoliticization of labour relations, and the emergence of a new class of private entrepreneurs; this, in turn, would prompt independent trade unions to organize around the defense of employees'

[33] This is the position taken in Bamber and Peschanski, 'Transforming Industrial Relations in Russia'.

[34] Bamber and Peschanski 'Transforming Industrial Relations in Russia', 81, for example, claimed in 1996 that 'the Russian state is beginning to adopt the role of a neutral third party'.

[35] Reported by Vadim Borisov, Director of the Moscow-based Institute for Comparative Research into Industrial Relations (ISITO), cited in Tony Weselowsky, 'Russia: Workers Still Waiting to Be Paid', *Radio Free Europe/Radio Liberty (RFE/RL) Daily Report*, 11 Feb. 1998.

[36] Philippa Fletcher, 'Russian Government Seeks to Keep Unions Out of Politics', *Reuters*, 12 Aug. 1998.

[37] Thirkell *et al.*, *The Transformation of Labor Relations*, 105.

interests at national, regional, and sectoral levels, leading to new forms of collective bargaining and conflict resolution similar to those that characterize corporatism in Western Europe.[38] But, whatever else it might mean and whatever variants it may have, 'corporatism' is a tripartite arrangement, predicated on the notion of three distinct actors: government, business, and labor. There might be competitive pressures and conflicts within each of these groups, but the dominant cleavage is generally assumed to be across the labor-business divide. In the context of post-Soviet Russia, however, the main division proved to be between those who, whether for political utility or genuine concern for social conditions, wanted to temper radical reforms initiated by the state (e.g., RUIE and FITUR), and those who, whether for political utility or genuine commitment to market capitalism, backed the state's policies and sought to weaken the influence of the old union leaders and industrialists. As a result, the state, not business, ended up as the focal point of labor's struggle for wages and social protection. Moreover, the government proceeded to act neither as a mediator, nor as an ally of the labor and business groups that embraced its reforms; rather, the Yeltsin administration dealt bilaterally and selectively with organized labor to stave off labor unrest, and subsequently went on the offensive to curtail the activities of organized labor. The question we must now turn to is what all this means for the future of organized labor in Russia.

The Irrelevance of Trade Unionism in Post-Soviet Russia?

That FITUR managed to retain control over its assets and maintain its position *vis-à-vis* other independent unions does not mean that it was actually able to advance its agenda or contribute to the collective strength of organized labor in the course of transition. In fact, on the whole, organized labor in post-Soviet Russia has remained divided, and where some collaboration is in evidence, the unions have been able to do little to shield workers from the adverse effects of radical market reforms.[39] In fact, neither FITUR, nor any of the other trade union federations, have been able to produce any tangible benefits for workers themselves, particularly in relation to the issue of wage arrears and social protection for laid-off workers.

When prolonged strikes have broken out, Yeltsin has been able to get away with simply promising modest wage increases in the short-run without having to take any concrete steps to ensure the timely payment of wages or offset the

---

[38] On the appeal of corporatism in post-socialist countries, see the discussion in Thirkell *et al.*, *The Transformation of Labor Relations*, 7; and Kubicek, 'Variations on a Corporatist Theme', 30–1. For an example of studies that interpret trends in post-Soviet industrial relations as a case of gradual convergence with industrial relations in advanced societies, see Bamber and Peschanski, 'Transforming Industrial Relations in Russia'.

[39] For a more comprehensive statement on the ineffectiveness of unions in the immediate aftermath of the collapse of the USSR, see Linda Cook, 'Workers in the Russian Federation: Responses to the Post Communist Transition, 1989–1993', *Communist and Post-Communist Studies*, 28 (March 1995), 13–32.

social impact of market-oriented economic reform. In regard to the wage arrears, one FITUR official noted in frustration: 'It's getting to be like a ritual. Workers protest, the government tells them everything will be paid soon. But the problem only worsens'.[40] Even the formerly cozy relationship between FITUR and the parliament is not paying dividends, as the parliament, especially since the 1998 financial crisis, has been passing legislation in support of the government's budgets to ensure continued IMF funding. In effect, FITUR has come to view its erstwhile political allies as collaborating too readily with the government and is now beginning to pursue its own agenda, separate from the KPRF's political platform. As FITUR's Andrey Isayev lamented:

Deputies failed to adopt a single socially significant law in the interests of workers. They set up a shamefully low minimum wage level, ignore the demands for enforcing legal responsibility of the employer for overdue wages. At the same time, they push through the anti-trade union law on labor and dutifully vote on all the budgets proposed by the government.[41]

The newer trade union federations, such as Sotsprof, and the more independent branch unions, such as the Independent Union of Miners or the air traffic controllers' union, have not fared any better in gaining concessions from the government. Miners did receive a modest wage increase from the government as a result of their support for Yeltsin in 1991, but their situation since that time has steadily deteriorated as wage arrears have mounted. Moreover, as the Russian government was pressured by the World Bank to end subsidies to the coal industry, some 10% of the country's miners faced lay-offs as a result of mine closures; in fact, those whose back wages have now been paid—largely through financial assistance from the World Bank—turned out to be the same miners who were being laid off![42] Other employees in coal-mining regions as well as teachers and health workers across Russia have seen their wages decline steadily. Given the continuing slack in labor demand, even branch unions in highly profitable sectors have been unable to ensure back payment of their wages, let alone bargain for wage increases in line with inflation.[43] The air traffic controllers, for example, were easily brushed aside when they complained that their wage packages were insufficient, especially relative to the wages and benefits offered to pilots.

[40] Galina Stela, Executive Secretary of FITUR, quoted in Fred Weir, 'Workers' Strikes, Social Unrest', *The Hindustan Times*, 19 Sept. 1997.
[41] Quoted in 'Russian Unions, Communists Disagree Over Strike Demands', *Interfax*, 13 Aug. 1998.
[42] The payment of back wages essentially constituted the severance pay for laid-off miners, but was woefully inadequate in the light of the lack of unemployment insurance and the sudden loss of enterprise-related non-wage benefits. See Stephanie Baker-Said, 'Paid Off, Then Laid Off', *Moscow Times*, 21 April 1998; and 'Miners Need More Than Just Back Pay', *Moscow Times* (20 May 1998).
[43] Louise Grogan, 'Arrears Enslave Labor', *Moscow Times*, 9 April 1998.

With neither FITUR nor the newer unions able to have any significant impact on social policy or on the problem of wage arrears, organized labor's clout has weakened considerably, and, as noted above, the government has been able to go on the offensive to limit the activities of trade unions. Thus, it is not surprising that the union federations are increasingly being disregarded by workers who see trade union leaders as either overly concerned with maintaining their own political clout or, at best, simply ineffective in delivering tangible benefits. In fact, surveys consistently show that the vast majority of workers view unions as powerless to protect their rights or livelihoods, with a surprisingly large segment reporting the absence of union organization at the workplace.[44] As Yuri Levada, Director of the All Russia Center for Public Opinion Research (VTsIOM; Moscow), puts it: 'We actually have no real trade unions, neither the old nor the new ones are fit for such a role. There are lobbyists, the regime's 'henchmen', great talkers, and the like, but no real trade unions. Hence the lack of trust'.[45]

That unions have been generally ineffective in post-Soviet Russia, however, does not mean that workers themselves have been passive. At the firm- or local-level, workers, whether union members or not, have been growing increasingly active on their own initiative. Strikes have been launched by trade union members in various sectors in various regions without authorization from higher level trade union officials and without any systematic coordination with affiliates in other regions or the national branch federations. Various groups of workers, ranging from miners to scientists, teachers and health workers, have engaged in strikes or walkouts in order to protest against declining real wages and delays in the payment of wages. Walkouts in Russia shot up dramatically between 1992 and 1997 from 200,000 worker-hours to 5.7 million worker-hours.[46] During the first nine months of 1997, local trade unions launched 2,000 individual and collective legal suits against employers, most without the backing of the national-level leadership.[47] In May and June 1998, a group of infuriated miners spontaneously organized a blockade of the Trans-Siberian Railroad, while in June 1998, coal-miners from Vorkuta and Inta, also without the encouragement of their trade union federations, came to Moscow and staged a 24-hour picket to demand the nationalization of the coal industry.

This increase in independent, sometimes uncoordinated, worker protest may be related to the decline in socio-economic conditions and the failure of

[44] In a 1995 survey, for example, 62% of the respondents believed that unions were powerless to defend their interests; see T. Chetvernina, P. Smirnov, and N. Dunaeva, 'Unions' Place At an Enterprise', *Economic Problems* [in Russian], 6 (1996), 86–7. In a 1993 survey conducted by VTsIOM, 67% of those polled in the private sector reported no union organization at the workplace. Both surveys are cited in Bamber and Peschanski, 'Transforming Industrial Relations in Russia', 80.

[45] Interview for Vitaly Golovachev, 'Humiliation', *Trud* [Work], 18 March 1998.

[46] Vladimir Radyunin, 'Kremlin Fails to Pay Off Back Wages', *The Hindu*, 20 Jan. 1998.

[47] Weselowsky, 'Russia: Workers Still Waiting To Be Paid'.

tripartism discussed in the previous two sections; but it also speaks to the inability of the trade union federations to shield workers from declining wages and standards of living.[48] It is thus the local- and workplace-level to which we must now turn our attention if we are to understand the post-Soviet transition from the perspective of individual workers and managers.

Non-market Norms and Relationships: Workers and Managers at the Enterprise Level

This section considers the norms and behavior of workers and managers at the level of firms and the networks and communities in which they are embedded. Given the failure of corporatism at the national level, this is the context in which workers and managers have had at least some opportunity to forge mutual understandings and develop strategies to cope with the uncertainties of the post-Soviet transition. Below, I consider some of the evidence in the behavior of managers and workers that points to the persistence of non-market norms and exchange relationships despite the new institutional environment. In the concluding section of this chapter, I attempt to relate these norms and relationships to the informal understandings developed during the Soviet era to cope with the 'immoral' features of the formal system of production.

To understand the attitudes of workers in the context of transition, it is necessary to go back to the late 1980s when labor unrest increased dramatically as Gorbachev's reforms increased hardship for many workers. It is important to note that the workers did not criticize reforms emphasizing collective responsibility for the joint performance of tasks by work brigades; nor did they vigorously object to Gorbachev's call to improve productivity and product quality. What they objected to most vehemently was, first, the notion that workers, rather than the system of production and distribution, bore the primary responsibility for the state of the economy, and second, the increased de-leveling of incomes that would result from Gorbachev's reliance on sharply differentiated material incentives to reward the discipline and productivity of individual workers.[49]

---

[48] On occasion, trade union officials have attempted to step in and support these independent protest activities, but often too late to provide leadership or coordination. For example, after coal-miners blockaded the Trans-Siberian Railroad in May and June, Anatoly Chekis, Chair of FITUR's Kuzbass regional body, declared that the 'trade unions will have to stand up for them and try to block the prosecution of the protesters'. See Yury Tyurin, 'Trade Union Leaders Accuse the Government of Breaking the System of Social Partnership, And Are Determined to Protect the Organizers of Coal Miners' Protests From Prosecution', *RIA Novosti*, 8 July 1998.

[49] Gorbachev attempted to simultaneously pursue brigade reforms emphasizing collective labor and market reforms within the enterprise emphasizing greater material rewards for individual 'effort and merit'. Gorbachev did not view the two strategies as based on inherently contradictory principles, although one placed responsibility on the individual for the performance of tasks, and one emphasized collectivities that would jointly determine the division of labor and the distribution of rewards. Workers, however, seemed to recognize the contradiction and mostly attacked the new incentive system. See Walter Connor, *The Accidental Proletariat* (Princeton: Princeton University Press, 1991), esp. 143–5 and 180–3.

The coal-miners' strikes of 1989 and 1991, although frequently portrayed as motivated by a desire for market reforms and further democratization, also pointed to the resilience of certain norms and expectations among workers. In 1989, workers were not leading a working-class revolt against every aspect of the Soviet enterprise system; they were mainly protesting the failure of the regime to deliver basic goods and supplies promised to workers by paternalistic enterprises. Moreover, workers in the steel industry, who continued to receive their non-wage benefits, resisted the pressures to join in the strikes, and in fact, some wrote letters urging the coal-miners to return to work.[50] The 1991 miners' strikes were even more confrontational, challenging Gorbachev and the Soviet regime while explicitly supporting Yeltsin's calls for more radical political and economic reforms. But, here too, the call for the 'market' was more noteworthy for its symbolic oppositional content than as a declaration of support for a full-scale capitalist economy; that is, the 'market' served as a symbol for greater enterprise autonomy in the light of the regime's inability to meet the just demands of the workers.[51] What most workers were concerned about was not so much whether capitalist economies were superior to socialist economies; they were mostly upset '. . . that people were not getting paid according to their labor: those who worked hard, and produced something of material value, were being cheated out of its value, while those who distributed and redistributed this wealth were enriching themselves without real work'.[52]

This attitude remained in evidence even after the post-Soviet transition got under way. Although many workers supported some basic restructuring of the economy and the enterprises, as Michael Burawoy and Pavel Krotov have shown, they were primarily acting to establish greater worker control on the shopfloor now that the state was seemingly 'withering away'.[53] In many cases, while trade union federations feared that market reforms could lead to large-scale lay-offs and bankruptcies, workers supported privatization, and even helped managerial elites to engineer 'insider privatization' as a means to retain greater control. As Simon Clarke notes, '[w]hile senior managers may see privatisation as a means of breaking from the tired rhetoric of socialism, the majority of workers see the economic and political independence of the enterprise as the basis on which the rhetoric of collectivism and workers' control can be given some reality'.[54] In the case of the 1994 privatization of the

[50] See Stephen Crowley, *Hot Coal, Cold Steel: Russian and Ukrainian Workers from the End of the Soviet Union to the Post-Communist Transformations* (Ann Arbor: University of Michigan Press, 1997).

[51] See Crowley, *Hot Coal, Cold Steel*, 193–207; and his 'Coal Miners, Cultural Frameworks, and the Transformation of the Soviet Political Economy', Paper presented at the Annual Meeting of the American Political Science Association, San Francisco, 29 Aug.–1 Sept. 1996.

[52] Ibid. 'Coal Miners', 15.

[53] Burawoy and Krotov, 'The Soviet Transition'.

[54] Simon Clarke, 'Privatisation and the Development of Capitalism in Russia', in Clarke *et al.* (eds), *What About the Workers? Workers and the Transition to Capitalism in Russia* (London: Verso, 1993), 240.

huge 'Zil' automobile factory, for example, privatization took the form of the plant's director, assistant director, and other management personnel buying up the vast majority of stock. Workers supported this transaction because, as a result, they were more likely to retain not only their jobs and incomes, but also to maintain the personal ties to supervisors and managers that formed the basis for enterprise paternalism in the Soviet era.[55]

In fact, despite mounting pressures for streamlining benefits delivered by large-scale enterprises to their employees, some scholars note that the expectation of 'guardianship' is still very much ingrained among both workers and managers, and that paternalistic understandings are likely to persist at the firm-level even market forces ultimately become entrenched in the wider economy.[56] A 1993 study of 277 privatized firms in Moscow found that managers typically continue to adhere to patriarchal norms, emphasizing familiar social relations, collective identification with the firm, and a blurring of the demarcation between the business and personal realms.[57] From the point of view of workers, as a 1995 survey indicates, while trade unions may still play a role in protecting workers jobs, it is the directors and managerial personnel who are viewed as the real defenders of the everyday needs and interests of workers.[58] A more recent study comparing labor relations across a large state firm, a smaller privatized firm, and a new joint venture company, found a strong expectation, even among white-collar engineers in the latter, that superiors should feel responsible for protecting subordinates even if this means violating formally prescribed rules about labor discipline and wage payment.[59] Evidently, one way of preserving and reproducing this paternalistic relationship was by bypassing the formal system of wages—technically based on output-related material stimuli and carefully graded pay scales—and relying on informal wage agreements and non-wage supplements so as to boost

[55] Victor Zaslavsky, 'From Redistribution to Marketization: Social and Attitudinal Change in Post-Soviet Russia', in Gail Lapidus (ed.), *The New Russia* (Boulder: Westview Press, 1996), 126.

[56] Petr Bizyukov, 'The Mechanisms of Paternalistic Management of the Enterprise', in Simon Clarke (ed.), *Management and Industry in Russia* (Brookfield, VT: Edward Elgar, 1995), 99–138. Similarly, there are cases such as the Tulachermet plant where labor has not only cooperated with management, but has continued to identify with the factory as an extended family. See Lisa Baglione and Carol Clark, 'Contemporary Labor Relations in Russian Industry: A Study of Two Metallurgical Enterprises', Paper presented at the Annual Meeting of the American Political Science Association, San Francisco, 29 Aug.–1 Sept. 1996, esp. 22.

[57] V. A. Radaev, 'Four Ways of Establishing Authority Within a Firm', *Sociological Magazine*, 2 (1994), 149–57; also cited in Elena Shershneva and Jurgen Feldhoff, *The Culture of Labour in the Transformation Process* (New York: Peter Lang, 1998), 26–7.

[58] The survey was conducted by the Centre for Labour Market Studies in 1995, with 41% of workers citing enterprise directors or management as the group most likely to defend their interests, and only 13% viewing the trade unions as serving this function. See Centre for Labour Market Studies, *Formation of Social Partnership in the Russian Federation* (Institute of Economics, Russian Academy of Sciences, 1995) 13–14; cited in Thirkell *et al.*, *The Transformation of Labour Relations*, 106. See also note 44.

[59] Shershneva and Feldhoff, *The Culture of Labour*, 72.

incomes and limit performance-related or skill-related pay differentials among workers of all grades.[60]

This same study also found that workers in all three cases, far from identifying with their particular job skills or with the working class at large, have continued to identify strongly with their workplace *kollektivs*, the informal face-to-face group corresponding to the formal administrative units within the factory, shop, or section. These *kollektivs* reflect dense social relations shared by workers in the same work-group, representing a source for the social identity of workers as well as a basis for mutual assistance, emotional support and social protection, both on the shopfloor and outside the enterprise.[61] This evidence may not definitively point to a distinctively Russian culture of labor, but it certainly suggests that workers' opposition to the old regime cannot be equated with their support for the kinds of labor practices that have evolved in the midst of the more individualistic market cultures of Western capitalist societies.

Among the new business elites, there are certainly those who have been innovative and who have adapted quickly to the new market environment. At the same time, a number of studies note the resilience of particularistic understandings and patterns of social exchange in the relations among enterprise directors. There remains, for example, a persistent tendency among many employers to ignore formally prescribed rules generally in favor of informal ethnical norms emphasizing personal loyalty, enterprise solidarity, paternalistic benevolence, and trust among customary business partners.[62] One study of managerial behavior shows how many newly privatized businesses continue to follow organizational practices developed in the context of a 'unique combination of "hard" and "soft" budget constraints' that directors faced in the Soviet era; these routines have been maintained by many business elites in an era of uncertainty and flux, with many enterprises retaining a large labor surplus, restraining from mass lay-offs, and accepting promissory notes from trusted partners in lieu of immediate payments, thus contributing to the spread of barter and the growth of inter-enterprise arrears.[63]

Even in seemingly reform-oriented St. Petersburg, one study finds that a large segment of the business elite continues to operate through norms and exchange relationships mediated by personal loyalty, trust among familiar

---

[60] Ibid. 70. The authors quote the head of the planning and finance department of a large state firm: 'To be honest, the piece rate system only exists formally. Payment depends on agreements with the shop management. This is true for everyone who works here. The sum is agreed upon when the worker is employed. In actual fact this is pay by time system. The piece rate system of payment becomes relevant only if the worker doesn't finish his task on time'.

[61] Ibid. 59–66.

[62] S. G. Klimova and L. V. Kunayevskii, 'New Entrepreneurs and Old Culture', *Sociological Studies* [in Russian] 5 (1993): 64–9; and V. A. Radaev, 'On Some Features of Normative Behaviour of Russia's Entrepreneurs', *World Economy and International Relations* [in Russian] 4 (1994): 31–8; cited in Shershneva and Feldhoff, *The Culture of Labour*, 25–6.

[63] Andrei Kuznetsov, 'Economic Reforms in Russia: Enterprise Behaviour as an Impediment to Change', *Europe-Asia Studies*, 46: 6 (1994), 964–6.

partners, and reputational concerns. This ethic is evident in the density of transactions among particular networks of directors who share close personal ties, rely on diffuse reciprocity, and give each other preferential treatment in terms of prices and payment schedules. While there is also a new group of business elites who are making impersonal decisions guided mainly by concerns for profit, the study finds no evidence as yet that non-market norms and mechanisms are in the process of steadily declining.[64]

It is also worth noting that there is little evidence to suggest that firms whose behavior is shaped by such particularistic norms and exchange relations perform more poorly than that of other firms. In the aforementioned St. Petersburg study, for example, businesses operating on the basis of informal ethical considerations and social networks fared no worse than those that relied more on market-driven logics and formal contracts.[65] Other empirical studies of firms across post-Soviet Russia demonstrate that some of the most successful enterprises in the post-privatization Russian economy are ones in which the traditional mechanisms of social exchange guide relations with other firms while forms of paternalistic management shape employment patterns and wage practices; in many of these cases, a large labor surplus is still maintained, shop heads and union leaders cooperate with enterprise administration, and the firms continue to provide important welfare services and benefits ranging from health care to children's summer camps.[66] Even in distant company towns thought to be bastions of conservatism, large enterprises have restructured production processes and external relations, while continuing to rely on reciprocal understandings among parent firms and subsidiaries, and paternalistic employment relations within the firm.[67] Whether or not these non-market norms and exchange relationships prove resilient over the longer term, the limited evidence to date suggests that we cannot simply dismiss these aspects as temporary remnants of the past or as stubborn obstacles to dynamic and flexible forms of production.

---

[64] Oleg Kharkhordin and Theodore Gerber, 'Russian Directors' Business Ethic: A Study of Industrial Enterprises in St. Petersburg, 1993', *Europe-Asia Studies*, 46: 7 (1994), 1075–107. Kharkhordin and Gerber identify two stable clusters of directors, corresponding to two distinct employers' associations and business ethics in St. Petersburg: the Association of Industrial Enterprises, whose members favored a more personalistic, trust-based business norms and opposed swift reforms, and the Association of Privatising and Private Enterprises, which was more market-oriented and supportive of the radical reforms. The former position may be viewed as consistent with the position of RUIE.

[65] Kharkhordin and Gerber, 'Russian Directors' Business Ethic', 1100.

[66] Simon Clarke, 'Post-Communism and the Emergence of Industrial Relations at the Workplace', in Richard Hyman and Anthony Ferner (eds), *New Frontiers in European Industrial Relations* (Oxford: Blackwell, 1994), 384–6.

[67] This is the case, for example, in the giant Tulachermet metallurgical concern in the Tula region; see Baglione and Clark, 'Contemporary Labor Relations in Russian Industry'.

The Moral Legacy of an 'Immoral Economy'?

The discussion above is not intended to serve as a definitive and uniform characterization of the Russian workforce or the new business elites, but it is
intended to raise the question of how some of the unusual trends and behaviors in post-Soviet industrial relations may relate to the legacies of Soviet economic institutions. In particular, I want to offer the suggestion that the
non-market norms and social relations evident among managers and workers
in post-Soviet Russia are nested within social networks and moral understandings that originated in the Soviet era. This is not the legacy of official
communist ideology or of the formal institutions set up by the Soviet regime;
it is a legacy of the *informal* norms and routines that guided the interactions
of workers, shop chiefs, and managers in an environment that appeared to
them to be chaotic—even 'immoral'—given the increasing and acknowledged
gap between official management practices and the ideals articulated by the
founders of the regime. In effect, I suggest that most workers and many managers continue to informally operate on the basis of their own 'moral economy' within the context of new formal institutions that appear to be no less
alienating or 'immoral' than the formal system of industrial relations that
crystallized after the October 1917 Revolution.[68]

In the months leading up to and immediately following the revolution,
Bolshevik leaders emphasized the principles of collective labor and egalitarianism, ideals that resonated with a new class of industrial workers previously
accustomed to the collectivist egalitarian ethos of the repartitional peasant
commune.[69] At the enterprise level the ideal of collective labor found concrete
expression in the principle of 'workers' control', suggesting some sort of
elected committee-type administration collectively making critical produc-

---

[68] This interpretation is adapted from my broader comparative-historical analysis of management ideologies and practices in Rudra Sil, *Managing 'Modernity':Work, Community, and
Authority in Late-Industrializing Japan and Russia* (Ann Arbor: University of Michigan Press,
forthcoming). I use the concept 'moral economy' here in much the same way that Jeffrey
Kopstein uses the term in Chapter 9 of this volume, although I emphasize the separation of for-
mal and informal aspects of industrial relations. The term 'moral economy' is originally from
E.P. Thompson's study of social relations in eighteenth-century England and was popularized by
James Scott's study of subsistence-oriented norms in peasant communities. See E. P. Thompson,
'The Moral Economy of the English Crowd in the Eighteenth Century', *Past and Present*, 50
(1971), 76–136; and James Scott, *The Moral Economy of the Peasant Rebellion and Subsistence in
Southeast Asia* (New Haven: Yale University Press, 1976).

[69] The Russian peasant commune (*mir*, or *obshchina*) was the primary source of collective
identity above the household level. The forums where collective decisions were reached included
the heads of all households regardless of wealth or status, and the commune regulated the common meadows and collective resources used by peasants. Most significantly, in the interest of distributive justice, the commune periodically redistributed land strips held by member households
giving due consideration to the quality of size and labor power available to each household. For
a discussion of how these norms and practices affected the behaviors and expectations of Russian
workers in the early twentieth century, see Rudra Sil, 'The Russian "Village in the City" and the
Stalinist System of Enterprise Management: The Origins of Worker Alienation in Soviet State-
Socialism', in Xiaobo Lu and Elizabeth Perry (eds.), *Danwei* (Armonk: M. E. Sharpe, 1997).

tion decisions, supervising production, and monitoring costs, all with the concurrence of factory personnel of all ranks and skill levels. In addition, in keeping with the egalitarian ideals of a 'classless' society, Lenin and the Bolsheviks initially upheld the ideals of 'equal wages for equal labor' in factories, downplaying variations in skill levels or efficiency. Workers themselves responded favorably to these pronouncements, setting up conferences, drawing up new decrees on wages and working hours, and organizing procedures for implementing workers' control.[70]

In the course of the civil war period (1918–21), however, Lenin and war commissar Leon Trotsky began to downplay the notions of 'workers' control' and wage egalitarianism in favor of a piece-rate wage system and managerial hierarchies under the 'bourgeois specialists' who previously managed the factories of Tsarist Russia. The trade union organization endorsed this shift in 1920, demonstrating that unions were beginning to be viewed as instruments of central party control rather than independent voices for factory workers.[71] Upon Stalin's rise to power in 1928, the old managers and specialists were purged and replaced *en masse* by a fairly unified new managerial elite loyal to Stalin and officially committed to meeting the targets of the Five Year Plans. As these new 'Red Directors' assumed power any remaining checks on managerial power from below disappeared while Stalin declared workers' criticism of management to be interfering with production; as a result, a steeply hierarchical system of 'one-man management' became firmly entrenched, and trade unions were forced to accept their role of 'transmission belts' of the party-state apparatus.[72] Finally, criticizing the 'bourgeois egalitarianism' of other party members, Stalin introduced sharply differentiated wage scales and individualized production norms for thousands of narrowly specialized tasks, and he encouraged 'socialist competitions' whereby selected individuals would be disproportionately rewarded for their productivity regardless of the effects of this productivity on factory machinery or the work group as a whole.[73]

[70] See Dewar, *Labour Policy in the USSR*, 18–26.

[71] See Azrael, *Managerial Power and Soviet Politics*, 13–17; and Kaplan, *Bolshevik Ideology*, 320–32.

[72] For a detailed discussion of the purge of the 'bourgeois specialists' and the emergence of one man management, see Azrael, *Managerial Power and Soviet Politics*, 52–77, 99–104; and Kuromiya, *Stalin's Industrial Revolution*, 545.

[73] Although Stalin criticized the Russian Taylorists for being too technical and for failing to tap into the revolutionary spontaneity of the workers, he retained Alexei Gastev, the 'Russian Taylor', to design the new wage scales and the system for determining individual production norms for thousands upon thousands of narrowly defined production tasks. Stalin's campaigns for 'socialist competition' and the glorification of 'shock workers' had a certain revolutionary quality, but within a broader comparative framework, these campaigns put the focus of individual performance evaluations and relied on sharply differentiated material incentives to spur individual productivity despite the regime's earlier glorification of collective labor and egalitarianism. In this respect, labor relations on the shopfloor under Stalin did not differ too dramatically from capitalist speed-ups under Western scientific management. On this point, see also Mark Beissinger, *Scientific Management, Socialist Discipline, and Soviet Power* (Cambridge: Harvard University Press, 1988), esp. 133–5; and Vladimir Andrle, *Workers in Stalin's Russia: Industrialization and Social Change in a Planned Economy* (New York: St. Martin's Press, 1988), 88–99.

This shift in official management doctrines had a dramatic impact on the attitudes, expectations, and behaviors of workers and managers, but not in the manner that Stalin had hoped or anticipated. During the massive urban migration of the 1920s–1930s, peasants-turned-workers were able to masquerade as loyal Soviet workers but also became frustrated with the steep managerial hierarchies, individualized production tasks, and the sharp wage differentials they found on the shopfloor. Wherever possible, they learned to bypass official work practices and rely on informal networks of collusion and mutual assistance, often in conjunction with supervisors and managers, in order to fulfill their norms and limit income differentials.[74] Thus, a sense of collectivism *did* emerge on the shopfloor, but it was a more particularistic, informal kind of collectivism quite different from the one the regime sought to foster, and the kind of cooperation it engendered was one that *undermined* the formal organization of production rather than support it.

In the post-Stalin era, the overt use of physical coercion and the threat of terror was largely abandoned, but the tensions inherent in the Stalinist system of industrial relations did not get resolved.[75] A number of scholars have pointed to new trends during the Brezhnev era (1964–82) as evidence of nascent labor incorporation, suggesting that a 'social contract' had been tacitly concluded between the regime, the industrial directors, and workers.[76] Indeed, the regime did offer guarantees of full employment, incremental wage increases for each plan period, access to cheap basic necessities, better welfare and pension plans, managerial bonuses, and some modest reductions in the base wages of different categories of workers. However, there was no effort to review official management practices in the light of increasing evidence of informal and quasi-legal activities among workers and enterprise directors. The formal system of individual-level norm-determination and performance evaluations remained intact, as did the formal structure of authority and the material rewards. The Brezhnev regime experimented on the margins, but stayed away from any fundamental transformation of the official enterprise system inherited from Stalin.

[74] For more detailed studies of workers' social relations, see David Hoffman, *Peasant Metropolis: Social Identities in Moscow, 1929–1941* (Ithaca: Cornell University Press, 1994); Steven Kotkin, *Magnetic Mountain: Stalinist as a Civilization* (Berkeley: University of California Press, 1995); and Kenneth Straus, *Factory and Community in Stalin's Russia* (Pittsburgh: University of Pittsburgh Press, 1998).

[75] In the late 1950s, Nikita Khrushchev called for more egalitarian wage scales and trumpeted the virtues of collective remuneration, and this would have represented a significant shift in official management practices, but he was unable to implement any concrete changes in formal management practices before being ousted.

[76] See, for example, Blair Ruble, 'Factory Unions and Workers' Rights', in Kahan and Ruble (eds), *Industrial Labor in the USSR* (New York: Pergamon, 1979); Valerie Bunce, 'The Political Economy of the Brezhnev Era: The Rise and Fall of Corporatism', *British Journal of Political Science*, 13 (April 1983), 129–58; and Linda Cook, *The Soviet Social Contract and Why It Failed* (Cambridge: Harvard University Press, 1993).

Moreover, any actual improvement in workers' standards of living and sense of security came about as a result of a growing reliance on the informal practices and informal networks of mutual support that had begun to emerge under Stalin. During the 1970s, the typical Soviet workplace and the surrounding community was characterized by the expansion of personalistic patron-client relations as well as the proliferation of informal networks based on kinship, friendship and reciprocity. The transactions that took place within the context of these informal networks were obviously not enforced through laws or regulations; they were part of a shadow economy, based entirely on diffuse reciprocity and trust among participating members, and some set of shared understandings and customs rooted in familiar social ties. The leveling in workers' incomes, for example, was only made possible by abandoning the formal rules for calculating bonuses (which were still based on sharp differentials linked to individual performance) in favor of informal wage-leveling practices managers began to invoke for the purpose of retaining compliant workers. By the end of the Brezhnev era, a set of stable norms and social exchange relationships had crystallized, rooted in informal understandings of what the workers needed to do and what the managers needed to provide so that both could just 'get by' within a formal system of production that was neither delivering the economic progress promised by the leaders, nor consistent with the moral sensibilities shared by workers on the shopfloor. If indeed a 'deal' had been struck between the regime, managers, and workers, it was one that required the latter to satisfy their needs outside the system. This only further highlighted the incongruities between formal management protocols and the informal norms and practices that had become prevalent throughout Soviet industry and were even tacitly acknowledged by the regime.[77]

Conclusion

In the course of the post-Soviet transition, the formal system of production and industrial relations has been transformed, but as yet, this has not resulted in the disappearance of the *informal* norms and practices at the enterprise level. While the dramatic changes since 1991 have generated some new opportunities and challenges for Russian workers and managers, their responses do not unambiguously reflect a consistent trend towards patterns of labor relations seen in the West. The attempt to create a new market economy in Russia and to integrate it into global capitalism has led to the entry of multinational firms and the privatization of state-owned enterprises, but global economic forces and the availability of new institutional models have had far less of an impact on the prevalent norms and attitudes of key economic actors at the

---

[77] On this point, see also Simon Clarke, 'Formal and Informal Relations in Soviet Industrial Production', in Clarke (ed.), *Management and Industry in Russia*.

local and enterprise levels. These actors continue to informally operate on the basis of existing moral understandings within formal market institutions that appear to be no more fair or predictable than the official Soviet system of industrial relations.

This may be why a new labor code proposed by Vladimir Putin's administration—which would make it easier for employers to issue temporary contracts, increase working hours, and even choose which unions to negotiate with—has been facing mounting opposition from most of the key trade union federations. Three of the federations, including FITUR, have just joined the International Confederation of Free Trade Unions (ICFTU) in the hope of mustering greater political clout and international support. Thus, a new showdown appears to be looming, although the most hotly contested issues are likely to be those related most closely to preexisting labor codes and enterprise practices. Whatever happens, it is not likely that the long-standing gap between formal economic institutions—whether Soviet or post-Soviet—and informal understandings will be eliminated anytime soon.

9

Globalization in One Country: East Germany between Moral Economy and Political Economy

Jeffrey Kopstein, University of Colorado at Boulder

The revolutions of 1989–91 propelled the states of Central and East Europe back into the international capitalist economy from which they had been cut off for half a century or more. Suddenly, the economies of the region were exposed to the full impact of international market forces, the rapid spread of tastes and values across frontiers, and the influence of international regimes and institutions—in short, the force of what political scientists have recently dubbed 'globalization'. Nowhere is this more true than in East Germany, a country that was absorbed into West Germany after 1990 just as the latter was about to enter its own globalization crisis. Post-socialist transformation and rapid reunification have brought home the force of global market pressures to most East German workers in an especially acute form. While other formerly communist states retained national sovereignty, and could thus regulate their re-entry into the global market through tariffs, taxes, and exchange rate policy, what is now eastern Germany re-entered the global market-place overnight without any of these protections. It is thus not a unique case that defies comparison, but it is an extreme case that can be useful for illustrating the effects of the new globalism.[1]

One effect, in particular, that I want to highlight in this essay is a much-discussed but little-studied feature of globalization: the tendency for the new universalism of the global market to produce new kinds of ethnic and regional particularism. Political theorists and social scientists have already speculated on the strange simultaneity of globalization and nationalism, of universalism and particularism in the present era, put most poignantly by Benjamin Barber as 'Jihad vs. McWorld'.[2] What remains unclear, however, is the causal relationship between the two that generate particularistic identities from universalist challenges.

What I want to argue is that the new cultural divide in Germany between easterners and westerners, one that appears to be deepening, is an illustration of the new globalism and particularism at work. Because Germans, eastern

---

[1] Andreas Pickel, 'The Jump Started Economy and the Ready-Made State: A Theoretical Reconsideration of the East German Case', *Comparative Political Studies*, 30: 2 (1997).

[2] Benjamin Barber, 'Jihad vs. McWorld', *The Atlantic Monthly*, 269: 3 (March 1992).

and western, share a common ethnicity, the politics of post-unification provide a laboratory of sorts for exploring the dynamics of globalization and
particularism in the post-cold war world that allows us, in effect, to hold
ethnicity constant. To anticipate the argument that follows: the ironic resurgence of an eastern German identity is the result of global market forces
confronting the work and leisure habits of a society that was systematically
cut off from the international division of labor for forty years. The new cultural divide in Germany is the product of two very different moral economies
confronting each other. One implication of this analysis is that the new particularism in other locales may stem from the clash not only of 'civilizations',
but, rather more prosaically, from the conflict between dominant labor and
leisure practices, and between notions of what is properly commodified and
what is best put outside of the market. These practices are being challenged
by global markets and the diffusion to the East of new tastes, values, and
institutions.

Moral Economy, Markets, and Particularism

One way of thinking about the cultural divide in Germany is in terms of ethnicity.[3] The language of cultural marker and stereotypical social exchange
that litters the writing on ethnicity has begun to creep into the analytical discourse on Germany.[4] Such a characterization is indeed tempting. Any number of statistical indicators could be used to support such an analysis.
Consider, for example, just one: marriages. In Berlin during 1995 there were
16,383 registered marriages. Of this number only 4% were 'intermarriages'
between East and West Berliners. In the same period Berliners married non-
Germans at almost eight times this rate.[5] This snapshot statistic suggests that
well after formal unification East and West Germans continued to interact as
'foreign' groups. As useful, however, as the ethnic analogy may be for understanding the character of cultural conflict, it has the disadvantage in the
German case of being just an analogy. The cultural divide in Germany may
be like ethnic conflict, but it is not ethnic conflict.

What is it then? It makes little sense to argue that there is something
immutably different between East and West Germans. Such essentialist
rhetoric is of little use to the social scientist, if for no other reason than the
fact that identities change over time, sometimes rapidly, sometimes slowly,
but they do change. I propose to explain how forty years of institutional separation created a very different moral economy in the East from the West,

---

[3] For an excellent argument exploring, and ultimately criticizing, this point of view, see Marc
Howard, 'A East German Ethnicity? Understanding the New Division of Unified Germany',
German Politics and Society, 13: 37 (1995), 49–70.
[4] Wolfgang Engler, *Die Ostdeutschen: Kunde von einem verlorenen Land* (Berlin: Aufbau,
1999); Luise Endlich, *Neuland: Ganz einfache Geschichten* (Transit, Berlin, 1999).
[5] 'Die Ost-West Ehe bleibt auch weiter die Ausnahme', *Berliner Zeitung* (9 Aug. 1996), 16.

and how this eastern moral economy is beginning to change the landscape of politics in Germany as a whole.

A word on moral economy is in order. The literature on this subject is now so vast as to constitute a subindustry within the social sciences. Although it is highly diverse in its claims, the notion of moral economy can be boiled down to a few simple propositions. It maintains that economic man is a historically contingent phenomenon and at best an ideal type. People tend to make trade-offs between goods only up to a certain point; thereafter, some things are not 'for sale'. For moral economists, most people have a fundamental sense of what is just and fair, and this sense forms their 'bottom line' beyond which exchange behavior will either not be engaged in or, when engaged in, it will be experienced as a moral violation. Furthermore, people will generally tolerate a social order only so long as an implicit social contract which lays down the bottom line of exchange is not violated. Of course, what this bottom line is, hence the nature of the moral economy, will differ from case to case. It therefore makes sense to speak of different moral economies in different societies. Interest remains an important category for moral economists but how interests are formed, the ultimate content of interests, and conditions under which interests become politically salient, is directly mediated by historical experience and cultural milieu.

A number of observable implications of this highly abstract principle can be discerned. Let me concentrate on just one: reactions to commodification. Since Karl Polanyi's work, we know that eras of commodification of land, capital, and labor are among the culturally most shocking and politically most volatile because, even though markets rapidly destroy old structures and norms, the terms of new implicit social contract are slow to be worked out. Although Polanyi casts the response to the commodification of the British economy in the eighteenth, nineteenth, and twentieth centuries in a kind of mushy, reified functionalism—of 'society protecting itself' through poverty laws, trade tariffs, welfare states, and currency debasements—that we may no longer find appealing, subsequent authors have easily recast his thought in terms of the ways in which received notions of 'fairness' and 'economic justice' shape interests in rapidly commodifying contexts.[6] Curiously, social scientists have yet to apply these categories to post-communist East Europe.

Yet nothing would seem to be more obvious, especially for East Germany. More than any other population in formerly communist East Europe, East Germans have confronted a sudden and almost complete commodification of their economy. While most analysts of post-communism have concentrated on the Leninist legacies and the barriers they pose to the successful construction of political democracy, very few have inquired or taken seriously the

---

[6] E. P. Thompson, 'The Moral Economy of the Crowd in Eighteenth Century England', *Past and Present*, February 1971; James C. Scott, *The Moral Economy of the Peasant* (New Haven: Yale University Press, 1976); Barrington Moore, *Injustice: The Social Basis of Obedience and Revolt* (Armonk: M. E. Sharpe, 1988).

cultural legacy of communist economics as opposed to politics. Few scholars have discussed the ways in which these economic legacies have contributed to the creation of new post-communist identities, precisely because the blatant economic inefficiencies of communism had let to its collapse in the first place.

Communism's collapse, however, should not dull our sense for how strongly Leninist economic institutions influenced not only social structures but also fundamental attitudes on issues of economic inequality, exchange relationships, employment, management, and even political participation. Neoliberal economics, with its assumption of instantaneous adjustment at both the individual and institutional level to altered incentives, may have kept us from appreciating this. At a material level, the assumption of instantaneous adjustment to new 'incentives' may be more or less true but at a cultural level it most certainly is not. The idea that such fundamental areas of human life as housing, schooling, and day care, as well as food and other staples, should be subject to cost-benefit calculations and the ups and downs of the market does not sit well with most East Germans, regardless of political orientation. Somehow the market, understood in this sense, offends their sensibilities even as they participate in it, understand that there is no practical alternative to it, and are prepared to do precious little to change it.[7] What might be described as an egalitarian moral economy of communist society appears to have persisted well into the capitalist transition.

Survey research on popular attitudes toward capitalist patterns of social stratification in post-communist societies has yielded contradictory results. In two papers using a telephone survey, written shortly after communism's collapse, Robert Shiller, Maxim Boycko, and Vladimir Korobov sought to show that attitudes toward equality and inequality across nations were quite similar and, remarkably, Russian and US attitudes were almost identical on issues of stratification and income distribution.[8] The assumption and conclusion of these studies was that communism did not really alter attitudes to commodification and equality, or to the extent that it did, such attitudes would change rapidly under a new incentive structure. Although these issues continue to be hotly debated in the scholarly community, it was only natural that East and West Germany became laboratory settings for similar research designs. The two Germanys seem to present the perfect control cases for the effects of immersion in different institutional orders on basic economic values in, what were before 1945, identical political cultures. Robert Rohrschneider, in several painstakingly researched articles on this topic, has come to the opposite conclusions of Shiller, Boycko, and Korobov. Using representatives from the

---

[7] In fact, most Germans now maintain that East Germans in their behavior and East Germany in its ethos are, if anything, *more* 'capitalist' than their Western counterparts.

[8] Robert Shiller, Maxim Boycko, and Vladimir Korobov, 'Popular Attitudes toward Free Markets: The Soviet Union and the United States Compared', *American Economic Review*, 81 (1991), 385–400; 'Hunting for Homo-Sovieticus: Situational versus Attitudinal Factors in Economic Behavior', *Brookings Papers on Economic Activity*, I (1992), 127–81.

Berlin parliament as respondents in face to face interviews, Rohrschneider consistently finds that regardless of party affiliation, respondents from East Berlin consistently support more egalitarian outcomes, greater governmental control over and intervention in the economy, and advocate the value of 'solidarity' more frequently than their West Berlin counterparts.[9]

The unification strategy has accommodated these differences in basic economic orientations. Unification with the West has permitted a special sort of post-communist economic policy in eastern Germany. It is at once both a shock therapeutic and a moral economic approach. On the one hand, more than any other post-communist country or region, eastern German industries and workers have been subject to the direct pressures of global economic competition, the results of which are discussed in greater detail below. On the other hand, unlike other post-communist countries, social stratification and income inequalities in eastern Germany have remained relatively stable since 1991. Comparing eastern Germany and Hungary, for example, Bruce Headly, Rudolf Andorka, and Peter Krause, using household panel data, found that after the revolution of 1989 income inequality increased very rapidly in Hungary, quickly surpassing that of West Germany. In East Germany, by contrast, 'net income inequality is almost unchanged since communist times and is much below West German levels'. Most surprising is that at the height of the unification shock, from March 1991 to March 1992, as measured by the German panel survey, there was no increase in inequality at all. The narrow distribution of net incomes in East Germany is a product primarily of federal taxes, transfers, and subsidies. Although others have shown that inequality is slowly increasing in East Germany, the influence of political and social considerations is far greater in East Germany than in Hungary, Russia, or probably any other country in formerly communist East Europe.[10]

This peculiar strategy was not merely the result of West Germany's capacity to underwrite a simultaneous market and welfare policy in the East. It also corresponded to the interests and attitudes of the main players on the ground during unification. The most commonly identified interest groups in determining the unification strategy of high wages and low inequality were the West German trade unions. After quickly colonizing the eastern German industrial landscape, the German trade unions lobbied successfully to move up eastern German wages faster than productivity in the hope of preventing wage competition from driving down wages in the West—wages that were

[9] Robert Rohrschneider, 'Cultural Transmissions versus Perceptions of the Economy: The Sources of Political Elites' Economic Values in the United Germany', *Comparative Political Studies*, 29, 1 (1996), 78–104; 'Report from the Laboratory: The Influence of Institutions on Political Elites' Democratic Values in Germany', *American Political Science Review*, 88: 4 (1994), 927–41.

[10] Bruce Headly, Rudolf Andorka, and Peter Krause, 'Political Legitimacy versus Economic Imperatives in System Transformation: Hungary and East Germany, 1990–1993', *Social Indicators Research*, 36 (1995), 247–73, quotation is from p. 261. See also *Das Parliament*, 17–24 January 1997, 1.

among the highest in the world. For their part, the leading politicians in what at the time of unification was the ruling party in Germany, the Christian Democratic Union (CDU), had no interest in staving off this trade union offensive. Nor did it express any interest in challenging East German conceptions of social justice. Such challenges might merely have created a solid bloc of potential Social Democratic (SPD) voters in the East by permitting social inequality to increase rapidly after 1991. By accommodating rather than attacking the prevailing moral economy of the East, the strategy of unification has served to perpetuate rather than overcome the cultural divide between East and West.

In the next section, I explain how this came to be. This requires an exploration of the origins of differing conceptions of economic and social justice in the East and the West in the post-World War II era. Because the story of the West is one that has been told before and, by now, is very well documented, I concentrate on the East, using the West only for contrasts. Explaining the current cultural divide, however, also necessitates a deeper enquiry into the origins of the unification strategy and its impact on East and West Germans. The next two portions of the chapter take on these tasks. The tentative conclusion is that while the continued cultural divide in German will not lead to the creation of two states, it will, as cultural divides have in other contexts, change the shape of national politics for good. The politics of unification mean that there is no going back to the old Federal Republic.

East German workers and Sovietization: A Twofold *Stunde Null* (Zero Hour)

Memoirs and archives have revealed how difficult and uncertain was the creation of the West German social market economy during the 1950s.[11] It was by no means certain that West German public opinion would tolerate what appeared at the time to be a protracted period of hardship after the 1948 currency reform that ultimately put the country on the path to self-sustained economic growth. It is now easily forgotten how poor most West Germans were in the late 1940s and early 1950s, how little they traveled, and how little they consumed. Consider, for example, a typical newspaper report in 1947 on the physical health of Berlin workers.

We came to the conclusion that the enterprise youth is not gaining but losing weight and that the overwhelming portion of young people are considerably underweight. One of the most shocking cases recently is that of Liselotte W., sixteen-and-half years old, who works in Tempelhof. She is 1.5 meters tall and weighs 26 kilos. Another youth from the same district is 1.69 meters tall and weighs 40 kilos. A fifteen-year-old is 1.38 meters tall and weighs 32 kilos.[12]

---

[11] This section is adapted from my book, *The Politics of Economic Decline in East Germany, 1945–1989* (Chapel Hill: University of North Carolina Press, 1997).

[12] *Tribüne* (3 March 1947). In Dietrich Staritz, *Die Gründung der DDR* (Munich: DTV, 1987), 206–7.

As we now know, West Germany during the 1950s succeeded in transforming not only most people's fundamental political values, but also altered conceptions of social justice that were prevalent in the first post-war years to allow for a market economy to develop. In the years immediately following unification in 1991, many western Germans looked back to the 1940s and 1950s as a model for repetition in the East: like western Germans, eastern Germans could and would eventually make their way to the economic promised land. If the West Germans had built a market economy from scratch in 1945, so too could the East Germans in 1991.

Forgotten in all of this is that the East Germans had already started from scratch once before in this century, in 1945, and were being asked to start from scratch once again. The East German *Stunde Null* was if anything even more trying than the one experienced in the West. The Soviet occupation authorities behaved atrociously by any standard one might imagine.[13] In the economy, industrial plant that was not dismantled as reparations for shipment to the Soviet Union, where a large part of it simply rotted on the rail spurs, was used as a source for reparations from running production. German labor, a highly skilled commodity, was probably regarded as one of the greatest trophies of the war.

But whatever the Soviets' hopes for the traditional German virtues of hard work and discipline in their own zone of occupation, the orientations and behavior of East Germans quickly changed under the impact of the difficult post-war conditions and Soviet labor practices. This is not to say that seventy years of German working-class culture could be wiped out overnight by 'sovietization'. It could not. Indeed, significant aspects of this culture were not at all incompatible with Soviet labor practices. Well into 1947, for example, the extensive system of vocational training developed during the *Kaiserreich* and extended into the Nazi period continued to operate, utilizing many of the principles associated with the 'company loyalty' school developed in the 1920s and 1930s by the conservative industrial pedagogue Carl Arnhold.

Sovietization, however, did change things, albeit not in a simplistic way. The history of work in postwar East Germany is less a story of implementing a master plan for sovietization than it is of crisis management. Of course, as in every country of eastern Europe, the Soviet military authorities precluded the development in East Germany of independent working-class organizations, especially after 1947. But suppressing working-class organizations could not begin to solve all the problems of labor motivation and productivity. Inducing East Germans to work set off a bitter conflict over wages and piece rates. The resolution of this conflict within the confines of the command economy created a new kind of German worker, and working class, with different habits, expectations, and definitions of what is just and proper, with a

---

[13] Norman Naimark, *The Russians in Germany* (Cambridge: Harvard University Press, 1995), esp. ch. 2, on rape.

different moral economy than that of its predecessor or what was beginning to take shape in the West.

As in the West, one finds in East Germany in the late 1940s and early 1950s moving reports in the newspapers of the day of severe malnourishment among young workers. The line between survival and starvation was one easily crossed. The collapse of the financial system, coupled with shortages in every sector of the economy under the weight of reparations payments, rendered monetary wages a weak instrument for tying labor to the workplace. With almost nothing to buy, it made little sense to work for money. Where money did matter, if one had a lot of it, was on the black market. Most East Germans spent several hours per day in the black market and several days each month roaming the countryside in search of food. Initially, then, it was not so much a matter of getting East Germans to work as they did before, but rather of inducing them to show up for work at all. In the years following the war, absenteeism remained high and labor discipline lax. Those who arrived at the factory gates often did so on empty stomachs or severely malnourished.

Of necessity, the economic ethos in this society was one that is strangely reminiscent of James Scott's peasant 'in water up to his neck'. The prevailing ethos was egalitarian, defensive, even cooperative, and inclined toward survival rather than the maximization of gain. The institutional expression of this ethic was the spontaneously formed enterprise council, which, with Soviet toleration, coordinated production and distributed equally to their employees a portion of production to trade against what little food and consumer goods that could be found. Enterprise councils have a rich history in German industrial relations, extending back to the Weimar period and in some cases before. In the post-war years, East German enterprise councils took on two new roles. First, they helped identify and root out active Nazis in industry, although in the case of management the Soviet record on removing these officials was mixed. Second, with many managers having fled to the West, councils performed the valuable service of getting production up and running again. But as they were composed primarily of Social Democratic and Communist workers, enterprise councils could hardly have been expected to increase labor discipline and productivity with the traditional tools of differential reward and labor segmentation.

It was not until the end of 1947 and the beginning of 1948, with the onset of the cold war and Zhdanov's articulation of the 'two camps' theory, that the Soviets made their move against the social bases of the post-war moral economy. In October 1947, the occupation authorities issued Order 234. In essence the order was a full blown transfer of Soviet-style labor institutions to East Germany. Enterprise councils were abolished or incorporated into centrally directed trade unions. The order also called for a number of social measures to address the most urgent needs of East Germans: industrial safety, strict limits on the use of child labor, longer vacation time for workers involved in physically exhausting labor, 'polyclinics' and nursing stations in the workplace, improved living conditions for workers, and increased wages for female workers. Most important, enterprises were put on special lists, called '234 lists', and received extra deliveries of food for preparation of hot meals served in the workers cafeteria and consignments of industrial consumer goods to be distributed at the workplace. Workers deemed to be especially productive or those involved in hard physical labor received a type 'A' meal. Those evaluated as less productive or performing less strenuous tasks received a less caloric and nutritious type 'B' meal. This principle was to be used in the direct distribution of consumer goods at the workplace as well.

The order also contained a number of measures to improve labor productivity. First and foremost came the fight against 'slackers and corruption'. Absentee workers who did not produce a medical excuse could now have their ration cards taken away. In extreme cases they could be assigned to clear rubble from bomb sites, which, along with construction, was among the most poorly paid work and was almost never included on the Order 234 lists of enterprises receiving extra food. Most important on the discipline side, the order called for the reintroduction of piece work (*Akkordarbeit*) and other forms of productivity-based wages throughout industry. To assist management in raising productivity, Soviet-style 'socialist competitions' were to be employed and those individual workers who contributed most to raising productive norms were to be designated 'activists' and receive financial and political rewards.

Thus began the process of 'sovietization' of the East German labor force. Through a combination of incentives and sanctions, the particular Soviet method of binding ordinary people to their place of work, of refashioning the factory as a social and political, as opposed to purely a economic institution had begun. Much of this, of course, was not new to German workers or managers. Siemens and Zeiss had been pioneers in designing social policies internal to the enterprise. Yet, as socially oriented as many German workers and industrialists may have been in the pre-war era, they operated in a political and economic environment far different from the one confronting workers and managers in Soviet-occupied Germany. For one thing, the presence of the Soviet military authorities precluded the formation of anything like the independent employer and employee organizations that had hammered out personnel and wage policy in the Weimar era, and now in West Germany. The absence of legitimate interest representation meant that any wage settlement would be viewed by everyone from the outset as suspect, as an expression of state policy or, worse, 'Russian' policy, rather than as the result of wage negotiations between nominally independent parties.

Beyond the legitimacy question which would, of course, never go away, East German management confronted a far different set of incentives than its pre-war counterparts. Pre-war German industry, for all the excesses of a highly organized internal market, still faced a modicum of domestic competition and the discipline of a highly competitive external market. These conditions no longer obtained for East German industry. Pervasive shortages and Soviet reparations policy all but guaranteed that the entire productive capacity of almost any given enterprise could be sold. Rather than being determined by demand, the success of East German managers was a function of their ability to secure the necessary inputs of production, of which labor was among the most important. It was this factor that yielded to labor a measure of power and ultimately determined the path of East German development.

Under these conditions, when the measures of Order 234 were implemented, the results were surprising and frustrating to both the Soviets and the East German communist authorities. Type A and B meals were never really doled out as intended; instead, complained one report to the center, workers continued to 'eat from the same pot'. Where management stiffened its resolve to increase the differential of reward, workers often spontaneously evened out differences by purchasing goods for each other. According to communist party reports from enterprises, many foremen could not be stopped from putting all the piece-work tickets of any one shift into a common urn in order to ensure equality of reward. Piece-work equipment was regularly sabotaged, and piece-work engineers and rate busters were often the targets of physical threats and intimidation. In short, 'everyday resistance' hindered the successful implementation of any plan by the authorities for a crypto-marketization of industrial relations in what was still an egalitarian moral economy.

The workers were assisted by managers who were under pressure from both the Soviets and the evolving East German state authorities to maximize production at any cost. Management's behavior was crucial, for however intrepid the resistance of ordinary people, once the Soviets wanted a policy there was no real way of stopping it. What management could and did do, however, is to corrupt the entire Taylorist apparatus set up by the Soviets, and continue to reward workers relatively equally. Most managers even used the onset of piece work to raise all wages beyond what they should have been. The East German communists and the Soviets wavered in their response to this retreat by management. Occasionally they attempted to make a run at the norm question, as during the rise and demise of the East German Stakhanovite movement in the late 1940s and early 1950s, but usually this amounted to little more than lip service. By turning what was supposed to be an economic measure into a socio-political one, East German managers were behaving quite rationally and shored up their position in a sellers market for labor.

This cat and mouse game between ordinary East Germans and the state continued unabated until 1953, when the regime took a quite serious run at the norm and wage question—interestingly, against the advice of the Soviets who had 'advisors' located in all strategic offices of the East German planning bureaucracy. Such runs were thought to be periodically necessary because wage competition between enterprises for scarce labor tended to increase solvent demand for consumer goods and the money supply beyond what was considered healthy. As in earlier years, the plan to raise output norms might once again have been undermined at the enterprise level had it not also been combined with price increases in transportation costs, consumer goods, and health care. The result was the first mass protest in the history of Soviet occupied eastern Europe. Over 500,000 people protested in 272 cities throughout the country on 17 June 1953. Wage demands quickly escalated to political demands, all of which could only be put down with Soviet tanks.

The 17 June 1953 strikes, and the aftermath in the weeks to come, clearly frightened the East German leadership as well as the Soviets. Although communist party leader Walter Ulbricht managed to keep his job—barely, we now know in retrospect—the June events had frightened him. In order to buy labor quiescence, the communist party, with Soviet approval, continued to corrupt the entire Taylorist apparatus set up for measuring old norms and implementing new ones. Gradually, the outlines of an implicit agreement (or 'social contract') between the workers' state and the working class began to take shape: production could rise so long as norms remained low and wages high, relative to productivity. Industrial unrest did reappear sporadically throughout the 1950s, as the regime tried time and again to manipulate wages and piece rates. But enterprise party organizations and management had little interest in creating unnecessary industrial conflict and both tended to cave in to whatever demands workers might make. Rather than attempt to change this moral economy, communist authorities from very early on capitulated to it, and this gave ordinary East Germans an extraordinary degree of 'blackmailing power' against the regime.

Throughout the 1950s wages rose faster than productivity in virtually every sector of industry, a problem that the leadership would repeatedly attempt to rectify, albeit with little success.[14] Never again would any East German leader attempt to implement development policies by asking for sacrifice from the population. East German leaders remained frightened of East German workers throughout the 1950s—which is why the Politburo built itself a specially guarded, and stocked, estate at Wandlitz—and even after the Wall was built in 1961. As an older generation of East Germans resumed its place and a new generation entered the workforce after 1945, both developed habits, orientations, and interests that were different from those of the working class of prewar Germany and what was starting to take shape in the West. The work ethic and culture of the East German working class had been completely refashioned. In the absence of a capitalist labor market, the egalitarian impulse developed in the early post-war years could not be broken as it was in the West.

---

[14] Twelve years after the June events, for example, when the management of the Oberspree Cable Works tried to adjust piece rates, a report of the Committee for Labor and Wages lamented that 'the workers declared that if new piece rates were introduced, they would take up work in another enterprise. Five workers took the discussion about the use of new rates, which would not have led to any wage reductions, as cause to quit'.

The long run impact of this moral economy was to preclude any meaningful economic reform. As it happens, the only period of economic reform in East Germany was the 1960s, and this was headed off as soon as it became apparent that its continuation would require raising prices for consumer goods and transferring workers away from inefficient enterprises. The latter issue caused a mini riot in the coal mines of Zwickau. By 1974, the State Planning Commission noted that officially set wages had lost whatever stimulative function they might have had. In many industries, wages had not changed in fifteen years; in metallurgy and machine building, twenty years. Piece-workers increased their wages through easily overfulfilling weak piece rates. With the specter of the workers uprising in June 1953 still haunting the communist party twenty years after the event, party and management refused to touch the issue. In consequence, piece rates became hopelessly outdated. In VEB Mikromat, for example, an electronics enterprise in Dresden, piece rates had not changed since 1956, and by the 1970s, were usually met at a rate of 160%.

Ignoring the center, management informally set wages as it saw fit. In 1974, a mere one-quarter of wages fell within the centrally determined guidelines, and in industry and construction only one-tenth. Notwithstanding official rules requiring significant wage differentials within an eight-tiered scheme, in practice, wage differentials remained small. The average aggregate figures can be seen in Table 9.1. As illustrative as these undifferentiated figures are, they nevertheless conceal some especially egregious cases of wage leveling in certain branches of the economy. In a number of enterprises, combines, and even entire industries, it was quite common for the average worker to earn more than a foreman. In the machine tools and heavy machine industries, for example, an average worker took home 63 and 50 marks respectively more per month than his immediate superior.

Table 9.1. Eastern Germany: Monthly average gross and net wages in industry: GDR Marks

Wage earner	Gross wage (Difference from worker)	Net wage (Difference from worker)
Worker	1014	899
Foreman	1312 (298)	1017 (118)
White-collar worker with higher education	1467 (453)	1137 (238)
White-collar worker without higher education	893 (−121)	688 (−211)

Source: Gunther Kusch *et al.*, 'Schlussbilanz—DDR', in *Fazit einer verfehlten Wirt schafts-und Sozialpolitik* (Berlin: Duncker & Humblot, 1991), 109.

Survey research done since 1989 has generally supported the argument that East Germans valued and continue to value equality. The failure of the East German state to devise and inculcate at a social level a vision of meritocratic inequality that could have withstood the creation of an advantaged political/economic class, ultimately set it apart from the West. In explaining the rapid demise of East Germany, a number of sociologists have argued that the decisive factor was the disparity between society of official meritocratic equality and a society that in reality consisted of fairly significant and growing inequalities.[15] I find the explanation fairly convincing. East Germans knew exactly whom to blame. What angered them and drove them into the streets in large numbers was the public revelations after November 1989 that their leaders lived in a style, however modest by western European upper-class standards, that was simply unobtainable for the vast majority of most East Germans. Unification provided the tantalizing possibility of having it all, lifestyles of the elites and a standard of living that would not drop. What most East Germans did not appreciate at the time, especially those who went out in the streets calling for unification late in December, was that an economic union with the West would bring not only new wealth but also an instant commodification of social and economic relations that had been decommodified for more than forty years.

East Germany between Development and Dependence

One thing that stands out about the economic commentary on German unification is how polarized the commentators are. Experts tend either to predict an inexorable march toward relative economic equality between East and West, based on the growth rates of the decade, or an unstoppable decline into a new German *Mezzogiorno*.[16] This is not the place to elucidate the assumptions and logic of these competing analyses. What is worth noting, however, are the most general trends.

The economic policies of the other ex-communist countries have shifted back and forth between neoliberal shock therapy and state-led industrial policy, as politicians and populations have learned to discard ideological formulas in favor of pragmatic solutions to problems of early capitalism. In eastern Germany, on the other hand, western German largesse has enabled the five

---

[15] Gordon Marshall, 'Was Communism Good for Social Justice: A Comparative Analysis of the Two Germanies', *British Journal of Sociology*, 47: 3 (1996), 397–420; J. Hunick and H. Solga, 'Occupational Opportunities in the GDR: A Privilege of the Older Generations', *Zeitschrift für Soziologie*, 23: 2 (1994), 237–53; H. Mayer and H. Solga, 'Mobilität und Legitimität. Zum Vergleich der Chancenstrukturen in der altern DDR und der Alten BRD order: Haben Mobilitatschancen zu Stabilität und Zusammenbruch der DDR beigetragen', *Köner Zeitschrift für Soziologie und Sozialpsychologie*, 46: 2 (1994), 193–208.

[16] In a recent issue of *Das Parliament*, the time frame for economic equality between East and West was put at 20–25 years and that the current levels of transfers will last that long as well! (17–24 January 1997, 1).

new states to sustain shock therapy over an extended period despite the significant social costs. At the same time, clearly eastern Germany has received more 'external' assistance than any other ex-communist country. From the time the GDR ceased to exist and joined the Federal Republic, on 3 October 1990, until the Autumn of 1995 nearly a trillion Deutschmarks of public money flowed from the west to the east, and the amount of support for the East continues to be astounding.

Western assistance has softened the shock considerably. Even so, the transition has not been smooth, nor has it gone according to plan. Predictions made at the time of unification, that the time needed for the East to catch up with the West was about five years, have been continually pushed into the future. Part of the explanation for the faulty forecasting was an underestimation of the economic disparities between East and West; few western Germans had a good grasp of the real economic situation in the East. But part of the reason was also a rather naive belief in the power of the 'market' in the West, a belief buttressed by eight years of solid economic growth in West Germany before unification. Such an illusion was also facilitated by a mythologized history of the 1950s during which Germans bootstrapped their way to prosperity. Ignored in all of this was the true nature of the German 'economic miracle'. It was in fact driven not only by the market but also by a complex set of non-market institutions that evolved slowly, mostly by trial and error, over a period of ten years during which the standard of living remained low and currency restrictions remained in force. By 1995, however, most German politicians had jettisoned facile comparisons with the post-war era and come to the realization that unification will be a very long-term process.

The German experience in the East suggests that, even under the most favorable conditions, when support exceeds anything given West Europe under the Marshall Plan, constructing capitalist institutions of self-sustained growth from scratch is an experiment in many ways just as ambitious as the communist one that just failed. This lesson may be obvious but it is one that reinforces what has long been supported by students of late economic modernization. Success in economic development is not only, or even primarily, dependent on the amount of capital available to an economy but, rather, on the economic institutions in place to utilize the capital at its disposal.[17] Capital and other resources may be transferred relatively quickly, especially in the 1990s, but the institutions and social structures designed to absorb and use them do not lend themselves to rapid transfer.

In 1990 most East Germans wanted unification for a very simple reason. Whether measured in terms of living standards or political and social freedoms, socialism was a failed experiment. Amalgamation with the most successful capitalist country in the world, West Germany, simply made sense as

---

[17] For the classic statement, see Chalmers Johnson, *MITI and the Japanese Economic Miracle* (Stanford, CA: Stanford University Press, 1986).

the best and most painless route to prosperity and freedom. With the choice thus put, a clear majority of East Germans voted for parties supporting rapid unification in the first free national election held in the GDR's history, on 18 March 1990. After that date, things moved quickly. By July 1990, an economic, monetary, and social union between the two countries was in place, and by year's end the GDR ceased to exist, its territory incorporated into western Germany as five new states within the German federal system.

A decade later, the results are impressive, especially if one ponders the counterfactual, 'what would eastern Germany have looked like without unification'. Between 1992 and 1995, the economy in the new German states grew between 7% and 10% per year, making Germany's east the fastest growing region in Europe at the time. Since then, however, growth has slowed considerably. East German productivity, which before unification had stood at about a third of West German levels, now stands at between a half and two-thirds, depending on the sector under consideration. Rudimentary economic infrastructure, such as roads, rail links, and telephone communications in the new states has been vastly improved by a steady stream of government investment.[18] But such overt signs of progress do not tell the whole story. For one thing, they mask very low starting points. Quite apart from the dismal state of the East German economy before unification, the immediate impact of unification between 1990 and 1992 was to unleash a depression in the east, the magnitude of which surpassed all expectations. Unable to compete with the West after the currency union—overnight this measure created a fourfold increase in the costs for east German goods and services—and subject to rapid privatization under the supervision of the German privatization agency, the Treuhand, East Germany industry collapsed.[19] Table 9.2 tells the story from industry and manufacturing, in which four out of five jobs have been lost since 1990, as well as other sectors. Unification has meant an unprecedented kind of forced occupational mobility. Very few East Germans today work at the same jobs as a decade ago. While such mobility might be common in the United States, it is neither common nor welcome in Germany.[20]

---

[18] Whereas in 1988 only 17% of East German households had telephones, corresponding to the level of Crete, between 1990 and 1993, 2.3 million new lines had been installed, with the expectation that the West German level would be attained by 1997. Manfred Wegner, 'Produktionsstandort Ostdeutschland', *Aus Politik und Zeitgeschichte*, B, 17/94 (29 April 1994), 20.

[19] In 1991, an American economist, George Akerlof, proposed that the shock be further cushioned by temporarily continuing support for uncompetitive enterprises which would shield them from 'foreign' competitors and predatory investors. His advice was never given any serious thought in policy circles. George Akerloff, Andrew Rose, and Janet Yellen, 'East Germany in from the Cold: The Economic Aftermath of Currency Union', *Brookings Papers on Economic Activity*, 1 (1991).

[20] Helga Welsh, ' Four Years and Several Elections Later: The Eastern Political Landscape after Unification', in David P. Conradt *et al.*, *Germany's New Politics* (Tempe: German Studies Review, 1995).

248   *Kopstein*

Table 9.2. Eastern Germany: Unemployment (1991–2000)

Year	Total (1,000's)	Total %	Men %	Women %
1991: 1st half	843	9.5	8.0	11.2
1991: 2nd half	1,038	11.8	8.9	14.7
1992: 1st half	1,123	14.2	10.0	18.9
1992: 2nd half	1,101	13.9	9.7	18.6
1993: 1st half	1,100	15.1	10.4	20.2
1993: 2nd half	1,175	16.2	11.2	21.5
1994: 1st half	1,117	15.7	10.4	21.3
1994: October	1,001	14.1	8.9	19.5
(1995–6: n.d.)				
1997: February	–	18.2	–	–
(1998–9: n.d.)				
2000: September	–	16.8	–	–

Source (1991–5 data) Eckart, 'Der wirtschaftliche Umbau in den neuen Bundes-landern', *Deutschland Archiv*, 26: 6 (June 1995), 585.

Table 9.2 shows aggregate unemployment rates since 1991. In assessing this table it must be noted that the figures do not include those on government-funded retraining programs, make-work programs, short-time work, or early retirement. If they did, the numbers would be closer to 30%, and in some areas higher. Notwithstanding this caveat, two items stand out. First, the real losers of unification are women. In fact, two-thirds of all unemployed East Germans are women.[21] Despite some success in bringing down male unemployment in 1994–5—though not from 1996 to 2000—little headway has been made in reducing female unemployment from an uncomfortably high level. As a result of these new pressures, the East experienced an unprecedented and much publicized decline in the birth and marriage rates immediately after unification, as young women delayed starting families until they found their footing in the new social order.[22] However, there is some evidence that the situation is now starting to 'normalize'. Second, aggregate unemployment rates started to bottom out only in the first half of 1994, well after the economy started to turn around. On the fifth anniversary of unification, official unemployment in the east hovered at approximately 14% with significant regional variation. The latest figures as of time of writing (September 2000) put unemployment in the East at 16.8%.

This latter observation—rapid economic growth in a stagnating (or even collapsing) labor market—suggests that the stabilization and turnaround of the East German economy has had little to do with sustained, 'domestically'

[21] Elke Horst and Jürgen Schupp, 'Aspekte der Arbeitsmarktentwicklung in Ostdeutschland', *Deutschland Archiv*, 28: 7 (July 1995), 737–42.
[22] Nicholas Eberstadt, 'Demographic Shocks in Eastern Germany 1989–1993', *Europe-Asia Studies*, 46: 3 (1994).

driven growth. Indeed, if one looks a little deeper, it is easy to see just how dependent on the West the East German economy was in the decade after unification. In 1995, the estimated DM158bn marks in transfers to East Germany ended up receiving from the federal government, other *Länder* (states), the European Union, and social security amounted to more than 25% of the resources available in East Germany for consumption and investment. Whereas East German demand for goods reached about DM610bn in 1995, only DM380bn goods were produced there. Trade flows tell a similar tale. In 1994, East Germany bought DM255bn from the West, while selling a mere DM45bn in return. There is not one major East German product that has a market throughout the Federal Republic; those that have managed to survive do so at a regional level. Despite high level commitments of major German producers to 'buy East', only about 10% of East German production is sold in the West and even less makes its way on to world markets.[23] Thus the balance of trade remains heavily tilted in the West's favor.

Much of the incoming capital has been spent on consumption and, as Table 9.3 suggests, much has flowed into construction. Besides the building of new homes and apartments, a wave of commercial and retail construction drove most of the initial East German recovery. According to one expert, however, the region simply does not require much of what was being built. For example, between 1990 and 1995, DM50bn were invested in metropolitan Leipzig, mostly in large shopping centers and the like. Meanwhile 17% of commercial real estate remains empty.[24] If the five new states are to be anything more than sales markets for West German firms, subsidized by large governmental transfers of wealth to the East German population, some sort of industrial policy must be put in place.

Table 9.3. Eastern Germany: Sectoral employment: in 1,000's (1991–4)

Sector	1981: 1st half	1991	1992	1993	1994
Agriculture and forestry	985	385	266	234	218
Energy and mining	306	209	164	134	124
Manufacturing	3,625	1,725	1,230	1,115	1,063
Construction	846	727	848	957	998
Trade and transport	1,652	1,206	1,141	1,135	1,115
Services	962	970	1,057	1,142	1,179
State	1,750	1,450	1,416	1,337	1,320
Total	9,766	6,672	6,122	6,054	6,017

Source: Karl Eckart, 'Der wirtschafliche Umbau in den neuen Bundeslandern', *Deutschland Archiv*, 28: 6 (June 1995), 585.

[23] Hans-Peter Brunner, 'German Blitz-Privatization', *Transition: The Newsletter About Reforming Economies*, 6: 4 (April 1995), 13.
[24] Herbert Henzler, 'Der Aufschwung Ost had noch viele matte Stellen', *Suddeutsche Zeitung* (10 Sept. 1995).

The central problem in the new German states is that the de-industrialization that occurred in the first years after unification has not been overcome. Measured against western standards, East Germany under communist rule was over-industrialized; now however it is clearly under-industrialized. Approximately one million people today work in industry in the East; by western standards this number should be 3.4 million. The rapid growth in the service sector after unification corrected what had been a typical weakness of a command economy. But further growth in this sector will depend on demand for services from industrial enterprises in the regions. It will also depend on the willingness of western firms investing in the east to use locally based service providers rather than relying solely on their tried and tested teams of external consultants, programmers, and market research from the West. Illustrating this problem, the head of a market research firm in Rostock complained to me in 1999 that 'since almost all large investment comes from the west, breaking into market research depends on developing connections with western firms who, in all honesty, have no need for new partners in the east. The fact of the matter is that West Germany and Europe produce more than enough to cover demand in east Germany and for that reason our situation is completely unlike that in the west after the second world war'.

Given the absence of large capital holders in the five new states, industrial investment will necessarily come from western Germany and other developed capitalist countries. Much of eastern Germany's future will thus depend on how attractive it is as an investment site. In comparison with other post-communist countries, eastern Germany enjoys a highly stable political and institutional environment for investors, which, in theory, should make it appealing for investors. In fact, the record since unification is mixed. While some areas in eastern Germany, such as Dresden and Leipzig have been successful, others have not. One problem continues to be labor costs. Fearing downward pressure on wages from cheaper eastern workers, German trade unions quickly dominated the eastern landscape and have consistently put upward pressure on eastern wage settlements. But with a persistent disparity in labor productivity, raising eastern wages rapidly up to the level of the West rendered unit labor costs for potential large investors even more threatening than they already are in western Germany. Describing the impact of high East German wages in the context of a globalized labor market in 1994, German economist Fred Klinger characterized the situation dramatically, 'Worldwide there is, by far, no more comparable production location that is simultaneously so expensive, so productively weak, and infrastructurally so poorly equipped'.[25] Thus, despite a good start after unification, productive investment has begun to lose pace.

---

[25] Fred Klinger, 'Aufbau und Erneuerung: Über die institutionellen Bedingungen der Standortentwicklung in Deutschland', *Aus Politik und Zeitgeschichte*, B, 17/94 (29 April 1994), 8.

High unit labor costs deter not only large corporate investors, they also make it difficult for small- and medium-sized businesses to stay afloat. The new medium-sized firms that sprouted after unification are currently undergoing a crisis of solvency; the majority are going bankrupt, a phenomenon not unusual in itself but alarming when one considers just how small the East German *Mittelstand* is compared to the West. As the subsidies and tax breaks from the federal government that are intended to promote enterprise in the east run out over the next few years, one can expect the bankruptcy rate to increase substantially.

With the Treuhand having finished its work of privatizing enterprises at the end of 1994, many Germans developed the sneaking suspicion that despite impressive gains in construction, infrastructure, and consumption, reestablishing a base of productive industry throughout the new states will not come about without some sort of regional economic policy. This is slowly becoming the consensus at both the federal and *Land* (state) level. Yet even with such a consensus, it is not clear whether Germany has either the political will or economic capacity to continue to pour in resources to the East at the rate of the past decade. Unification has not only created new problems, it has also brought old ones to a head more quickly than expected. In particular, the German welfare state, a staple of national integration since Bismarck's time, will most likely continue to be downsized in the coming years, as the Federal government searches for ways to defray the costs of high unemployment, industrial restructuring, an aging population, and economic uncertainty in the new states. The flexibility and adaptability of German-style organized capitalism is currently being pushed to the limit by the costs of unification.[26]

For this reason, most economists now predict that levels of development in the new German states will be far more differentiated than in pre-unification West Germany.[27] One can already see the contours of this differentiation. Whereas unemployment levels in Dresden are already lower than in such crisis-ridden western cities as Bremen and Wilhelmshaven, such traditionally backward areas of East Germany as Mecklenburg-Western Pomerania or Brandenburg, where the old communist government made some effort to even out the differences, will probably resume their status as sparsely populated and poor areas. More than a generation ago, Albert Hirschman argued that small differences in levels of development tend to reinforce the backwardness of the backward region and the advantage of the advanced region because small differences quickly accumulate into large advantages.[28]

---

[26] Calculated at between DM120m and DM140bn per year, the total support of the West for the East is between 4% and 5% of the West's GDP.

[27] From a socio-demographic perspective, this also marks a return to the pre-war pattern of emigration. During that era German governments had customarily allowed backward areas to stagnate and encouraged the poor in those areas to emigrate to the West. Today, this has again more or less become the pattern in Germany.

[28] Albert O. Hirschman, *The Strategy of Economic Development* (New Haven: Yale University Press, 1958), 185–211.

Although post-war Germany policy managed to even out regional economic differences through administratively intricate financial transfers, this policy was designed to work among regions with economies at roughly the same level of development. Extending the policy eastward after 1990, however, has put a severe strain on the German budget which, if continued, will necessitate either higher taxes or significantly lower social benefits for Germans today and in the future. Budgetary considerations will therefore ultimately reinforce the advantages currently enjoyed by Germany's richer regions.

Persistence of Regional Identities: Workers and Politics in the Long Run

Even though East Germans are eating better food, receiving better health care, buying more consumer durables, living in better apartments, travelling abroad more frequently and to pricier destinations, and breathing better air at home, many still complain that the skills and communal habits acquired under socialism have been devalued by the transition to capitalism and a Western culture that belittles the lives lived in the GDR's forty-year history. This is true even for the vast majority of East Germans who continue to say that unification was both a good idea and a necessary step. West Germans, for their part still supportive of a unified Germany if somewhat irritated at the cost, recognize too that neither political nor economic unification are substitutes for nation-building. As one West German admitted in a conversation in Fall 1998, 'my positive feelings about unification do not contradict the fact that from the standpoint of basic values I still probably have more in common with Danes, Frenchmen, and the Dutch than with most east Germans'. Surveys continue to show that most western Germans rarely visit eastern Germany.

Undoubtedly, the strains of unification have exacerbated the cultural divide that was already in place when unification occurred. Most Germans have the uneasy feeling that unification has somehow changed everything; there is no going back to the old *Bundesrepublik*. Often overlooked in the literature is how unification has changed not only East Germany but also the West. The changes are subtle but important, and they range from the mundane to the strategic. The future of such bedrocks of West German political stability as the welfare state and Germany's strict subordination to the US lead in foreign policy are now quite open to debate.

Notwithstanding these new challenges to western Germans' source of identity, they pale in comparison to the changes experienced in the East. Public opinion in the East is volatile and difficult to gauge from the polls. As already noted, the vast majority of East Germans continue to judge unification with the West to have been a good idea. Few would want to go back to 'really-existing socialism'. There is nevertheless a widespread feeling among East Germans, much more widespread than expressed in the public opinion polls, that something is wrong with the new order that has descended upon them. Such amorphous sentiments cannot be explained by relative deprivation. Rather, they are related to the sudden and almost complete commodification of the economy. After all, measured purely in terms of living standards East Germans are the true winners of communism's collapse. Even though most East Germans earn more money and consume better products than before unification, the idea that such fundamental areas of human life such as housing, schooling, day care, as well as food and other staples, should be subject to cost-benefit calculation remains morally malodorous. The 'moral economy' of communist society appears to have persisted well into the transition period.

West Germans have very little understanding or sympathy for this moral economy; understandably so, since addressing its core elements would mean dismantling an order that has given them an enviable standard of living. Such fundamental differences in opinion between East and West Germans complicate the task of nation-building. Differences between East and West will persist for some time. Not surprisingly, political elites have been quick to adapt. While the major political parties are careful not to play the East off against the West, politicians of all persuasions have learned to pitch their messages differently depending on the regional audience. Successful politicians and administrators usually have dual cultural competencies that allow them to swim in both eastern and western waters. When they do not, they do not survive long.

The federal elections of 1994 and 1998, and the regional elections in 1999, provided a litmus test of sorts for unified Germany.[29] West Germans, never asked at the ballot box whether they wanted unification, could use the opportunity to vent their frustrations with the costs of unification, which at the very least amounts to a yearly personal and corporate income tax surcharge. East Germans, after years of vicariously experiencing an idealized capitalism through television, could now vote on what they thought of 'really-existing capitalism'.

In 1994, although the Social Democrats (*Sozialdemokratische Partei Deutschlands*; SPD), managed to capitalize on voter anger in several regional and local contests, improving economic news at the beginning of the year and a general sentiment that there was no alternative to the Christian Democrats at the federal level allowed for the re-election of Helmut Kohl for his last term in office. By 1998, voters had tired of the CDU which had been in power since 1982. At the same time, Gerhard Schröder, the new leader of the Social

---

[29] Matthias Jung and Dieter Roth, ' Kohls knappster Sieg'; Jürgen Falter and Markus Klein, 'Die Wähler der PDS bei der Bundestagswahl 1994'; and Urstila Feist, 'Nichtwähler 1994': all in *Aus Politik und Zeitgeschichte* (B, 51–52/94, 23 Dec. 1994). In English, see the excellent series of articles in Conradt *et al.*, *Germany's New Politics*. For the 1998 results, see Russell J. Dalton, 'Germany's Vote for the "New Middle" ', *Current History*, 98: 626 (1999), 176–80. The following discussion draws on these various studies.

Democrats, had managed to refashion the message of his party in the manner of Tony Blair and Bill Clinton so that it would appeal to voters at the center of the political spectrum. The makeover worked and in the 1998 elections the SPD won a plurality and formed a coalition government with the Greens. One year later, however, in the wake of a growing impression that the SPD/Green government was no more competent than its CDU predecessor, the SPD suffered a series of stunning defeats in a number of state (*Land*) level elections, which, in the German political system, is reflected at the national level in the makeup of the upper house of parliament, the *Bundesrat*. In 2000, Schröder managed to stabilize his authority not because of any changes in policy but rather thanks to the corruption scandal that enveloped the opposition CDU.

How is the cultural divide between East and West Germans reflected in differences in voting behavior? The big difference between West and East German voting behavior has been in the performance of the smaller parties which under Germany's proportional representation system have a relatively good chance of capturing seats. In 1998, the Free Democratic Party (FDP), which had been a coalition partner in every CDU government since 1982 and currently advertises itself as a party of free enterprise, sustained its support in the West at just over 7%, at the same time it all but collapsed in the East, garnering a mere 3.3% of the eastern vote. In the 1999 state elections in the East, it performed worse than several right-wing radical parties, failing to receive the 5% minimum to be allotted seats in the state parliaments. Given the weak development of East German business, few East Germans had much interest in the Free Democrats. Similarly, the Greens, who had done poorly in the 1990 elections, fared much better in the West in 1994, easily clearing the 5% hurdle in nearly every state level election as well as in the federal campaign. But in the East they lost much of the support they enjoyed after 1990, ending up with a mere 4.3% of the eastern German vote. In the 1998 federal elections the Greens fared slightly worse than in the 1994 campaign and were unable to improve their position in the East. Whereas the FDP had trouble finding a chic upper middle-class constituency in the East, the Greens had trouble finding a solid 'post-materialist' constituency among East German voters.

The largest divergence between East and West Germany, however, has been the performance of the Party of Democratic Socialism (PDS), the successor to the old communist party. While receiving a paltry 0.9% of the western vote in 1994, the PDS consistently booked nearly 20% of the East German vote at both the federal and state levels, and 34.7% in East Berlin. In the 1998 federal elections, PDS sustained and even increased its share of votes among East Germans. Furthermore, in the 1999 state elections in four East German states, the PDS often outperformed the Social Democrats and in East Berlin it received an astounding 40.6%. Such consistently high levels of support for an 'anti-system' party that is still uncomfortable with its own Leninist past is a source of quiet concern to many Germans in the West. The PDS campaigns have been cleverly formulated and implemented. The PDS portrays itself as a 'socialist alternative' to all the other parties, as a party that represents the ideals and interests of its old communist clientele, while simultaneously fighting for the interests of those who feel somehow disenfranchised by unification. The PDS has also gained in strength by mobilizing voters in the East who had simply stopped voting altogether. In addition to an unanticipated strong vote among young people, the fact that 27% of white-collar workers and 35% of civil servants in eastern Germany voted PDS in 1994 suggests that party loyalty runs deeper than expected, even among East Germans who successfully negotiated the transition.[30]

Whether the PDS will be able to sustain its strength in the East, expand its voter base into the West, or simply fade away as the material and spiritual difficulties of unification become less salient remains an open question. Some evidence suggests that it will be a part of the eastern German political landscape for some time to come.[31] First, the PDS has had an usually persistent clientele. Four-fifths of its 1990 voters remained loyal to the party in the 1994 election and these numbers were sustained into the 1998 and 1999 elections. Such a level of party loyalty puts it above any other party in the East. Almost 70% of its voters are long-time members of the party, which suggests that in an era of declining party identification, the PDS constitutes an important exception. Second, the social characteristics of PDS voters indicate that changes in the economic or social conditions in eastern Germany will not affect the party loyalty of PDS voters. They tend to have above average education levels, to be politically alienated and distrustful of the Federal Republic's political institutions, and overwhelmingly 'socialist' in orientation, believing that the GDR had more good than bad points. It is possible that such a nostalgic outlook will pass as conditions in the East improve, but this will more likely result from a new generation coming to accept the new Germany as inevitable and natural. Whether the PDS will be able to adapt to a changing generation of voters remains an open question.

Apart from voting behavior there appears to be a long-term sense of disappointment in the East with the institutions of representative liberal democracy. Commentators on the left have tended to attribute this malaise to a nascent discursive political culture of 1989 that was destroyed by the electoral professionals. There is probably some validity to this argument but it may also be worth looking deeper into the East German past in order to understand why so many people are dissatisfied with liberal institutions. One German psychologist, for example, has argued that although few East Germans would want to return to 'really-existing socialism', the *de facto* blackmailing power of the population in the GDR gave them a sort of immediate access to power—'if you don't come and fix my heating, I won't vote in

---

[30] Gerald R. Kleinfeld, 'The Return of the PDS', in *Germany's New Politics*, 209.
[31] The following evidence is drawn from Falter and Klein, 'Die Wähler der PDS', 24.

your rigged elections'—that is missing in a representative democracy, where power is necessarily indirect and distant.[32] In the East German workplace and neighborhoods, with their continuous cycles of party, trade union, and educational meetings, politics was experienced not only as something oppressive, and even laughable, but also as something that was, as the Germans say, 'skin near'. Politics in the new order is experienced as something distant and irrelevant and the PDS has profited from this at the local level by cultivating a strategy of grassroots politics—the only party to have succeeded in doing this in the East.

Conclusion: Globalization and Moral Economy

East Germany's globalization crisis, an extreme variation on a common post-socialist theme, has reinforced old identities and even created new cultural differences that might have otherwise been ignored. I have argued here that what is driving the new particularisms in Germany today is the impact of global markets on conceptions of work and the market that reflect the legacy of forty years of Leninist economic institutions. Although East Germans have improved their material quality of life, they continue to feel a lack of recognition for the distinctive moral economy that they brought into unified Germany. Political theorists, such as Charles Taylor and Axel Honneth, have recently argued that the 'need for recognition' runs as deep as that other bedrock of interest based political analysis—the need for self-preservation.[33] If their analysis is correct, then the mode of unification, which cast aside forty years of East German history while preserving the economic equalities that were the basis of that history, explains the nature of the continuing cultural divide in Germany today. Such divisions and boundaries can be easily 'ethnicized' and taken advantage of by political entrepreneurs. Germans will surely not be politically divided again in the manner of pre-1989, if only because the elites on both sides of the old borders are, for the most part, committed to making unification work. In a 'Europe of regions', however, the kinds of regional tensions in culture, interests, and identity may gradually erode what were considered after 1991 to be sovereign inevitabilities.

The strategy of unification which accommodated the old communist moral economy appears to have helped perpetuate the divide between East and West in unexpected ways. It is not clear that an alternative strategy of unification, that of leaving the East to fend for itself in a market with high tariffs, would have worked much better. While it might have altered fundamental attitudes towards economic inequality, it would also probably have produced

---

[32] Lydia Lange, 'Warum so viele Ostdeutsche von der repräsentativen Demokratie enttäuscht sind',' *Die Zeit* (10 Jan. 1997), from www.zeit.de

[33] Charles Taylor, *Multiculturalism and the Politics of Recognition* (Princeton: Princeton University Press, 1992); Axel Honneth, *The Struggle for Recognition* (Cambridge: Cambridge University Press, 1995).

more unrest. We do know, however, that the new divide, whatever its ultimate causes, is slowly and permanently changing Germany. First, regional variations in development will probably grow in the years to come as the budget is stretched to its limits by the costs of unification which remain at approximately 4–5% of West German GDP. Second, the need to compete politically in the East will probably alter the structure and governance of the major parties. If the PDS survives or thrives at the local level, decisions will eventually have to be made on acceptable forms of cooperation because, a decade after unification, it remains the most firmly rooted party in the East. Third, the German model of industrial relations is quickly being undermined by the growing fiscal crisis of the state—brought on in part by the costs of reunification—and the continuing stagnation of the labor market in the East. These considerations, when taken together, suggest that the costs of Germany's globalization crisis of unification have been, and will continue to be, much higher, than anyone would have dared imagine a decade ago.

10

Corporatist Renaissance in Post-communist Central Europe?

Mitchell A. Orenstein, Syracuse University and
Lisa E. Hale, Los Alamos National Laboratory

The displacement of the communist international system by a hegemonic, capitalist-democratic world order is a driving force of socio-economic transformation in Central and East Europe. In the area of labor relations, joining the capitalist global economy meant relinquishing the full employment guarantee that lay at the heart of the socialist system. There is no question, therefore, that globalization has forced the creation and liberalization of labor markets in Central and East Europe.

Withdrawal of the full employment guarantee had a major impact on welfare in post-communist societies. Unemployment rates shot up to 10–15% in most countries, causing poverty in many affected households. Average wages fell sharply as a result of economic contraction. Most governments allowed minimum wages to fall, until they were transformed from mechanisms of social support into instruments of immiseration.[1] At the same time, trade union membership collapsed due to privatization and the end of compulsory affiliation (Table 10.1). Trade unionists remained mostly passive in the face of these economic challenges to their well-being.[2] And trade union organizations generally supported the market reforms that seemed certain to erode their institutional power. This was particularly true of trade unions, like Solidarity in Poland, that participated in anti-communist opposition and saw markets as a key method of dismantling communism.[3] Trade union support for liberal market reforms appears suicidal to many analysts, a bizarre exam-

Special thanks to Javier Astudillo and Natalia Tsvetkova for their detailed comments on a previous draft. Thanks also to Donna Leicach for her capable research assistance.

[1] 'Guy Standing and Daniel Vaughan-Whitehead, 'Introduction', in Standing and Vaughan-Whitehead, *Minimum Wages in Central and Eastern Europe* (Budapest: Central European University Press, 1995), 2.

[2] Stephen Crowley, *Hot Coal, Cold Steel* (Ann Arbor: University of Michigan Press, 1997); Bela Greskovits, *The Political Economy of Protest and Patience* (Budapest: Central European University Press, 1998).

[3] David Ost and Marc Weinstein, 'Unionists Against Unions: Toward Hierarchical Management in Post-Communist Poland', *East European Politics and Societies*, 13: 1 (Winter 1999).

Table 10.1. Central Europe: Trade union density: percentage of the non-agricultural labor force (1985–95)

Year	Hungary	Czech Republic	Poland
1985	74.1	–	–
1989	–	–	47.1
1990	–	76.8	–
1995	52.5	36.3	27.0

Source: International Labour Office, *World Labour Report 1997–98*, 238. These figures are based on self-reported membership. In the authors' estimation, trade union density in Central Europe is in the 20–30% range in 1999, based on public opinion polls, interviews, and other available data sources.

ple of 'false consciousness' that challenges rational choice understandings of interest group behavior and raises fundamental questions about the future of organized labor in the East. Many have concluded that organized labor's failure to adapt quickly to new economic and political conditions has rendered it 'emasculated' or 'politically feeble'.[4]

However, as the forces of economic liberalization swept through post-communist Central Europe, with seemingly devastating effects on worker welfare and organized labor, a countervailing trend—a surprising rebirth of national corporatist institutions—was also underway. The countries examined in this chapter—Hungary, the Czech Republic, and Poland—all founded macro-level corporatist institutions of interest intermediation between 1988 and 1994 with the assistance of the International Labour Organization (ILO). They were joined by many of their Central European neighbors, including Bulgaria, Slovakia, and Slovenia.[5] This striking advent of corporatism in Central Europe has led scholars, including Iankova[6] and Garrett, to point to the Central European experience as evidence of a potential revival of European national corporatism. Garrett, for instance, writes, 'there is no reason why social democratic corporatism should not be presented as a viable alternative to the neoclassical perspective for developing and prospering in the era of global markets'. He suggests the Czech Republic as an example of this possibility, since it shares key 'common threads' with the other countries

---

[4] Paul Kubicek, 'Organized Labor in Postcommunist States: Will the Western Sun Set on It, Too?', *Comparative Politics*, 32: 1 (October 1999), 83–92.

[5] Reinhard Heinisch, 'The State of Corporatism in a Central Europe in Transition', in Irwin Collier *et al.* (eds), *Welfare States in Transition: East and West* (New York: St. Martin's Press, 1999); International Labour Office, *World Labour Report 1997–98* (Geneva: ILO, 1998); Robert Kyloh (ed.), *Tripartism on Trial: Tripartite Consultations and Negotiations in Central and Eastern Europe* (Geneva: ILO, 1995).

[6] Elena Iankova, 'The Transformative Corporatism of Eastern Europe', *East European Politics and Societies*, 12: 2 (Spring 1998), 222–64.

that have engaged in 'recent successful experiments with social democratic corporatism'.[7]

What accounts for the rise of institutions of corporatist interest concertation in the midst of economic globalization in Central Europe? Why Central Europe? Why now? And to what effect? Have corporatist institutions played a fundamental role in transitions to democracy? Are they influencing the shape of capitalism in the region? Does the revival of corporatism reflect a societal response to the pressures of globalization? Or are corporatist institutions mechanisms of state control over organized labor—a sham corporatism that serves mainly liberal goals? Do they indicate a return to historic patterns of interest representation, mimic Western models, or point to a distinctive new form of industrial relations in the East?

This chapter examines the genesis and efficacy of corporatist institutions in three Central European countries. We argue that the genesis of corporatist institutions in Central Europe should not be confused with the development of a fully articulated, West European-style corporatist society characterized by 'a monopolistic union movement without ideological cleavages or competing craft unions and with a high degree of organization; a similar degree of organizational concentration on the employer side; centralized collective bargaining; and participation by the peak organizations of labor and capital in the formulation of government economic and social policy'.[8] Corporatist institutions in Central Europe have a different meaning, captured in Iankova's phrase, 'transformative corporatism'.[9] Central Europe's transformative corporatism arose as part of social democratic state strategies to provide mechanisms of interest concertation during a painful and potentially conflictual transition to capitalism. However, state dominance in these institutions remains too strong, and trade unions and employers' organizations too fragmented to call post-communist Central European societies corporatist.[10]

Establishment of institutions for corporatist interest concertation has been a consistent feature of leftist government strategies for transformation in post-communist Central Europe, part of an attempt to structure a new role for organized labor in a democratic capitalist society. Critics may be right that Central Europe's corporatist institutions will die a slow death in the face of labor fragmentation and the forces of liberal economic globalization. However, we argue that despite the failure to develop a strongly corporatist form of labor relations and wage bargaining to date, Central Europe's national tripartite institutions have played a significant role in the post-communist socio-economic transformation. Furthermore, their existence holds open the possibility for enhanced and expanded corporatist bargaining

---

[7] Geoffrey Garrett, *Partisan Politics in the Global Economy* (Cambridge: Cambridge University Press, 1998), 156.

[8] Fritz Scharpf, *Crisis and Choice in European Social Democracy* (Ithaca: Cornell University Press, 1987), 9.

[9] Iankova, 'Transformative Corporatism'.   [10] Heinisch, 'The State of Corporatism'.

in the future, though the chances may appear slim at present. Following a brief discussion of overall trends, we present country studies of Hungary, the Czech Republic, and Poland that evaluate the genesis and efficacy of corporatist institutions in each case. A final section is devoted to analyzing emergent patterns of state-society relations in post-communist Europe and to placing corporatist institutions within this broader framework.

Why Corporatism?

The paradoxical rise of corporatist institutions at a time of economic liberalization can be explained by the conjunction of several key factors. In essence, the establishment of corporatist institutions between 1988 and 1994 reflected an attempt by left-leaning governments to incorporate organized labor into economic policy discourse at a time when liberalizing economic reforms were taking a heavy toll on the interests of labor. In the early years of the post-communist transformation, analysts and governments alike expected organized labor to play a significant role in the process of change.[11] This expectation was grounded on two observable facts. First, despite most unions' strong and delegitimizing associations with the communist system, trade unions remained the largest civil society organizations, with considerable potential for popular mobilization. Trade unions in Poland, Hungary, and even Czechoslovakia, for instance, played a major role in the events that toppled the communist system in 1988–9. Despite widespread claims of trade union frailty, most Central and East European governments in 1988–94 regarded trade unions as non-negligible players in post-communist society. Further considering that all post-communist governments wanted to initiate painful programs of economic reform whose impact would fall hardest on the working class, governments identified trade unions as being among the few civilian groups that could mobilize mass resistance to unemployment or other unpopular aspects of the reform. In all three countries studied, organized labor periodically reminded governments of its mobilization potential.

Policymakers' attitudes towards organized labor and corporatist institutions differed along a nascent left-right divide. Economic liberals and their allies on the right were generally hostile to trade unions, and took a confrontational approach towards organized labor. Prime Minister Václav Klaus of the Czech Republic, for instance, excoriated trade union action in public, calling the unions Stalinist and dredging up past trade union support for the communist regime in an effort to delegitimize even the mildest and most reasonable trade union action. Poland's economic liberals after 1990 quickly distanced themselves from the Solidarity trade union that helped bring many of them to power. And Hungary's Alliance of Young Democrats Party (FIDESZ) disbanded the Labor Ministry after its election to government in 1998. On the

[11] Kubicek, 'Organized Labor', 83.

other hand, left-leaning politicians and governments took a consensus-driven approach to labor relations. Believing in the legitimacy of organized labor, being allied with trade unions in left party coalitions, and adopting political and economic strategies that attempted to avoid social conflict, leftist governments and politicians saw corporatist institutions as a mechanism for resolving inevitable disputes over economic liberalization before they resulted in widespread social unrest. Right-wing liberal politicians only came to accept this role for corporatist institutions after periods of massive social conflict.

As a result of the transition strategies of left politicians and parties, corporatist institutions quickly became part of the institutional repertoire of industrial relations in Central Europe. Historical and international factors further enabled the rapid adoption of these institutions.

Corporatism played a significant role in the politics of some Central European countries not only during the inter-war period, the main democratic point of reference in the region, but also during the communist period. Central Europe has a strong, living legacy of direct bargaining between trade unions and the state. In both Leninist theory and practice, trade unions had served as a 'transmission belt' between the party and the working class. This meant that trade union leaders were co-opted into party and state structures and robbed of their independence, but also that trade unionists were accustomed to representation at the highest levels of the bureaucratic apparatus. Trade unions actively participated in communist legislative processes, sometimes initiating work legislation.[12] One could say, therefore, that communist industrial relations had some corporatist features—despite questions of authenticity and representation. When the socialist pattern of trade union representation in the workers' states fell apart in 1988 and 1989, actors on all sides felt the need to replace old institutional ties with something new. Democratic corporatism offered a ready alternative model. Thanks to these historical and cultural legacies, corporatism in East-Central Europe did not need to be justified or explained, but rather molded into a form compatible with a democratic society and freedom of association. Left governments, in particular, were ready to give trade unions institutional guarantees and legitimacy they lacked in exchange for negotiated acquiescence in liberal economic reforms.

The development of corporatism in post-communist East-Central Europe was also spurred by the availability of a clear western model provided by the International Labour Organization (ILO) in Geneva. The ILO quickly set up a Central and Eastern European Team to promote the development of tripartite bargaining in the region. The ILO tripartite bargaining model has heavily influenced most new corporatist institutions.[13]

---

[12] Iankova, 'Transformative Corporatism', 12.
[13] Mitchell Orenstein and Raj Desai, 'State Power and Interest Group Formation: The Business Lobby in the Czech Republic', *Problems of Post-Communism*, 44: 6 (1997).

Thus, a combination of needs to smooth social conflict during transition, deep historical trends and experiences, domestic politics, and international pressures combined to allow for the development of corporatist institutions between 1988 and 1994. Hungary came first. The final communist-led government founded a tripartite National Interest Reconciliation Council in 1988 in an attempt to bring organized labor into the process of liberalization. Its activities were suspended, reconsidered, and then renewed by the first democratically elected government in 1990, when the name of the body changed to the Interest Reconciliation Council. In the Czech Republic, corporatism was the brainchild of the first Civic Forum government, which sought to create structures to bring the trade unions into the process of economic reform in order to perpetuate 'social peace'. Surprisingly, Poland was a laggard. Although trade unions participated at the roundtable discussions that ushered in the transition to democracy, a national tripartite body was not founded in Poland until 1994 because of a deep divide between Solidarity, the leftist All-Poland Alliance of Trade Unions (OPZZ), and the government of Solidarity liberals, which opposed excessive trade union input in decisions of government.

Efficacy Concerns

After their swift emergence, corporatist institutions proved difficult to institutionalize in post-communist Central Europe for several reasons. First, as opposed to the development of corporatism in West Europe, there has been no strong elite consensus in the political system on the desirability of corporatist institutions as a means of interest concertation.[14] In Austria, for example, corporatist intermediation grew out of the strong negative experience of social conflict in the Nazi period that convinced leaders on all sides of the need for institutions of compromise. In post-communist Europe, no such systemic agreement exists. Left-leaning politicians and parties have supported corporatist bargaining, but right-wing liberals have not. Often when in power, the latter have taken significant steps to undermine the effectiveness of corporatist institutions. Without a strong left-wing and right-wing consensus, the functioning of corporatist institutions depends greatly on changing governmental priorities and who is in power at a particular moment. Thus, effective bargaining episodes have been sporadic, further contributing to the difficulties of institutionalizing corporatist institutions. In sharp contrast to West Europe, then, Central European corporatism has been 'top-down', driven from above by state priorities and initiatives, rather than from below by societal concerns. Corporatism in Western Europe often developed from below, as a means of coordination between strong trade unions and employers' associations. In the Austrian model, employers are organized into

---

[14] Heinisch, 'The State of Corporatism'.

mandatory chambers, insuring a breadth of representation in monopoly organizations. Central European trade unions are generally fragmented and politicized,[15] while employers' associations are nascent and weak.[16] Corporatist institutions have served at the whim of passing state interests, as conceived by ever-changing governments of the left and right.

For these reasons, the performance of corporatist institutions has been sporadic, but not entirely unimportant. Further evidence of their value both to the state and to other actors affecting social change is provided by the case studies below. Although Hungary and the Czech Republic created corporatist institutions as part of early state strategies for transformation, and before any serious demand-driven reasons emerged, the case of Poland shows that the demand was there. Poland founded corporatist institutions after a series of strike waves raised the necessity of greater social coordination. McKitrick[17] provides strong evidence to suggest that this corporatist intermediation changed the face of labor relations in Poland by introducing face-to-face consultations that affected the course of privatization at the enterprise level. Case studies show that corporatist institutions were formed to respond to real needs for integrating labor into consultative and decision-making processes during the transition to capitalism. It is one thing to compare Central European to Austrian corporatism and find that the former comes up short.[18] However, this does not capture the purpose of Central Europe's transformative corporatism. Corporatist institutions in Central Europe should probably be judged by the ends they were designed to serve, and how far they served them, rather than by West European preconceptions and standards. And when one undertakes this latter exercise, as in the case studies below, the record of corporatist institutions in Central Europe does not appear so poor. Corporatist institutions have achieved moderate goals towards providing a forum for negotiation and interest reconciliation between organized labor and the state at critical moments of post-communist transition in each country under examination. These institutions are unlikely to produce corporatist societies or labor markets on the West European model. But the following case studies show that they have had sporadic successes and continue to provide an important forum for labor inclusion in discourse and policymaking in countries in transition.[19] Should labor and management ever become more organized in Central Europe, these institutions could provide an organizational channel for greater interest coordination in the future. Case studies below discuss the founding of national tripartite councils and their basic functions, the structure of interest repres-

[15] International Labour Office, *World Labour Report 1997–98*, 145.

[16] Orenstein and Desai, 'State Power'.

[17] Sean McKitrick, 'Managing Mistrust: Corporatist Intermediation and Economic Reform in Poland, 1989–1994', MS (Claremont Graduate University, 1999).

[18] Heinisch, 'The State of Corporatism'.

[19] International Labour Office, *World Labour Report 1997–98*, 151.

entation at the macro level, and finally provide an initial evaluation of the efficacy and evolution of these institutions in the post-1989 period.

Hungary

Hungary's Interest Reconciliation Council (IRC) has had a rocky time since its inception in 1988. Originally called the National Interest Reconciliation Council (NIRC), the Hungarian council was founded by a government seeking social support for its program of transformation. In this case the government was communist. In 1988, Hungary was consumed by an economic crisis, and affected by spontaneous strikes. It seemed important to the government at that time to set negotiations with the official trade union federation on a new footing, to redraft labor legislation, and to codify and regulate a right to strike previously denied under communism.[20] As originally conceived, the national tripartite council would negotiate indicative wage bargains at the national level and participate in setting the minimum wage. After the 1990 elections brought the Magyar Democratic Forum to power, the Interest Reconciliation Council was renamed and restarted with the same initial purpose, to win social support for reform through partnership negotiations. However, the IRC was never given its own legal statute, so the scope of its authority was defined only in part by the Labor Code, which gave the council authority to negotiate the minimum wage and maximum wage increases, regulated by a punitive tax system until 1992. Otherwise, the functions of the IRC were set by government initiative.[21] All existing trade unions and employers' associations were invited to join.[22]

By 1992, Hungary already experienced a high level of fragmentation among employee and employer interest groups. Trade unions had gone through a difficult period of formation and reformation between 1988 and 1990. The official communist union organizations, the National Council of Trade Unions (SZOT) split in 1989, and dissolved itself entirely in March 1990. Its main successor organization was the National Confederation of Hungarian Trade Unions (MSZOSZ). A number of independent union confederations formed as well, playing a substantial role in roundtable negotiations and the transition

[20] By 1988, there was already a plurality of trade union organizations, but only the official union federation, SZOT, was invited to bargain in the NIRC with the government.

[21] Heinisch, 'The State of Corporatism', 67–9; S. J. Ingleby, 'The Role of Indigenous Institutions in the Economic Transformation of Eastern Europe: The Hungarian Chamber System—One Step Forward or Two Steps Back?', *Journal of European Public Policy*, 3: 1 (March 1996), 102–21.

[22] Maria Ladó, 'Representation of Workers' and Employers' Interests in Changing Industrial Relations in Hungary', in Jerzy Hausner, Ove K. Pedersen, and Karsten Ronit (eds), *Evolution of Interest Representation and Development of the Labour Market in Post-Socialist Countries* (Cracow: Cracow Academy of Economics and Friedrich Ebert Stiftung, 1995), 323. By 1990 there were more than 200 trade unions organized under four main confederations. Employers' associations, which had not truly participated in bargaining at the NIRC before 1990, also started to proliferate and join the council.

to democracy in Hungary. According to Ladó, 'These parallel developments were deeply interwoven and jointly led to a rather fragmented trade union movement'.[23] Rivalry developed between the newly formed and reconstituted trade unions over members and resources. In mid-1990 a Trade Union Round Table was set up to distribute the resources of the formerly monopolistic association, SZOT, and to create some unity within the trade union movement. However, dialogue collapsed in early 1991.

In 1991, the Hungarian government intervened to help the trade unions settle their disputes. Parliament passed two laws in 1991, one on the protection of trade union property and a second on the voluntary nature of trade union dues. Because they required employees to elect to join or rejoin a union of their choice, these laws were broadly favorable to the newly formed trade unions. However, neither of these laws was fully implemented. Former SZOT assets were finally distributed on the basis of an agreement among the trade unions in 1992, and the strength of the various trade unions was measured in elections to the national social security boards and to newly created enterprise works councils in 1993. Unions had considerable power in the early years of transition. Until 1998, trade union representatives elected by employees dominated the national social insurance and pension fund boards. In 1993, the reformed MSZOSZ won approximately 50% of the votes on these boards, and 70% in enterprise works councils.[24]

Employers' associations also proliferated in the first years of the transition, until three dominant organizations emerged: the National Association of Employers, the National Association of Entrepreneurs, and the National Association of Hungarian Industrialists.[25] In 1991, under pressure from the Hungarian Chamber of Commerce, the Hungarian government began to draft a law establishing a mandatory chamber organization for business, based on the Austrian model, which was finally passed in spring 1994. From this time, all Hungarian businesses had to join one of three mandatory chambers in agriculture, trades, and industry, in addition to any employers' organizations that provided representation on the IRC, adding to the fragmentation of employer representation.[26]

The Hungarian Interest Reconciliation Council (IRC) provided a forum for the negotiation and resolution of a number of important strike threats in 1990–1. Especially notable was the council's contribution to resolving a taxi drivers' strike in Budapest in autumn 1990, a strike that caused the capital city to grind to a halt. 'Although that mass demonstration had little to do with industrial relations or labour issues, it was, eventually, settled by the IRC. The successful mediation gave a firm legitimacy to the tripartite forum as well as to the key actors of negotiation'.[27] Since that crucial time, however, the influence of the council has been thrown into question. Trade union agree-

---

[23] See Ladó, 'Representation of Workers', 294.   [24] Ibid. 297–307.
[25] Heinisch, 'The State of Corporatism', 68.   [26] Ingleby, 'Indigenous Institutions'.
[27] Ladó, 'Representation of Workers', 323.

ment has proven difficult to reach. Negotiations in 1992 and 1993 become information sessions rather than decision-making ones. And broader efforts to reach an elusive national social pact ultimately fell flat.

In summer 1994, the newly elected center-left government of the Hungarian Socialist Party and the Alliance of Free Democrats (liberals), announced their intention to negotiate a broad national agreement through the IRC on the continuation of reforms. This process is described in some detail by Lajos Héthy, a labor relations scholar and former head of the government negotiating team. The center-left coalition hoped to use the negotiation of a broad transition agreement to emphasize a difference in policy style from the previous center-right government. The previous government had come under heavy criticism for its elitism and aloofness. It had been seemingly impermeable to extensive criticism of its reform strategies. Both the socialist and the liberal party hoped that a general transition agreement would help to re-establish some common ground in the transition process among a variety of social actors after the preceding period of fragmentation and contention. However, there were important obstacles to reaching an agreement. First, the trade unions and employers' associations were organizationally and philosophically fragmented. Second, all the different parties, including the two government parties, had different conceptions of what a general transition agreement should include. The result was that talks within the IRC in 1994 became increasingly diffuse. Third, parties to the talks changed their bargaining positions over time. Most importantly, the trade unions, which had initially been persuaded to give up their emphasis on comprehensive labor law reform after meeting firm resistance from employers' groups, eventually decided to re-establish this as a priority. This decision to press labor law reform followed labor's agreement to a set of radical budget-cutting measures in November 1994. After the budget debates, the trade unions decided that they 'had gone to the final limit of possible concessions' and had to establish an intransigent position on labor law. Employers also raised additional points for discussion in the fall of 1994. The Hungarian government tried to set a deadline for talks to conclude in January 1995, but by then the economic situation had altered so radically that attempts to reach a general agreement were scrapped.[28] Instead, the socialist-liberal government announced a radical series of austerity measures in February 1995 that were prepared quickly by the new Minister of Finance in a type of shock therapy or surprise attack approach,[29] eschewing corporatist bargaining, although the new Finance Minister, Lajos Bokros, did present his program to the IRC.

[28] L. Héthy, 'Negotiated Social Peace: An Attempt to Reach a Social and Economic Agreement in Hungary', in Attila Agh and Gabriella Ilonszki (eds), *Parliaments and Organized Interests* (Budapest: Hungarian Centre for Democracy Studies, 1996), 150–3; International Labour Office, *World Labour Report 1997–98*, 152.

[29] David Stark and László Bruszt, *Postsocialist Pathways* (Cambridge: Cambridge University Press, 1998), 173–4.

The failure to reach a broad and widely discussed social pact followed by the unilateral announcement of austerity measures was a severe blow to corporatism in Hungary. But the IRC survived the attack. In 1997, the IRC provided a critical forum for the negotiation of Hungary's dramatic pension reform, during which several important compromises were reached between the socialist-liberal government and the socialist trade unions.[30] The IRC also negotiated an agreement in February 1997 to strengthen collective bargaining and the application of labor legislation in Hungary.[31]

The Hungarian case exemplifies the limited role that corporatist-type bargaining has played in East-Central European transformations. Hungary's last communist government founded the National Interest Reconciliation Council as part of a strategy to maintain social peace during a contentious market transition. However, the emergence of a fragmented structure of interest representation between 1988 and 1990, both among trade unions and employers, presented enormous challenges for structures of concertation. While corporatist negotiations allowed the state to retain some level of institutionalized social dialogue between trade unions, employers' associations, and governments during a period of radical transition, this dialogue has not produced enduring societal agreement. The experience of Hungary's attempt to reach a general transition agreement in 1994 demonstrates the difficulties of reaching a social pact in the absence of powerful, centralized, and cohesive interest organizations, particularly in economic crisis conditions. The future of corporatism in Hungary and elsewhere in the region will depend upon strengthening interest organization. Still, despite high levels of fragmentation, the IRC continues to have sporadic success in resolving disputes on important transition issues.

The Czech Republic

Corporatism in the Czech Republic was an integral part of its social-liberal strategy for transformation from the outset. Czech social-liberalism was born of a compromise between radical neoliberals around finance minister Václav Klaus and social democrats in the first Civic Forum governments of Czechoslovakia. While Klaus and his neoliberal allies pushed through radical stabilization, liberalization, and privatization programs, other policy areas, including labor relations and social policy, were governed by social democratic-minded members of the broad Civic Forum coalition. Labor minister Petr Miller, Prime Minister Marian Čalfa, and Deputy Prime Minister Václav Valeš successfully pushed for the establishment of a national tripartite coun-

---

[30] Mitchell A. Orenstein, 'How Politics and Institutions Affect Pension Reform in Three Postcommunist Countries', World Bank Social Protection Discussion Paper 2310 (March 2000); R. Palacios and R. Rocha, 'The Hungarian Pension System in Transition', World Bank Social Protection Discussion Paper 9805 (1998).
[31] International Labour Office, *World Labour Report 1997–98*, 153.

cil in April 1990, despite the objections of finance minister Václav Klaus.[32] A Council for Economic and Social Agreement was established in October 1990, after negotiations with the major trade union federations and the establishment of a central employers' association. It was explicitly intended to provide a mechanism for insuring 'social conciliation' during the transition to capitalism.[33] Václav Klaus never approved of corporatist interest intermediation, however, and after he became prime minister in 1993, he attempted to do away with national corporatism, but only with limited success. The Czech tripartite council was already fairly well institutionalized at the time of Klaus' assaults, and a wave of labor unrest coupled with poor economic performance in 1996 and 1997 forced Klaus to retreat and accept a broader role for corporatist intermediation.[34]

The Czech Republic provided better social conditions for the establishment of corporatist bargaining than other Central European countries because the Czech Republic's trade union movement was only moderately fragmented. Most Czechoslovak trade unions were initially grouped in a single national federation, the Czech and Slovak Chamber of Trade Unions (ČSKOS).[35] An independent Confederation of Arts and Culture (KUK) was also represented in the tripartite council, and these two trade union federations have remained the sole representatives of labor on the national tripartite council. Other trade unions exist in the Czech Republic, outside the central federation, but they continue to be marginal in terms of size and political importance.[36] The ČSKOS played an ambiguous role in the process of democratization in Czechoslovakia. On the one hand, a nationwide movement of enterprise strike committees arose overnight within the trade union structure to demand an end to the communist regime. Igor Pleskot, a sociologist who had lost his academic position in 1968, became one of the leaders of this spontaneous independent movement and was later elected the first Chairman of the Czech and Slovak Chamber of Trade Unions (ČSKOS), the successor organization to the communist-era Revolutionary Trade-Union Movement (ROH).[37] Pleskot helped to lead strike committees that organized a nationwide two-hour strike on 27 November 1989. This strike played an important role in bringing down the communist regime, since it shocked communist leaders

---

[32] Igor Tomeš [advisor to the labor minister], interview (19 Jan. 1995).

[33] Council of Economic and Social Agreement of the Czech Republic, *Council of Economic and Social Agreement of the Czech Republic* (Prague 1993), 1.

[34] Jiři Kleibl and Zuzana Dvořáková, 'Industrial Relations in the Czech Republic', *Prague Economic Papers*, 3 (1999), 228.

[35] After the split of Czechoslovakia, the Czech parts of ČSKOS re-established themselves as the Czech and Moravian Chamber of Trade Unions (ČMKOS). Republic-level tripartite institutions also took the place of the Czechoslovak tripartite council, but its structures, practices, and members continued with minimal changes.

[36] Kleibl and Dvořáková, 'Industrial Relations', 221.

[37] For more details on the origins of this movement, see Igor Pleskot, 'Czech and Slovak Trade Union Movement in the Period of Transformation to a Civil Democratic Society, 1989–1993', mimeo (Czech-Moravian Chamber of Trade Unions, 1994).

with an unexpected display of working-class support for the students and townspeople demonstrating in Prague. However, at the same time, the ROH remained in the hands of the old communist leaders and became a target of mass denunciation in November and December 1989. Leaders of the democratic strike committees were later elected to take over ROH, but only in March 1990 when it was re-established as ČSKOS. They then faced the daunting task of overhauling the organization. Czech and Slovak trade unions retained most of the former property of the old ROH, and these extensive property holdings provided the trade unions with some vital resources in the early years of democratization. Yet continuity with the past also meant that the Czech trade unions were regarded with suspicion by the population at large, as yet another 'old structure' in a dubious posture of renovation. Still, the relative unity of the trade union movement provided the basis for a corporatist system of wage bargaining.

Employers' associations were initially weaker, less representative, and more fragmented than their trade union counterparts. A national umbrella employers' association was created at the request of the government for the purpose of participating in tripartite negotiations in 1990, but this association had only a fictitious existence. It was meant to provide some unity to the multiplicity of employers' associations that arose or transformed themselves after 1989 and suddenly arrived at the bargaining table. Rapidly, the Union of Industry, and later the Union of Transport, rose to dominance on the employers' side, although an active Association of Entrepreneurs representing mainly small businesspeople and a few other sectoral organizations were also represented. Czech employers' associations did not inherit massive property holdings, as the trade unions did, but instead depended on large companies in each sector for financing and premises.[38] Employers' associations, overshadowed in the tripartite council by the government and trade unions, have also been slow to develop and coordinate independent agendas. As in Hungary, a mandatory chamber law was proposed by the former communist chamber of commerce, but it was rejected by Václav Klaus and other liberals in the first Civic Forum governments. Therefore, business interest representation remains voluntary but concentrated around a dominant employers' organization.

As part of an effort by the government to win 'social peace' at a time of radical structural reform, the Council for Economic and Social Agreement (RHSD) started in October 1990 to bring together representatives of government, trade unions, and employers' associations to discuss legislative proposals in economic, labor, and social affairs. Importantly, and in contrast to other tripartite bodies throughout the region, government legislative and regulatory proposals in these areas had to be submitted to the tripartite council for discussion before they were presented to parliament or enacted through

---

[38] Orenstein and Desai, 'State Power'.

the ministries. In addition, the tripartite council was supposed to reach indicative wage bargains on a yearly basis and to conclude a General Agreement for the year—a sort of social contract on the main directions of the transformation. Minimum wages were negotiated in the tripartite council, along with other government wage regulations. Agreements reached in the tripartite council were non-binding, but the government was required to forward the results of the negotiations, and the positions of the three 'social partners', to the parliament.[39] The Czech tripartite council was initially considered better organized than others in East-Central Europe because of its clear demarcation of powers with the parliament. The tripartite council debates government legislative drafts and sends its opinions to parliament, but parliament ultimately makes final decisions. Relations between the two bodies are considerably more confused in Hungary, where there has been a running conflict over the import of tripartite agreements and no clear enabling legislation or statement of purpose.

Corporatist intermediation was one pillar of a broader Czech governmental strategy for maintaining 'social peace' during the transition. In essence, the strategy was based on a low-wage, low-unemployment trade-off designed to maintain relatively full employment in the economy. Exchange rate policy and wage controls were used to keep Czech wages low in dollar terms, lower than in other Central European economies, though labor productivity and GDP per capita in the Czech Republic were higher in purchasing-power-parity terms. Low wages in domestic and international comparative terms served to keep more workers employed, and thus reduced a main social cost of transition, unemployment. Until recently, unemployment was far lower in the Czech Republic than in any other economy in transition in the region (see Table 10.2), a notable fact, since unemployment is one of the primary causes of poverty in Central Europe. The Czech Republic was for a long time one of the only post-communist countries without a significant problem with long-term unemployment.[40] Czech policymakers planned for and used active labor market policies, such as retraining and jobs programs, earlier and more extensively than those of any other post-communist countries.[41]

Corporatist intermediation was viewed by the government as a means of obtaining trade union acquiescence in the low wage policy, a policy objective that came under increasing pressure after 1995.[42] The first major act of the tripartite council, founded in October 1990, was to debate the government's proposal and to enact a General Agreement for 1991 that accepted the principle of real wage cuts and created a formula for maintaining them within

[39] Kleibl and Dvořáková, 'Industrial Relations', 230.

[40] Tito Boeri, 'Learning from Transition Economies: Assessing Labor Market Policies across Central and Eastern Europe', *Journal of Comparative Economics*, 25, 368.

[41] Boeri, 'Learning from Transition Economies', 384.

[42] Anna Pollert, 'The Transformation of Trade Unionism in the Capitalist and Democratic Restructuring of the Czech Republic', *European Journal of Industrial Relations*, 3: 2 (1997).

Table 10.2. Central Europe: Unemployment, prices, and wages (1991–7)

Country	1991	1992	1993	1994	1995	1996	1997
Hungary							
Unemployment (%)	7.4	12.3	12.1	10.4	10.4	10.5	10.4
Consumer prices[a]	35.0	23.0	22.5	18.8	28.2	23.6	18.3
Average wages[a]	25.6	25.9	24.7	23.5	21.3	21.6	22.1
Czech Republic							
Unemployment (%)	4.1	2.6	3.5	3.2	2.9	3.5	5.2
Consumer prices[a]	56.6	11.1	20.8	10.0	9.1	8.8	8.5
Average wages[a]	16.7	19.6	23.8	15.7	17.0	17.4	13.5
Poland							
Unemployment (%)	11.8	13.6	16.4	16.0	14.9	13.2	10.5
Consumer prices[a]	70.3	43.0	35.3	32.2	27.8	19.9	14.9
Average wages[a]	63.1	38.7	35.4	36.7	32.7	26.9	21.5

[a] Average annual percentage increase.

Source: *EBRD Transition Report Update*, April 1999. Average wages are gross average monthly earnings in manufacturing/industry.

accepted levels. In the event, real wage declines were far more severe than initially expected, as consumer prices skyrocketed by 60% after price liberalization in January 1991. This embroiled the tripartite council in the first of a series of disputes over wage controls that lasted until they were officially lifted in 1995. Tax-based wage limits represented a phased dismantling of the former communist system of wage controls. Neoliberal reformers were afraid that full labor market deregulation would spur inflation. Therefore, they replaced the old communist system of job categories and seniority for individual workers, except for the so-called 'budgetary' sector, with a new system of punitive taxes on 'excess' increases in an enterprise's average wage bill, above annual percentage limits agreed in the tripartite council. Almost as soon as the system was in place, the trade union federation began lobbying for its abatement, and by 1993 for its cancellation, but the federation never took a tough stand on the issue until a new trade union president, Richard Falbr, was elected in 1994. Trade unions were able to bargain successfully for increases in the minimum wage and they also received institutional benefits from participation in the tripartite process, including the enactment of trade union friendly labor legislation. Thus, there is strong evidence to suggest that the Czech tripartite council was successful in achieving wage controls in an atmosphere of social peace until 1995, when the trade unions began to take a more active stance in favor of wage increases.[43]

[43] Pollert, 'The Transformation of Trade Unionism in the Capitalist and Democratic Restructuring of the Czech Republic', 213.

Czech trade unions received important institutional guarantees by participating in the tripartite system. At a time when the finance minister was a self-declared Thatcherite imposing radical structural reform, the trade unions could have fared far worse. In fact, though, the trade unions won a substantial concession in the Collective Bargaining Act of 1991 that established a new system of collective labor relations. Written with strong trade union and International Labour Organization (ILO) participation, the act was negotiated through the tripartite framework. In conjunction with the Act on Wages of 1991 and the much-amended Labor Code, the Collective Bargaining Act constitutes a generally favorable system of labor relations. For instance, unions do not need to undergo long recognition battles as in the United States or Britain, but are instantly recognized and must be bargained with once formed within a workplace. Czech workers also enjoy relatively strong protection against job dismissal. Trade union bargaining power and the right to strike are protected in accordance with ILO norms. Czech trade unions have used these institutional guarantees to begin collective bargaining at the enterprise and branch level, an important mobilizing tool, and to launch important nationwide strikes between 1995 and 1997.

As Pollert eloquently describes, Czech labor relations moved away from the social consensus model in the early years of the Klaus administration (1993–7), and decisively towards greater conflict in 1995. Klaus disliked special representation for trade unions and business organizations, and tried to pull the government out of the tripartite council. One result of his government's more confrontational approach was that a General Agreement was not signed after 1994. Klaus wanted Czech labor relations to evolve towards a more bipartite model, focused more narrowly on wages and working conditions, with limited state involvement or responsibility for consultation. The Klaus government was able to achieve a renegotiation of the tripartite statute in 1995 that significantly reduced the scope of tripartite bargaining.[44] However, this agreement did not last long. 1996 and 1997 were marked by increasing strikes, particularly among public sector employees, including doctors, nurses, teachers, and railway workers.[45] A railway strike paralyzed the country in 1997, showing that organized labor's potential for mobilization was not entirely dissipated. And as the Czech economic miracle soured in 1997, the Klaus government was unable to resist trade union pressure to reinstate the original tripartite structure. Klaus agreed to renegotiate and broaden the scope of negotiations, government participation, and to restore the original name of the RHSD in exchange for trade union acquiescence in his government's ill-fated 'little package' of economic austerity measures.[46] ('Economic' had been removed from the title in 1995.)

---

[44] Kleibl and Dvořáková, 'Industrial Relations', 228.
[45] Pollert, 'Transformation', 213.
[46] Kleibl and Dvořáková, 'Industrial Relations', 228.

In short, corporatism in the Czech Republic was the product of an explicit government strategy of 'social peace' pursued by left-wing politicians within the broad Civic Forum coalition. Facing a relatively unified trade union movement, the government was able to provide institutional guarantees to the trade unions in exchange for acquiescence in wage controls from 1990–5. In 1995, when wage controls were lifted and the trade unions began to take a more confrontational approach, the work of the tripartite council slowed to a standstill. The government of Václav Klaus attempted to withdraw from the tripartite council in 1995, yet the trade unions fought for continued government participation and won their battle on the strength of a growing strike wave. Furthermore, when the liberal Klaus government ran into economic difficulties in 1997, it approached the trade unions with a proposal to restart tripartite negotiations about a 'little package' of economic reforms. The durability of the tripartite council is significant, demonstrating its continuing importance to both the trade unions and to governments, although at different times and for different reasons. The national tripartite council has become an integral part of the Czech system of industrial relations. It has played an important role in forging social consensus during the transition to capitalism and democracy, continues to engage in mandatory consulting on government social and economic legislation, and may provide a forum for corporatist wage bargaining in the future.

Poland

During the communist period, Poland was renowned for its powerful, encompassing independent labor movement, Solidarity. Solidarity's most famous leader, Lech Wałęsa, was the representative of the opposition that the communist government chose to approach during the late 1980s in order to negotiate a path toward peaceful reforms. It was also the Solidarity union movement that was credited with staging the strikes and protests that brought about the collapse of the Polish communist party-state.[47]

On this basis, one might have expected Poland's post-communist political economy to be social democratic in nature, characterized by effective national corporatist structures. However, the first post-communist Solidarity-led governments instead suppressed labor participation in policy debates and took no steps to establish formal, centralized bargaining structures. Since Solidarity had direct access to the government between 1989 and 1993, liberal economic reformers in the new governments feared labor influence would undermine desperately needed, and fragile, reforms. They believed that any formal bargaining structure would be overwhelmed by Solidarity's power. Furthermore, because Solidarity was theoretically already represented in the

---

[47] Although, by 1989, there was already a plurality of opposition labor organizations involved in organizing the protests and strikes.

government itself, and because there was relative calm among workers during the early, triumphant stages of the post-communist period, it was widely believed that labor already was sufficiently represented at the central level. Some discussion of a tripartite forum took place at the labor ministry early on,[48] but since employers' organizations were still nascent, and because of Solidarity's fierce rivalry with the formerly 'official' trade union federation OPZZ, the discussions did not result in any action.

In addition, Lech Wałęsa played a singular role in encouraging the institutional confusion that characterized labor relations in Poland during the first period of reform. In 1989, Wałęsa was the one individual capable of knitting together the diverse strands of the Solidarity movement, including the workers, the Church, the intellectual advisors, and the activists. He had a tremendous sense of political balance that allowed him to keep all of these forces in line and moving in the same direction. This was vital for Solidarity in the period when it faced a hostile, communist state. However, Wałęsa believed that he should continue to play this unifying role as president. Wałęsa hoped to turn the presidential office into an informal site for trade union representation and bargaining with the government. In an effort to guard this role for himself, to personally remain the pivot of the Solidarity movement, Wałęsa opposed institutionalization within the trade unions, the Solidarity movement, the government, and the field of labor relations, seeing any such measures as threats to his own position.[49] Wałęsa wanted to be the personal ambassador of labor to the government of Poland and he therefore had no interest in formalizing corporatist bargaining structures. However, Wałęsa's efforts to provide an 'umbrella' for liberal reforms ultimately failed to quell labor protests.

In 1992 and 1993, two massive strike waves gripped the country,[50] marking the end of the period of labor and government consensus in Poland. Starting in the summer of 1992, there were thousands of strikes, involving hundreds of thousands of workers and costing over 1.5 million lost working days.[51]

[48] Jacek Kuroń [First Minister of Labor], interview with Lisa Hale (Warsaw, Poland, 14 Feb. 1996).

[49] On Polish citizens' committees, see Tomek Grabowski, 'From a Civic Movement to Political Parties: The Rise and Fall of the Solidarity Committees in Poland, 1989–1991', Paper presented at the Annual Meeting of the American Political Science Association, 1995. Published in revised form in *East European Politics and Societies*.

[50] In 1988 and 1989, there were nearly 1,000 strikes each year. In 1990 and 1991, there were 250 and 305 strike actions, respectively. By 1992 and 1992, these numbers grew astronomically. In 1992, there were 6,351 strikes and in 1993, 7,364 strikes. The initial period of labor peace had ended. For details on these strike waves, see Carol Timko, 'The 1992–1993 Strike Wave and the Disorganization of Worker Interests in Poland', Paper presented at the 1996 Annual Meeting of the American Political Science Association (September 1996). For more general discussions on labor relations in this period see L. E. Hale, 'Poland's Right Turn: Solidarity as Opposition, Government and Union in the Capitalist Transition', PhD dissertation (Northwestern University, June 1999). Also, Mark Kramer, 'Polish Workers and the Post-communist Transition, 1989–1993', *Communist and Post-Communist Studies*, 28: 1 (1995), 71–114.

[51] Hausner, 'The State Enterprise Pact'.

Strikes paralyzed the Silesian coal mines, the aviation industry in Mielec, the copper mines in Lubin, and the FSM Fiat auto plant in Tychy. The FSM strike was especially significant, since it threatened a major foreign investor in Poland. Another striking feature of the workers' actions at this time was that formerly communist and anti-communist unions were teaming up to oppose the Solidarity government's liberal reforms, the first time this had happened since the fall of communism.[52] Solidarity trade unions had no choice but to go along with strikes organized by their rival, OPZZ. Solidarity trade union leaders began to criticize government policy, mainly because their own membership was striking in many factories. Thus the strikes of 1992 served to radicalize Solidarity, forcing it to break with Wałęsa and the government, and encouraging the union to organize its own massive teachers' and public sector strikes in 1993.

In the wake of the strikes and the fragmented situation in parliament at the beginning of 1992, there was a widespread sense in Solidarity circles that things could not proceed as they had for the past three years and that trade unions had to be included in the process of economic reform. Jacek Kuroń, a popular, former Solidarity dissident and leader of the 'Solidarity left', was among the first to argue for a corporatist solution to integrating the trade unions into the political process. He re-entered the Ministry of Labor with the Suchocka government in Summer 1992 calling for a Pact on State Enterprises that would resolve most of the basic conflicts between trade unions and the government. The pact was aptly named. It was meant to be a mega-deal between the government and labor to achieve social peace and put new life into the privatization portion of Balcerowicz's shock therapy reform plan. Trade unions and enterprise employee councils would agree to draw up a privatization strategy for their enterprise within six months. In exchange, the government would fulfill a long list of trade union wishes in state enterprises, including providing worker shares in the privatized enterprise. If, after six months, the employee council had not designed and approved its own privatization package, the government would step in, take control, and privatize the enterprise in a top-down manner. Tadeusz Syryczyk, the first Solidarity Minister of Industry, captured the essence of the pact when he defined it 'as the buying out of certain previously acquired employee rights'.[53] The pact also included provisions for a national tripartite council, based on the ILO model, to provide a standing mechanism for social concertation in the future.

The process of negotiating the Pact on State Enterprises, however, ran into difficulties because of the opposing views and political rivalry of the two main trade union federations, Solidarity and OPZZ. The unions' representatives refused to sit at the same table and after a few initial sessions, government representatives had to conduct separate negotiations with each federation,

[52] *RFE/RL Research Report*, 28 (Aug. 1992).
[53] Quoted in Hausner, 'The State Enterprise Pact', 114.

walking between separate rooms at the Ministry of Labor. Several smaller but still significant unions left the talks altogether. In the end, the Pact, signed on 22 February 1993 after six months of negotiation, was actually three separate agreements with Solidarity, OPZZ, and seven other large branch unions in industry and transport, respectively. The Polish government, represented by Minister Kuroń, and the Confederation of Polish Employers signed all three pacts. They were largely parallel agreements, differing sometimes only in detail, but sometimes in significant ways. For example, OPZZ refused to agree on the proposed system of collective agreements that the other unions agreed to.

Ultimately, the Pact was introduced to parliament just before the Suchocka government fell in 1993 and enabling legislation was not passed in time. When a leftist government made up of the former communist Alliance of the Democratic Left (SLD) and the Polish Peasant Party (PSL) came to power after elections in September 1993, it withdrew all pact legislation, except for legislation on the tripartite committee which it founded in February 1994. However, many elements of the pact, including provisions on privatization, state enterprise restructuring, insolvency protection, and wage controls, remained subjects of tripartite discussion and were eventually implemented under the SLD-PSL government. In the opinion of the World Labour Office, 'It is generally accepted in Poland that the part of the pact dealing with social questions has been applied in its entirety'.[54]

Bargaining over the terms of the new labor code was the first instance in which the tripartite council was active in producing consensus. Labor code negotiations took place primarily during 1995 and 1996. The fact that this issue was bargained at the tripartite level forced a modest amount of institutionalization of interest representation among the actors affecting change in Poland. Once the labor code became the subject of tripartite negotiations, employers, who were not especially well organized prior to the establishment of the tripartite council, began to use their disparate organizations to articulate a common position on the new labor code. Various business organizations and employers' unions finally decided on a series of preferences which they communicated to the leader of the official employers' union and the official representative of employers at the tripartite council, the Confederation of Polish Employers (KPP).

Unions did not overcome their general competitiveness and animosity toward each other on the issue of the labor code. OPZZ and Solidarity remained divided over the optimal number of hours in the working week through the end of labor code negotiations. Had they been more unanimous in their view of working week hours, they probably would have reached an even more favorable resolution of this issue at the tripartite level. However, the tripartite constituencies all accepted the labor code outcomes without

[54] International World Labour Office, 'World Labour Report', 1998, 154.

protest due to their involvement in negotiating the terms of the code changes. This marked a substantial improvement over their ability to accept past policy decisions, as evidenced by the level of strike and protest activity, which declined sharply. Thus the tripartite council achieved its first aim in Poland, to reduce social conflict.

As part of its new Strategy for Poland, Poland's post-communist left-wing government also tried to use the new tripartite council as a means to talk down inflation and reach economy-wide indicative wage bargains. Both major trade union federations participated in tripartite wage negotiations. However, the intensely politicized nature of trade unions in Poland, and their close relations with the major political parties, made cooperation difficult at times. Employers' associations were also quite fragmented. Still, indicative wage agreements were reached and employers' associations probably share some of the credit for the left government's victory over inflation between 1993 and 1997. Private enterprises still had substantial room to negotiate exceptions and the freedom to exceed national indicative wage agreements. State-owned enterprises could be called to account, however. And workers in the 'budgetary sector', including those in the civil service, health, and education fields, actually had their average wage raises established through tripartite negotiations, although these were set far below the national level.[55]

Social issues were negotiated at the tripartite level and while none of the parties to these negotiations claim to be wholly pleased with the policies decided there, they are ready to accept them as fairly bargained.[56] Social security reform provisions were extensively negotiated at the tripartite council during 1996, 1997, and 1998. And minimum wage bargains were revisited there frequently.

While these important social issues were, and continue to be, negotiated at the tripartite council, representing an important contribution of this corporatist institution to social peace and democratic institutionalization of interest mediation, the tripartite council has not shaped the overall nature of political and economic reforms in Poland. In contrast with the Czech Republic where social bargaining was part of the underlying strategy of early decision-making on political and economic reforms, Poland's first post-communist leaders implemented the overall framework of the reform program with virtually no social input whatsoever. It was only after significant protest and political instability that the tripartite council was accepted as an appropriate venue for bargaining over social policies.

As in Hungary and the Czech Republic, Poland's tripartite committee was founded by politicians of the left as part of a strategy to achieve social peace during market transition. Right-wing liberals either opposed these efforts at concertation on principle,[57] or accepted them as a necessary cost of buying

[55] Ibid. 154–5.
[56] Hale interviews with leaders of many employers and trades unions during 1995 and 1996.
[57] For instance, see Marek Dąbrowski, 'Utopia Paktowania' [Pacted Utopia], *Gazeta Wyborcza*, 2: 4, stycznia 1993.

trade union support for the market transition after a massive strike wave. A fragmented, polarized, and politicized trade union movement impeded both the establishment of corporatist institutions in Poland—until 1994, making Poland one of the last Central European countries to adopt such institutions—and their further development. At the national level, the two main trade union federations are quasi-political parties. Solidarity is a constituent member of the Solidarity Electoral Action coalition that won parliamentary elections in 1997, while the OPZZ is part of the post-communist Alliance of the Democratic Left. Trade union leaders sit in parliament as representatives of both major parties. Therefore, trade unions often grandstand and campaign for votes and media attention, rather than pursue the economic interests of their membership. Likewise, trade union leaders often have an interest in pursuing a political, rather than a union, career. In tripartite negotiations, the unions sometimes prefer to prevent progress and behave as an opposition party rather than allow the government to take credit for mutually beneficial solutions. Despite this, Poland's tripartite council has played a moderately effective role in indicative wage bargaining and in negotiating crucial social reforms. However, alliances between the main trade union federations and major political parties may place limits on the possibilities of future corporatist interest concertation in Poland.

Conclusion: Interest Representation in Post-communist Europe

The rebirth of corporatist institutions (Table 10.3) in post-communist East-Central Europe has to be seen as a form of institutional experimentation in an uncertain and disorganized social environment. Representation of interests in post-communist Europe tends towards the informal. Official structures are often not as useful as personal contacts. Civil society organizations tend to be disorganized, and clear channels of civil society-state relations have yet to be established. Legal rules are unstable and the powers of mobilizable interest groups have yet to be tested.

On the advice of the International Labour Organization (ILO) and at their own initiative, many states in post-communist East-Central Europe have experimented with tripartite councils in line with historical models. Corporatist bargaining can be seen as an outgrowth of corporatist arrangements that existed under communism, and during the inter-war period. The founding of tripartite councils offered states a means of maintaining dialogue with the trade unions and employers' associations during a difficult period of initiating new labor legislation and establishing a new system of labor relations based on collective bargaining.

Whether and to what extent this experimentation has produced any useful results is a matter of debate, and much remains to be seen. We would venture the tentative conclusion that corporatist intermediation in East-Central

Table 10.3. Central Europe: Corporatist institutions

Country	Name	Foundation	Fragmentation of interests
Hungary	Interest Reconciliation Council	1988; founded by liberalizing communist government to maintain social peace	High
Czech Republic	Council for Economic and Social Agreement	1990; founded at the initiative of leftists within the broad Civic Forum coalition as part of strategy of social peace	Medium
Poland	Tripartite Committee for Socio-Economic Issues	1994; founded by left government to further dialogue with trade unions after massive strike waves in 1992 and 1993	High

Europe has played an important, though limited role in the transition to capitalism and democracy, and that tripartite councils will remain part of the institutional landscape of the region for decades to come. In Hungary, the Interest Reconciliation Council helped to settle a critical taxi drivers' strike in Budapest in 1990, created a forum for discussion between the government and important interest groups, and played a central role in an attempt to reach a general socio-economic agreement after the 1994 elections. This attempt ended abruptly in 1995, when the government suddenly announced a sharp package of austerity measures, but the Council enjoyed a revival in 1997, when it took on a more limited, but still important set of issues for negotiation. The Czech tripartite council played a major role in drafting new labor legislation, creating a system of collective bargaining, and setting wage levels. It played a fundamental institutional role in protecting 'social peace' during the early part of the transformation. In Poland, the tripartite committee was founded later and successfully reduced social tensions that had emerged as a result of early transition policies. It facilitated indicative wage bargaining and negotiated labor code and social security reforms. However, its late arrival to the transition in Poland limited its ability to affect underlying transformation strategies and principles. Furthermore, while the tripartite council has furthered the institutionalization of employers' organizations, it has not improved inter-union relations significantly.

Institutional factors, especially the level of fragmentation of the trade union federations and their linkages with political parties, explain some of the success and failure of corporatist bargaining. Politicization of trade unions in Poland and Hungary would seem to limit the possibility for the development of corporatist wage bargaining and other forms of concertation. Conversely, relatively high levels of trade union centralization and the unions' political independence initially enabled the Czech Republic to establish an atmosphere of social peace through tripartite bargaining, though this was quickly undone by a shift in government strategies towards more confrontational labor relations under the Klaus government.

Interestingly, we find that government strategies are the major factor governing the genesis and efficacy of the state-dominated corporatist institutions in post-communist Central Europe. Leftist parties and politicians advanced corporatist institutions as a strategy for managing social conflict during the transition to capitalism with sporadic success. In doing so, they drew upon historical legacies of corporatist interest mediation and the availability of a Western model promoted by the ILO through its Geneva and Budapest offices. On the other hand, neoliberal governments and politicians took a more confrontational approach to organized labor and downplayed or attempted to cancel institutions of corporatist intermediation. The resulting lack of a left-wing and right-wing consensus on the benefits of corporatist institutions remains the single greatest obstacle to their further development.[58] In conclusion, we find that tripartite councils in Central Europe were formed as a result of explicit governmental strategies to embark on a process of negotiation with the leading trade union federations. Their performance depends on continuing government commitment to this goal, although their durability in the face of explicit rejection by neoliberal governments, in the Czech case, suggests that these institutions may take on a life of their own as interest organizations strengthen.

While we have noted in this chapter some of the successes of corporatist interest concertation in Central Europe, it is important not to exaggerate, and to keep some caveats in mind. First of all, there is a crucial difference between the establishment of corporatist institutions which have played a limited role in the transformation process and the development of a 'corporatist society'. Iankova, one of the most astute observers of East-Central European corporatism, argues the rather extreme position that since the emergence of Solidarity in 1980, the entire transition can be characterized as an episode of 'transformative corporatism', which goes 'far beyond the pure economic exigencies typical of west European corporatist settlements'.[59] 'During the post-communist transformations, bargained exchange between organized interests and the state is both more frequent, extensive, and intensive than is normal for corporatism in relatively stable market economies'.[60] Our case studies

---

[58] F. Traxler, 'European Transformation and Institution Building in East and West: The Performance of and Preconditions for Neocorporatism', in R. W. Kindley. and D. F. Good (eds), *The Challenge of Globalization and Institution Building* (Boulder: Westview Press, 1997), 169.

[59] See Iankova, 'Transformative Corporatism', 1.   [60] Ibid. 19.

show that while the range of issues and functions assigned to post-communist corporatist bodies might be more extensive than usual, the level of bargaining, concertation, and negotiation can in no way be considered more intensive than in corporatist West European states. Newly institutionalized corporatist bodies in East-Central Europe have often proven incapable of reaching consensus, and the significance of their decisions is often in doubt. Unless these bodies become more institutionalized, it would be false to characterize East-Central European societies as 'corporatist'. These countries have corporatist institutions that have played an important, but limited role in the transition to democratic capitalism. While these bodies may develop into defining fora for interest representation, they may also atrophy, making it premature to assign the corporatist label to these societies or their systems of interest representation.[61]

Finally, to what extent do corporatist institutions of interest reconciliation in East-Central Europe reflect a response to new pressures of globalization? Katzenstein argued that small states in Europe used corporatist bargaining to respond flexibly to shocks from the world economy.[62] The transformative corporatism of East-Central Europe, by contrast, responds to challenges posed by systemic transformation, thus largely to domestic pressures. To the extent that de-communization is synonymous with a reinsertion of Central Europe into the world economy, we can see the corporatist experience of this region through Katzenstein's lens. However, the involvement of the ILO in providing a specific form for corporatist interest concertation in Central Europe illustrates a second dimension of globalization. These institutions not only react to global pressures, they are themselves foreign imports. Corporatist institutions have blown in from the West on the same winds that carried the music of Michael Jackson, the McDonald's French fry, the philosophy of Karl Popper, skinheads, and jackboots. What Central Europeans will make of this in the future is unknown. But the presence of these corporatist bodies themselves is important, since they provide an institutional form wherein processes of interest concertation can take on a life of their own.

---

[61] See Hausner, Pedersen, and Ronit (eds), *Evolution of Interest Representation and Development of the Labour Market in Post-Socialist Countries* (1995), 365.

[62] Peter J. Katzenstein, *Small States in World Markets: Industrial Policy in Europe* (Ithaca: Cornell University Press, 1985).

Conclusion

11

Institutional Legacies and the Transformation of Labor: Late-industrializing and Post-socialist Economies in Comparative-Historical Perspective

Rudra Sil, The University of Pennsylvania and
Christopher Candland, Wellesley College

The chapters in this volume shed light on some of the most important questions at the intersection of comparative industrial relations and international political economy. What common economic challenges do workers face in societies undergoing economic adjustment or post-communist economic transitions? How have labor organizations responded to new, often unprecedented, challenges to existing labor institutions in an increasingly interdependent global economy? Is the decline in union membership and the weakening of organized labor likely to continue, resulting in the unfettered commodification of labor while the mechanisms for the 'self-protection of society' disappear?[1] Are there institutional arrangements that can simultaneously enhance the competitiveness of firms and national economies and protect the livelihoods and rights of workers in the global age? Does the emergence of post-Fordist production necessitate even less control over the production process for workers, or does it pave the way for alternative channels for workers' participation? To what extent are changes in labor institutions and the renegotiation of social pacts similar across countries or regions, and to what extent do variations reflect the persistence of existing institutional arrangements in the face of the homogenizing pressures of global economic forces?

The contributions here incorporate insights and analyses that suggest the outlines of a general comparative framework—not a unifying paradigm or model—for analyzing the effects of economic reform on workers and labor institutions, and the effects of workers' expectations, behaviors (i.e. labor institutions) on economic development and on the strategies of key economic factors. The intention is to recast concerns normally considered to be within the domain of industrial relations specialists in the context of issues that more generally concern students of international political economy and

---

[1] The term 'self-protection of society' is from Karl Polanyi, *The Great Transformation* (Boston: Beacon, 1966).

comparative politics. First, each of the authors provides some background into the labor regime that emerged, whether at the national, local or factory level, over the course of state-guided or socialist industrialization programs during much of the period between the 1950s and the 1980s. Second, each of the chapters considers the processes through which labor institutions are being transformed and increasingly exposed to the pressures of an increasingly interdependent global economy. In some cases, these processes were set in motion by dramatic social events such as the East European 'velvet revolution' or the collapse of the USSR; in others, the initiative came from governments or managers. In either scenario, the studies analyze the shifts in labor institutions, as well as in the concerns and strategies of unions.

Four of the chapters have examined contemporary late-industrializers, tracing how the shift from state-led development to economic liberalization or privatization have produced different kinds of responses from workers and unions to such common problems as the loss of job security, imposed wage restraints, and increased managerial control over new, more flexible labor processes. Four of the chapters have examined 'post-socialist' transitions, analyzing the varying degrees and directions of change in labor-management relations following the introduction of market-oriented reforms in China and the collapse of communism in East Europe and the former Soviet Union. One other chapter has considered whether the Japanese system of industrial relations can still be considered a viable alternative to West European corporatist models of bargaining or to traditional Fordist models of mass production given that the Japanese 'model' itself is undergoing an important paradigm shift under the pressures of a global economy.

This concluding chapter briefly considers what is gained by juxtaposing these varied analyses within a common framework for analyzing the common pressures of globalization and the effects of distinctive institutional legacies on the responses to these pressures. We begin by considering some of the shared features of industrial relations under late and socialist industrialization and by noting some factors that make it difficult to apply models based on the experiences of Organization for Economic Cooperation and Development (OECD) countries to the analysis of labor regimes elsewhere. Next, we analyze important ways in which industrial relations in socialist countries differed from those in post-colonial contexts, and the ways in which these differences may contribute to different patterns and outcomes in the transformation of industrial relations in the two contexts. In the section that follows, we consider the distinctive, even unique, institutional legacies that are shaping the responses of workers and the transformation of labor institutions at national, regional, and factory levels. We then identify further questions on the basis of certain patterns of change that occur within or cut across our categories of post-socialist and post-colonial settings. We suggest that the concept of globalization is most useful when it is employed not as a universal model for projecting trajectories of institutional change but as a more restricted framework for capturing the common threats facing labor during economic adjustment.

Labor, the State and Late-industrialization: Some Common Legacies and Challenges

Most of the similarities between late-industrialized and socialist economies—and the differences between these and the advanced industrial economies of the West—can be traced to the enormous role the state has played in coordinating economic development and, in the process, establishing the institutional frameworks for labor regimes. The role of the state in coordinating economic activities in late-industrialization is explicit in Gerschenkron's comparative analysis of economic backwardness in Europe—in particular, his analysis of the role of the Russian state which provided an 'historical substitute' for the English entrepreneur in order to enable Russian industrialization to take off.[2] Subsequent studies of bureaucratic-authoritarianism in Latin America and the capitalist developmental state in East Asia pointed to the importance of the state in promoting and designing industrialization programs, limiting the effects of the international economy on domestic industry, mediating between the public and private sectors, and insulating the economic policy bureaucracy from social pressures.[3]

Despite Marx's contention that the state would eventually 'whither away' in the transition to communism, the logic of the developmental state is applicable to socialist industrialization as well. The revolutionary destruction of pre-communist economic and social structures and the subsequent quest for autarkic socialist industrialization required a strong party-state apparatus. As Lenin himself argued, although the state would eventually 'whither away', the arrival of socialism in underdeveloped regions meant that a 'dictatorship of the proletariat' (that is, a communist party-state) would have to ensure the

[2] See Alexander Gerschenkron, *Economic Backwardness in Historical Perspective* (Cambridge: Harvard University Press, 1962). Gerschenkron's treatment of the Russian case—which was the most 'backward' of the four countries he examined—may be viewed as a model for state-led late-industrialization in most post-colonial and socialist economies given the level of challenge in overcoming relative backwardness. The idea that the state should play a dominant role in the development and protection of domestic industry can be found as far back as the mid-nineteenth century in the writings of Johann Fichte and Friedrich List, both of whom made a strong case for state intervention so as to enable Germany (or Prussia) to catch up with England. See Johann-Gottlieb Fichte, 'Der geschlossene Handelsstaat' [The Closed Trading State], in Fichte, *Ausgewahlte Werke* [Selected Works], v. 3 (Darmstadt: Wissenschaftliche Buchgesellschaft, 1964), 417–544; Friedrich List, *The National System of Political Economy*, trans. Sampson S. Lloyed (London: Longmans, 1916); and the discussion of these pieces in Andrew Janos, 'The Politics of Backwardness on Continental Europe', *World Politics*, 41: 3 (April 1989), 327, fn. 6.

[3] See, for example, Guillermo O'Donnell, *Modernization and Bureaucratic-Authoritarianism: Studies in South American Politics* (Berkeley: Institute of International Studies, University of Californa at Berkeley, 1973); and Chalmers Johnson, 'Political Institutions and Economic Performance: The Government-Business Relationship in Japan, South Korea, and Taiwan', in Frederic C. Deyo, *The Political Economy of the New Asian Industrialism* (Ithaca: Cornell University Press, 1987).

destruction of the remnants of the bourgeois state machinery, coordinate socialist accumulation, and 'telescope' the bourgeois and socialist stages of development.[4] Stalinist collectivization and the first Five Year Plan (1928–33) marked a dramatic event establishing the role of the state's economic ministries in directly controlling all sectors of the economy, even agriculture. Mao's 'socialism with Chinese characteristics' and, later, economic experiments conducted by East European communist regimes did result in economic programs that would differ from the Soviet command economy in important respects.[5] But, in all cases, the role of the party-state apparatus, the system of central planning, and the reliance on state-owned enterprises contributed to quite similar economic institutions and practices in the course of socialist industrialization.

Modernizing elites in late-industrializing economies, regardless of the extent of their commitment to particular ideologies or to particular political or economic systems, have tended to be almost as reliant on large and strong state sectors as has been the case with socialist industrialization. In the case of post-colonial late-industrializers, not only did the new national elites face the standard challenges of relative economic backwardness that all late-industrializers have faced, but they also had to coordinate the shift from an economy organized around primary exports and dependent on formerly imperial countries to an industrial economic base upon which national sovereignty could be secured. For decades, governments throughout the late-industrializing world enthusiastically adopted a Keynesian framework for economic policy, in conjunction with economic ideologies ranging from the neoclassical to the socialist. These governments promoted domestic industry through high import tariffs, restrictions on foreign ownership and investment, and various forms of tax concessions, concessional credit, export draw-backs and other forms of support to domestic private industry. Moreover, the middle classes at the time of industrial take-off were either small or lacked the resources and inclination to establish industrial production facilities, the state had to directly set up the basic industries—minerals, iron and steel, electricity, chemicals and fertilizers, engineering, and machines—that were required as the foundation for downstream industries. In short, throughout much of Latin America, Asia and Africa, industrial manufacturing was thought to be a public good that only the state could provide for the foreseeable future.

---

[4] See V. I. Lenin, 'Two Tactics of Social Democracy in the Democratic Revolution', in *Selected Works* (Moscow: Progress Publishers, 1977), 475–83; and Lenin, 'The State and Revolution', from Robert Tucker (ed.), *The Lenin Anthology* (New York: Norton, 1975).

[5] For example, even during collectivization, Mao invested proportionately more in the agricultural sector than did Stalin (insisting that, unlike the USSR, China would 'walk on two legs'). Poland was the one Soviet bloc country in which collectivization was not attempted at all. Hungary, while not eager to repeat the kinds of policies that led to the Prague Spring in 1968 in Czechoslovakia, proceeded to establish a 'New Economic Mechanism' during the 1970s through market-based price structures for certain sectors.

It is not surprising, therefore, that in both socialist and late-industrializing settings—including Japan until the 1970s—we find the state playing a central role in shaping the character of labor regimes. In fact, the role of the state in controlling—if not dictating—the process of labor incorporation and emergent patterns of labor relations has been so dominant that in none of the countries studied in this volume is there much evidence of the 'societal corporatism' that has characterized labor relations in most western societies for much of the post-World War II period.[6] This is certainly true in the case of socialist countries where, as Sil and Orenstein and Hale suggest, the extent of party-state control over trade union federations and factory trade union committees rendered the very concept of 'corporatism' meaningless in the analysis of labor relations at both the national or factory levels.[7] This is also largely true of post-colonial late-industrializers such as India, Pakistan, Mexico, and Brazil where governments—whether democratic or authoritarian—played a pivotal role in determining the character and scope of the labor movement, the formal process of labor incorporation, the creation of labor laws, the resolution of industrial disputes, and the rights of workers and employers. In these cases, if labor relations were systematically corporatized at all, the result was closer to the 'state corporatist' variety than to societal corporatism.[8] In

[6] 'Corporatism' is generally defined in Schmitter's classic essay as '. . . a system of interest representation in which the constitutent units are organized into a limited number of singular, compulsory, non-competitive, hierarchically ordered, and functionally differentiated categories, recognized or licensed (if not created) by the state and granted a deliberate representational monopoly within their respective categories in exchange for observing certain controls on their selection of leaders and articulation of demands and supports'. Societal corporatism is a type of corporatism found in political systems with relatively autonomous, multilayered territorial units; open, competitive electoral processes and party systems; and ideologically varied, coalitionally based executive authorities. As Schmitter himself notes, societal corporatism appears to be most common in liberal, advanced capitalist, organized democratic welfare states. See Philippe Schmitter, 'Still the Century of Corporatism?' in Schmitter and Gerhard Lehmbruch (eds), *Trends Towards Corporatist Intermediation* (Beverly Hills: Sage, 1979), 13, 22–3.

[7] As Sil and Orenstein and Hale note in Chapters 8 and 10 of this volume, trade unions in the USSR and communist East Europe, although theoretically regarded as independent representatives of the proletariat, were essentially turned into 'transmission belts' for the communist party-state. This was justified on the basis of the notion that the party represented the 'vanguard' of the proletariat and no conflicts of interest were thought to be possible between workers and the communist party-state. Schmitter describes the Soviet system of industrial relations as a 'monist' type of corporatism, but also acknowledges that this type stretches the general definition of corporatism given the extent of party-state control over the definition and articulation of labor's interests; see Schmitter, 'Still the Century of Corporatism?', 16.

[8] In post-colonial authoritarian regimes, labor incorporation was managed, and even engineered, by populist dictators and the parties they created (as evident in Brazil and Mexico), and labor relations for long periods of time resembled, if anything, a state corporatist model. In more pluralist settings, elements of state corporatism were less viable, but nor did societal corporatism take root; the state still played a dominant role in shaping labor regimes by providing a common framework—through labor laws, factory inspection systems, business licensing laws, mediation in labor disputes, and less direct methods of administrative guidance—for standardizing relations between business groups and trade unions. In India, as Candland notes, while a legal trade union could be formed by a handful of employees, trade union federations were formed across sectors and became affiliated with political parties. On state corporatism, see Schmitter, 'Still the Century of Corporatism?', 16.

fact, in the case of India, where distinct trade union federations are linked to competing political parties and studies of industrial relations generally 'focus on the state's rather than capital's relations to labor, because the state is labor's most important counterplayer'.[9] Even in the case of post-war Japan, as Weathers notes, thanks to the 'legacy of forced economic development', much of the annual wage bargaining actually took place between management and the enterprise union at the firm level through standardized procedures and within parameters established by a powerful economic bureaucracy.[10] In each of the cases studied in this volume, the state was not merely one of three relatively equal actors in a tripartite bargaining relationship; it virtually set the terms for labor incorporation and determined the character of labor regimes at the national level and at the regional or firm levels.

At the level of the enterprise, there are other important similarities that are related to the dynamics of late development in both socialist and post-colonial settings. Command economies in the former and large public sectors in the latter both tended to emphasize large-scale industrial enterprises that planners expected to spur rapid industrialization and economic growth. In addition, many large firms in the private sector with close ties to government elites received significant preferential treatment in the form of government subsidies, special licensing agreements, and the support of the government in quelling industrial unrest. Production processes in all of these large-scale enterprises were heavily influenced by technologies and Fordist mass production techniques borrowed from the West, and managers frequently relied on some variation of a piece-rate system of wages in order to motivate and discipline the workforce.[11] However, in the absence of competition, these large-scale firms, many of them monopolies in their respective sectors or regional domains, retained large, often redundant, workforces, and were not penalized for the poor use of industrial capacity or the inefficient allocation of inputs. At the same time, in the midst of urbanization and rapid socio-economic

---

[9] See Lloyd Rudolph and Susanne Rudolph, *In Pursuit of Lakshmi* (Chicago: University of Chicago Press, 1987), 260.

[10] Weathers notes that trade union federations at the national level could be distinguished in terms of their ties to left-wing and right-wing parties and organizations, but this did not change the relatively homogeneous features of cooperative enterprise unionism across firms and sectors. Some, such as Jacoby, view the post-war Japanese system of industrial relations as a unique 'statist micro corporatism', to be distinguished from the 'macro corporatism' of Austria, Germany, and Scandinavia, while others refer to Japanese industrial relations as 'corporatism without labor'. See, respectively, Sanford Jacoby, 'Social Dimensions of Global Economic Integration', in Jacoby (ed.), *The Workers of Nations* (New York: Oxford University Press, 1995), 21–2; and T. J. Pempel and Kiichi Tsunekawa, 'Corporatism Without Labor? The Japanese Anomaly', in Schmitter and Lehmbruch (eds), *Trends Towards Corporatist Intermediation*, 231–70.

[11] Ironically, although socialist intellectuals had initially criticized Taylorism and Fordism as exploitative, after the Bolshevik Revolution, Lenin entusiastically supported the establishment of Taylorist practices, including a piece-rate wage system, over the objections of the trade unions. See Kendall Bailes, 'Alexei Gastev and the Soviet Controlversy over Taylorism, 1918–24', *Soviet Studies*, 29: 3 (July 1977), 373–94.

change, the large enterprises did contribute to the creation and maintenance of social order by providing employment and wage security and by serving as a key channel for the controlled allocation of many basic necessities. These ranged from company housing and rationed goods to recreational facilities. The privileged position given to large state enterprises, and to some private sector firms, produced noticeable differences in the wages, benefits, and status gained by permanent employees in these enterprises, resulting in a highly stratified workforce.[12] In sum, the imperative of catch-up industrialization combined with the simultaneous desire to overcome constraints posed by existing socio-economic structures—whether influenced by colonialism or pre-revolutionary feudal relations—to make the post-colonial and socialist state the dominant actor in inducing and managing economic and social change, and, in the process, shaping the character of labor relations.

Over the last decade or two, however, there has been a marked reduction in the level of state intervention in the management of industrial relations throughout all of these countries. Where the former socialist regimes have been replaced by new democratic regimes attempting to promote market-oriented economic reforms, the state has engaged in large-scale liberalization and privatization schemes and has deliberately sought a more restricted role for itself in the management of labor relations, in keeping with the suggestions of international financial institutions and western economic advisers. In most post-colonial settings, including such countries as India, Mexico, and Brazil, the state has significantly shifted course and has initiated reforms oriented towards economic liberalization, sometimes under the leadership of the same political elites that previously embraced state-led industrialization. In all of these cases, the old social pacts have given way to pressures for wage restraint and more flexible employment practices in the interest of enabling firms and national economies to become more efficient and productive in the face of global competition.

Thus, in both late-industrializing and post-socialist settings, many workers previously employed in large state-sector firms are seeing a sharp reduction in wage levels, employment security and welfare benefits as many of these firms are being privatized or are being forced to become more competitive and self-sufficient. It is not surprising, then, that organized labor in countries as diverse as Russia, India, and Mexico is struggling, through different strategies, to preserve the economic and social benefits they were previously accustomed to as firms are now being privatized or forced to reduce input costs associated with

---

[12] That is, the industrial workforce was not just differentiated into such standard categories as skilled, semi-skilled, and unskilled. In post-colonial late-industrializing countries, sharp differences appeared between workers in the informal sector, usually underpaid and lacking in benefits or employment security, and workers employed by large-scale public sector enterprises. In state-owned enterprises in socialist economies, employees in large 'closed enterprises'—usually in the heavy industry or defense sectors—received higher wages, additional benefits and privileges, as well as access to special goods than the most skilled workers in other state enterprises.

labor. Moreover, even if overall unemployment rates may not have risen every-where, the rates of underemployment, the inability of workers to secure enough work to meet minimum standards of living, have risen in most late-industrial-izing and post-socialist settings.[13] As a result, unskilled or semi-skilled work-ers, especially female workers, have had little choice but to take up jobs in the informal sector, and the growth of the latter, in turn, has increased the difficul-ties in defining and protecting the rights of workers in these sectors. In sum, there are important similarities in the difficulties and challenges that workers worldwide are now facing as a direct result of economic liberalization and of the subsequent exposure of previously shielded national and local economic actors to the pressures of global economic competition. The question that must then be addressed concerns the extent to which the potential solutions to these similar problems will also prove to be similar throughout the world.

Towards Tripartitism? Common Obstacles to Societal Corporatism

With the state retreating from the economy and the private sector growing in size and importance, one might expect that now, perhaps, industrial relations in post-colonial and post-socialist may be reframed in terms of a more bal-anced tripartite bargaining framework as part of a genuine 'societal corpo-ratism'. In a few instances, this has indeed been the case: in Ireland, as Doherty notes, corporatism is being renewed and strengthened, and in East-Central Europe, as Orenstein and Hale note, corporatist labor relations have been established and appear to be resilient. However, it must be remembered that the initiative for the (re)construction of corporatism has come from the state, and that Ireland, Hungary, the Czech Republic, and Poland are each relatively small states with relatively small, stable informal sectors and closer ties to the European Union. These characteristics are discussed further below, but for now, it is worth noting that they do not apply to most of the post-colonial and post-socialist economic transformations analyzed here. In most of these latter cases, balanced, effective tripartite bargaining frameworks have not been successfully established; the process through which social pacts are being renegotiated certainly involve organized labor, business, and the state, but there is nothing to suggest a convergence on a corporatist system of industrial relations. Three specific points are worth noting in this regard.

First, as noted in most of the chapters, including those by Doherty and Orenstein and Hale, although economic adjustment and market transitions suggest a retreat of the state from the management of industrial relations and

---

[13] In 1994, there were at least 120 million people registered as unemployed worldwide. This figure did not include the estimated 700 million people who were underemployed. In addition, since the 1980s and into the 1990s, more than 400,000 employees have been laid off each year by the world's largest firms. See Ankie Hoogvelt, *Globalization and the Postcolonial World* (Baltimore: Johns Hopkins University Press, 1997), 112–13, 139–40; and J. Rifkin, *The End of Work* (New York: Putnam's, 1995), esp. ch. 12.

from the economy at large, the state remains a major player not only in designing and implementing economic reform but also in influencing the transformation of existing labor institutions. In post-socialist and post-colonial
societies, ranging from China and Russia to India and Brazil, workers may
increasingly look to regional and firm-level social networks in their quest to
maintain or improve their livelihoods, but it is still the state—not business—
that is the focal point of the political struggles being waged over the efforts to
maintain wage and income security and over the renegotiation of social pacts.
To the extent that the private sector is larger and more active, it remains constrained in its ability to conclude formal pacts with organized labor without
the state's involvement in such matters as the reformulation of labor laws, the
establishment of new labor standards, and the overhauling of social welfare
systems.[14] Even the corporatist solutions in Ireland and East-Central Europe
have been engineered primarily by state elites attempting to maintain social
peace in the midst of economic liberalization. In other words, recent shifts in
the relative weights of state, business, and labor has not reduced the dominant
position of the former, particularly from the point of view of labor.

Second, corporatism requires peak business associations, but it is difficult
to identify the collective interests of 'business' in many of the post-socialist
and post-colonial economies studied in this volume. Medium-sized enterprises and even some large-scale enterprises are often enmeshed in regional
economies and have different interests and different approaches to wage bargaining and labor relations than do large-scale state enterprises operating on
a national level. Employers in sectors previously privileged by the state are
often at odds with employers in other sectors when it comes to adjusting their
approaches to labor relations as a result of economic liberalization. In addition, as Martin's analysis of automobile plants in Brazil and Mexico suggests,
sectors that are making the shift towards flexible production systems must
deal with different kinds of challenges than many of the traditional heavy
industrial sectors such as mining or steel. Variations in the interests of business actors by firm size and sector, of course, may be found even in the model
corporatist countries such as Austria, Germany, or the Scandinavian countries. The problem in post-colonial and post-socialist countries has to do with
the fact that, even within a given sector, business elites differ significantly
in terms of their political alliances, their dependence on state contracts,
and their orientations towards liberalization policies.[15] In post-socialist

[14] In India, for example, labor laws that make it difficult for firms to fire workers remain in
place and make it difficult for firms to release redundant workers despite the government's professed interest in becoming more competitive. Similarly, in Russia, it is the state that must come
up with an alternative solution to deal with pensions and accumulating wage arrears. In both
cases, company-level pacts do exist, but organized labor is looking at the state as its main negotiating partner.

[15] In India, for example, the Tata Corporation has not relied on government contracts and has
adopted its own form of enterprise paternalism including the establishment of company towns
for regular employees; the Birla Corporation, by contrast, relies heavily on government contracts
and has close ties to key bureaucracies or agencies.

economies, many of the new entrepreneurs are old party apparatchiks who had the initial capital to purchase stock in state-enterprises. In the case of Russia, as Sil notes, the failure of tripartitism can be traced to the very different kinds of interests and attitudes that characterize different groups of businessmen. While some private firms are managed by entrepreneurs eager to speed up market-oriented economic reforms, many directors of privatized firms have sought to slow down economic liberalization and maintain the social networks and understandings they developed under the command economy when they colluded with each other and with workers and party officials in order to meet plan targets, maximize their bonuses, and expand their black market activities. Thus, the growth of the private sector does not automatically point to the emergence of 'business' as a coherent, unified actor that can take its place alongside the state as a near-equal partner in a tripartite bargaining relationship.

Third, organized labor has also been struggling to define and advance a common agenda in both post-colonial and post-socialist contexts. In postcolonial settings, union membership rates have either dropped or national-level unions are finding themselves having to compete with local, firm-level, or sector-level workers' organizations in order to remain relevant. Candland notes the drop in membership rates among trade union federations in India as the continuing pattern of political unionism, wherein each trade union federation is linked to a national political party, has rendered unions less flexible and less able to deal with the new challenges facing workers. Similarly, as Murillo notes, while the CTM's relationship to the ruling party (PRI) may make it tolerant of economic liberalization policies initiated by Salinas, some of its sectoral affiliates (electricity, for example) have opposed economic reform. In post-socialist settings where the party-state apparatus collapsed, the trade union system may not have collapsed altogether, and this has far-reaching consequences for the prospects of organized labor. In Russia, for example, FITUR (Federation of Independent Trade Unions of Russia) inherited the leadership and the resources of the old trade union apparatus, and has attempted to retain these resources at all costs while regularly criticizing economic reformers; however, many of its sectoral affiliates as well as new trade union federations have often embraced economic liberalization, not so much because of their commitment to a market economy as because of their attempt to reduce the FITUR's position within organized labor. At the local level, as Lu and Sil note, the continued dependence of workers on their firms, whether privatized or not, for many crucial resources, along with sharp differences related to the resources available to the firms and their communities, suggests that workers will have a difficult time creating an independent and united labor movement.

Finally, there is also the question of the growing informal economy. In South Asia and Latin America, the informal economy has always accounted for a substantial portion of economic activity, but now, post-Soviet Russia and China, too, have large and growing informal sectors. And in many post-colonial and post-socialist settings, market-oriented economic reforms are resulting in workers becoming more dependent on these informal sectors for survival, although the informal workforce may be more fragmented and powerless in some places and more unified and locally effective in others.[16] The significant differences in the interests of organized labor and workers in the informal sector may not be new in the case of post-colonial late-industrializing countries as it is in post-socialist settings. However, the problems created for labor institutions everywhere by the partial retreat of the state from the management of the economy do give these differences new meanings. The creation or maintenance of working-class solidarity under these conditions is likely to prove extremely difficult.[17]

Defining elements of the overarching framework that emerge from the previous chapters are that there are some similar trends, legacies, and challenges in evidence in the evolution of industrial relations in countries where the state, after having played a dominant role in shaping the labor regime, is now undertaking significant economic reforms designed to reduce its role in the economy, but that significant variations across economies, regions, and firms continue to exist. Convergence of labor relations is not in evidence. The following two sections examine, in turn, variations related to the distinctive legacies of post-colonial underdevelopment and socialist development, and other, more context-specific, sources of variation within and across post-colonial and post-socialist regions.

Labor Relations in Late-industrializing and Socialist Economies: Two Distinct Legacies

The chapters in Part I and Part II of this volume, considered alongside each other, point to some important differences between labor relations in the contexts of post-colonial and socialist development. Certainly, in many respects, post-colonial countries embracing protectionist policies and economic nationalism are comparable to socialist countries, which set up command economies. However, it is significant that the former had some experience with a substantial private sector and some exposure to global capitalism. Thus, whereas globalization has certainly led to changes in post-colonial economies, in post-socialist regions, where state-run monopolies dominated the economy and where labor and management were both shielded from

[16] See Bryan Roberts, 'Informal Economy and Family Strategies', *International Journal of Urban and Regional Research*, 18 (March 1994), 6–23.

[17] However, as the emergence of new corporatist trends in Ireland and East-Central Europe suggest, where the workforce is less differentiated and where the informal sector is small and stable, it may be possible for organized labor to remain or become a relevant and unified actor in negotiating economic restructuring or transition. See the contributions of Doherty and Orenstein and Hale, Chapters 5 and 10 respectively.

international economic forces for decades, we are now witnessing the *creation* of an open market economy. Related to this general distinction are some other important variations between the kinds of labor regimes that emerged in the course of post-colonial and socialist late-industrialization.

To begin with, it is significant that labor regimes in post-colonial late indus-trializers were shaped by the nature of colonial administration and the char-acter of labor relations in the industries set up by colonial powers. In addition, post-independence labor regimes were influenced by the nature of the independence struggle, the manner in which post-independence political regimes were established, and the economic ideology that informed the coun-try's development strategy and the role assigned therein to labor.[18] At the same time, the quest for late-industrialization in all but a few 'Third World' countries was typically influenced by both western capitalism and socialist industrialization and, thus, tended to involve both public and private sec-tors.[19] State enterprises may have served as a model for private sector enter-prises, and the middle classes may have been relatively small and weak, but in most post-colonial countries, a private sector did exist, and upper and middle classes did own some of the means of production.[20] Under these conditions, organized labor may have been co-opted by ruling parties or populist dicta-tors, but developmental elites in post-colonial countries—ranging from India and Ireland to Mexico and Brazil—accepted the idea that workers had dis-tinct interests (at least *vis-à-vis* private sector employers) and required distinct bodies for representing those interests. As a result, a tradition of independent

---

[18] In Ireland, for example, Doherty notes that the fragmentation of organized labor can be traced back to the split between unions organized by the British and the new Irish unions which emerged after 1923. In India, the creation of a trade union wing under the Indian National Congress, combined with the subsequent dominance of the Congress Party during the first four decades of independence, set the stage the present system of political unionism with each trade union federation affiliated with a political party.

[19] Most newly independent countries very deliberately set out to find what Nehru called a 'third way' between capitalism and socialism. In the case of India, this 'third way' consisted of an economy in which the public and private sectors each accounted for 50% of the GNP. Elsewhere, the balance between public and private sectors may have varied considerably, but the point remains that leaders of most post-colonial countries, as a matter of principle, chose to established mixed economies in an effort to emulate the best of each system. Latin American countries, of course, became formally independent much earlier, but the quest for rapid industrialization and the effort to reduce dependence on more industrialized capitalist countries did not begin in earnest until the 1930s. Thus, although Latin American governments were far less enthusiastic about the concept of the 'Third World', they did adopt development programs that were more or less similar to those of more recently established post-colonial nations.

[20] This may not apply to such rare cases as Ne Win's Burma, Sukarno's Indonesia, or Uganda and Mozambique during the 1970s, but these cases are the exception rather than the rule. Even during Julius Nyerere's attempt to promote 'African socialism' in Tanzania, for example, the cre-ation of an autarkic statist economy and the collectivization of agriculture *(ujaama vijijini)* was not accompanied by the elimination of the private sector or the small but active urban middle class (largely consisting of Indians) which owned many small- and medium-sized businesses and engaged in money-lending activities.

trade unionism has emerged even in countries where trade union federations are affiliated with, or have been co-opted by, political parties.[21]

In marked contrast, in countries that came under the control of communist parties, the private sector was insignificant, the middle class was virtually non-existent, the industrial proletariat was glorified, and the developmental ideology was specifically based on the eventual elimination class conflict and of private property. Under these conditions, whatever role workers' organizations may have played in the establishment of communist regimes, trade unions were denied an independent role in the representation of workers' interests on the basis of an ideological faith in the absolute convergence of interests between the proletariat and the party that claimed to be its vanguard. Trade union federations were headed by party members and controlled by party elites who set the agenda for local or sectoral trade union committees. In effect, trade unions became little more than 'transmission belts' for communicating policies adopted by party-state elites to workers and managers in different branches and firms.[22] Moreover, in socialist countries, the state directly employed virtually the entire industrial workforce. The state set wages under non-market conditions, established internal passports to limit labor mobility, and made workers dependent on the enterprise for the allocation of even the most basic necessities, ranging from housing and education to basic foodstuffs and recreational facilities. Such problems as labor turnover, production slack, informal networks of collusion, and a burgeoning black market may have represented limits to the regime's control over the workforce. This does not alter the fact that there were few, if any, formal channels for the independent representation of workers' interests in socialist economies.

There are further differences between post-colonial and post-socialist countries related to the degrees and instruments of control the state exerted over workers and organized labor. The post-colonial state is typically much less autonomous and much less of a unitary actor. It is certainly true that labor institutions in post-colonial countries have been shaped from above by national and local legislation and the intervention of state administrative apparatuses, such as labor courts, factory inspectors, trade union registrars, and workers' welfare bodies; it is also true that the state has frequently been

---

[21] In the case of Mexico, for example, witness the ability of CTM's sectoral unions to pursue objectives and strategies that are quite different from what the CTM's national federation might call for. Similarly, in India, party affiliation does not keep organized labor as a whole from attempting to obstruct any changes in labor laws and block the lay-offs of redundant workers.

[22] Trade unions were sometimes mobilized for the purpose of purging management (as was the case during Stalin's attempt to replace en masse the directors of enterprises in the 1930s), but union members had little say in this as the initiative came from the party leadership. Since the 1960s, with increased discussions of 'socialist legalism', trade unions did begin to play a small role in cases where directors may have dismissed workers illegally or may have withheld pay. However, trade unions continued to work closely with the communist party leadership, the state ministries, and enterprise administration.

the largest, and often the model, employer, directly engaging in wage-setting, providing key resources and access to rationed goods, controlling the labor process, and recruiting and socializing workers. However, this does not change the fact that the post-colonial state is far more constrained in its ability to control or direct labor regimes when compared to socialist states. Government intervention in industrial relations, for example, may produce a segment of professional trade union leaders who themselves leave factory work, who are motivated by interests that may be different from those of the workers whom they represent, and who may be co-opted by government or by employers. Given the higher levels of mobility in the labor market and the possibility of alternative employment opportunities, workers in post-colonial settings, especially in smaller private sector firms, were much less dependent on their enterprises for basic economic necessities and social benefits.

This stands in marked contrast to the direct control exerted by the party-state apparatus in socialist countries. Even after the decline of overt coercion since the 1940s in the USSR and since the 1960s in China, the state was able to severely limit the mobility of workers. Mechanisms included an internal passport system that limited the opportunities for individuals to switch their places of residence, a system of labor books that kept a detailed record of individual workers' performance, including absences and violations of work rules, and a system of 'organized dependence' that kept workers reliant on state-owned enterprises for access to key goods and services.[23] Turnover did occur regularly; workers did find connections who would help them find jobs and apartments in different locations; and in labor-short economies, firms did have to compete with each other to retain a surplus labor force. But, the fact remains that labor 'markets' in socialist command economies severely constrained the mobility of workers except within a given enterprise.

At the same time, however, it is important to note that the industrial workforce in socialist economies did enjoy a significantly higher standard of living than has been the case for most workers in post-colonial regions. Even the most crowded apartments in Moscow, Prague or Budapest represented a 'great leap forward' over the slum dwellings found along the outskirts of (or even within) overcrowded cities such as Bombay, Rio de Janeiro or Mexico City. Despite periods of famine that were brought on by mass collectivization in the USSR and China, all socialist countries became self-sufficient in their food supply. The number of doctors and hospital beds available to the sick or injured grew rapidly while life-expectancy rose steadily. Literacy rates and skill levels climbed steadily among the industrial workforce as well as among the population at large. And for all the instruments available to the party-

[23] On 'organized dependence', see Andrew Walder, *Communist Neo-Traditionalism* (Berkeley: University of California Press, 1986). In the labor-short Soviet economy, there was more of a 'mutual dependence' as managers needed to maintain a surplus labor supply; see Stephen Crowley, 'Barriers to Collective Action: Steelworkers and Mutual Dependence in the Former Soviet Union', *World Politics*, 46: 4 (July 1994), 589–615.

state elite for controlling the workers, socialist states were theoretically workers' states. This meant that workers were guaranteed not only employment, but also generous welfare benefits ranging from educational and recreational facilities to subsidized foodstuffs, generous maternity leaves, child care, and automatic pensions, even for non-retirees. This also meant that despite the privileges accorded to political and economic elites, wage differentials across categories of workers, and between workers and management, were substantially narrower than is typically the case in most post-colonial societies, and in many advanced industrial countries. Workers may not have been satisfied with their jobs and they may have resented their managers or political leaders, but most did enjoy a far greater standard of living compared to the majority of workers in post-colonial societies.

By contrast, even in the most economically advanced and pluralistic postcolonial societies, the majority of workers—in most cases, the vast majority— have had to contend with conditions of mass urban and rural poverty. Most manufacturing workers toil for subsistence or below-subsistence wages under miserable working conditions and live in urban slums where high rates of mortality and malnutrition tend to be high.[24] This poverty, along with the persistence of feudal property structures and a high concentration of capital, often combine to severely distort labor markets to the point where they are hardly 'markets' in any meaningful sense. A choice between starvation or employment at subsistence or sub-subsistence wages cannot involve genuine freedom of contract.[25] The army of the unemployed—that is, a virtually inexhaustible pool of semi-skilled and unskilled labor—places a heavy downward pressure on wages. It is not surprising, then, that workers, as sellers of labor, often enter into 'agreements' of debt bondage, whereby they become lifelong indentured servants. Nor is it surprising, therefore, that the sale of labor power is often negotiated by representatives of labor without direct input of the workers themselves. Moreover, while the most skilled employees in large public-sector firms may receive wages and benefits commensurable with their counterparts in socialist state-owned enterprises, the differentials in the wages and benefits received by skilled and unskilled workers in different sectors tend to be dramatically higher. Thus, industrial labor in post-colonial settings tends to be far more stratified than was the case with the industrial

[24] In India, for example, recent studies note that the greater proportion of India's poor live in urban areas, and that rates of illness and mortality in urban slums are almost like those during the Industrial Revolution. See Robert Repetto *et al.*, *The 'Second India' Revisited* (Washington, DC: World Resources Institute, 1994); cited in William Stevens, 'Green Revolution is Not Enough, Study Finds', *New York Times* (6 Sept. 1994).

[25] This is not merely a rhetorical or theoretical point. Workers have starved to death in India because of late payment of wages. In May 1994, for example, nine workers starved to death on a tea plantation in Hailakandi district because their wage payments were delayed for several weeks, while four others were killed by police when they demanded immediate payment of their back-wages. *Reuters*, 'Indian Police Kill Four Tea Plantation Workers' (6 May 1994).

labor in socialist countries,[26] resulting in a much more significant informal sector in the former.

Closely related to the standard of living and the character of the labor market in socialist and post-colonial settings is the extent of the workers' ties to rural communities and to non-capitalist forms of production. Industrial development in the post-colonial world, even in Latin American countries, which are more urbanized than other post-colonial regions, has tended to produce dualistic economies with relatively small modern industrial enclaves operating within predominantly agricultural economies. As a result, many laborers still work in urban areas seasonally, returning to rural areas frequently. This permits industrialization in some cases to form parasitic relationships with non-capitalist forms of exploitation, with particular consequences for women and other non-paid producers and reproducers of labor power. Given the extent of poverty and the absence of adequate income or welfare security, a considerable portion of the industrial workforce in post-colonial countries, the vast majority in many cases, continues to maintain close ties that become essential to survival in the absence of adequate income or welfare provisions. In contrast, socialist countries, with the notable exception of China, have generally experienced a far more rapid pace of urbanization, with the vast majority of workers living in cities and working in factories while the size of the agrarian population and the contribution of agriculture to the GNP have both sharply declined since the World War II. This does not mean that regional identities were erased by urbanization or industrialization; it does mean that a much more permanent urban proletariat emerged in socialist settings than is the case with post-colonial settings where connections to rural economies remain an important feature of the labor market.

Finally, in many post-colonial countries, kinship ties and regional and ethnic identities are manipulated far more regularly for the purpose of more efficiently controlling wages, undermining workplace solidarity, and keeping labor disorganized. To be sure, networks based on kinship, region, or ethnicity have been in evidence in China, Russia, and other socialist countries. And the strong ties between workers in given sectors and the communities in which their enterprises are located have served as a substitute for ethnicity or kinship in socialist settings insofar as these ties have prevented the joint articulation of shared working-class interests. Nevertheless, these ties have not been manipulated by employers for controlling workers to the extent that they have been in many post-colonial countries. This is, in part, because workers were already constrained by the party-state apparatus and because of the universalist character of communist ideology in which primordial ties

---

[26] On the nature and extent of wage stratification in socialist settings, see Walter Connor, *Socialism, Politics and Equality* (New York: Columbia University Press, 1979); David Lane, *Soviet Labour and the Ethic of Communism* (Boulder: Westview Press, 1987), esp. 178; and Walder, *Communist Neo-Traditionalism*, esp. 227–40.

are deemed to be primitive and ethno-national identities are deemed to be bourgeois social constructions.

None of this suggests that workers were any more content or 'modern' under socialist regimes than in post-colonial, late-industrializing societies, as evident in the participation of workers in the East European 'velvet revolutions' of 1989 and in the miners' strikes of 1989 and 1991 that ultimately enabled Yeltsin to engineer the break-up of the USSR. Nor was the level of workers' solidarity in socialist settings higher than in post-colonial settings where the stratification of the workforce and the strength of ethnic or regional identities have more explicitly affected labor recruitment and management strategies for controlling workers. In both contexts, as noted above, economic crises and the collapse of communism have resulted in similar kinds of pressures in the wake of economic liberalization, state enterprises have been privatized, the downsizing of firms, and cutbacks in social spending. In both contexts, organized labor is struggling to define and advance an agenda that will appeal to a broader stratum of the industrial workforce. Nevertheless, for the purposes of comparing the responses of workers and organized labor to market-oriented economic reforms sweeping through these countries, it is worth bearing in mind that the workers previously employed by socialist factories were more urbanized and literate, were accustomed to a higher standard of living, and experienced a lower degree of stratification than is the case for most workers in post-colonial countries.

Thus, the decline in employment levels, real wages, and living standards for most workers in post-Soviet Russia is much more noticeable than is the case for the majority of workers in post-colonial countries who have been fighting off absolute poverty, malnutrition, disease, and early death for decades. Absolute immiseration may not necessarily provide a more powerful impetus for social movements than relative immiseration, but the objectives and dynamics of these movements are likely to be different in important ways. For example, wage arrears in post-socialist countries may lead workers to regularly complain and join in protests organized by trade unions, but these workers have not yet faced the kind of situation in post-colonial settings where the late payment of subsistence wages may result in death (see note 25). In addition, an unemployment rate of 9% or 10% is a source of much greater anxiety for workers previously accustomed to full employment than for workers in Brazil or India. As a result, organized labor is likely to gain more mileage out of the unemployment issue in post-socialist settings than in post-colonial settings. It is not surprising, therefore, that workers without job or income security in post-colonial settings maintain their ties to rural communities or to the informal sector in order to have some sort of a safety net, as has been the case in much of South Asia and Latin America, while those in post-socialist settings press for some form of continuing enterprise paternalism and state-supported welfare system, as is already evident in Russia and China.[27]

[27] Sil, Lu, and Kopstein point to the continuing tendency of workers in post-socialist contexts to treat their employers as the providers of not only regular salaries but also a range of social

In sum, while the ability of organized labor to increase or maintain its unity and strength may not systematically vary across post-socialist and post-colonial contexts, the expectations formed by different categories of workers based on their previous experiences are likely to affect how they define their goals and what individual and collective strategies they adopt in pursuing those goals in the face of new economic pressures stemming from liberalization and globalization. Thus, while the end of the cold war and the onset of globalization has made talk of a 'Second' and 'Third' world less meaningful, an overarching comparative framework for the study of contemporary trends in industrial relations must at least partially incorporate the systematic differences arising from the distinct experiences of workers and the nature of labor institutions that evolved under socialist and post-colonial industrialization.

Institutional Persistence and Historical Legacies: Other Sources of Variation

Given the differences noted above in the labor regimes formed under post-colonial and socialist settings, it is unlikely that labor, management, and the state in the two settings will gravitate towards any single institutional solution, corporatist or otherwise. However, it is just as unlikely that labor relations in post-socialist and post-colonial regions will travel along only two distinct trajectories towards two different outcomes. Rather, as the contributions in this volume suggest, if existing institutional arrangements are likely to play an important role in shaping the distinctive paths being traveled by organized labor and by workers at the national, sectoral and firm levels in different countries or regions, then a number of other sources of variation are likely to be found both within and across our categories of post-colonial and post-socialist political economy. These other sources of variation are likely to lead to a far more diverse set of outcomes than any one or two models will be able to account for. At least five points, each pointing to important questions deserving of further research, emerge from a more nuanced comparison of some of the cases covered in this volume.

First, whether we are discussing post-socialist or post-colonial economic reform, the influence of existing institutional arrangements or understandings on contemporary relations will vary depending on historical circumstances, leadership strategies, and international contexts. Indeed, in several of the cases discussed in this volume, institutional legacies are less constraining than in others, and the variation in the effects of these legacies is often significant. For example, as Candland points out, the repressed labor movement in Pakistan, which previously exerted very little influence over economic policy, has now began to adopt new, factory-level strategies and is beginning to have

benefits workers may not otherwise have access to. In contrast, in post-colonial settings, Candland, Murillo, and Doherty all emphasize the distinctions between trade union strategies adopted at the national level and the more fragmented strategies adopted by workers who rely more on their ties to local communities for safety nets.

some limited success in improving the position of some workers as Pakistan's economy undergoes structural adjustment. On the other hand, the continuity of large-scale political unionism in India has undermined the inability of organized labor to define a new agenda to cope with the new challenges facing workers since the late 1980s. And in Ireland, as Doherty notes, the past legacy of fragmentation among Irish trade union federations—a legacy that is evident at the firm and sectoral levels and that dates back to the split between British-organized unions and new Irish unions shortly after independence—remains evident at the firm or sectoral levels despite the establishment of a new social partnership, 'Partnership 2000', at the national level. Within post-socialist contexts, too, despite the fact that existing social institutions may continue to influence the behavior of workers and managers, in the former Soviet bloc, political and economic institutions were virtually replaced en masse. Under these conditions, institutional legacies of the past are unlikely to prevent economic actors from reaching new, unprecedented types of arrangements and social partnerships. Thus, while Lu, Sil, and Kopstein point to the continuing influence of existing moral understandings, as Orenstein and Hale's chapter suggests, the legacy of the old trade union structure is not much in evidence in East-Central Europe where the emergence of corporatist labor practices appears to signal a new era of industrial relations. Even in the case of Russia, where the old trade union federation has managed to survive and reorganize, the shift from a party-state-controlled trade union system to a more independent federation that opposes government policies is a significant one. The point is that differences in past institutional arrangements influence aspects of contemporary industrial relations in ways that cut across the post-socialist and post-colonial categories. Further, these differences have important consequences for variations in national, regional, sectoral, or firm-level labor institutions.

A second set of observations that cut across post-socialist and post-colonial settings relates to the response of organized labor to market-oriented economic reforms and globalization and to the extent to which this response is shaped by the overall structure of trade unionism. Organized labor has not universally opposed economic liberalization despite the consequences of liberalization for the wage levels, employment security, and welfare benefits for many categories of workers. In Mexico, Ireland, and East-Central Europe, the major trade union federations have cooperated with the government and have acknowledged the need for wage restraint during periods of economic adjustment. Even in Japan, a consensus is finally building towards a major restructuring of the economy. As Weathers notes, while workers will seek to uphold the tradition of 'lifetime' employment, there is little question that unions remain weak. Indeed, there seems to be an increasing awareness that some of the features of the Japanese 'model' of industrial relations will have to be sacrificed as part of the social cost of economic restructuring. In Russia, where the largest trade union (FITUR) continues to oppose radical economic reforms, many of the newer trade union organizations have embraced the reforms. As a result, FITUR has, in common with Indian trade unions, the dilemma of doggedly attempting to slow down the pace of economic liberalization, while being regarded by many segments of the population, including many categories of workers, as conservative or even irrelevant. Moreover, the contrast between India and Mexico—with organized labor in India generally obstructing such reforms as privatization, and the CTM federation in Mexico supporting key economic reforms—further suggests that the existence of political unionism does not by itself explain organized labor's support for market-oriented economic policies. Clearly, there remains more research to be done on the question of what factors generally incline some trade unions to accept economic policies that they find to have negative consequences for workers. The level of organized labor's support for various government economic policies may be easily explained in particular contexts, but a more nuanced framework is required to identify whether certain shared institutional features more generally account for organized labor's responses to economic reform and globalization.

The first two sets of observations directly relate to a third interesting pattern of variation. Continuities or changes in national industrial relations systems may or may not correlate with shifts in sectoral, local, or firm-level patterns of industrial relations. In some cases, especially where national trade union federations have had to support economic liberalization for political reasons, there have been direct splits between trade union federations and their sectoral affiliates. These variations in the linkages between national organized labor and labor movements or workers' behaviors at the subnational level suggest that the case for convergence in a global economy is even more tenuous. Perhaps the most obvious case of a split between national and regional patterns of industrial relations is evident in Germany where, as Kopstein notes, a new particularism has emerged among workers in East Germany as a result of distinct moral understandings linked to labor practices in the German Democratic Republic and very different from the (West) German system of industrial relations. In contrast, Orenstein and Hale's study of the emergence of corporatist labor practices in East-Central Europe does not suggest any significant differences between national and sectoral or firm levels as organized labor is proving to be relatively successful in representing the interests of most workers and delivering important social benefits. In Russia, in fact, FITUR's dogged opposition to Yeltsin's economic policies have prompted some of the competing trade unions and even some of the sectoral affiliates to embrace economic reform in order to weaken FITUR's position and improve their own standing among trade unions. In some postcommunist settings, as in the case of China and post-Soviet Russia, the impact of global economic forces has been mediated by regional or enterprise-based informal networks and practices that continue to survive despite the weakening or collapse of the official trade union federations created by the communist regimes. In post-colonial settings, this is most obvious in the case of Mexico where, as Murillo notes, the CTM's affiliation to the ruling PRI has prevented it from challenging Salinas' economic reforms, thus opening the door for challenges from CTM affiliates at the sectoral level. In cases such as India and Russia, where large, well-organized, national trade union federations are obstructing economic reform, the inability of organized labor to protect workers jobs and improve wage levels and income security has prompted workers to rely on informal bargains struck with either their firms or communities. In addition, Martin points out that the social ties binding workers' representatives to managers and local social forces have survived the impact of globalization and the arrival of flexible employment systems, and are now shaping the distinctive paths through which transitions to flexibility are being negotiated. In Ireland, changes in industrial relations appear to be coming from above rather than below. Despite the continuing fissures at the local level, a concerted effort is now under way to extend national-level social partnership so as to encompass firms and sectors facing new difficulties in the course of continuing liberalization.

This brings us to a fourth point. There is significant variation in the possibilities for societal corporatism in post-colonial and post-socialist contexts. As noted above, in Ireland and in a few of the countries in East-Central Europe, we do find the successful establishment of corporatist institutions explicitly modeled after western European corporatism. These cases, however, are not typical. First of all, as Doherty and Orenstein and Hale suggest, the emergence of corporatism had less to do with the inexorable logic of globalization than with particular historical circumstances and choices made by key elites at critical junctures. In East-Central Europe, as Orenstein and Hale note, the establishment of tripartitism can be traced back to the role of workers during the 'velvet revolution' and the strategies subsequently adopted by politicians, newly emergent business associations, and a reorganized labor movement following the establishment of new regimes and new legal and institutional frameworks since 1989. More importantly, several features are worth noting in regard to why these cases where corporatism appears to be succeeding may be the exception rather than the rule. Ireland, Poland, Hungary, and the Czech Republic are each relatively small economies. None has as diverse a labor force or as large an informal sector as large industrializing countries such as India, Brazil, Russia, or China. Each is in close proximity to advanced industrial economies, and each is the process of being more closely integrated into a larger, supranational economic union. These similarities may not point to a model *per se*. They do, however, raise questions about the prospects for societal corporatism where such features as a large and diverse labor market, a large and growing informal sector, and continued economic dependence upon advanced industrial countries are in evidence.[28]

---

[28] This emergent hypothesis is based in part on a logic not unlike the one underlying Peter Katzenstein's comparative study of how small European states design industrial policies in similar ways. See his *Small States in World Markets* (Ithaca: Cornell University Press, 1985).

Finally, there is the question of old and new democracies. Of the cases examined in this volume, China alone has yet to experience competitive multiparty elections, and China and Pakistan probably represent the two countries where trade union federations have had the least independent influence on national economic and social policy. On the other end, India and Ireland have relatively stable parliamentary democracies that have been around for decades, and genuine national and regional multiparty competition has now emerged in the place of the domination of post-independence parties. Yet, India and Ireland have produced very different systems of industrial relations, with trade union federations in the former continuing to exist as wings of competing parties and trade unions in the latter seeking to negotiate as a separate entity with management and the state. The vast majority of the regions examined in this volume are emergent democracies, ranging from post-1985 Brazil to post-1989 eastern Europe and post-1991 Russia. The stability and effectiveness of democratic institutions clearly varies across these countries, although in all cases, strong executive branches have emerged as key players in the crafting of economic reforms. Clearly, the nature of existing political systems or the institutions emerging in the course of post-authoritarian transitions are having an important influence on the strategies of organized labor as it seeks to maintain or improve workers' livelihoods. In East-Central Europe, for example, the parliaments have a more significant role to play compared to Russia, where the president frequently decrees key laws and economic policies, and this may account for the success of tripartitism in the former and its utter failure in the latter. Similarly, as Candland's comparative study shows, authoritarian leaders in Pakistan prevented militant labor movement from influencing economic policy to the extent that Indian unions are able. However, this may also account for the somewhat greater success Pakistani labor has had more recently at the local level or firm level in the midst of economic restructuring. These observations suggest that it would be worthwhile to conduct further comparative research on the opportunities and constraints encountered by unions and workers as a direct result of particular features of political regimes and political transitions.

In sum, while economic reform and the subsequent exposure to global economic forces has created some common problems, and while the differences between labor regimes formed during post-colonial and socialist industrialization may lead to important, systematic differences in post-colonial and post-socialist labor relations, there are a variety of other patterns that have emerged from the analyses presented in this volume. These patterns are not fully accounted for here, but they do point to further questions that need to be systematically researched within more nuanced comparative frameworks. Why are institutional legacies more persistent and more consequential in some cases than in others? Are there specific factors that account for the response of organized labor to market-oriented economic reforms initiated by governments? Are there particular causes and consequences derived from the manner in which national systems of industrial relations are tied to local, sectoral, or firm-level labor practices? What factors generally account for the emergence of stable tripartite bargaining frameworks? And how do the differences between different kinds of authoritarian regimes and parliamentary or presidential democratic systems affect the responses of organized labor to new economic policies and new economic conditions? We do not pretend to have the answers to these questions, but the discussions above can provide a basis for further, systematic comparative research into how certain clusters of historical circumstances, institutional characteristics, and international factors can combine to produce particular combinations of opportunities and constraints for workers and unions as they respond to global economic forces.

Conclusion

The question of workers' changing conditions in the global economy is an extremely important one. It has received some serious attention recently, but most of this attention deals with how workers and unions in advanced industrial countries are being affected by transnational flows of goods, capital, and technology. Workers in countries such as China, India, Russia, and Brazil represent a very large percentage of the world's labor force. While some workers are benefiting from new job opportunities created by transformations in the global economy, many other workers find themselves losing whatever material benefits, rights, and protection they were beginning to enjoy. At the same time, nowhere in the world and at no time in history have workers remained passive for long in the face of new threats to their livelihoods or living standards. Even if they lack the means to resist the changes in work organization, political unionism, or employment terms accompanying globalization, they have diverse experiences and diverse 'repertoires of contention' to draw upon as they seek to get by under the changing conditions and as they seek to strike formal and informal bargains with employers, governments, local communities, and even other workers.

The chapters in this volume trace the fundamental changes under way in industrial relations, at national, sectoral, local, or workplace levels, while examining the distinctiveness of the institutions and emergent strategies in each of the countries analyzed. They provide the empirical foundation for the contention that the dynamics of the increasingly interdependent global economy are better understood not as a set of inexorable forces producing convergent trends, policies, and institutions, but rather as a set of relationships between workers, owners, and state managers. Most of the authors recognize that globalization has generally weakened the political power of organized labor, but they do not find evidence of workers passively accepting their fates. Rather, the studies here find workers making attempts to redefine their roles and find new strategies for protecting and advancing their shared interests. Distinctive institutional practices and historical legacies inherited by different categories of workers, and by political and business elites, condition workers' expectations, interests, and behaviors as they redefine their goals and devise individual and collective strategies to achieve those goals.

BIBLIOGRAPHY

'9 killed in U.P. firing on workers', *Times of India* (4 June 1991).

AGH, ATTILA and GABRIELLA ILONSZKI, *Parliaments and Organized Interests: The Second Steps* (Budapest: Hungarian Centre for Democracy Studies, 1996).

AGUILAR, GARCÍA JAVIER and LORENZO ARRIETA, 'En la fase más aguda de la crisis y en el inicio de la reeestructuración o modernización', in Javier García Aguilar (ed.), *Historia de la CTM: 1936–1990*, 2 (Mexico City: Instituto de Investigaciones Sociales, UNAM, 1990).

AHMED, KHURSHID [General Secretary, Pakistan WAPDA Hydroelectric Central Labour Unions], interview, (Lahore, Pakistan, 8 December 1995).

AHMED, MUNEER, 'The November Mass Movement in Pakistan', *Political Sociology: Perspectives on Pakistan* (Lahore: Punjab Adbi Markaz, 1978/1974), 1–56.

AKERLOFF, GEORGE, ANDREW ROSE, and JANET YELLEN, 'East Germany in from the Cold: The Economic Aftermath of Currency Union', Brookings Papers on Economic Activity, 1 (1991).

ALBROW, MARTIN, *The Global Age* (Stanford, CA: Stanford University Press, 1996).

ALEXANDER, JEFFREY C., 'Modern, Anti, Post and Neo', *New Left Review*, 210 (March–April 1995).

ALI, SUBASHINI [Communist Party of India Member of Parliament from Kanpur district], interview (Kanpur, 22 December 1991).

All Pakistan State Enterprises Workers' Action Committee, 'Accord signed with the Govt', mimeograph, 1991. (Summarized in GoP, *Economic Survey 1991–92*, Islamabad, 1992.)

ALLEN, KIERAN, *Fianna Fail and Irish Labour* (Chicago: Pluto Press, 1997).

ALVARADO, ARTURO, 'La fundación del PNR', in *El Partido en el Poder*, (Mexico City: IEPES, 1991).

ALVES, MARIA HELENA MOREIRA, *State and Opposition in Military Brazil* (Austin, TX: University of Texas Press, 1985).

AMIN, ASH (ed.), *Post-Fordism: A Reader* (Oxford: Blackwell, 1994).

APTER, DAVID, 'System, Process and the Politics of Economic Development', in B. F. Hoselitz and W. E. Moore (eds), *Industrialization and Society* (The Hague: Mouton, 1963).

ARBIX, GLAUCO, *Uma Aposta no Futuro: Os Tres Primeiros Anos da Câmara Setorial da Industria Automotiva Brasileira* (São Paulo: Scritta, 1996a).

—— 'Trabalho: Dois Modelos de Flexibilização', *Lua Nova*, 37 (1996b), 171–90.

—— and IRAM JÁCOME RODRIGUES, 'The Transformation of Industrial Relations in the Brazilian Automotive Industry', in John P. Tuman and John T. Morris (eds), *Transforming the Latin American Automobile Industry: Unions, Workers, and the Politics of Restructuring* (Armonk, NY: M. E. Sharpe, 1998b), 77–94.

ARNAUD, ALBERTO, 'Historia de una Profesión: Maestros de Educatión Primaria en México: 1887–1993'. Unpublished MA thesis (Centro de Estudios Internacionales, El Colegio de México, 1993).

ARNULFO, ARTEAGA, 'La reestructuración de la industria automotriz en México y sus repercusiones en el viejo núcleo fabril', in Arnulfo Arteaga (ed.), *Proceso de Trabajo y Relaciones Laborales en la Industria Automotriz en México* (Mexico City: Fundación Ebert and UAM-Iztapalapa, 1992).

ARTEAGA, ARNULFO, 'Ford: un largo y sinuoso camino', in Graciela Bensusán and Samuel León (eds), *Negociación Colectiva y Conflicto Laboral en México* (Mexico City: Fundación Ebert and Flacso, 1990).

—— *Proceso de Trabajao y Relaciones Laborales en la Industria Automotriz en México* (México, DF.: Universidad Autónoma Metropolitana, Unidad Iztapalapa, and Fundación Friedrich Ebert, Representación en México, 1992).

ASLUND, ANDERS, 'The Russian Road to the Market', *Current History* (October 1995), 311–16.

ASPE, PEDRO, *El Camino Mexicano de la Transformación Económica* (Mexico City: Fondo de Cultura Económica, 1993).

AZIZ NASSIF, ALBERTO, *El Estado Mexicano y la CTM* (Mexico City: Ed. La Casa Chata, 1989).

AZRAEL, JEREMY, *Managerial Power and Soviet Politics* (Cambridge: Harvard University Press, 1966.

BABSON, STEVE, *Lean Work: Empowerment and Exploitation in the Global Auto Industry* (Detroit: Wayne State University Press, 1995).

BACZKOWSKI, ANDRZEJ, 'In Search of Optimum Solutions', in *Tripartism and Industrial Relations in Central and Eastern European Countries* (Warsaw: Ministry of Labour and Social Policy, 1994).

BAGLIONE, LISA and CAROL CLARK, 'Contemporary Labor Relations in Russian Industry: A Study of Two Metallurgical Enterprises', Paper presented at the Annual Meeting of the American Political Science Association (San Francisco, 20 August–1 September 1996).

BAILES, KENDALL, 'Alexei Gastev and the Soviet Controversy over Taylorism, 1918–24', *Soviet Studies*, 29: 3 (July 1977), 373–94.

BAKER-SAID, STEPHANIE, 'Paid Off, Then Laid Off', *Moscow Times* (21 April 1998).

BAKSHI, C. R., 'Bailadila Privatisation', *Trade Union Record* (20 October and 5 November 1995), 35–6.

BAKSHI, RAJNI, 'The Legacy of a Marathon Struggle', *The Hindu* (20 September 1992).

BALANANDAN, E., 'Presidential Address to the Working Committee Meeting (annual) of the All India Trade Union Congress, 2 November 1995 (Bhilai)', *The Working Class*, 25: 4 (December 1995) (New Delhi: AITUC), 5–6.

BAMBER, GREG J., and VALENTIN PESCHANSKI, 'Transforming Industrial Relations in Russia: A Case of Convergence With Industrialized Market Economies?', *Industrial Relations Journal*, 27: 1 (1996), 74–88.

BANURI, TARIQ and EDWARD AMADEO, 'Words Within the Third World: Labour Market Institutions in Asia and Latin America', in Tariq Banuri (ed.), *Economic Liberalization: No Panacea, The Experiences of Latin America and Asia* (Oxford: Clarendon Press, 1991), 171–220.

BARBER, BENJAMIN, 'Jihad vs. McWorld', *The Atlantic Monthly*, 269: 3 (March 1992).

BARTLETT, DAVID, *The Political Economy of Dual Transformations: Market Reform and Democratization in Hungary* (Ann Arbor: University of Michigan Press, 1997).

Beijing Review (Beijing).

BEISSINGER, MARK, *Scientific Management, Socialist Discipline, and Soviet Power* (Cambridge: Harvard University Press, 1988).

BELANGER, JACQUES, P. K. Edwards, and Larry Haiven (eds), *Workplace Industrial Relations and the Global Challenge* (Ithaca, NY: ILR Press, 1994).

BENDERS, JOS, 'Leaving Lean? Recent Changes in the Production Organization of Some Japanese Car Plants', *Economic and Industrial Democracy*, 17 (1996), 9–38.

BENDIX, REINHARD, *Work and Authority in Industry: Ideologies of Management in the Course of Industrialization* (New York: Wiley, 1956).

BENNETT, DOUGLAS C., and KENNETH E. SHARPE, *Transnational Corporations Versus the State: The Political Economy of the Mexican Auto Industry* (Princeton: Princeton University Press, 1985).

BENSUSÁN, GRACIELA, 'Institucionalización laboral en México. Los años de la definición (1917–1931)', PhD dissertation (UNAM, 1992).

——and CARLOS GARCÍA, 'Entre la estabilidad y el conflicto: Relaciones laborales en Volkswagen de México', in Arnulfo Arteaga (ed.), *Proceso de Trabajao y Relaciones Laborales en la Industria Automotriz en México* (México, DF: Universidad Autónoma Metropolitana, Unidad Iztapalapa, and Fundación Friedrich Ebert, Representación en México, 1992).

——'Los determinantes institucionales de la flexibilización laboral', in *Revista Mexicana de Sociología*, 1 (1994), 45–78.

——and CARLOS GARCÍA, *Opiniones Sindicales sobre la Reforma Laboral* (Mexico City: Fundación Ebert, 1993).

————'Entre la tradición y el cambio: El corporativismo sindical en México', in Silvia Portella (ed.), *Sindicalismo Latinoamericao entre la Renovación y la Resignación* (Caracas: Nueva Sociedad, 1995), 67–82.

——and SAMUEL LEÓN, *Negociación colectiva y conflicto laboral en México* (Mexico City: Fundacion Ebert-Flacso, 1990).

BERGER, SUZANNE and RONALD DORE (eds), *National Diversity and Global Capitalism* (Ithaca, NY: Cornell University Press, 1996).

BERGGREN, CHRISTIAN, *Alternatives to Lean Production: Work Organization in the Swedish Auto Industry* (Ithaca, NY: ILR Press, 1992).

BERTRANÚ, JULIÁN, 'La política de la reforma a la seguridad social en México', MS, *Flacso-Sede México* (Mexico City, 1994).

BHATT, ELA, 'SEWA is Heading Towards Full Employment at the Household Level', interview with Sindhu Menon, in *Labour File*, 2: 4 (April 1996), 19–22.

BIRD, RICHARD, ROBERT EBEL, and CHRISTINE WALLICH (eds), *Decentralization of the Socialist State: Intergovernmental Finance in Transition Economies* (Washington, DC: World Bank, 1995).

BIZBERG, ILÁN, *Estado y sindicalismo en México* (Mexico City: El Colegio de México, 1990).

BIZYUKOV, PETR, 'The Mechanisms of Paternalistic Management of the Enterprise', in Simon Clarke (ed.), *Management and Industry in Russia: Formal and Informal Relations in the Period of Transition* (Brookfield, VT: Edward Elgar, 1995).

BLACK, BERNARD, REINIER KRAAKMAN, and ANNA TARASSOVA, 'Russian Privatization and Corporate Governance: What Went Wrong?', *John M. Olin Program in Law and Economics Working Paper No. 178* (Stanford Law School, September 1999).

BLASI, JOSEPH R., MAYA KROUMOVA, and DOUGLAS KRUSE, *Kremlin Capitalism: Privatizing the Russian Economy* (Ithaca, NY: Cornell University Press, 1997).

BLAUNER, ROBERT, *Alienation and Freedom* (Chicago: University of Chicago Press, 1964).

BLUNDY, ANNA, 'Youth Suicides Plague Russia', *The Times (UK)* (3 November 1998).

BLYTON, PAUL and J. MORRIS (eds), *A Flexible Future: Prospects for Employment and Organization* (New York: Walter de Gruyter, 1991).

BOERI, TITO, 'Learning from Transition Economies: Assessing Labor Market Policies across Central and Eastern Europe', *Journal of Comparative Economics*, 25: 3 (December 1997), 366–84.

BOITO, ARMANDO, 'Reforma e persistência da estrutura sindical Brasileira', in Armando Boito (ed.), *O Sindicalismo Brasileiro nos Anos 80* (Rio de Janeiro: Paz e Terra, 1991).

BOSWELL, TERRY and DIMITRIS STEVIS, 'Globalization and International Labor Organizing: A World-System Perspective', *Work and Occupations*, Special Issue on Labor in the Americas, 24: 3 (August 1997), 288–307.

BOYD, ROSALYND, ROBIN COHEN, and PETER GUTKIND (eds), *International Labour and the Third World: The Making of a New Working Class* (Brookfield, VT: Avebury, 1987).

BOYER, ROBERT, 'Do Labour Institutions Matter for Economic Development? A "Regulation" Approach for the OECD and Latin America With an Extension to Asia', in Gerry Rodgers (ed.), *Workers, Institutions and Economic Growth in Asia* (Geneva: International Institute for Labour Studies, 1995).

—— 'The Convergence Hypothesis Revisited: Globalization But Still the Century of Nations?', in Berger and Dore (eds), *National Diversity and Global Capitalism* (Ithaca, NY: Cornell University Press, 1996).

BRANDELL, INGA (ed.), *Workers in Third-World Industrialization* (New York: St. Martin's Press, 1991).

BRESCIANI, LUIZ PAUL, 'The Challenge to the "ABC" Region: Productive Restructuring and Metal Workers' Strategies in Brazil's Auto Industry Heart', Paper presented at the Fifth Colloquium of GERPISA (Paris, June 1997).

BROWN, CLAIR, YOSHIFUMI NAKATA, MICHAEL REICH, and LLOYD ULMAN, *Work and Pay in the United States and Japan* (New York/Oxford: Oxford University Press, 1997).

BRUNNER, HANS-PETER, 'German Blitz-Privatization', *Transition: The Newsletter About Reforming Economies*, 6: 4 (April 1995).

BRYANT, RALPH, 'Global Change: Increasing Economic Integration and Eroding Political Sovereignty', *Brookings Review*, 12: 4 (Fall 1994), esp. 42–5.

BUNCE, VALERIE, 'The Political Economy of the Brezhnev Era: The Rise and Fall of Corporatism', *British Journal of Political Science*, 13 (April 1983), 129–58.

—— and JOHN ECHOLS, 'Soviet Politics in the Brezhnev Era: "Pluralism" or "Corporatism"', in Donald Kelly (ed.), *Soviet Politics in the Brezhnev Era* (New York: Praeger, 1980).

BURAWOY, MICHAEL, 'View From Production: The Hungarian Transition from Socialism to Capitalism', in Chris Smith and Paul Thompson (eds), *Labour in Transition: The Labour Process in Eastern Europe and China* (London: Routledge, 1992), 180–99.

—— 'The State and Economic Involution: Russia Through a China Lens', *World Development*, 24 (June 1996), 1105–17.

——and PAVEL KROTOV, 'The Soviet Transition from Socialism to Capitalism: Worker Control and Economic Bargaining in the Wood Industry', *American Sociological Review*, 57 (February 1992).

——and JANOS LUKACS, *The Radiant Past: Ideology and Reality in Hungary's Road to Capitalism* (Chicago: University of Chicago Press, 1992).

BURGESS, KATRINA, 'Thresholds of Institutional Change: Economic Reform and Party-Labor Relations in Mexico', Paper prepared for delivery at the conference 'Economic Reform and Civil Society in Latin America', David Rockefeller Center for Latin American Studies, Harvard University (12 April 1996).

BURT, RONALD S., *Toward a Structural Theory of Action: Network Models of Social Structure, Perception, and Action* (New York: Academic Press, 1982).

'Cabinet Decides to Privatize IISCO', *The Statesman* (27 November 1993).

CABLE, VINCENT, 'The New Trade Agenda: Universal Rules Amid Cultural Diversity', *International Affairs*, 72: 2 (April 1996), 227–46.

CALDERÓN, FELIPE [Secretary-General of the PAN], personal interview (Mexico City, 14 April 1995).

CALLAGHY, THOMAS, 'Toward State Capacity and Embedded Liberalism in the Third World: Lessons for Adjustment', in Nelson (ed.), *Fragile Coalitions: The Politics of Economic Adjustment* (New Brunswick, NJ: Transaction Books, 1989), 115–38.

CALMFORS, LARS and JOHN DRIFFILL, 'Centralization and Wage Barganing', *Economic Policy*, 3: 1 (1988), 13–61.

CAMACHO, MANUEL, *El futuro inmediato* (Mexico City: Ed. Siglo XXI, 1980).

CAMERON, DAVID, 'Social Democracy, Corporatism, Labor Quiescence, and the Representation of Economic Interest in Advanced Capitalist Society', in John Goldthorpe (ed.), *Order and Conflict in Contemporary Capitalism* (New York/Oxford: Oxford University Press, 1984).

CAMP, RODERIC AI, *Politics in Mexico: The Decline of Authoritarianism* (3rd edn) (New York: Oxford University Press, 1999).

CAMPUZANO MONTOYA, IRMA, 'El impacto de la crisis en la CTM', *Revista Mexicana de Sociología*, 3 (1990), 161–90.

CANDLAND, CHRISTOPHER, 'Trade Union Development and Industrial Restructuring in India and Pakistan', *Bulletin of Concerned Asian Scholars*, 27: 4 (October–December 1995), 63–78.

CARDOSO, ADALBERTO MOREIRA, 'Globalização e relações industriais na indústria automobilístico Brasileiro: Um estudo de caso', *Avances de Investigacíon. Bremen, Germany, and São Paulo: Transformación Económica y Trabajo en América Latina: Proyecto Comparativo Internacional*, 2 (September 1995).

CARDOSO, FERNANDO HENRIQUE and ENZO FALETTO, *Dependencia y Desarrollo en América Latina* (Buenos Aires: Ed. Siglo XXI, 1969).

CARRIERE, JEAN, NIGEL HAWTHORN, and JACQUELINE RODDICK, *The State, Industrial Relations and the Labour Movement in Latin America* (Basingstoke, UK: Macmillan, 1989).

CARRILLO, JORGE, 'La Ford en México: restructuración industrial y cambio en las relaciones sociales'. Unpublished PhD dissertation (México, DF: Centro de Estudios Sociológicos, El Colegio de México, 1993).

Centre for Labour Market Studies, *Formation of Social Partnership in the Russian Federation* (Institute of Economics, Russian Academy of Sciences, 1995).

CERNY, PHILIP, 'Globalization and the Changing Logic of Collective Action', *International Organization*, 49: 4 (Autumn 1995), 595–625.

CHAN, ANITA, 'Revolution or Corporatism? Workers and Trade Unions in Post-Mao China', *The Australian Journal of Chinese Affairs*, 29 (1993), 31–61.

——'Chinese Danwei Reforms: Convergence with the Japanese Model?', in Xiaobo Lu and Elizabeth Perry (eds), *Danwei: The Changing Chinese Workplace in Historical and Comparative Perspective.* (Armonk, NY: M. E. Sharpe 1997), 169–94.

CHANDRA DAS, PRAFULLA, *Trade Union and Politics in India: A Study of Orissa* (New Delhi: Discovery Publishing House, 1990).

CHATTERJI, RAKHAHARI, *Unions, Politics and the State: A Study of Indian Labour Practices* (New Delhi: South Asian Publishers, 1980).

CHETVERNINA, T., P. SMIRNOV, and N. DUNAEVA, 'Unions' Place At an Enterprise', *Economic Problems* [in Russian], 6 (1996), 83–9.

CHIROT, DANIEL, 'The Corporatist Model and Socialism', *Theory and Society*, 9 (1980), 363–81.

CHUMA HIROYUKI, KENSHO, *Nihon-gata 'koyo chosei'* [Investigation: Japanese-style 'Employment Adjustment'] (Tokyo: Shueisha, 1994).

CLARK, CAROL, 'The Transformation of Labor Relations in Russian Industry: The Influence of Regional Factors in the Iron and Steel Industry', *Post-Soviet Geography and Economics*, 37: 2 (1996), 88–112.

CLARK, MARJORIE RUTH, *Organized Labor in Mexico* (Chapel Hill: University of North Carolina Press, 1934).

CLARK, RODNEY, *The Japanese Company* (New Haven, CT: Yale University Press, 1979).

CLARKE, SIMON, 'Privatisation and the Development of Capitalism in Russia', in Peter Clarke, Michael Burawoy, Peter Fairbrother, and Pavel Krotov (eds), *What About the Workers? Workers and the Transition to Capitalism in Russia* (London: Verso, 1993).

——'Post-Communism and the Emergence of Industrial Relations at the Workplace', in Richard Hyman and Anthony Ferner (eds), *New Frontiers in European Industrial Relations* (Oxford: Blackwell, 1994).

——'Formal and Informal Relations in Soviet Industrial Production', in Simon Clarke (ed.), *Management and Industry in Russia: Formal and Informal Relations in the Period of Transition* (Brookfield, VT: Edward Elgar, 1995a), 1–27.

—— *Management and Industry in Russia: Formal and Informal Relations in the Period of Transition* (Brookfield, VT: Edward Elgar, 1995b).

—— MICHAEL BURAWOY, PETER FAIRBROTHER, and PAVEL KROTOV (eds), *What About the Workers? Workers and the Transition to Capitalism in Russia* (London: Verso, 1993).

CLIFTON, JUDITH CATHERINE, 'The Politics of Privatization in Mexico: Telecommunications and State-Labour Relations (1988–1994)', *Papeles de Trabajo de América Latina Contemporánea 0397*, (Madrid: Instituto Universitario Ortega y Gasset, 1997).

COLE, ROBERT E., 'Japanese Workers, Unions and the Marxist Appeal', *The Japan Interpreter*, 6: 2 (Summer 1970), 114–34.

—— *Japanese Blue Collar: The Changing Tradition* (Berkeley/Los Angeles: University of California Press, 1971).

——*Strategies for Learning: Small-group Activities in American, Japanese, and Swedish Industry* (Berkeley/Los Angeles/Oxford: University of California Press, 1989).

COLLIER, RUTH BERINS, 'Popular Sector Incorporation and Political Supremacy', in Sylvia Ann Hewlett and Richard S. Weinert (eds), *Brazil and Mexico: Patterns in Late Development.* (Philadelphia: Institute for the Study of Human Issues, 1982).

——and DAVID COLLIER, *Shaping the Political Arena: Critical Junctures, the Labor Movement and Regime Dynamics in Latin America* (Princeton: Princeton University Press, 1991).

——and JAMES SAMSTAD, 'Mexican Labor and Structural Reform: New Unionism or Old Stalemate?', in Riordan Roett (ed.), *The Challenge of Institutional Reform in Mexico* (Boulder, CO: Lynne Rienner, 1995).

COLLINGSWORTH, TERRY, J. WILLIAM GOOLD and PHARIS J. HARVEY, 'Time for a Global New Deal', *Foreign Affairs* (January–February 1994), 8–13.

Committee for the Study of Labor Issues, Japan Federation of Employers' Associations (Nikkeiren), 'Structural Reform—The Search for a Third Option. Employment Stability and Improved National Quality of Life', Nikkeiren Position Paper for 1997.

CONNOR, WALTER, *Socialism, Politics and Equality: Hierarchy and Change in Eastern Europe and the USSR* (New York: Columbia University Press, 1979).

——*The Accidental Proletariat: Workers, Politics, and Crisis in Gorbachev's Russia* (Princeton: Princeton University Press, 1991).

——*Tattered Banners: Labor, Conflict, and Corporatism in Postcommunist Russia* (Boulder, CO: Westview, 1996).

CONRADT, DAVID P. *et al.*, *Germany's New Politics* (Tempe, AZ: German Studies Review, 1995).

COOK, LINDA, *The Soviet Social Contract and Why It Failed: Welfare Policy and Workers' Politics from Brezhnev to Yeltsin* (Cambridge: Harvard University Press, 1993).

——'Russia's Labor Relations: Consolidation or Disintegration?', in Douglas W. Blum (ed.), *Russia's Future: Consolidation or Disintegration?* (Boulder, CO: Westview, 1994).

——'Workers in the Russian Federation: Responses to the Post-Communist Transition, 1989–1993', *Communist and Post-Communist Studies*, 28 (March 1995), 13–32.

CORNELIUS, WAYNE A., 'Mexican Politics in Transition: The Breakdown of a One-Party-Dominant Regime', Monograph series 41 (San Diego: University of California, San Diego, Center for U.S.-Mexican Studies, 1996).

Council of Economic and Social Agreement of the Czech Republic (Prague 1993).

COVARRUBIAS, ALEJANDRO, 'Actitudes obreras y compromiso organizacional en la industria automotriz mexicana: Transformaciones bajo sistemas de produccion flexibles', Paper presented at the conference 'Globalização, Reestruturação Produtiva e Transformação nas Relações Capital-Trabalho no Complexo Automobílistico', Centro Brasileiro de Análise e Planejamento (São Paulo, August 1996), 26–8.

CRAWFORD, BEVERLY (ed.), *Markets, States, and Democracy: The Political Economy of Post-Communist Transformation* (Boulder, CO: Westview, 1995).

CROWLEY, STEPHEN, 'Barriers to Collective Action: Steelworkers and Mutual Dependence in the Former Soviet Union', *World Politics*, 46: 4 (July 1994), 589–615.

—— 'Coal Miners, Cultural Frameworks, and the Transformation of the Soviet Political Economy', Paper presented at the Annual Meeting of the American Political Science Association (San Francisco, 29 August–1 September 1996).

—— *Hot Coal, Cold Steel: Russian and Ukrainian Workers from the End of the Soviet Union to the Post-Communist Transformations* (Ann Arbor: University of Michigan Press, 1997).

CTM, *Memorias de la CXI Asamblea Ordinaria de la CTM* (Mexico City, 1990).

—— *Memorias de la CXII Asamblea Ordinaria de la CTM* (Mexico City, 1991).

—— *La CTM y la Economia de los Trabajadores* (Mexico City, 1993).

—— *Memorias de la CXV Asamblea Ordinaria de la CTM* (Mexico City, 1993).

—— *Memorias de la CXVI Asamblea Ordinaria de la CTM* (Mexico City, 1994).

—— 'Congreso Nacional de Empresas y Organismos del Sector Social', in *CTM: Cincuenta Años de Lucha Obrera* (Mexico City: Instituto de Capacitación Política del PRI, 1994).

DALTON, RUSSELL, 'Germany's Vote for the "New Middle"', *Current History*, 98: 626 (1999), 176–80.

Das Parliament (Bonn), 17/24 January 1997, 1.

DATAR, B. N., 'Trade Union Recognition', (Bombay: Lala Lajpat Rai College of Commerce and Economics, 1983).

DE LA GARZA TOLEDO, ENRIQUE, 'Quién ganó en Telmex?', *El Cotidiano*, 32 (November–December 1989), 33–4.

—— *Reestructuración Productiva y Respuesta Sindical en México* (México, DF: UNAM/UAM-Iztapalapa, 1993).

—— and ALFONSO BOUZAS, 'La flexibilidad del trabajo en México', Paper presented at the first meeting of the International Working Group on Subnational Economic Governance in Latin America and Southern Europe, Institute of Latin American and Iberian Studies (Columbia University, 20–22 September 1997).

DE LARA RANGEL, MARIA EUGENIA, 'De la dispersión a la unificación del movimiento obrero', in Javier Aguilar García (ed.), *Historia de la CTM: 1936–1990* (Mexico City: Instituto de Investigaciones Sociales de la UNAM, 1990).

DEL ALIZAL, LAURA, 'Las reglas de orígen en el TLC', in Gustavo Emmerich (ed.), *El Tratado de Libre Comercio: Texto y Contexto* (México, DF: UAM-Iztapalapa), 73–83.

DEL CAMPO, JESÚS MARTÍN [PRD official and SNTE leader], personal interview (Mexico City, 12 April 1995).

Der Spiegel, 36/1995.

DEWAR, MARGARET, *Labour Policy in the USSR, 1917–1928* (London: Royal Institute of International Affairs and Oxford University Press, 1956).

DEYO, FREDERIC, *Beneath the Miracle: Labor Subordination in the New Asian Industrialism* (Berkeley: University of California Press, 1989).

—— (ed.), *Social Reconstructions of the World Automobile Industry: Competition, Power, and Industrial Flexibility* (New York: St. Martin's Press, 1996).

DÍAZ, PAUL BERNARDO [former local union leader in the Ford plant at Cuahutitlán], personal interview (Mexico City, 28 February 1995).

'Die Ost-West Ehe bleibt auch weiter die Ausnahme', *Berliner Zeitung* (9 August 1996), 16.

DIESSE (Departamento Intersindical de Estatistica e Estudos Socio-Economicos), 'A reestruturação negociada na industria automobilística Brasileira', *Boletim DIEESE 168* (March 1995), 18–20.

DIWAN, ISHAC and MICHAEL WALTON, 'How International Exchange, Technology, and Institutions Affect Workers: An Introduction', *The World Bank Review*, 11: 1 (1997), 1–15.

DOMÍNGUEZ, JOSÉ [advisor to the secretary of education of CTM], personal interviews (Mexico City, 21 and 26 February 1995).

DORE, RONALD, *British Factory, Japanese Factory* (Berkeley: University of California Press, 1973).

DUNLOP, JOHN, *Industrial Relations Systems* (Carbondale: Southern Illinois University Press, 1958).

DURÁN, JORGE [former secretary of External Relations of the SME], personal interview (Mexico City, 28 March 1995).

EBERSTADT, NICHOLAS, 'Demographic Shocks in Eastern Germany 1989–1993', *Europe-Asia Studies*, 46: 3 (1994).

Economist Intelligence Unit, *The Motor Industries of South America and Mexico: Poised for Growth*, Research Report (London/New York/Hong Kong, 1995).

Economic Research Institute, Japan Society for the Promotion of Machine Industry, *Engineering Industries of Japan*, 30 (May 1996).

Economic Review, 'Privatization—Need for Checks and Balances' (February 1992).

EDWARDS, SEBASTIAN and NORA LUSTIG, *Labor Markets in Latin America: Combining Social Protection with Market Flexibility* (Washington, DC: Brookings Institution, 1997).

ELGER, TONY and CHRIS SMITH (eds), *Global Japanization? The Transnational Transformation of the Labour Process* (London: Routledge, 1994).

ELGUEA, JAVIER [Director of Human Resources of Telmex], personal interview (Mexico City, 15 February).

ERICKSON, KENNETH PAUL, and KEVIN J. MIDDLEBROOK, 'The State and Organized Labor in Brazil and Mexico', in Sylvia Ann Hewlett and Richard S. Weinert (eds), *Brazil and Mexico: Patterns in Late Development* (Philadelphia: Institute for the Study of Human Issues, 1982).

ERMIDA URIARTE, OSCAR, 'El futuro del Derecho del Trabajo y las relaciones laborales', in Silvia Portella (ed.), *Sindicalismo Latinoamericao entre la Renovación y la Resignación* (Caracas: Nueva Sociedad, 1995), 47–56.

EVANS, PETER, 'The State as Problem and Solution: Predation, Embedded Autonomy, and Structural Change', in Haggard and Kaufman (eds), *The Politics of Economic Adjustment* (New Brunswick, NJ: Transaction Books, 1989), 139–81.

——*Embedded Autonomy: State and Industrial Transformation* (Princeton: Princeton University Press, 1995).

FALTER, JÜRGEN and MARKUS KLEIN, 'Die Wähler der PDS bei der Bundestagswahl 1994', *Aus Politik und Zeitgeschichte* (23 December 1994), B 51–2.

FANG, WEIZHONG (ed.), *Guanyu Gaohao Guoyou Qiye de Diaocha* [Investigations on How to Improve SOEs] (Beijing: Zhongguo wenshi chubanshe, 1995).

FEIST, URSTILA, 'Nichtwähler 1994', *Aus Politik und Zeitgeschichte* (23 December 1994), B 51–2.

FICHTE, JOHANN-GOTTLIEB, 'Der geschlossene Handelsstaat' [The Closed Trading

State], in *Ausgewählte Werke* [Selected Works], 3 (Darmstadt: Wissenschaftliche Buchgesellschaft, 1964).

FILTZER, DON, 'Economic Reform and Production Relations in Soviet Industry, 1986–90', in C. Smith and P. Thompson (eds), *Labor in Transition: The Labor Process in Eastern Europe and China* (London: Routledge, 1992), 110–48.

FLETCHER, PHILIPPA, 'Russian Government Seeks to Keep Unions Out of Politics', Reuters, 12 August 1998.

FLOREK, LUDWIK, 'Problems and Dilemmas of Labor Relations in Poland', *Comparative Labor Law Journal*, 13: 2 (Winter 1992), 111–28.

FOOTE, DANIEL H., 'Law an an Agent of Change? Governmental Efforts to Reduce Working Hours in Japan', in Harald Baum (ed.), *Japan: Economic Success and Legal System* (Berlin/New York: Walter de Gruyter, 1997), 252–301.

FRENKEL, STEPHEN, 'Patterns of Workplace Relations in the Global Corporation: Toward Convergence?', in Jacques Bélanger *et al.* (eds), *Workplace Industrial Relations and the Global Challenge* (Ithaca, NY: ILR Press, 1994), 240–74.

——and JEFFREY HARROD, *Industrialization and Labor Relations: Contemporary Research in Seven Countries* (Ithaca, NY: ILR Press, 1995).

FRIEDEN, JEFFREY, *Debt, Development and Democracy: Modern Political Economy and Latin America, 1965–1985* (Princeton: Princeton University Press, 1991).

FUJIMOTO, TAKAHIRO, 'An Evolutionary Process of Toyota's Final Assembly Operations—The Role of Ex-post Dynamic Capabilities' (Tokyo: The University of Tokyo, Faculty of Economics, Research Institute for the Japanese Economy, Discussion Paper F-Series, January 1996).

FUKUYAMA, FRANCIS, 'The End of History?', *The National Interest*, 16 (Summer 1989), 3–18.

GALENSON, WALTER, *Labour and Economic Growth in Five Asian Countries: South Korea, Malaysia, Taiwan, Thailand, and the Philippines* (New York: Praeger, 1992).

GARCÍA, G. ALEJANDRO, and LARA R. ARTURO, 'Cambio tecnológico y aprendizaje laboral en G.M.: Los casos de Silao y D.F.', in Huberto Juárez Nuñez and Steve Babson (eds), *Enfrentando el Cambio: Obreros del Automóvil y Producción Esbelta en América del Norte* [Confronting Change: Auto Labor and Lean Production in North America] (Puebla, Mexico/Detroit: Universidad Autónoma de Puebla/Wayne State University, Labor Studies Center, 1998), 207–22.

GARCÍA, P. ROBERTO and STEPHEN HILLS, 'Meeting "Lean" Competitors: Ford de México's industrial relations strategy', in Huberto Juárez Nuñez and Steve Babson (eds), *Enfrentando el Cambio: Obreros del Automóvil y Producción Esbelta en América del Norte* [Confronting Change: Auto Labor and Lean Production in North America] (Puebla, Mexico/Detroit: Universidad Autónoma de Puebla/Wayne State University, Labor Studies Center, 1998), 143–54.

GARETT, GEOFFREY, *Partisan Politics in the Global Economy* (Cambridge: Cambridge University Press, 2000).

GARGUILO, MARTÍN and MARIO BENASSI, 'The Dark Side of Social Capital'. Unpublished manuscript (1998).

GARON, SHELDON, *The State and Labor in Modern Japan* (Berkeley: University of California Press, 1987).

GARRETT, GEOFFREY, *Partisan Politics in the Global Economy* (Cambridge: Cambridge University Press, 1998).

——and PETER LANGE, 'The Politics of Growth: Strategic Interaction and Economic Performance in the Advance Industrial Democracies:1974–80', *Journal of Politics*, 47 (1985), 792–827.

—— ——'Political Responses to Interdependence: What's "Left" for the Left?', *International Organization*, 45 (Autumn 1991), 539–64.

GEERTZ, CLIFFORD, *Agricultural Involution: The Processes of Ecological Change in Indonesia* (Berkeley: University of California Press, 1963).

GERSCHENKRON, ALEXANDER, *Economic Backwardness in Historical Perspective* (Cambridge: Harvard University Press, 1962).

GOLDEN, MIRIAM, *Heroic Defeats: The Politics of Job Loss* (New York: Cambridge University Press, 1997).

GOLOVACHEV, VITALY, 'Humiliation', *Trud* (18 June 1998).

GÓNGORA, JANETTE and HORACIO VÁZQUEZ, 'El sindicalismo mexicano ante el Tratado de Libre Comercio', *Trabajo*, 5–6 (1991), 4–6.

GORDON, ANDREW, *The Evolution of Labor Relations in Japan: Heavy Industry, 1853–1955* (Cambridge: Council on East Asian Studies, Harvard University, 1985).

——'Contests for the Workplace', in Andrew Gordon (ed.), *Postwar Japan as History* (Berkeley: University of California Press, 1993), 373–94.

GOSWAMI, OMKAR *et al.*, 'Report of the Committee on Industrial Sickness and Corporate Restructuring'. Submitted to the Union Minister of Finance, Government of India, July 1993.

GOTHOSKAR, SUJATA, PRIYA HALAL, SHARAD DUDHAT, ODILE FLAVIA, and GIRISH VAIDYA (eds), 'Job Losses and Closures: Management Strategies and Union Counter-Strategies', mimeograph (1990).

GOUREVITCH, PETER, *Politics in Hard Times: Comparative Responses to International Economic Crises* (Ithaca, NY: Cornell University Press, 1986).

Government of India, Ministry of Finance, Board for Industrial and Financial Reconstruction, *Industrial Sickness—Case Studies: Metallurgical*, 1: 4, mimeograph (July 1991).

——Ministry of Labour, *The Indian Labour Yearbook*, various issues.

Government of Ireland, website, http://www.irlgov.ie

Government of Pakistan, Ministry of Labour, Manpower and Overseas Pakistanis, *Pakistan Labour Gazette* (Islamabad: Printing Corporation of Pakistan Press), various issues.

——*Pakistan Essential Services (Maintenance) Act, 1952* (Karachi: Manager of Publications, 1952).

GRABOWSKI, TOMEK, 'From a Civic Movement to Political Parties: The Rise and Fall of the Solidarity Committees in Poland, 1989–1991', Paper presented at the Annual Meeting of the American Political Science Association, 1995. Later published in revised form in *East European Politics and Societies*.

GRAHAM, LAURIE, 'How Does the Japanese Model Transfer to the United States? A View from the Line', in Tony Elger and Chris Smith (eds), *Global Japanization? The Transnational Transformation of the Labour Process* (London: Routledge, 1994).

GRANOVETTER, MARK, 'The Strength of Weak Ties', *American Journal of Sociology*, 91 (1973), 481–510.

——*Getting a Job: A Study of Contacts and Careers* (Cambridge: Harvard University Press, 1974).

GRANOVETTER, MARK, 'Economic Action and Social Structure: The Problem of Embeddedness', *American Journal of Sociology*, 91 (1985), 481–510.

——and RICHARD SWEDBERG (eds), *The Sociology of Economic Life* (Boulder, CO: Westview Press, 1992).

GRESKOVITS, BELA, *The Political Economy of Protest and Patience* (Budapest: Central European University Press, 1998).

GRINDLE, MERILEE and JOHN THOMAS, *Public Choices and Policy Change* (Baltimore: The Johns Hopkins University Press, 1991).

GROGAN, LOUISE, 'Arrears Enslave Labor', *Moscow Times* (9 April 1998).

GUNNIGLE, PATRICK, 'More Rhetoric than Reality: Enterprise Level Industrial Relations in Ireland', *The Economic and Social Review*, 28: 4 (1997).

GUTHRIE, DOUGLAS, 'Organizational Uncertainty and Labor Contracts in China's Economic Transition', *Sociological Forum*, 13 (1998), 457–94.

GUTKIND, PETER (ed.), *Third World Workers: Comparative International Studies* (New York: E. J. Brill, 1988).

HAGGARD, STEPHAN, *Pathways from the Periphery: The Politics of Growth in the Newly Industrializing Countries* (Ithaca, NY: Cornell University Press, 1990).

——and CHUNG H. LEE, *The Politics of Finance in Developing Countries* (Ithaca, NY: Cornell University Press, 1993).

——and ROBERT KAUFMAN (eds), *The Politics of Economic Adjustment* (Princeton: Princeton Unviersity Press, 1992).

—— ——'Introduction: Institutions and Economic Adjustment', in Stepan Haggard and Robert Kaufman (eds), *The Politics of Economic Adjustment International Constraints, Distributive Conflicts, and the State* (Princeton: Princeton University Press, 1993).

—— ——*The Political Economy of Democratic Transitions* (Princeton: Princeton University Press, 1995).

HALE, LISA E., 'Poland's Right Turn: Solidarity as Opposition, Government and Union in the Capitalist Transition'. Unpublished PhD dissertation (Evanston, IL: Northwestern University, June 1999).

HANSENNE, MICHEL, 'Promoting Social Justice in the New Global Economy', *Monthly Labor Review*, 117 (September 1994), 3–4.

HANSON, GORDON and HELEN SHAPIRO with RICARDO DOMINGUEZ, 'Volkswagen de México's North American Strategy' (Cambridge: Harvard Business School Case 9-794-104, 1994).

HAUGHTON, JONATHAN, 'The Historical Background', in J. W. O'Hagan (ed.), *The Economy of Ireland: Policy and Performance of a Small European Country* (New York: St. Martin's Press, 1995).

HAUSNER, JERZY, 'The State Enterprise Pact and the Potential for Tripartism in Poland', in Robert Kyloh (ed.), *Tripartism on Trial: Tripartite Consultations and Negotiations in Central and Eastern Europe* (Geneva: International Labour Organization, 1995).

——and WITOLD MORAWSKI, 'Tripartism in Poland'. Unpublished manuscript (University of Warsaw Department of Sociology, 1994).

——OVE K. PEDERSEN and KARSTEN RONIT (eds), *Evolution of Interest Representation and Development of the Labour Market in Post-Socialist Countries* (Cracow: Cracow Academy of Economics and Friedrich Ebert Stiftung, 1995).

HEADLY, BRUCE, RUDOLF ANDORKA, and PETER KRAUSE, 'Political Legitimacy versus

Economic Imperatives in System Transformation: Hungary and East Germany, 1990–1993', *Social Indicators Research*, 36 (1995), 247–73.

HEINISCH, REINHARD, 'The State of Corporatism in a Central Europe in Transition', in Irwin Collier *et al.* (eds), *Welfare States in Transition: East and West* (New York: St. Martin's Press, 1999).

HELBURN, I. B. and JOHN SCHARER, 'Human Resources and Industrial Relations in China', *Industrial and Labor Relations Review*, 38 (1984), 3–15.

HELLEINER, GERALD, *The New Global Economy and the Developing Countries: Essays in International Economics and Development* (Brookfield, VT: Edward Elgar, 1990).

HENZLER, HERBERT, 'Der Aufschwung Ost had noch viele matte Stellen', *Süddeutsche Zeitung* (10 September 1995).

HEREDIA, BLANCA, 'Making Economic Reform Politically Viable: The Mexican Experience', in William Smith, Carlos Acuña, and Eduardo Gamarra (eds), *Democracy, Markets and Structural Reform in Latin America* (New Brunswick, NJ: North-South Center and Transaction Publishers, 1994).

HERNÁNDEZ, JUAREZ [Secretary-General of the STRM], personal interview (Mexico City, 19 April 1995).

HERRERA LIMA, FERNANDO, 'Reestructuración de la industria automotriz en México y respuesta sindical', in *El Cotidiano*, 46 (March–April 1992), 21–4.

HETHY, LAJOS, 'Negotiated Social Peace: An Attempt to Reach a Social and Economic Agreement in Hungary', in Attila Agh and Gabriella Ilonszki (eds), *Parliaments and Organized Interests: The Second Steps* (Budapest: Hungarian Centre for Democracy Studies, 1996).

HIRSCHMAN, ALBERT O., *The Strategy of Economic Development* (New Haven: Yale University Press, 1958).

HOFFMAN, DAVID, *Peasant Metropolis: Social Identities in Moscow, 1929–1941* (Ithaca, NY: Cornell University Press, 1994).

HONNETH, ALEX, *The Struggle for Recognition* (Cambridge: Cambridge University Press, 1995).

HOOGVELT, ANKIE, *Globalization and the Postcolonial World* (Baltimore: The Johns Hopkins University Press, 1997), 112–13, 139–40.

HORI HARUHIRO, 'Rodo kumiai no keizaiteki kino' [The economic function of unions], *JIL Risaachi*, 29 (Spring 1997), 22–5.

HORST, ELKE and JÜRGEN SCHUPP, 'Aspekte der Arbeitsmarktentwicklung in Ostdeutschland', *Deutschland Archiv*, 28: 7 (July 1995), 737–42.

HOSEI DAIGAKU OHARA SHAKAI MONDAI KENKYUJO (ed.), *'Rengo Jidai' no Rodo Undo: Saihen no Michinori to Shintenkai* [The Labor Movement of the 'Rengo era': The Journey Toward Restructuring and New Developments] (Tokyo: Sogo Rodo Kenkyujo, 1992).

HOWARD, MARC, 'A East German Ethnicity? Understanding the New Division of Unified Germany', *German Politics and Society*, 13: 37 (1995), 49–70.

HOWELL, JUDE, 'The Myth of Autonomy: The Foreign Enterprise in China', in Chris Smith and Paul Thompson (eds), *Labor in Transition: The Labor Process in Eastern Europe and China* (London: Routledge, 1992).

HUMPHREY, JOHN, *Capitalist Control and Workers' Struggle in the Brazilian Auto Industry* (Princeton: Princeton University Press, 1982).

——'Industrial Reorganization in Developing Countries: From Models to Trajectories', *World Development*, 23: 1 (1995), 149–62.

HUNICK, J. and H. SOLGA, 'Occupational Opportunities in the GDR: A Privilege of the Older Generations', *Zeitschrift für Soziologie*, 23: 2 (1994), 237–53.

HYODO and TOTSUKA, *Chiiki Shakai to Rodo Kumiai* [Regional Society and Labor Unions: 'Industrial Hollowing' and the Search for a Regional Strategy] (Tokyo: Nihon Keizai Hyoronsha, 1995).

IANKOVA, ELENA A., 'The Transformative Corporatism of Eastern Europe', *East European Politics and Societies*, 12: 2 (Spring 1998), 222–64.

IGARASHI JIN, 'Rengo no seisaku seido sanka' [Rengo's policy and institutional participation], *Kikan Rodo Ho* (Autumn 1994), 6–24.

INGLEBY, S. J., 'The Role of Indigenous Institutions in the Economic Transformation of Eastern Europe: The Hungarian Chamber System—One Step Forward or Two Steps Back?', *Journal of European Public Policy*, 3: 1 (March 1996), 102–21.

INKELES, ALEX and DAVID SMITH, *Becoming Modern: Individual Change in Six Countries* (Cambridge: Harvard University Press, 1974).

International Labour Office, 'India: Tripartite Cooperation for Structural Adjustment', *Social and Labour Bulletin* (June, 1992), 143–5.

—— *World Labour Report 1997–98: Industrial Relations, Democracy and Social Stability* (Geneva: ILO, 1998).

International Organization, special issue, 39, 3 and 4 (World Peace Foundation with the University of Wisconsin, Madison, 1986).

Irish Trade Web, http://www.itw.ie

ISHIDA MITSUO, 'Jinji shogu no kobetsuka to rodo kumiai kino' [The individualization of personnel treatment and labor union functions], *Nihon Rodo Kyokai Zasshi*, 460 (October 1998), 40–8.

JACKMAN, RICHARD, 'Wage Policy in the Transition to a Market Economy: The Polish Experience', in Fabrizio Coricelli and Ana Revenga (eds), *Wage Policy during the Transition to a Market Economy: Poland 1990–91*, World Bank Discussion Papers 158 (Washington, DC: World Bank, 1992).

JACOBY, SANFORD (ed.), *The Workers of Nations: Industrial Relations in a Global Economy* (New York: Oxford University Press, 1995).

—— Preface, in Sanford Jacoby (ed.), *The Workers of Nations: Industrial Relations in a Global Economy* (New York: Oxford University Press, 1995a).

—— 'Social Dimensions of Global Economic Integration', in Sanford Jacoby (ed.), *The Workers of Nations: Industrial Relations in a Global Economy* (New York: Oxford University Press, 1995b), 3–34.

JANOS, ANDREW, 'The politics of backwardness on Continental Europe', *World Politics*, 41: 3 (April 1989).

JIANG, LIU et al., *1996–97 Zhongguo Shehui Xingshi Fenxi yu Yuce* [Analysis and Predictions of China's Social Situation in 1996–97] (Beijing: Zhongguo shehui kexue chubanshe, 1997).

Jingji Ribao [Economic Daily] (Beijing).

JOHNSON, CHALMERS, *MITI and the Japanese Economic Miracle* (Stanford, CA: Stanford University Press, 1986).

—— 'Political Institutions and Economic Performance: The Government-Business Relationship in Japan, South Korea, and Taiwan', in Frederic C. Deyo (ed.), *The Political Economy of the New Asian Industrialism* (Ithaca, NY: Cornell University Press, 1987).

JUNG, MATTHIAS and DIETER ROTH, 'Kohls knappster Sieg', *Aus Politik und Zeitgeschichte* (23 December 1994), B 51–2.

KAHLER, MILES (ed.), *The Politics of International Debt* (Ithaca, NY: Cornell University Press, 1986).

——'Trade and Domestic Differences', in Suzanne Berger and Ronald Dore (eds), *National Diversity and Global Capitalism* (Ithaca, NY: Cornell University Press, 1996).

KAPLAN, FREDERICK, *Bolshevik Ideology and the Ethics of Soviet Labor, 1917–1920* (New York: Philosophical Library, 1968).

KAPLINSKY, RAPHAEL, 'Technique and System: The Spread of Japanese Management Techniques to Developing Countries', *World Development* , 23: 1 (1995), 57–71.

KATZENSTEIN, PETER, *Small States in World Markets: Industrial Policy in Europe* (Ithaca, NY: Cornell University Press, 1985).

KECK, MARGARET, 'The New Unionism in the Brazilian Transition', in Alfred Stepan (ed.), *Democratizing Brazil: Problems of Transition and Consolidation* (New York/Oxford: Oxford University Press, 1989), 252–98.

——*The Workers Party and Democratization in Brazil* (New Haven/London: Yale University Press, 1992).

KENNEDY, KIERAN A., 'Ireland: The Revolution Unfinished', in Kieran A. Kennedy (ed.), *Ireland in Transition* (Cork: published in collaboration with Radio Telefis Eireann by the Mercier Press, 1986).

KENNEY, MARTIN and RICHARD FLORIDA, *Beyond Mass Production, The Japanese System and Its Transfer to the U.S.* (New York: Oxford University Press, 1993).

KEOGH, DERMOT, *Twentieth Century Ireland: Nation and State* (New York: St. Martin's Press, 1995).

KEOHANE, ROBERT O. and JOSEPH S. NYE, *Power and Interdependence: World Politics in Transition* (Boston: Little, Brown, 1977).

KERN, HORST and CHARLES SABEL, 'Trade Unions and Decentralized Production: A Sketch of Strategic Problems in the German Labour Movement', in Marino Regini (ed.), *The Future of Labour Movements* (London: Sage, 1992), 217–49.

KERR, CLARK, J. T. DUNLOP, F. H. GARBISON and C. A. MYERS, *Industrialism and Industrial Man* (Cambridge: Harvard University Press, 1960).

KESTER, W. CARL, 'American and Japanese Corporate Governance: Convergence to Best Practice?', in Suzanne Berger and Ronald Dore (eds), *National Diversity and Global Capitalism* (Ithaca, NY: Cornell University Press, 1996), 107–37.

KHAN, A. R. [Chief Economist, Pakistan Planning Commission], interview (Islamabad, Pakistan, 29 November 1995).

KHAN, NOOR [Air Marshal (retired) and former Deputy Martial Law Administrator (1968–69)], interview (Karachi, Pakistan, 3 April 1995).

KHARKHORDIN, OLEG and THEODORE GERBER, 'Russian Directors' Business Ethic: A Study of Industrial Enterprises in St. Petersburg, 1993', *Europe-Asia Studies*, 46: 7 (1994), 1075–107.

KINGSTONE, PETER, *Crafting Coalitions for Reform: Business Preferences, Political Institutions, and Neoliberal Reform in Brazil* (University Park, PA: Pennsylvania State University Press, 1999).

KLANDERMANS, P. BERT, 'Linking the "Old" and the "new": Movement Networks in The Netherlands', in R. J. Dalton and M. Keuchler (eds), *Challenging the Political Order: New Social and Political Movements in Western Democracies* (New York: Oxford University Press, 1990).

KLEIBL, JIRI and ZUZANA DVORAKOVA, 'Industrial Relations in the Czech Republic', *Prague Economic Papers*, 3 (1999).

KLEINFELD, GERALD R., 'The Return of the PDS', in David P. Conradt *et al.* (eds), *Germany's New Politics* (Tempe, AZ: German Studies Review, 1995).

KLIMOVA, S. G. and L. V. KUNAYEVSKII, 'New Entrepreneurs and Old Culture', *Sociological Studies* [in Russian], 5 (1993), 64–9.

KLINGER, FRED, 'Aufbau und Erneuerung: Über die institutionellen Bedingungen der Standortentwicklung in Deutschland', *Aus Politik und Zeitgeschichte*, B 17/94 (29 April 1994).

KNOKE, DAVID, *Political Networks: The Structural Perspective.* (Cambridge/New York: Cambridge University Press, 1990).

KOCHAN, THOMAS A., RUSSELL D. LANSBURY, and JOHN PAUL MACDUFFIE (eds), *After Lean Production: Evolving Employment Practices in the World Auto Industry* (Ithaca, NY: ILR Press, 1997).

KOPSTEIN, JEFFREY, *The Politics of Economic Decline in East Germany, 1945–1989* (Chapel Hill: University of North Carolina Press, 1997).

KOTKIN, STEPHEN, *Magnetic Mountain: Stalinism as a Civilization* (Berkeley: University of California Press, 1995).

KRAMER, MARK, 'Polish Workers and the Post-communist Transition, 1989–1993', *Communist and Post-Communist Studies*, 28: 1 (1995), 71–114.

KREUGER, ANNE (ed.), *Political Economy of Policy Reform in Developing Countries* (Cambridge: MIT Press, 1993).

KUBICEK, PAUL, 'Variations on a Corporatist Theme: Interest Associations in Post-Soviet Ukraine and Russia', *Europe-Asia Studies*, 48: 1 (1996), 87–106.

—— 'Organized Labor in Post-Communist States: Will the Western Sun Set on It, Too?', *Comparative Politics* (October 1999), 83–102.

KUMAZAWA, MAKOTO, ANDREW GORDON (ed.), A. GORDON and MIKISO HANE (trans.), *Portraits of the Japanese Workplace: Labor Movements, Workers, and Managers* (Boulder, CO: Westview Press, 1996).

KUROMIYA, HIROAKI, *Stalin's Industrial Revolution: Politics and Workers, 1928–1932* (Cambridge: Cambridge University Press, 1988).

KUZNETSOV, ANDREI, 'Economic Reforms in Russia: Enterprise Behaviour as an Impediment to Change', *Europe-Asia Studies*, 46: 6 (1994).

KYLOH, ROBERT (ed.), *Tripartism on Trial: Tripartite Consultations and Negotiations in Central and Eastern Europe* (Geneva: International Labour Organization, 1995).

LADO, MARIA, 'Representation of Workers' and Employers' Interests in Changing Industrial Relations in Hungary', in Jerzy Hausner, Ove K. Pedersen, and Karsten Ronit (eds), *Evolution of Interest Representation and Development of the Labour Market in Post-Socialist Countries*, (Cracow: Cracow Academy of Economics and Friedrich Ebert Stiftung, 1995), 285–336.

'Landmarks', *Business India* (14–27 August 1995), 32.

LANE, DAVID, *Soviet Labour and the Ethnic of Communism: Full Employment and the Labour Process in the USSR* (Boulder, CO: Westview, 1987).

LANGE, LYDIA, 'Warum so viele Ostdeutsche von der repräsentativen Demokratie enttäuscht sind', *Die Zeit*, 10 January 1997, from *Die Zeit* website: www.zeit.de, 27 September 1995.

LANGE, PETER, MICHAEL WALLERSTEIN, and MIRIAM GOLDEN, 'The End of Corporatism? Wage Setting in Nordic and Germanic Countries', in Sanford Jacoby (ed.), *The Workers of Nations: Industrial Relations in a Global Economy* (New York: Oxford University Press, 1995*b*).

LASH, SCOTT, 'The End of Neo-Corporatism? The Breakdown of Centralised Bargaining in Sweden', *British Journal of Industrial Relations*, 23 (1985), 215–39.

LAWRENCE, ROBERT, *Single World, Divided Nations: International Trade and OECD Labor Markets* (Washington, DC: Brookings Institution Press, 1996).

LEAL, FELIPE, *Agrupaciones y Burocracias Sindicales en México, 1906–1938* (Mexico City: Ed. Terranova, 1985).

——'Las estructuras sindicales', in Pablo González Casanova (ed.), *Organización y Sindicalismo* (Mexico City: Ed. Siglo XXI, 1986).

LEITE, MÂRCIA DE PAULA, ROQUE DA SILVA, LUIS PAULO BRESCIANI, and JEFFERSON JOSÉ DA CONCEIÇÃO, 'Reestruturação produtiva e relações industriais: Tendências do setor automotivo Brasileiro', *Revista Latinoamericana de Estudios del Trabajo*, 2: 4 (1996), 79–110.

LEJARZA, MATEO [advisor to the Secretary-General of the STRM], personal interviews (Mexico City, 27 February and 28 March 1995).

LENIN, V. I., 'The State and Revolution', in Robert Tucker (ed.), *The Lenin Anthology* (New York: Norton, 1975).

——'Two Tactics of Social Democracy in the Democratic Revolution', in *V. I. Lenin: Selected Works in Three Volumes* (Moscow: Progress Publishers, 1977).

LEÓN, SAMUEL, 'Del partido de partido al partido de sectores', in *El Partido en el Poder* (Mexico City: IEPES, 1990).

LERNER, DANIEL, *The Passing of Traditional Society* (rev. edn) (New York: Free Press, 1964).

LEVY, MARION, *Modernization and the Structure of Societies* (Princeton: Princeton University Press, 1966).

LEWIS, W. ARTHUR, 'Economic Development with Unlimited Supplies of Labour', *The Manchester School of Economic and Social Studies*, 22: 2 (May 1954), 139–91.

Liaowang [Outlook New Weekly] (Beijing).

LIPPOLDT, DOUG, 'Social Benefits in Transition: An Introduction', in *Organization for European Cooperation and Development (OECD), The Changing Social Benefits in Russian Enterprises* (OECD, August 1996), website: www.oecd.org/sge/ccet/cpru 2309/present.htm

LIST, FRIEDRICH, *The National System of Political Economy*, Sampson S. Lloyed (trans.) (London: Longman, 1916).

LOCKE, RICHARD M., 'The Demise of the National Union in Italy: Lessons for Comparative Industrial Relations Theory', *Industrial and Labor Relations Review*, 2: 4 (January 1992), 229–49.

——*Remaking the Italian Economy* (Ithaca, NY/London: Cornell University Press, 1995).

——THOMAS KOCHAN, and MICHAEL PIORE, 'Reconceptualizing Comparative Industrial Relations: Lessons from International Research', *International Labour Review*, 134: 2 (1995).

LOYOLA, RAFAEL, and LILIANA MARTÍNEZ, 'Petróleos Mexicanos: La búsqueda de un nuevo modelo empresarial', *Estudios Sociológicos*, 12 (1994).

LOYOLA, RAFAEL, '1938: El despliegue del corporatismo partidario', in *El Partido en el Poder* (Mexico City: IEPES, 1990).

Lu, Xiaobo, 'Enterprise Paternalism and Transition to Market Socialism: The Political Economy of State Sector Reform In State Socialist Systems', *Mondes en Développement*, 25 (1997), 41–56.
—— and Lowell Dittmer, 'Personal Politics in the Chinese Danwei Under Reform', *Asian Survey* , 36 (1996), 246–67.
—— and Elizabeth Perry (eds), *Danwei: The Changing Chinese Workplace in Historical and Comparative Perspective* (Armonk, NY: M. E. Sharpe, 1997).
Lustig, Nora, 'The Mexican Peso Crisis: The Foreseeable and the Surprise', *Brookings Discussion Papers in International Economics* (Washington, DC, 1995).
Ma, Lianjie and Haning, Chen, 'Lun waishang touzi qiye de laozi guanxi' [Labor relations in foreign invested enterprises], *Jingji Wenti* [Economic Problems], 4 (1996), 31–8.
MacDuffie, John Paul, 'International Trends in Work Organization in the Auto Industry: National-Level vs. Company-Level Perspectives', in Kristen Wever and Lowell Turner (eds), *The Comparative Political Economy of Industrial Relations* (Madison, WI: Industrial Relations Research Association, 1995), 71–113.
Maddison, Angus, *Class Structure and Economic Growth: India and Pakistan since the Moghuls* (New York: W. W. Norton, 1971).
Madhavan, Narayanan, 'India: Indian Mining Plans Draws Opposition Ire', Reuters News Service (31 March 1996).
Mainwaring, Scott, 'Brazil: Weak Parties, Feckless Democracy', in Scott Mainwaring and Timothy Scully (eds), *Building Democratic Institutions: Party Systems in Latin America* (Stanford, CA: Stanford University Press, 1995).
—— 'Presidentialism in Brazil: The Impact of Strong Constitutional Powers, Weak Partisan Powers, and Robust Federalism', Working papers 225 (Woodrow Wilson International Center for Scholars, Latin American Program, 1997).
Majone, Giandomenico, 'From the Positive to the Regulatory State: Causes and Consequences of Changes in the Mode of Governance', *Journal of Public Policy*, 17 (1997), 139–67.
Mani, Mohan, 'New Attempt at Workers' Resistance', *Economic and Political Weekly*, 7 October 1995.
Marbrán, Ignacio, 'La dificultad del cambio (1968–1990)', in *El Partido en el Poder* (Mexico City: IEPES, 1990).
Marmolejo, Pilar [training manager at Inttelmex, the training institute of Telmex], personal interview (Mexico City, 20 February 1995).
Marshall, Gordon, 'Was Communism Good for Social Justice: A Comparative Analysis of the Two Germanies', *British Journal of Sociology*, 47: 3 (1996), 397–420.
Martin, Scott B., 'As Câmaras Setoriais e o Meso-Corporativismo', *Lua Nova*, 37 (1996), 139–70.
—— 'Beyond Corporatism: New Patterns of Representation in the Brazilian Auto Industry', in Douglas C. Chalmers, Carlos M. Vilas, Katherine Hite, Scott B. Martin, Kerianne Piester, and Monique Segarra (eds), *The New Politics of Inequality in Latin America: Rethinking Participation and Representation*. (Oxford/New York: Oxford University Press, 1997), 45–71.
—— 'Social Networks and Workplace Citizenship in Brazil's New Democracy: The Case of the Automobile Industry. Uunpublished manuscript (1998).
—— 'Embedding Labor Flexibility Amidst Globalization: Comparative Perspectives on the Automobile Industry of the Americas (Brazil, Mexico, and the United

States)', Paper presented at the Second Workshop of the International Research Network on Subnational Economic Governance in Latin America and Southern Europe, (São Paulo: CEBRAP and Institute of Latin American and Iberian Studies of Columbia University 26–8 June 1999).

—— 'Working in the Global Factory: The Social Embedding of Flexibility'. Unpublished PhD dissertation (Department of Political Science, Columbia University, May 2000).

MATHUR, AJEET N. [Indian Institute of Technology industrial relations expert], interview (Calcutta, India, December 1991).

—— 'The Experience of Consultation during Structural Adjustment in India (1990–92)', *International Labour Review*, 132: 3 (1993), 331–45.

MATTHEW, BABU [President, Bharat Electronics Employees Union], interview (Bangalore, India, 24 June 1996).

MAXFIELD, SYLVIA, *Gatekeepers of Growth: The International Political Economy of Central Banking in Developing Countries* (Princeton: Princeton University Press, 1997).

MAYER, H. and H. SOLGA, 'Mobilität und Legitimität. Zum Vergleich der Chancenstrukturen in der alten DDR und der alten BRD Order: Haben Mobilit-Uatschancen zu Stabilität und Zusammenbruch der DDR beigetragen?', *Kölner Zeitschrift für Soziologie und Sozialpsychologie*, 46: 2 (1994), 193–208.

McKITRICK, SEAN, 'Managing Mistrust: Corporatist Intermediation and Economic Reform in Poland, 1989–1994'. Manuscript (1999).

McLERNON, DOUGLAS S., 'Ireland', in Joan Campbell (ed.), *European Labor Unions* (Westport, CT: Greenwood Press, 1992).

MELGOZA, JAVIER, 'Avances e incertidumbres en la modernización del sector eléctrico', *El Cotidiano*, 46 (March–April 1992), 45–7.

—— 'El SME y la productividad: los saldos de la negociación', *Polis*, 93 (1994), 155–92.

MENDEZ BERRUETA, LUIS and JOSÉ QUIROZ TREJO, *Modernización Estatal y Respuesta Obrera: Historia de una Derrota* (Mexico City: UAM, 1994).

MIDDLEBROOK, KEVIN J., *The Paradox of Revolution: Labor, the State, and Authoritarianism in Mexico* (Baltimore: The Johns Hopkins University Press, 1995).

MIKHALEV, VLADIMIR, 'Social Security in Russia Under Economic Transformation', *Europe-Asia Studies*, 48: 1 (1996), 5–25.

'Miners Need More Than Just Back Pay', *Moscow Times* (20 May 1998).

MIYATA YOSHIJI, *Kumiai Zakkubaran* [Speaking Frankly about Unions] (Tokyo: Toyo Keizai Shimposha, 1982).

MOLINAR, JUAN, *El Tiempo de la Legitimidad* (Mexico City: Cal y Arena, 1991).

MONTIEL, YOLANDA and LUDGER PRIES, *Proceso de Trabajo, Acción Sindical y Nuevas Tecnologías en Volkswagen de México*. (México, DF: CIESAS/Ediciones de la Casa Chata, 1991).

—— —— 'Organización del trabajo y relaciones laborales: El reto de la flexibilidad (Avances de investigación)', Working paper (El Colegio de Puebla, Mexico, 1992).

Moore, Barrington, *Injustice: The Social Basis of Obedience and Revolt* (Armonk, NY: M. E. Sharpe, 1988).

MORVANT, PENNY, 'Workers Stage Protests', *Open Market Research Institute (OMRI) Daily Digest* (28 March 1997).

MUNCK, RONNIE, *Ireland: Nation, State, and Class Struggle* (Boulder, CO: Westview Press, 1988).

MUNSLOW, BARRY and M. H. J. Finch (eds), *Proletarianisation in the Third World: Studies in the Creation of a Labour Force Under Dependent Capitalism* (London: Croom Helm, 1984).

MURAKAMI, KANJI, 'IMF–JC no taito' [The rise of the IMF–JC], *Asahi Jaanaru* (25 June 1967), 94–100.

MURILLO, MARIA VICTORIA, 'Latin American Unions and Social Sector Reform: Industrial Competition and Policy Choice', OCE Working Paper 332 (Inter-American Development Bank, Washington, DC, 1996).

——'A Strained Alliance: Continuity and Change in Mexican Labour Politics', in Mónica Serrano (ed.), *Mexico: Assessing Neo-Liberal Reform* (London: Institute of Latin American Studies, University of London, 1997).

MURPHY, R. TAGGGART, *The Weight of the Yen: How Denial Imperils America's Future and Ruins an Alliance* (New York/London: W. W. Norton, 1997).

Muttahida Labour Federation, 'An Introduction to the Muttaheeda Labour Federation', pamphlet (May 1992).

MUZUMDAR, KAMAL [former INTUC official], interview (New Delhi, India, 28 November 1991).

NAGARIK MANCHA, *Against the Wall: West Bengal Labour Scenario* (Calcutta: Spokesman, 1991).

NAIK, HARIBEN [President, Rashtriya Mills Mazdoor Sangh], interview (Bombay, India, 20 April 1992).

NAIMARK, NORMAN, *The Russians in Germany* (Cambridge: Harvard University Press, 1995).

NAKAMURA, KEISUKE, HELMUT DEMES, and HITOSHI NAGANO, 'Work organization in Japan and Germany: A research on VCR production (1)' (Tokyo: Deutsches Institut für Japan Studien, 1994).

NAKATANI IWAO, 'Nikyokubun ga susumu Nihon keizai' [The progressive bipolarization of Japan's economy], *Asahi Shimbun* (20 March 1997), 4.

NAUGHTON, BARRY, 'Danwei: The Economic Foundations of a Unique Institution', in Xiaobo Lu and Elizabeth Perry (eds), *Danwei: The Changing Chinese Workplace in Historical and Comparative Perspective* (Armonk, NY: M. E. Sharpe, 1992), 169–94.

NELSON, JOAN (ed.), *Fragile Coalitions: The Politics of Economic Adjustment* (New Brunswick, NJ: Transaction Books, 1989).

——(ed.), *Economic Crisis and Policy Choice: The Politics of Adjustment in the Third World* (Princeton: Princeton University Press, 1990).

NILAND, JOHN, RUSSELL LANSBURY, and CHRISSIE VEREVIS (eds), *The Future of Industrial Relations* (Thousand Oaks, CA: Sage, 1994).

O'DONNELL, GUILLERMO, *Modernization and Bureaucratic-Authoritarianism: Studies in South American Politics* (Berkeley: Institute of International Studies, University of Californa at Berkeley, 1973).

——*Counterpoints: Selected Essays on Authoritarianism and Democratization* (Notre Dame: University of Notre Dame Press, 1999).

O'GRADA, CORMAC, *A Rocky Road: The Irish Economy Since the 1920s* (Manchester: Manchester University Press, 1997).

O'HEARN, DENIS, *Inside the Celtic Tiger* (London: Pluto Press, 1998).

—— 'The Irish Case of Dependency: An Exception to the Exceptions?' *American Sociological Review*, 54 (1989).

—— 'The Road from Import-Substituting to Export-Led Industrialization in Ireland: Who Mixed the Asphalt, Who Drove the Machinery, and Who Kept Making Them Change Directions?', *Politics & Society*, 18: 1 (1990).

OHMAE, KENICHI, *The Borderless World: Power and Strategy in the Interlinked Economy* (New York: Harper Perennial, 1993).

—— 'Putting Global Logic First', in Kenichi Ohmae (ed.), *The Evolving Global Economy* (Boston: Harvard Business Review, 1995), 141–60.

OKUNISHI YOSHIO, 'Kigyo-nai chingin kakusa no genjo to sono yoin' [Intrafirm wage differentials and their causes], *Nihon Rodo Kenkyu Zasshi*, 460 (October 1998), 2–16.

OLIVER, NICK and BARRY WILKINSON, *The Japanization of British Industry* (Oxford: Blackwell, 1988).

OLSON, MANCUR, *The Rise and Decline of Nations* (New Haven: Yale University Press, 1982).

ONOMICHI, HIROSHI, *Kore ga Rengo da!* [This is Rengo!] (Tokyo: Takeuchi Shoten, 1987).

ORENSTEIN, MITCHELL, 'How Politics and Institutions Affect Pension Reform in Three Postcommunist Countries', World Bank Social Protection Discussion Paper (March 2000).

—— and RAJ DESAI, 'State Power and Interest Group Formation: The Business Lobby in the Czech Republic', *Problems of Post-Communism*, 44: 6 (November/ December 1997), 43–52.

ORTTUNG, ROBERT, 'Russia Becoming a Series of Closed Markets', *Open Market Research Institute (OMRI) Russian Regional Report* (26 March 1997).

OST, DAVID and WEINSTEIN, MARC, 'Unionists Against Unions: Toward Hierarchical Management in Post-Communist Poland', *East European Politics and Societies*, 13: 1 (Winter 1999).

OSTRY, SYLVIA, 'New Dimensions of Market Access: Overview from a Trade Policy Perspective', in Eileen M. Doherty (ed.), *Japanese Investment in Asia: International Production Strategies in a Rapidly Changing World* (Berkeley, CA: The Berkeley Roundtable on the International Economy and The Asia Foundation, 1995).

OTSUBO, SHIGERU, *Globalization: A New Role for Developing Countries in an Integrating World* (Washington, DC: World Bank, 1996).

Pakistan Institute for Labour Education and Research, 'Trade Union Leadership Development Course', mimeograph (February 1989).

PALACIOS, ROBERT and ROBERTO ROCHA, 'The Hungarian Pension System in Transition', World Bank Social Protection Discussion Paper 9805 (1998).

'Panel favours IISCO's revival through SAIL', *The Statesman* (29 December 1993), 13.

PARSONS, TALCOTT, *The Social System* (New York: Free Press, 1951).

—— and EDWARD SHILS, *Toward a General Theory of Action* (New York: Harper and Row, 1951).

PAYNE, LEIGH, *Brazilian Industrials and Democratic Change* (Baltimore: The Johns Hopkins University Press, 1994).

PEMPEL, T. J. and KIICHI TSUNEKAWA, 'Corporatism Without Labor? The Japanese Anomaly', in Philippe Schmitter and Gerhard Lehmbruch (eds), *Trends Towards Corporatist Intermediation* (Beverly Hills, CA: Sage, 1979), 231–70.

'Pension reform debated', *Open Market Research Institute (OMRI) Daily Digest* (5 February 1997).

PÉREZ FERNÁNDEZ DEL CASTILLO, GERMÁN, 'Del corporativismo de estado al corporativismo social', in Carlos Bazdresch, Nisso Bucay, Soledad Loaeza, and Nora Lustig (eds), *México, Auge y Crisis* (Mexico City: Ed. Fondo de Cultura Económica, 1992).

PÉREZ, GABRIEL, 'El SME ante el reto de la modernización del sector eléctrico', in *El Cotidiano*, 58 (October–November 1993), 12–16.

PERRY, ELIZABETH, 'Labor's Battle for Political Space: Tthe Role of Worker Associations in Contemporary China', in Deborah Davis, Richard Kraus, Barry Naughton, and Elizabeth Perry (eds), *Urban Spaces in Contemporary China* (Washington, DC: Woodrow Wilson Center Press, 1995).

PESCHARD, JACQUELINE, 'El partido hegemónico: 1946–1972', in *El Partido en el Poder* (Mexico City: IEPES, 1990).

PICKEL, ANDREAS, 'The Jump-Started Economy and the Ready-Made State: A Theoretical Reconsideration of the East German Case', *Comparative Political Studies*, 30: 2 (1997).

PIORE, MICHAEL and CHARLES SABEL, *The Second Industrial Divide: Possibilities for Prosperity* (New York: Basic Books, 1984).

PLESKOT, IGOR, 'Czech and Slovak Trade Union Movement in the Period of Transformation to a Civil Democratic Society, 1989–1993', mimeograph (Czech-Moravian Chamber of Trade Unions, 1994).

POLANYI, KARL, *The Great Transformation* (New York: Farrar & Rinehart, 1944; Boston: Beacon, 1966).

POLLERT, ANNA, 'The Transformation of Trade Unionism in the Capitalist and Democratic Restructuring of the Czech Republic', *European Journal of Industrial Relations*, 3: 2 (July 1997), 203–28.

POWELL, WALTER W., and LAUREL SMITH-DOERR, 'Networks and Economic Life', in Neil Smelser and Richard Swedberg (eds), *The Handbook of Economic Sociology* (Princeton: Princeton University Press/Russell Sage, 1994), 368–402.

PRAVDA, ALEX and BLAIR RUBLE, *Trade Unions in Communist States* (Boston: Allen & Unwin, 1986).

PRZEWORSKI, ADAM, *Democracy and Markets* (New York: Cambridge University Press, 1991).

——and HENRY TEUNE, *The Logic of Comparative Social Inquiry* (New York: Wiley, 1970).

PRIES, LUDGER (with GABRIELA GARCÍA, CÉSAR GUTIÉRREZ and FERNANDO HERRERA), 'Relaciones industriales en la industria automotriz', in *Las Relaciones Laborales en el Proceso de Tranformación en América Latina: El Caso de México* (Bremen, Germany: Universität Bremen, May 1998).

Qiaobao [Overseas Chinese Daily] (New York).

RADAEV, V. A., 'Four Ways of Establishing Authority Within a Firm', *Sociological Magazine* [in Russian], 2 (1994), 149–57.

——'On Some Features of Normative Behaviour of Russia's Entrepreneurs', *World Economy and International Relations* [in Russian], 4 (1994), 31–8.

RADYUNIN, VLADIMIR, 'Kremlin Fails to Pay Off Back Wages', *The Hindu* (20 January 1998).

RAMASWAMY, E. A., *Worker Consciousness and Trade Union Response* (Delhi: Oxford University Press, 1988).

RAMÍREZ, MIGUEL, 'The Political Economy of Privatization in Mexico, 1983–92', Occasional Paper 1 (Latin American Studies Consortium of New England, 1993).

REMMER, KAREN, 'Democracy and Economic Crisis: The Latin American Experience', *World Politics*, 42: 3 (1991), 315–35.

Renmin Ribao (RMRB) [People's Daily] (Beijing).

REPETTO, ROBERT *et al.*, *The 'Second India' Revisited* (Washington, DC: World Resources Institute, 1994).

Reuters, 'Indian Police Kill Four Tea Plantation Workers', 6 May 1994.

RFE/RL. Radio Free Europe/Radio Liberty Research Reports.

RIFKIN, J., *The End of Work, The Decline of the Global Labor Force and the Dawn of the Post-Market Era* (New York: Putnam's, 1995).

ROBERTS, BRYAN, 'Informal Economy and Family Strategies', *International Journal of Urban and Regional Research*, 18 (March 1994), 6–23.

ROBINSON, NANCY, 'The Politics of Low Income Housing in Mexico: A Case Study of Infonavit, the Workers' Housing Institute'. MA thesis (Stanford University, CA, 1980).

RODRIGUES, IRAM JACOMÉ, *Sindicalismo e Política: A Trajetória da CUT* (São Paulo: Scritta, 1997).

RODRÍGUEZ L. JAVIER, 'Transformaciones productiva y relaciones laboarles en NISSAN Mexicana (planta CIVAC)', in Arnulfo Arteaga García (ed.), *Proceso de Trabajao y Relaciones Laborales en la Industria automotriz en México* (México, DF: Universidad Autónoma Metropolitana, Unidad Iztapalapa, and Fundación Friedrich Ebert, Representación en Mexico, 1992), 57–110.

RODRÍGUEZ, JOSÉ ANTONIO [advisor to former secretary general of the SNTE Elba Esther Gordillo], personal interview (Mexico City, 4 April 1995).

ROHLEN, THOMAS P., *For Harmony and Strength: Japanese White-Collar Organization in Anthropological Perspective* (Berkeley: University of California Press, 1974).

ROHRSCHNEIDER, ROBERT, 'Cultural Transmissions versus Perceptions of the Economy: The Sources of Political Elites' Economic Values in the United Germany', *Comparative Political Studies*, 29: 1 (1996), 78–104.

—— 'Report from the Laboratory: The Influence of Institutions on Political Elites' Democratic Values in Germany', *American Political Science Review*, 88: 4 (1994), 927–41.

ROMO, HORACIO [secretary of External Relations of the SME], personal interview (Mexico City, 7 April 1995).

ROSTOW, WALT W., *The Stages of Economic Growth* (Cambridge: Cambridge University Press, 1962).

ROXBOROUGH, IAN, *Unions and Politics in Mexico: The Case of the Automobile Industry* (Cambridge: Cambridge University Press, 1984).

—— 'Inflation and Social Pacts in Brazil and Mexico', *Journal of Latin American Studies*, 24 (1992), 639–64.

—— 'The Urban Working Class and the Labour Movement in Latin America Since 1930', in Leslie Bethell (ed.), *The Cambridge History of Latin America: vol. 4, Part II. Latin America Since 1930* (Cambridge: Cambridge University Press, 1997), 307–78.

—— and ILÁN BIZBERG, 'Union Locals in Mexico', *Journal of Latin American Studies*, 15: 1 (May 1983).

'RS Call for Probe into U.P. Firing', *Times of India* (5 June 1991).

RUBLE, BLAIR, 'Factory Unions and Workers' Rights', in Arcadius Kahan and Blair Ruble (eds), *Industrial Labor in the USSR* (New York: Pergamon, 1979).
—— *Soviet Trade Unions* (Cambridge: Cambridge University Press, 1981).
RUDOLPH, LLOYD and SUZANNE HOEBER RUDOLPH, *In Pursuit of Lakshmi: The Political Economy of the Indian State* (Chicago: University of Chicago Press, 1987).
RUESCHEMEYER, DIETRICH, EVELYN HUBER STEPHENS, and JOHN STEPHENS, *Capitalist Development and Democracy* (Chicago: University of Chicago Press, 1992).
'Russia: Facts and Figures', *Radio Free Europe/Radio Liberty (RFE/RL) 1996 Country Report*, website: http://www.rferl.org
'Russian Death Rate Almost Twice As High as in West', Agence France Presse (13 November 13, 1998).
'Russian Unions, Communists Disagree Over Strike Demands', Interfax (13 August 1998).
SABEL, CHARLES, *Work and Politics: The Division of Labor in Industry* (New York: Cambridge University Press, 1982).
—— 'Can the End of Social Democratic Trade Unions Be the Beginning of a New Kind of Social Democratic Politics?', in Stephen R. Sleigh (ed.), *Economic Restructuring and Emerging Patterns of Industrial Relations* (Kalamazoo, MI: Upjohn Institute for Employment Research, 1993*a*), 137–65.
—— 'Studied Trust: Building New Forms of Cooperation in a Volatile Economy', in Richard Swedberg (ed.), *Explorations in Economic Sociology* (New York: Russell Sage Foundation, 1993*b*), 104–44.
SACHS, JEFFREY D., and ANDREW M. WARNER, 'Economic Reform and the Process of Global Integration', Brookings Papers on Economic Activity, 1 (1995).
—— —— 'Achieving Rapid Growth in the Transition Economies of Central Europe', Discussion Paper 544, Harvard Institute for International Development (July 1996).
SALINAS DE GORTARI, CARLOS, *El Reto* (Mexico City: Editorial Diana, 1988).
—— *Cuarto Informe de Gobierno, Anexo Estadístico* (Mexico City: Poder Ejecutivo Federal, 1992).
—— *Sexto Informe de Gobierno, Anexo Estadístico* (Mexico City: Poder Ejecutivo Federal, 1994).
SAMANT, DATTA [President, Kamgar Aghadi (Workers Party)], interview (Bombay, India, 3 March 1993).
SAMUELS, BARBARA C. II, *Managing Risk in Developing Countries: National Demands and Multinational Response* (Princeton: Princeton University Press, 1990).
SÁNCHEZ, JORGE [former secretary general of the SME], personal interview (Mexico City, 7 April 1995).
SANFORD, JACOBY (ed.), *The Workers of Nations: Industrial Relations in a Global Economy* (New York: Oxford University Press, 1995*a*).
—— Preface, in Sanford Jacoby (ed.), *The Workers of Nations: Industrial Relations in a Global Economy* (New York: Oxford University Press, 1995*b*), ix–xii.
SARWAR, BEENA, 'Pakistan: Greens to Blockade Import of Danish Ship', Interpress Services (15 November 1994).
SCHARPF, FRITZ, *Crisis and Choice in European Social Democracy* (Ithaca, NY: Cornell University Press, 1987).
SCHLEIFER, A. and D. VASILIEV, 'Management Ownership and Russian Privatization', in R. Frydman, C. W. Gray, and A. Rapaczynski (eds), *Corporate Governance in Central Europe and Russia* (Budapest: Central European University Press, 1996).

SCHMITTER, PHILIPPE, 'Still the Century of Corporatism?', *Review of Politics*, 36 (1974), 85–131. Also reprinted in Philippe Schmitter and Gerhard Lehmbruch (eds), *Trends Towards Corporatist Intermediation* (Beverly Hills, CA: Sage, 1979), 7–52.

——and GERHARD LEHMBRUCH (eds), *Trends Towards Corporatist Intermediation* (Beverly Hills, CA: Sage, 1979).

SCHOR, JULIET, and JONG-IL YOU (eds), *Capital, the State and Labour: A Global Perspective* (Brookfield, VT: Edward Elgar, 1995).

SCOTT, JAMES C., *The Moral Economy of the Peasant: Rebellion and Subsistence in Southeast Asia* (New Haven: Yale University Press, 1976).

SETALVAD, TEESTA, 'Workers Mean Business', *Business India* (6–19 July 1992), 99–100.

SHAHEED, ZAFAR, 'The Organisation and Leadership of Industrial Labour in Pakistan (Karachi)'. Unpublished PhD dissertation (Department of Politics, University of Leeds, 1977).

SHAIKEN, HARLEY, 'Lean Production in a Mexican Context', in Steve Babson (ed.), *Lean Work: Empowerment and Exploitation in the Global Auto Industry* (Detroit: Wayne State University Press, 1995), 247–59.

SHERSHNEVA, ELENA, and JURGEN FELDHOFF, *The Culture of Labour in the Transformation Process: Empirical Studies in Russian Industrial Enterprises* (New York: Peter Lang, 1998).

SHIGERU OTSUBO, *Globalization: A New Role for Developing Countries in an Integrating World* (Washington, DC: World Bank, 1996).

Shijie Ribao (SJRB) [*World Journal*] (New York).

SHILLER, ROBERT, MAXIM BOYCKO, and VLADIMIR KOROBOV, 'Popular Attitudes toward Free Markets: The Soviet Union and the United States Compared', *American Economic Review*, 81 (1991), 385–400.

—— —— ——'Hunting for Homo-Sovieticus: Situational versus Attitudinal Factors in Economic Behavior', Brookings Papers on Economic Activity, 1 (1992), 127–81.

SHIMADA, HARUO, 'Japan's industrial culture and labor-management relations', in Shumpei Kumon and Henry Rosovsky (eds), *The Political Economy of Japan: Vol. 3. Cultural and Social Dynamics* (Stanford, CA: Stanford University Press, 1992), 267–91.

SHROUTI, ARVIND, 'New Economic Policy, Changing Management Strategies— Impact on Workers and Trade Unions' (New Delhi: Friedrich Ebert Stiftung, 1994).

——[researcher, Maniben Kara Institute], interview (Bombay, India, 25 June 1996).

SIDDHANTA, T. N., 'Brutal Killings at Dalla Cement Factory' (New Delhi: AITUC Publication, August 1991).

SIL, RUDRA, 'The Russian "Village in the City" and the Stalinist System of Enterprise Management: The Origins of Worker Alienation in Soviet State-Socialism', in Xiaobo Lu and Elizabeth Perry (eds), *Danwei: The Changing Chinese Workplace in Historical and Comparative Perspective* (Armonk, NY: M. E. Sharpe, 1997).

—— *Managing 'Modernity': Work, Community, and Authority in Late-Industrializing Japan and Russia* (Ann Arbor: University of Michigan Press, forthcoming).

SILVA HERZOG, JESÚS, *Lázaro Cárdenas. Su Pensamiento Económico, Social y Político* (Mexico City: Editorial Nuestro Tiempo, 1975).

SIMITS, S., 'The Juridification of Labor Relations', *Comparative Labor Journal*, 7 (1986), 93–142.

SIQUIERA NETO, JOSÉ FRANCISCO, *Contrato Coletivo do Trabalho: Perspetiva de Rompimento com a Legalidade Repressiva* (São Paulo: Editora Limitada, 1991).

SKLAIR, LESLIE, *Foreign Investment and Irish Development: A Study of the International Division of Labour in the Midwest Region of Ireland*, Progress in Planning Series, 29: 3 (New York: Pergamon, 1988).

SLIDER, DARRELL, 'Gorbachev's First Reform Failure: Work-Place Democratization', *Journal of Communist Studies*, 9: 2 (June 1993), 62–85.

SME, *Estatutos* (Mexico City: Mexican Union of Electricity Workers, 1992).

—— *El Nuevo Organismo, Triunfo y Nuevo Reto del Sindicato* (Mexico City: Mexican Union of Electricity Workers, 1994).

SMELSER, NEIL, *Social Change in the Industrial Revolution* (Chicago: University of Chicago Press, 1959).

—— and RICHARD SWEDBERG (eds), *The Handbook of Economic Sociology* (Princeton: Princeton University Press, 1993).

SMITH, CHRIS and PAUL THOMPSON (eds), *Labor in Transition: The Labor Process in Eastern Europe and China* (London: Routledge, 1992).

SMITH, PETER, *Labyrinths of Power: Political Recruitment in Twentieth Century Mexico* (Princeton: Princeton University Press, 1979).

SMITH, WILLIAM C., CARLOS H. ACUÑA, and EDUARDO GAMARRA (eds), *Democracy, Markets, and Structural Reform in Contemporary Latin America: Argentina, Bolivia, Brazil, Chile, and Mexico* (New Brunswick, NJ: Transaction Publishers, 1994).

SNTE, *Estatutos* (Mexico City: National Union of Education Workers, 1992).

STANDING, GUY and DANIEL VAUGHAN-WHITEHEAD (eds), *Minimum Wages in Central and Eastern Europe: From Protection to Destitution* (Budapest: Central European University Press, 1995).

—— ——'Introduction', in Guy Standing and Daniel Vaughan-Whitehead, *Minimum Wages in Central and Eastern Europe: from Protection to Destitution* (Budapest: Central European University Press, 1995).

STARITZ, DIETRICH, *Die Gründung der DDR* (Munich: DTV, 1987).

STARK, DAVID, 'Bending the Bars of the Iron Cage: Bureaucratization and Informalization in Capitalism and Socialism', *Sociological Forum*, 4 (1989), 637–64.

—— and LÁSZLÓ BRUSZT, *Postsocialist Pathways: Transforming Politics and Property in East Central Europe* (Cambridge: Cambridge University Press, 1998).

STARR, S. FREDERICK, 'The Changing Nature of Change in the USSR', in Seweryn Bialer and Michael Mandelbaum (eds), *Gorbachev's Russia and American Foreign Policy* (Boulder, CO: Westview Press, 1988).

STEVENS, WILLIAM, 'Green Revolution is Not Enough, Study Finds', *New York Times* (6 September 1994).

STPS, *Memoria de Labores* (Mexico City: Secretaría de Trabajo y Previsión Social, 1989).

—— *Memoria de Labores* (Mexico City: Secretaría de Trabajo y Previsión Social, 1994).

—— 'Emplazamientos y huelgas estalladas en empresas de jurisdicción federal', Secretaría de Trabajo y Previsión Social, subsecretaría 'B' (Mexico City 1995).

STRAUS, KENNETH, 'The Soviet Factory as Community Organizer', in Xiaobo Lu and Elizabeth Perry (eds), *Danwei: The Changing Chinese Workplace in Historical and Comparative Perspective* (Armonk. NY: M. E. Sharpe, 1997), 142–68.

——*Factory and Community in Stalin's Russia* (Pittsburgh: University of Pittsburgh Press, 1998).

STREECK, WOLFGANG, *Social Institutions and Economic Performance: Studies of Industrial Relations in Advanced Capitalist Economies* (Beverly Hills: Sage, 1992*a*).

——'Training and the New Industrial Relations: A Strategic Role for Unions?', in Marino Regini (ed.), *The Future of Labour Movements* (London: Sage, 1992*b*), 225–69.

——'Lean Production in the German Automobile Industry: A Test Case for Convergence Theory', in Suzanne Berger and Ronald Dore (eds), *National Diversity and Global Capitalism* (Ithaca. NY: Cornell University Press, 1996), 138–70.

STRM, 'Comisión de Modernización. Proyecto', XII National Ordinary Democratic Convention of the Telephone Workers (Mexico City, 1988).

SUTELA, PEKKA, 'Insider Privatisation in Russia: Speculations on Systemic change', *Europe-Asia Studies*, 47: 3 (1994), 417–35.

SWEDBERG, RICHARD (ed.), *Explorations in Economic Sociology* (New York: Russell Sage, 1993).

SWENSON, PETER, 'Bringing Capital Back In, Or Social Democracy Reconsidered', *World Politics*, 43: 4 (1991), 513–44.

——*Fair Shares: Unions, Pay and Politics in Sweden and Germany* (Ithaca, NY: Cornell University Press, 1989).

TABATA, HIROKUNI, 'Changes in Plant-Level Trade Union Organizations: A Case Study of the Automobile Industry', University of Tokyo Institute of Social Science Occasional Papers in Labor Problem and Social Policy (1989).

TAKAGI IKURO, 'Nihon rodo kumiai undo ni okeru "uha" no keifu: Sodomei to JC-gata no doshitsusei to ishitsusei' [The genealogy of the 'right-wing' of the Japanese labor movement: Sodomei and JC-type homogeneity and heterogeneity], in Shimizu Shinzo (ed.), *Sengo Rodo Kumiai Undo shi Ron* [Debates on the Postwar History of Labor Unions] (Tokyo: Nihon Hyoronsha, 1982), 373–99.

TAYLOR, CHARLES, *Multiculturalism and the Politics of Recognition* (Princeton: Princeton University Press, 1992).

TELLO, CARLOS, *La Nacionalización de la Banca* (Mexico City: Ed. Siglo XXI, 1984).

THANKAPPAN, D. [Director, Centre for Workers' Management], letter to P. Chidambaram [Minister of Finance], 15 June 1996.

The Irish Times on the Web, http://www.ireland.com

THELEN, KATHLEEN, *Union of Parts: Labor Politics in Postwar Germany* (Ithaca. NY: Cornell University Press, 1991).

THIRKELL, J. E. M., K. PETKOV, and S. A. VICKERSTAFF, *The Transformation of Labour Relations: Restructuring and Privatization in Eastern Europe and Russia* (New York: Oxford University Press, 1998).

THOMPSON, E. P., 'The Moral Economy of the English Crowd in the Eighteenth Century', *Past and Present*, 50 (1971), 76–136.

TIDD, JOSEPH, *Flexible Manufacturing Technologies and International Competitiveness* (London: Pinter, 1991).

TIMKO, CAROL C., 'The 1992–1993 Strike Wave and the Disorganization of Worker Interests in Poland', Paper presented at the Annual Meeting of the American Political Science Association (San Francisco, September 1996).

TIWARI, T. *et al.*, 'Report of the Committee to Examine the Legal and Other

Difficulties Faced by Banks and Financial Institutions in Rehabilitation of Sick Industrial Undertakings and Suggest Remedial Measures Including Changes in the Law' (Bombay: Reserve Bank of India, 1984).

TOTSUKA HIDEO and HYODO TSUTOMU (eds), *Chiiki Shakai to Rodo Kumiai* [Regional Society and Labor Unions] (Tokyo: Nihon Keizai Hyoronsha, 1995).

TRAXLER, R., 'European Transformation and Institution Building in East and West: The Performance of and Preconditions for Neocorporatism', in R. W. Kindley and D. F. Good (eds), *The Challenge of Globalization and Institution Building: Lessons from Small European States* (Boulder, CO: Westview Press, 0000).

Tribüne (Berlin) 3 March 1947.

TSURU, TSUYOSHI and JAMES B. REBITZER, 'The Limits of Ent Them', BRIE Working Paper 111 (December 1997).

TUMAN, JOHN P., 'The Political Economy of Restructuring in Mexico's "Brownfield" Plants: A Comparative Analysis', in John P. Tuman and John T. Morris (eds), *Transforming the Latin American Automobile Industry: Unions, Workers, and the Politics of Restructuring* (Armonk, NY: M. E. Sharpe, 1998), 148–78.

TURNER, LOWELL, *Democracy at Work: Changing World Markets and the Future of Labor Unions* (Ithaca. NY: Cornell University Press, 1991).

—— and PETER AUER, 'A Diversity of New Work Organization: Human-centered, Lean and In-between', in F. C. Deyo (ed.), *Social Reconstructions of the World Automobile Industry: Competition, Power and Industrial Flexibility* (New York: St. Martin's Press, 1996).

TYURIN, YURY, 'Trade Union Leaders Accuse the Government of Breaking the System of Social Partnership, And Are Determined to Protect the Organizers of Coal Miners' Protests From Prosecution', *RIA Novosti* (8 July 1998).

UNCTAD (United Nations Conference on Trade and Development), *World Investment Report, 1994: Transnational Corporations, Employment, and the Work-place* (New York/Geneva, 1994).

UZZI, BRIAN, 'Social Structure and Competition in Interfirm Networks: The Paradox of Embeddedness', *Administrative Science Quarterly*, 42 (1997), 35–67.

VAN WERSCH, HUBERT, *The Bombay Textile Strike 1982–83* (Bombay: Oxford University Press, 1992).

VÁZQUEZ RUBIO, OSCAR, 'Los telefonistas cruzaron el pantano: concertaron con Telmex', *El Cotidiano*, 21 (September–October, 1989), 31–2.

—— 'Conseguimos avanzar, pero esto no garantiza un triunfo', *El Cotidiano*, 35 (May–June 1990), 25–6.

—— 'El telefonista sostiene su apuesta', *El Cotidiano*, 35 (May–June 1990), 18–21.

VEGA LOPEZ, EDUARDO, 'La política económica de México durante el período 1982–1994', *El Cotidiano*, 67 (March–April 1995), 31–3.

VERMA, ANIL, T. KOCHAN, and R. LANSBURY, *Employment Relations in the Growing Asian Economies* (New York: Routledge, 1995).

VERNON, RAYMOND, *Sovereignty at Bay: The Multinational Spread of U.S. Enterprises* (New York: Basic Books, 1971).

VOGEL, STEVEN, *Freer Markets, More Rules: Regulatory Reform in Advanced Industrial Countries* (Ithaca, NY: Cornell University Press, 1996).

VON BULOW, MARISA, 'Reestructuración productiva y estrategias sindicales. El caso de la Ford en Cuahutitlán 1987–1993'. MA thesis (FLACSO-Mexico, 1994).

—— 'Reestructuración productiva y estrategias sindicales. El caso de la Ford en

Cuahutitlán 1987–1994', Paper presented at the Latin American Studies Association XIX International Congress (Washington, DC, 28–30 September 1995).

VON PRONDZYNSKI, FERDINAND, 'Ireland: Between Centralism and the Market', in Anthony Ferner and Richard Hyman (eds), *Industrial Relations in the New Europe* (Cambridge, MA: Blackwell Business, 1992).

WADE, ROBERT, 'Globalization and Its Limits: Reports of the Death of the National Economy are Greatly Exaggerated', in Suzanne Berger and Ronald Dore (eds), *National Diversity and Global Capitalism* (Ithaca, NY: Cornell University Press, 1996), 60–88.

WADHAM, NICK, 'Study: One-Third of Russians in Poverty' (Associated Press, 20 July 1999).

'Wage Arrears Mount', *Open Market Research Institute (OMRI) Daily Digest* (16 December 1996).

WALDER, ANDREW, *Communist Neo-Traditionalism: Work and Authority in Chinese Industry* (Berkeley: University of California Press, 1986).

WANG, BOJUN, 'Shichanghua dachao zhongde zhigong quanyi baozhang' [Worker rights protection in the market reform], *Taosuo yu Zhengming* [Inquiries and Debates], 4 (1995), 23–7.

WANG, JIAXIN (ed.), *Zhongguo Laodong Nianjian 1992–1994* [Chinese Labor Yearbook] (Beijing: Zhongguo laodong chubanshe, 1996).

WARNER, MALCOLM, *The Management of Human Resources in Chinese Industry* (New York: St. Martin's Press, 1995).

WEATHERS, CHARLES, 'The 1999 Shunto and the Restructuring of Wage Setting in Japan', *Asian Survey*, 39: 6 (June 1999), 960–86.

WEGNER, MANFRED, 'Produktionsstandort Ostdeutschland', *Aus Politik und Zeitgeschichte*, B 17/94 (29 April 1994), 20.

WEIR, FRED, 'Workers' Strikes, Social Unrest', *The Hindustan Times* (19 September 1997).

WELSH, HELGA, ' Four Years and Several Elections Later: The Eastern Political Landscape after Unification', in David P. Conradt *et al.*, *Germany's New Politics* (Tempe, AZ: German Studies Review, 1995).

WESELOWSKY, TONY, 'Russia: The Roots of Labor Malaise', Radio Free Europe/Radio Liberty (RFE/RL) Report (11 February 1998).

—— 'Russia: Workers Still Waiting to Be Paid', Radio Free Europe/Radio Liberty (RFE/RL) Daily Report (11 February 1998).

WEVER, KIRSTEN and LOWELL TURNER (eds), *The Comparative Political Economy of Industrial Relations* (Madison, WI: Industrial Relations Research Association, 1995*a*).

—— ——'A Wide Angle Lens for a Global Marketplace', in Kristen Wever and Lowell Turner (eds), *The Comparative Political Economy of Industrial Relations* (Madison, WI: Industrial Relations Research Association, 1995*b*), 1–8.

WEYLAND, KURT GERHARD, *Democracy without Equity: Failures of Reform in Brazil* (Pittsburgh: University of Pittsburgh Press, 1996).

WHITE, HARRISON C., *Chains of Opportunity: System Models of Mobility in Organizations* (Cambridge: Harvard University Press, 1970).

WHITEHEAD, LAWRENCE, 'Political Democratization and Economic Liberalization: Prospects for Their Entrenchment in Eastern Europe and Latin America. Unpublished manuscript, 1995.

WOMACK, JAMES, DANIEL JONES, and DANIEL ROOS, *The Machine That Changed the World* (New York: Rawson/Macmillan, 1990).

WOOD, ELLEN MEIKSINS, PETER MEIKSINS, and MICHAEL YATES (eds), 'Rising From the Ashes? Labor in the Age of "Global" Capitalism', special issue of *Monthly Review*, 49: 3 (July–August 1997).

WOOD, STEPHEN (ed.), *The Transformation of Work* (London: Unwin Hyman, 1989).

World Bank, *Pakistan: Country Economic Memorandum FY93: Progress Under the Adjustment Program* (Washington, DC: World Bank, 23 March 1993).

—— *Reformas Laborales y Económicas en América Latina y el Caribe* (Washington, DC: World Bank, 1995).

XELHUANTZI LÓPEZ, MARÍA, *Sindicato de Telefonista de la República Mexican. 12 años: 1976–1988* (Mexico City: Mexican Union of Telephone Workers, 1989).

—— 'Reforma del Estado Mexicano y sindicalismo'. MA thesis (UNAM, 1992).

—— [advisor to the secretary general of the STRM Francisco Hernández Juarez], personal interview (Mexico City, 5 April 1995).

YAQOOB, MOHAMMAD [Chairman All Pakistan State Employees Workers Action Committee], interview (New Delhi, India, 29 March 1992).

YOSHIMURA, YOSUKE, *Daikigyo Roshi no Kenka Matsuri* [Ritualistic Quarrels between Labor and Management at Large Companies] (Tokyo: Japan Institute of Labor, 1982), 29–56.

ZAMORA, GERARDO, 'La política laboral del estado mexicano, 1982–88', *Revista Mexicana de Sociología*, 3 (1990), 23–48.

ZAPATA, FRANCISCO, *El conflicto sindical en América Latina* (Mexico City: El Colegio de México, 1986).

—— 'Labor and Politics: The Mexican Paradox', in Edward Epstein (ed), *Labor Autonomy and the State in Latin America* (Boston: Unwin Hyman, 1989).

—— 'Crisis en el sindicalismo en México?', *Revista Mexicana de Sociología*, 1 (1994), 79–88.

—— *El Sindicalismo Mexicano Frente a la Restructuración México* (México, DF: El Colegio de México, Centro de Estudios Sociológicos/Instituto de Investigaciones de las Naciones Unidas para el Desarrollo Social, 1995).

ZASLAVSKY, VICTOR, 'From Redistribution to Marketization: Social and Attitudinal Change in Post-Soviet Russia', in Gail Lapidus (ed.), *The New Russia: Troubled Transformation* (Boulder, CO: Westview Press, 1996).

ZEPEDA, MARIO, 'El Pronasol, la política y la pobreza', *Memoria*, 36 (1990), 6–7.

Zhongguo Gonghui Tongji Nianjian [Trade Union Statistic Yearbook of China] (Beijing: Zhongguo tongji chubanshe, 1994).

Zhongguo Jingji Nianjian [Economic Statistic Yearbook of China] (Beijing: Zhongguo tongji chubanshe, 1996).

Zhongguo Laodong Tongjin Nianjian [Labor Statistic Yearbook of China] (Beijing: Zhongguo laodong chubanshe, 1996).

Zhongguo Tongji Nianjian [Statistical Yearbook of China] (Beijing: Zhongguo tongji chubanshe, 1996).

Zhonghua Quanguo Zonggonghui [All China Federation of Trade Unions], *Jianguo Yilai Zhonggong Zhongyang Guanyu Gongren Yundong Wenjian Xuanbian* [Selected CCP Central Committee Documents on Workers Movements] (Beijing: Gongren chubanshe, 1989).

Zweig, Ferdynand, *The Worker in an Affluent Society: Family Life and Industry* (London: Heinemann, 1961).

INDEX

Pérez Fernández del Castillo, G. 34n
Perry, E. 10n, 22n, 228n
  and China 182n, 184n, 185n, 187n, 198n
Peschanski, V. 214n, 215n, 219n, 220n, 222n
Peschard, J. 37n
Petkov, K. 215n
Philippines 27n, 195
Pickel, A. 233n
PILER (Pakistan Institute of Labour
  Education and Research) 91
Piore, M. 9n, 12n, 15n, 103n
Pleskot, I. 269
PNR (National Revolutionary Party,
  Mexico) 37
Poland 25, 26, 184, 198, 207
  corporatist renaissance 258–61, 264, 272,
    274–81
  institutional legacies and transformation of
    labor 288n, 292–3, 306
Polanyi, K. 6, 93, 235, 285n
Politburo 243
political parties 106, 109, 136, 219, 254–5,
  279, 280
political liberalization, reform, transition 32,
  33, 66, 202
political unionism *see* unions and unionism
Pollert, A. 271n, 272n, 273
Popper, K. 282
popularism *see* economic development
  ideologies
Portella, S. 101n
post-Fordism 12, 20, 103, 285
  see also Fordism
post-socialism 3, 4, 9, 15, 16–18, 129, 286
poverty 19, 81, 147, 150, 211, 258
Powell, W. W. 104n
Prague 270, 299
  Prague Spring (1968) 288n
Pravda, A. 184n
PRC *see* China
PRD (Party of the Democratic Revolution,
  Mexico) 32n, 38, 50, 54n
PRI (Institutional Revolutionary Party,
  Mexico) 19, 294, 305
  partisan loyalty and union competition
    31–4, 37–41, 42n, 44–62, 64–6, 68
Pries, L. 106n, 107, 115n, 126n
privatization 15, 24, 31, 41, 42, 44, 58, 65, 69,
  99, 166, 192, 200, 207–12, 247, 268, 276,
  286
  labor responses to 19, 44–5, 58, 60, 78–87,
    224
Privatisation Commission (Pakistan) 79
PRM (Party of the Mexican Revolution) 37
Programme for Competitiveness and Work
  (Ireland, 1994–6) 147
Programme for Economic and Social
  Progress (Ireland, 1991–3) 147

Programme for National Recovery (Ireland,
  1988–90) 147
Prondzynski 136n, 146n
Przeworski, A. 5n, 98n
PSE (Pact of Economic Solidarity, Mexico,
  1982) 40–1, 42
PSL (Polish Peasant Party) 277
PT (Workers' Party, Brazil) 110–11, 113, 114
PWC (Pakistan Workers' Confederation)
  90–1

Qiaobao 200n
Quinn, R. 148, 152n, 153n
Quiroz Trejo, J. 49n

Radaev, V. A. 225n, 226n
Radyunin, V. 222n
Raipur 81
Rajya Sabha 81
Ram, S. 83n
Ramaswamy, A. 84n
Ramírez, M. 44n
Rapaczynski, A. 210n
Ravi Alkalis 91
Rebitzer, J. B. 163n
Regini, M. 129n
Reich, M. 165n
religion 70, 71, 110–11, 275
Remmer, K. 5n
Rengo 161, 163–5, 173, 176n, 177
Repetto, R. 299n
Reuters 299n
RHSD (Council for Economic and Social
  Agreement) 270, 273
Rifkin, J. 292n
Rio de Janeiro 299
RMMS (National Mill Workers' Union) 85,
  86
RMRB (*Renmin Ribao*) 190n–191n, 192,
  193n, 196n, 197, 199n–200n
Roberts, B. 295n
Robinson, N. 46n
Rocha, R. 268n
Roddick, J. 10n
Rodgers, G. 93n
Rodrigues, I. J. 100n, 123n
Rodríguez, J. A. 53n-54n, 56n
Roett, R. 50n
Rogowski, R. 35n
ROH (Revolutionary Trade-Union
  Movement) 269, 270
Rohlen, T. 158
Rohrschneider, R. 236–7
Romo, H. 58n
Ronit, K. 265n, 282n
Roos, D. 21n, 103n
Rose, A. 247n
Rosovsky, H. 164n

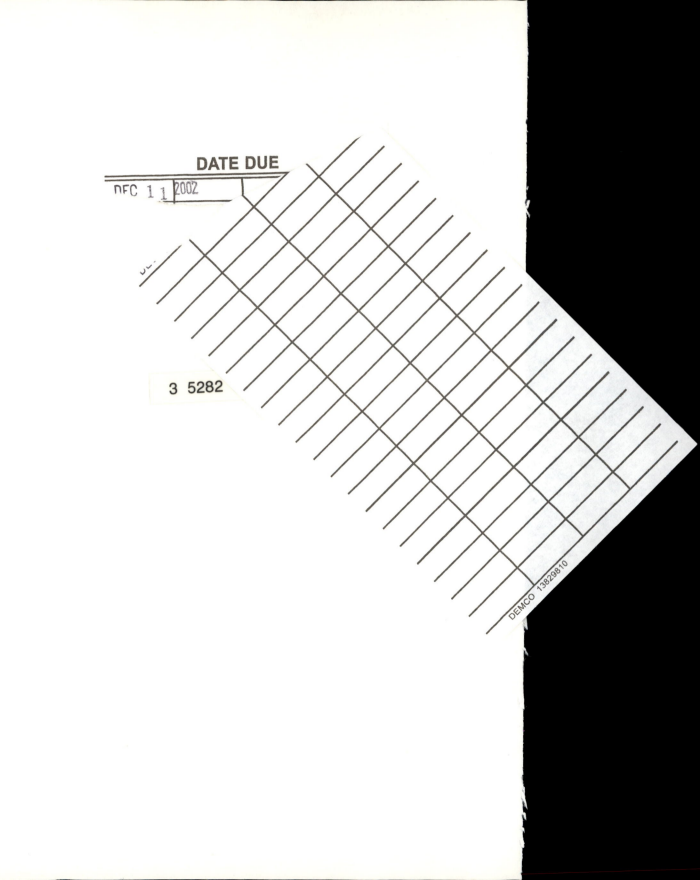